Continuity and Change

RESEARCH COMPANION with the WEEKLY EXPLORER

Program Authors

James Banks, Ph.D.
Kerry and Linda Killinger Endowed Chair in Diversity Studies
Director, Center for Multicultural Education
University of Washington
Seattle, Washington

Kevin P. Colleary, Ed.D.
Curriculum and Teaching Department
Graduate School of Education
Fordham University
New York, New York

William Deverell, Ph.D.
Director of the Huntington-USC Institute on California and the West
Professor of History, University of Southern California
Los Angeles, California

Daniel Lewis, Ph.D.
Dibner Senior Curator
The Huntington Library
Los Angeles, California

Elizabeth Logan Ph.D., J.D.
Associate Director of the Huntington-USC Institute on California and the West
Los Angeles, California

Walter C. Parker, Ph.D.
Professor of Social Studies Education
Adjunct Professor of Political Science
University of Washington
Seattle, Washington

Emily M. Schell, Ed.D.
Professor, Teacher Education
San Diego State University
San Diego, California

mheducation.com/prek-12

Copyright © 2019 McGraw-Hill Education

All rights reserved. No part of this publication may be reproduced or distributed in any form or by any means, or stored in a database or retrieval system, without the prior written consent of McGraw-Hill Education, including, but not limited to, network storage or transmission, or broadcast for distance learning.

McGraw-Hill Education
120 S. Riverside Plaza, Suite 1200
Chicago, IL 60606

ISBN: 978-0-07-692525-4
MHID: 0-07-692525-0

Printed in the United States of America.

4 5 6 7 8 9 LWI 23 22 21 20 19

Program Consultants

Jana Echevarria, Ph.D.
Professor Emerita
California State University
Long Beach, California

Douglas Fisher, Ph.D.
Professor, Educational Leadership
San Diego State University
San Diego, California

Carlos Ulloa, Ed.D.
Principal, Escondido Union School District
Escondido, California

Rebecca Valbuena, M.Ed.
K-5 Teacher on Special Assignment/Academic Coach
Glendora Unified School District
Glendora, California

Program Reviewers

Gary Clayton, Ph.D.
Professor of Economics
Northern Kentucky University
Highland Heights, Kentucky

Lorri Glover, Ph.D.
John Francis Bannon, S.J. Professor of History
Saint Louis University
St. Louis, Missouri

Thomas Herman, Ph.D.
Project Director, Center for Interdisciplinary Studies of Youth and Space
Department of Geography
San Diego State University

Nafees Khan, Ph.D.
Department of Teaching and Learning
Social Studies Education
Clemson University
Clemson, South Carolina

Clifford Trafzer, Ph.D.
Distinguished Professor of History
Rupert Costo Chair in American Indian Affairs
University of California
Riverside, California

Letter from the Authors

Dear Social Studies Detective,

Why did people settle in California? Who were the first people who lived in your community—and why did they choose to live there? In this book, you will find out more about communities. You will think about the issues important in your community and what **you** can do to help!

As you read, be an investigator. What do you wonder about? Write your own questions and read closely to find the answers. What in this book interests you? What do you find exciting? Take notes about it and analyze your notes. Then you can use your notes to do a project to share what you've learned. Take a closer look at photos of real people and places. Use maps and timelines to think about how California and your community have changed.

Enjoy your investigation into the amazing world of social studies—a place where people live in communities that grow and change, a place where **you** can make a difference!

Sincerely,

The IMPACT Social Studies Authors

PRIMARY SOURCE

San Francisco Bay Bridge in the 1940s

©2017 Smithsonian

Contents

Reference Sources

Communities in California

How Does Geography Impact California Communities?

American Indians of the Local Region

How Have California Indians Influenced the Local Region?

How and Why Communities Change Over Time

How Has Life Changed for People in My Community Over Time?

American Citizens, Symbols, and Government

How Do Our Government and Its Citizens Work Together?

Economics of the Local Region

How Do People in a Community Meet Their Needs?

Skills and Features

Literature

Did You Know?

Map and Globe Skills

Then and Now

InfoGraphics

A Day in the Life

Biography

Perspectives

Primary Sources

Field Trips

Citizenship

Timeline

Point of View

Around the World

Charts, Graphs, and Diagrams

Maps

Primary Source Quotes

Getting Started

You have two social studies books that you will use together to explore and analyze important Social Studies issues.

IMPACT
CALIFORNIA
SOCIAL STUDIES
Continuity and Change
INQUIRY JOURNAL
IMPACT
CALIFORNIA SOCIAL STUDIES
Continuity and Change
RESEARCH COMPANION
3

The Inquiry Journal

The Inquiry Journal is your reporter's notebook where you will ask questions, analyze sources, and record information.

The Research Companion

The Research Companion is where you'll read nonfiction and literature selections, examine primary source materials, and look for answers to your questions.

Every Chapter

Chapter opener pages help you see the big picture. Each chapter begins with an **Essential Question**. This **EQ** guides research and inquiry.

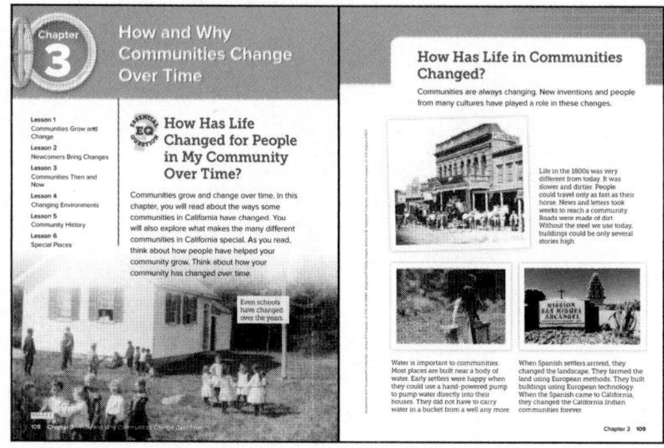

Chapter 3
How and Why Communities Change Over Time
How Has Life Changed for People in My Community Over Time?
How Has Life in Communities Changed?

In the **Research Companion**, you'll explore the EQ through words and photographs.

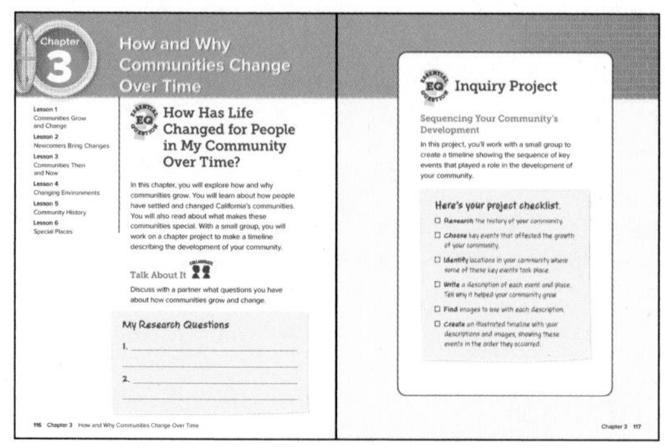

In the **Inquiry Journal**, you'll talk about the EQ and find out about the EQ Inquiry Project for the chapter.

StasKhom/iStock/Getty Images

Explore Words

Find out what you know about the chapter's academic vocabulary.

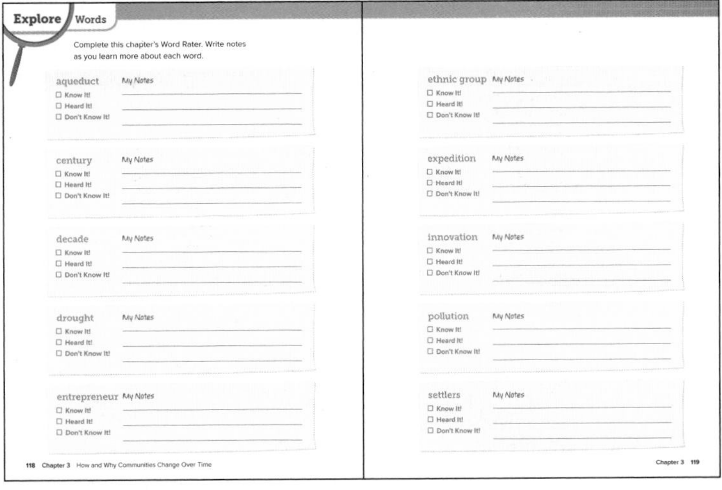

Explore Words

Complete this chapter's Word Rater. Write notes as you learn more about each word.

Word	Rating	My Notes
aqueduct	☐ Know It! ☐ Heard It! ☐ Don't Know It!	
century	☐ Know It! ☐ Heard It! ☐ Don't Know It!	
decade	☐ Know It! ☐ Heard It! ☐ Don't Know It!	
drought	☐ Know It! ☐ Heard It! ☐ Don't Know It!	
entrepreneur	☐ Know It! ☐ Heard It! ☐ Don't Know It!	
ethnic group	☐ Know It! ☐ Heard It! ☐ Don't Know It!	
expedition	☐ Know It! ☐ Heard It! ☐ Don't Know It!	
innovation	☐ Know It! ☐ Heard It! ☐ Don't Know It!	
pollution	☐ Know It! ☐ Heard It! ☐ Don't Know It!	
settlers	☐ Know It! ☐ Heard It! ☐ Don't Know It!	

118 Chapter 3 How and Why Communities Change Over Time

Chapter 3 119

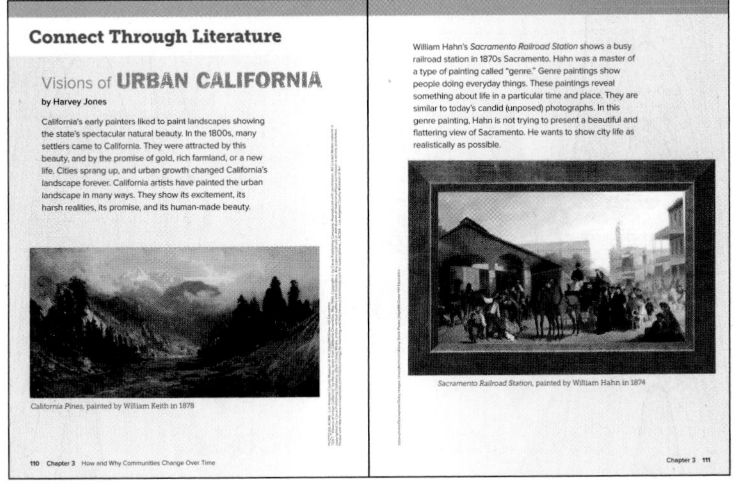

Connect Through Literature

Visions of **URBAN CALIFORNIA**

by Harvey Jones

California's early painters liked to paint landscapes showing the state's spectacular natural beauty. In the 1800s, many settlers came to California. They were attracted by this beauty, and by the promise of gold, rich farmland, or a new life. Cities sprang up, and urban growth changed California's landscape forever. California artists have painted the urban landscape in many ways. They show its excitement, its harsh realities, its promise, and its human-made beauty.

California Pines, painted by William Keith in 1878

William Hahn's *Sacramento Railroad Station* shows a busy railroad station in 1870s Sacramento. Hahn was a master of a type of painting called "genre." Genre paintings show people doing everyday things. These paintings reveal something about life in a particular time and place. They are similar to today's candid (unposed) photographs. In this genre painting, Hahn is not trying to present a beautiful and flattering view of Sacramento. He wants to show city life as realistically as possible.

Sacramento Railroad Station, painted by William Hahn in 1874

110 Chapter 3 How and Why Communities Change Over Time

Chapter 3 111

Connect Through Literature

Explore the chapter topic through fiction, informational text, and poetry.

People You Should Know

Learn about the lives of people who have made an impact in history.

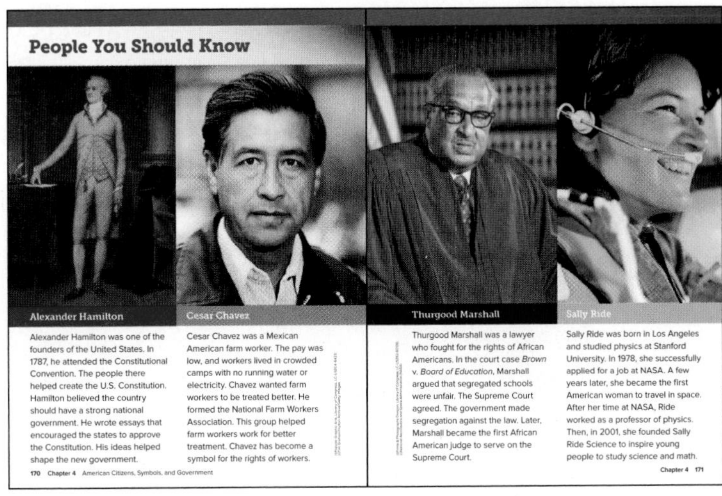

People You Should Know

Alexander Hamilton

Alexander Hamilton was one of the founders of the United States. In 1787, he attended the Constitutional Convention. The people there helped create the U.S. Constitution. Hamilton believed the country should have a strong national government. He wrote essays that encouraged the states to approve the Constitution. His ideas helped shape the new government.

Cesar Chavez

Cesar Chavez was a Mexican American farm worker. The pay was low, and workers lived in crowded camps with no running water or electricity. Chavez wanted farm workers to be treated better. He formed the National Farm Workers Association. This group helped farm workers work for better treatment. Chavez has become a symbol for the rights of workers.

Thurgood Marshall

Thurgood Marshall was a lawyer who fought for the rights of African Americans. In the court case *Brown v. Board of Education*, Marshall argued that segregated schools were unfair. The Supreme Court agreed. The government made segregation against the law. Later, Marshall became the first African American judge to serve on the Supreme Court.

Sally Ride

Sally Ride was born in Los Angeles and studied physics at Stanford University. In 1978, she successfully applied for a job at NASA. A few years later, she became the first American woman to travel in space. After her time at NASA, Ride worked as a professor of physics. Then, in 2001, she founded Sally Ride Science to inspire young people to study science and math.

170 Chapter 4 American Citizens, Symbols, and Government

Chapter 4 171

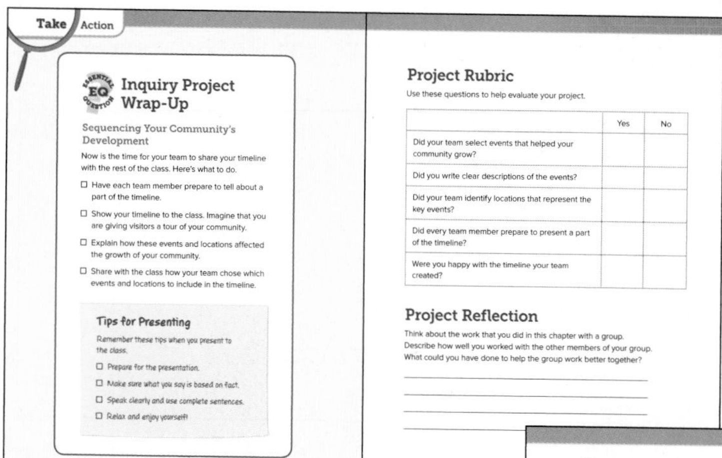

Take Action

Inquiry Project Wrap-Up

Sequencing Your Community's Development

Now is the time for your team to share your timeline with the rest of the class. Here's what to do.

- ☐ Have each team member prepare to tell about a part of the timeline.
- ☐ Show your timeline to the class. Imagine that you are giving visitors a tour of your community.
- ☐ Explain how these events and locations affected the growth of your community.
- ☐ Share with the class how your team chose which events and locations to include in the timeline.

Tips for Presenting

Remember these tips when you present to the class.

- ☐ Prepare for the presentation.
- ☐ Make sure what you say is based on fact.
- ☐ Speak clearly and use complete sentences.
- ☐ Relax and enjoy yourself!

174 Chapter 3 How and Why Communities Change Over Time

Project Rubric

Use these questions to help evaluate your project.

	Yes	No
Did your team select events that helped your community grow?		
Did you write clear descriptions of the events?		
Did your team identify locations that represent the key events?		
Did every team member prepare to present a part of the timeline?		
Were you happy with the timeline your team created?		

Project Reflection

Think about the work that you did in this chapter with a group. Describe how well you worked with the other members of your group. What could you have done to help the group work better together?

Take Action

Present your Inquiry Project to your class and assess your work with the project rubric. Then take time to reflect on your work.

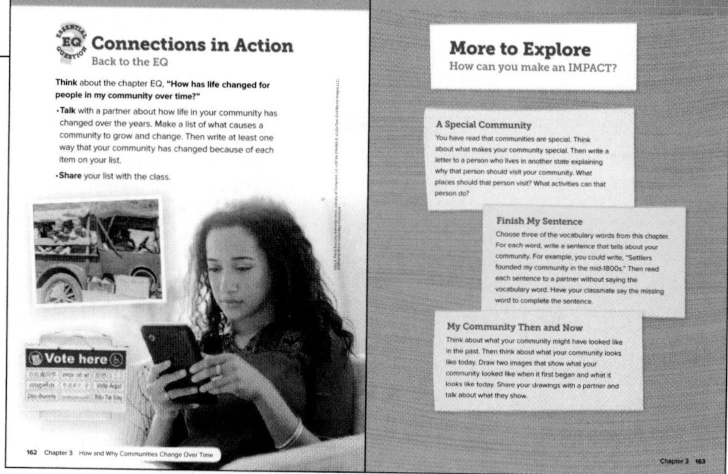

Connections in Action

Back to the EQ

Think about the chapter EQ, **"How has life changed for people in my community over time?"**

- **Talk** with a partner about how life in your community has changed over the years. Make a list of what causes a community to grow and change. Then write at least one way that your community has changed because of each item on your list.
- **Share** your list with the class.

162 Chapter 3 How and Why Communities Change Over Time

More to Explore

How can you make an IMPACT?

A Special Community

You have read that communities are special. Think about what makes your community special. Then write a letter to a person who lives in another state explaining why that person should visit your community. What places should that person visit? What activities can that person do?

Finish My Sentence

Choose three of the vocabulary words from this chapter. For each word, write a sentence that tells about your community. For example, you could write, "Settlers founded my community in the mid-1800s." Then read each sentence to a partner without saying the vocabulary word. Have your classmate say the missing word to complete the sentence.

My Community Then and Now

Think about what your community might have looked like in the past. Then think about what your community looks like today. Draw two images that show what your community looked like when it first began and what it looks like today. Share your drawings with a partner and talk about what they show.

Chapter 3 163

Connections in Action

Think about the people, places, and events you read about in the chapter. Talk with a partner about how this affects your understanding of the EQ.

Every Lesson

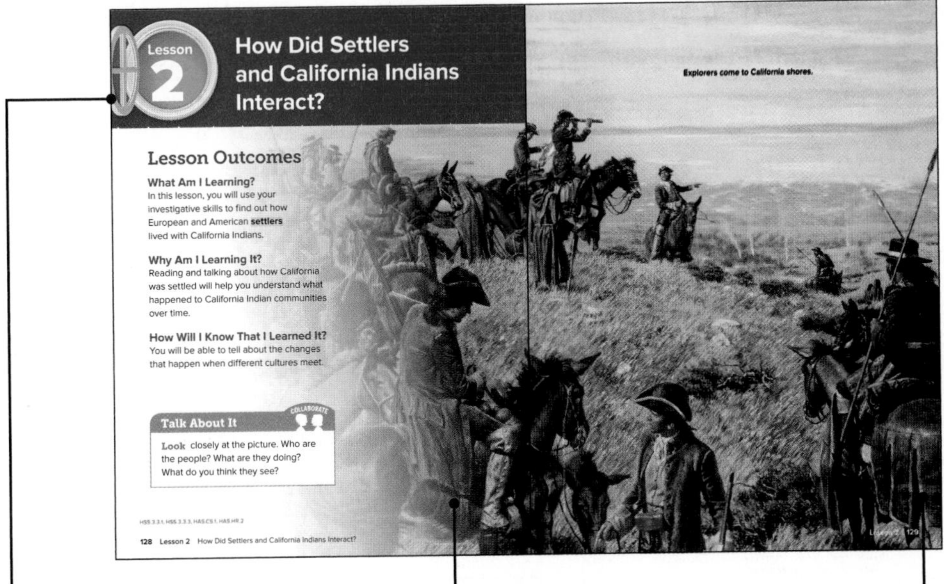

Lesson Question lets you think about how the lesson connects to the chapter EQ.

Lesson Outcomes help you think about what you will be learning and how it applies to the EQ.

Images and text provide opportunities to explore the lesson topic.

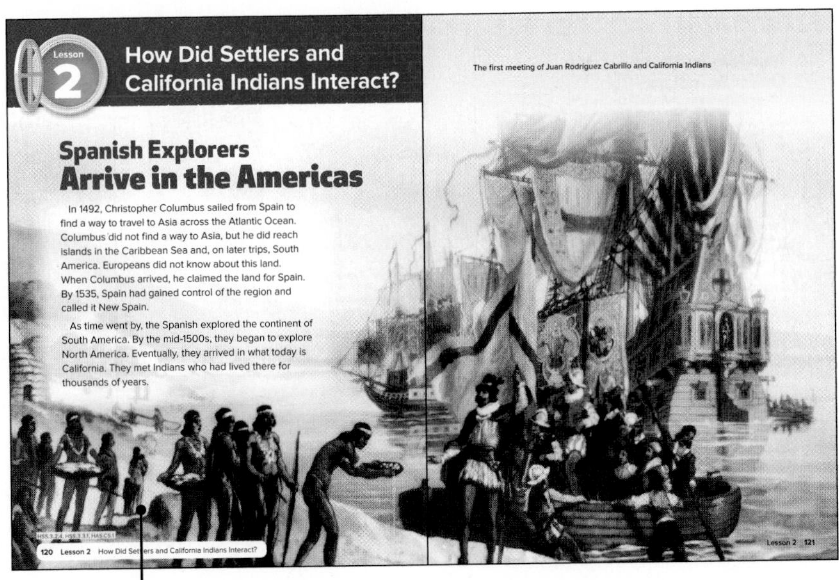

Lesson selections help you develop a deeper understanding of the lesson topic and the EQ.

Analyze and Inquire

The Inquiry Journal provides the tools you need to analyze a source. You'll use those tools to investigate the texts in the Research Companion and use the graphic organizer in the Inquiry Journal to organize your findings.

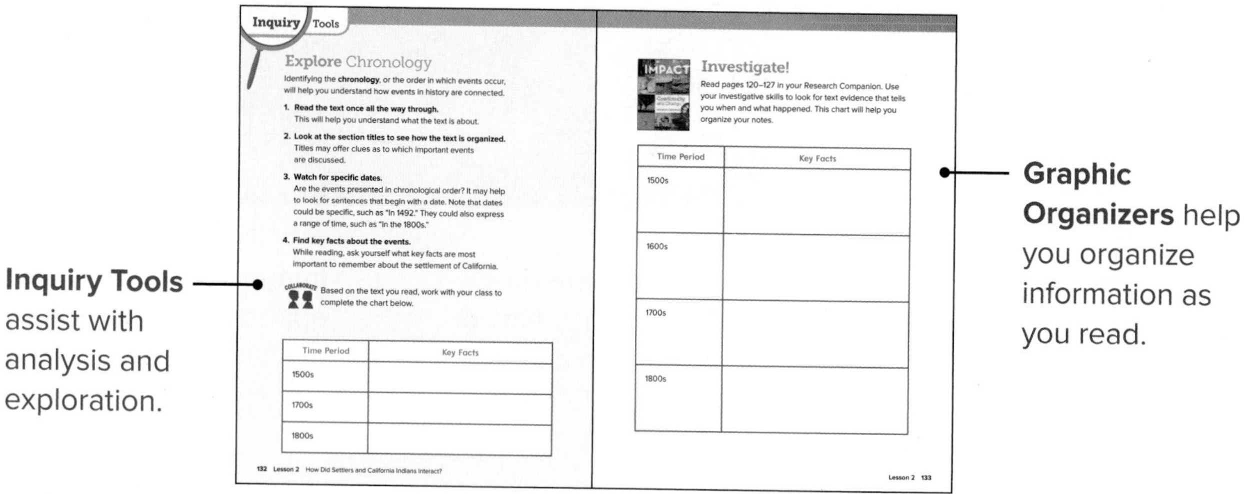

Inquiry Tools assist with analysis and exploration.

Graphic Organizers help you organize information as you read.

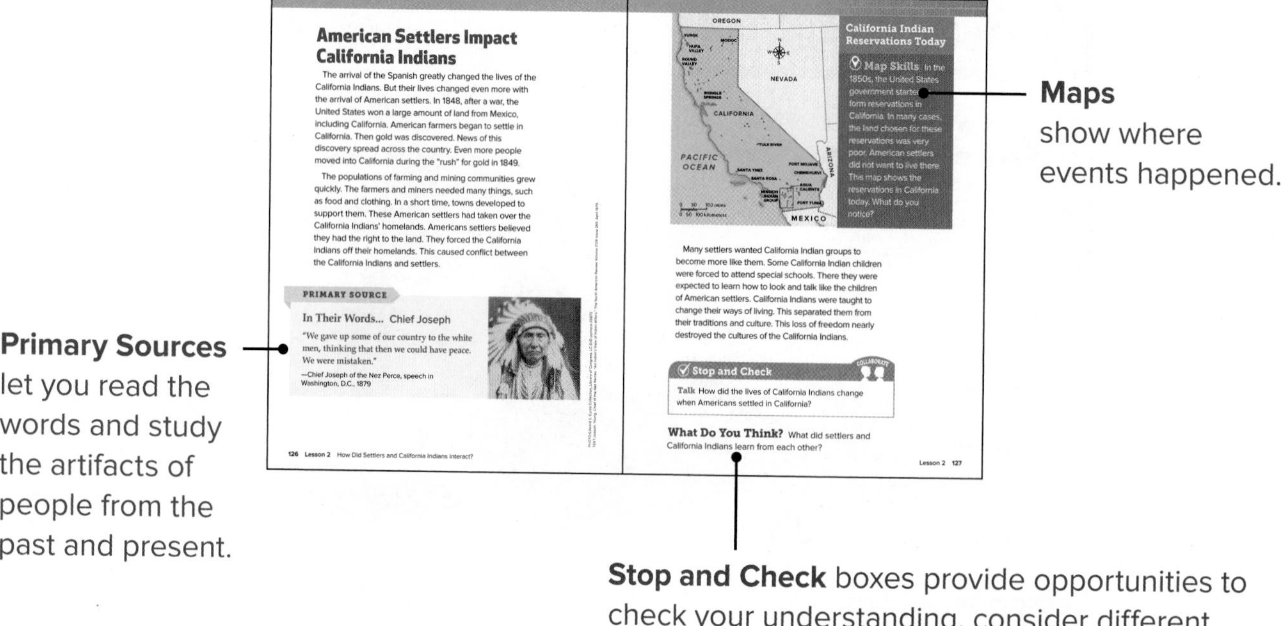

Primary Sources let you read the words and study the artifacts of people from the past and present.

Maps show where events happened.

Stop and Check boxes provide opportunities to check your understanding, consider different perspectives and make connections.

Report Your Findings

At the end of each lesson you have an opportunity in the Inquiry Journal to report your findings and connect back to the EQ. In the Research Companion, you'll think about the lesson focus question.

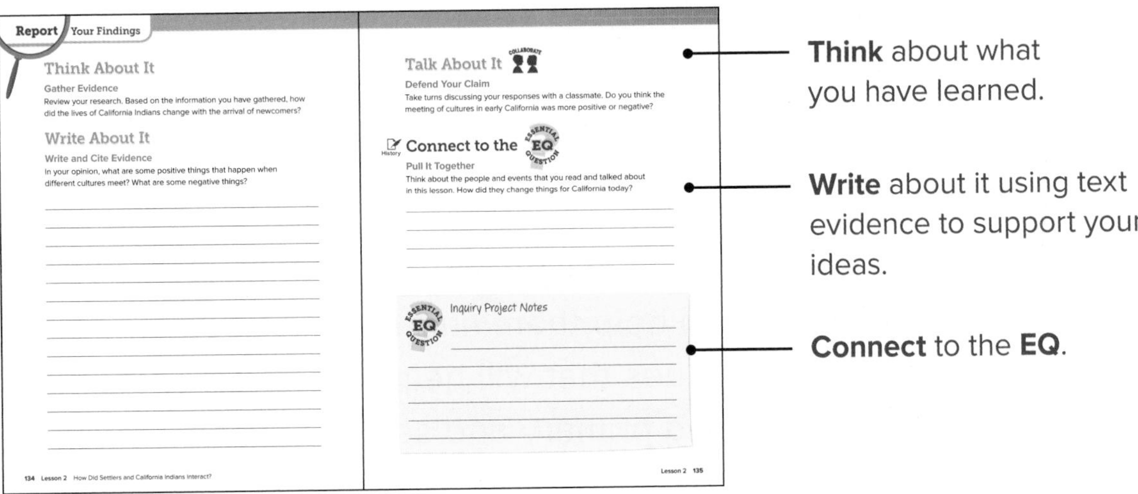

Report Your Findings

Think About It

Gather Evidence

Review your research. Based on the information you have gathered, how did the lives of California Indians change with the arrival of newcomers?

Write About It

Write and Cite Evidence

In your opinion, what are some positive things that happen when different cultures meet? What are some negative things?

Talk About It

Defend Your Claim

Take turns discussing your responses with a classmate. Do you think the meeting of cultures in early California was more positive or negative?

Connect to the EQ

Pull It Together

Think about the people and events that you read and talked about in this lesson. How did they change things for California today?

Inquiry Project Notes

134 Lesson 2 How Did Settlers and California Indians Interact?

Lesson 2 135

Think about what you have learned.

Write about it using text evidence to support your ideas.

Connect to the **EQ**.

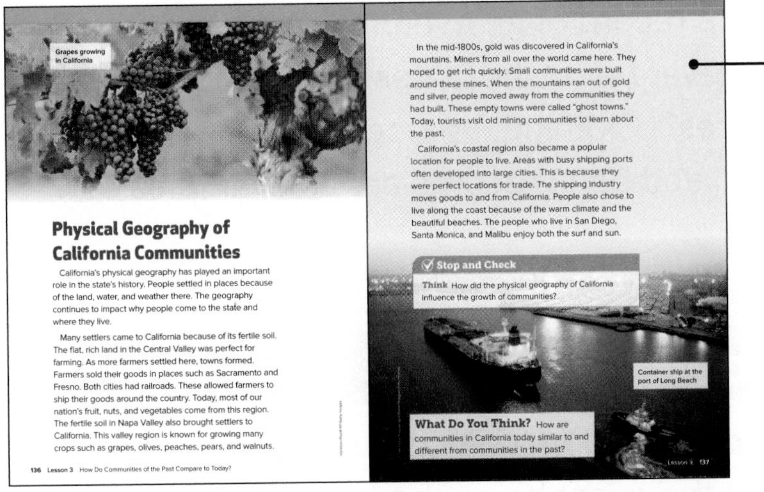

Grapes growing in California

Physical Geography of California Communities

California's physical geography has played an important role in the state's history. People settled in places because of the land, water, and weather there. The geography continues to impact why people come to the state and where they live.

Many settlers came to California because of its fertile soil. The flat, rich land in the Central Valley was perfect for farming. As more farmers settled here, towns formed. Farmers sold their goods in places such as Sacramento and Fresno. Both cities had railroads. These allowed farmers to ship their goods around the country. Today, most of our nation's fruit, nuts, and vegetables come from this region. The fertile soil in Napa Valley also brought settlers to California. This valley region is known for growing many crops such as grapes, olives, peaches, pears, and walnuts.

In the mid-1800s, gold was discovered in California's mountains. Miners from all over the world came here. They hoped to get rich quickly. Small communities were built around these mines. When the mountains ran out of gold and silver, people moved away from the communities they had built. These empty towns were called "ghost towns." Today, tourists visit old mining communities to learn about the past.

California's coastal region also became a popular location for people to live. Areas with busy shipping ports often developed into large cities. This is because they were perfect locations for trade. The shipping industry moves goods to and from California. People also chose to live along the coast because of the warm climate and the beautiful beaches. The people who live in San Diego, Santa Monica, and Malibu enjoy both the surf and sun.

Stop and Check

Think How did the physical geography of California influence the growth of communities?

Container ship at the port of Long Beach

What Do You Think? How are communities in California today similar to and different from communities in the past?

136 Lesson 3 How Do Communities of the Past Compare to Today?

Lesson 3 137

Think about what you read in the lesson. How does this give you a new understanding about the lesson focus question?

Be a Social Studies Detective

How do you learn about people, places, and events? Become a Social Studies Detective!

Explore! Investigate! Report!

Investigate Primary Sources

Detectives solve mysteries by asking questions and searching for clues to help them answer their questions. Where can you get clues that will help you learn about the past? By analyzing primary and secondary sources!

What are Primary Sources?

A **primary source** is a record of an event by someone who was present at whatever he or she is describing. **What are some primary sources?** Clothing, photographs, toys, tools, letters, diaries, and bank records are all examples of primary sources.

Did You Know?

A **secondary source** is information from someone who was not present at the event he or she is describing. Secondary sources are based on primary sources, such as a newspaper article.

StasKhom/iStock/Getty Images

A classroom long ago

Social Studies Detective Strategies

Inspect

- Look closely at the source.
- Who or what is it?
- How would you describe it?

Find Evidence

- Where did the event take place?
- When did it happen?
- What are the most important details?

Make Connections

- Is this source like others you found?
- Are there other perspectives that you need to consider?
- What information supports your idea?

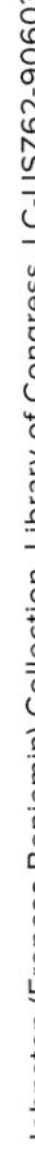

Social Studies Detectives make connections to learn about the past. Look closely at the image below. Use the Social Studies Detective Strategy to analyze the image.

PRIMARY SOURCE

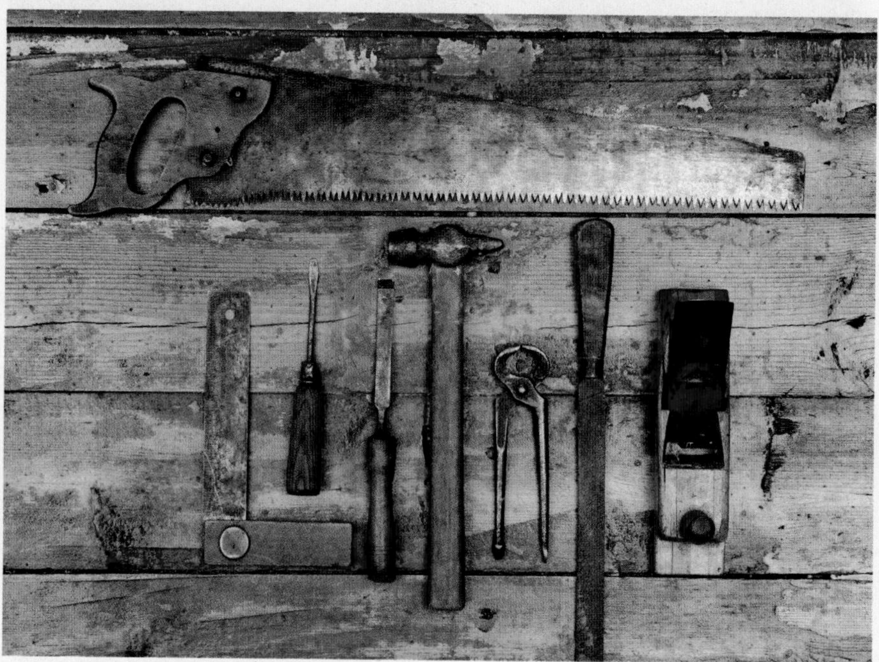

Social Studies Detective Strategies

1. Inspect
2. Find Evidence
3. Make Connections

Talk About It

After you look closely and ask questions about the image and find evidence to support your ideas. Look for evidence, or details in the picture that support your ideas. Share your evidence and make connections to what you know.

ronstik/Shutterstock.com

Here is another source. Inspect the source, and look for clues to answer your questions and make connections.

NO PLACE LIKE SAGAMORE HILL

(To Ethel, at Sagamore Hill)
White House, June 11, 1906.

BLESSED ETHEL:
I am very glad that what changes have been made in the house are good, and I look forward so eagerly to seeing them. After all, fond as I am of the White House and much though I have appreciated these years in it, there isn't any place in the world like home—like Sagamore Hill, where things are our own, with our own associations, and where it is real country.

MORE ABOUT QUENTIN

White House, Nov. 22, 1908.

DEAREST ARCHIE:
I handed your note and the two dollar bill to Quentin, and he was perfectly delighted. It came in very handy, because poor Quentin has been in bed with his leg in a plaster cast, and the two dollars I think went to make up a fund with which he purchased a fascinating little steam-engine, which has been a great source of amusement to him. He is out to-day visiting some friends, although his leg is still in a cast. He has a great turn for mechanics.

from *Theodore Roosevelt's Letters to His Children*

Roosevelt, Theodore, Theodore Roosevelt's Letters To His Children, Edited by Joseph Bucklin Bishop. New York, NY: Charles Scribner's Sons, 1919.

Explore Geography

Geographers are social studies detectives who study the Earth's surface, plants, animals, and people. They use tools to help them investigate. Here are a few of the tools you need to be a geographer.

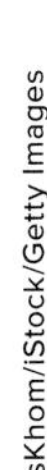

Reading a Map

A map is a drawing of a place. This map shows the United States. Most maps have features that help us use them.

Map Title The map title names the areas shown on the map. The title may also tell you the kind of information shown on the map, such as roads or landforms.

Inset Map An inset map is a small map included on a larger map. The inset map might show an area that is too large, too small, or too far away to be included on the main map.

Boundary Lines Boundary lines show divisions between states and countries. The boundaries between states usually are drawn differently from the boundaries between nations.

Locator Map A locator map is a small map on a larger map. It shows the area of the map in a larger region.

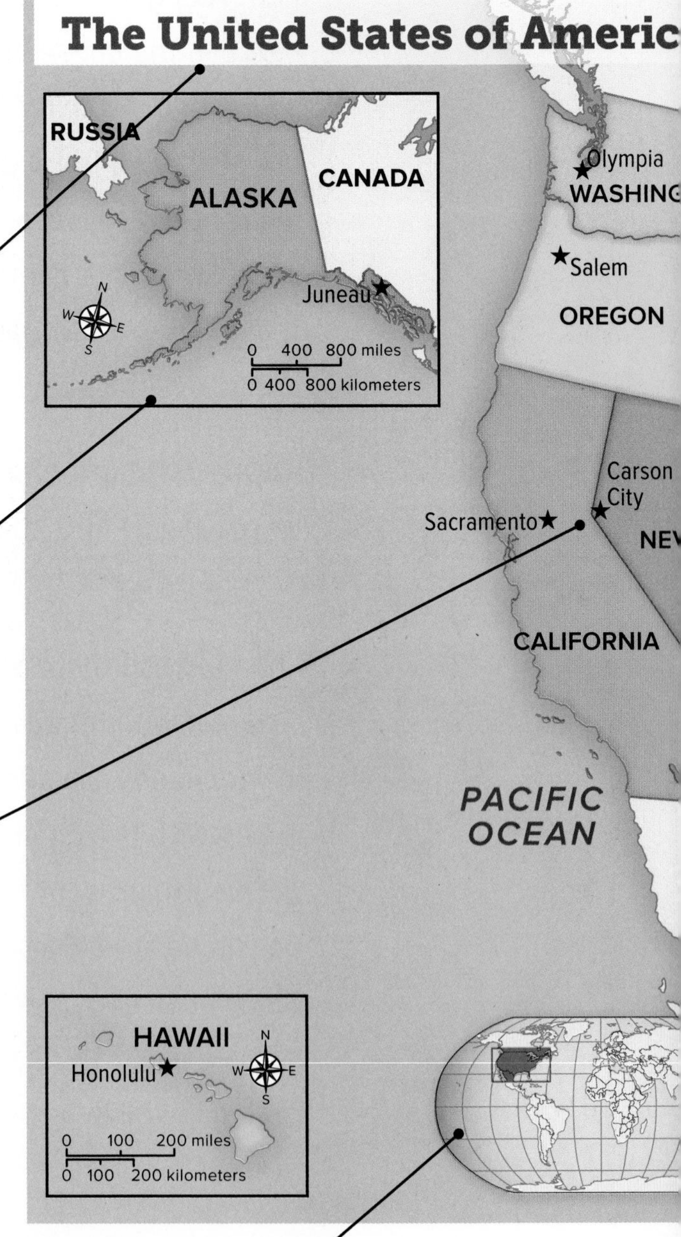

Scale Distances on Earth are too far to show on a map. To figure out the real distance between two places on a map, you use the scale. The scale shows the relationship between distances on a map and real distances.

Compass Rose
The compass rose shows where north, south, east, and west are on the map.

Map Key The key on a map helps you understand the symbols or colors on the map.

Special Purpose Maps

Maps can show different kinds of information about an area such as how many people live there, where mountains and rivers stretch, and where the roads are. These kinds of maps detailing geographical features are called special purpose maps. Below is an example of a special purpose map.

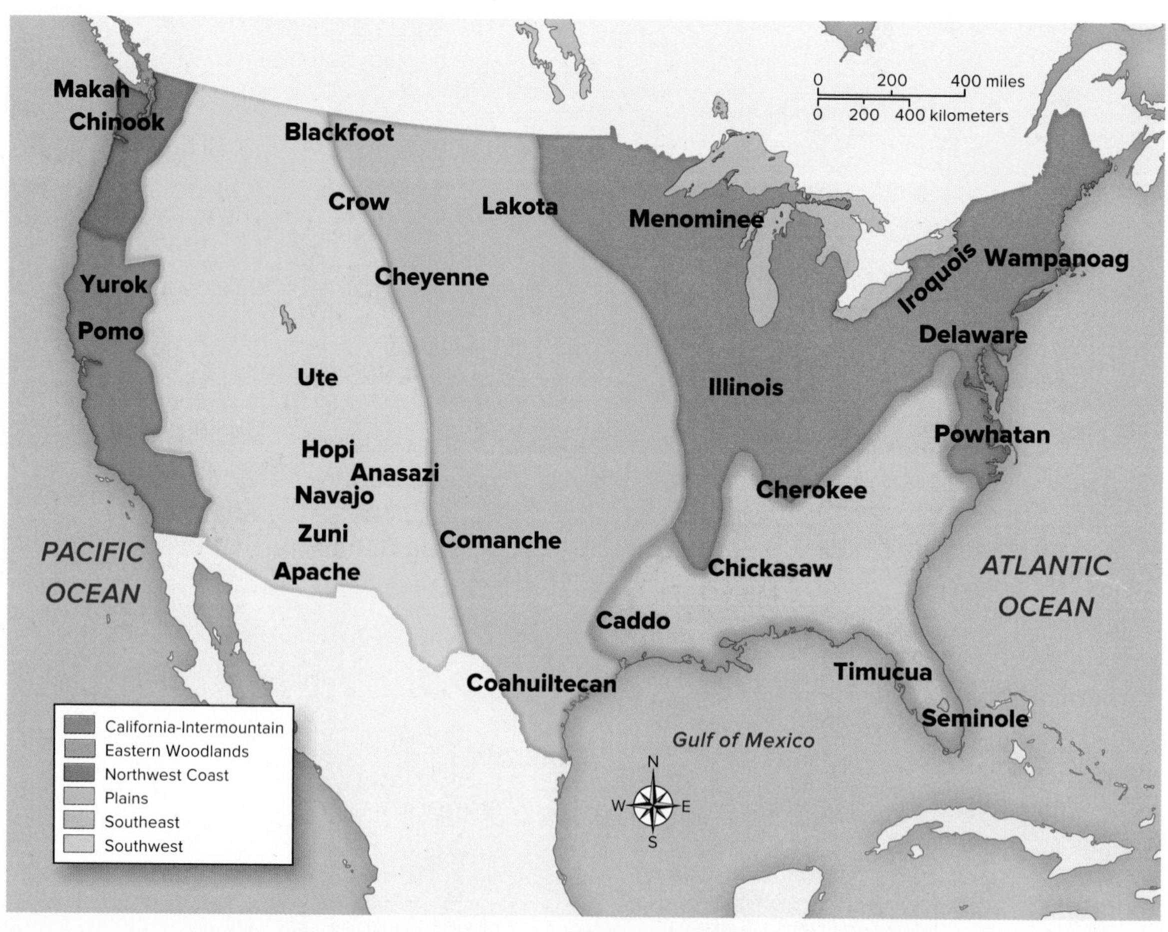

Historical Maps

Historical maps tell a story about a time in the past. This map shows where American Indian tribes lived.

Globes

A globe is a special map that is shaped like a ball. It is a small model of Earth. A model is a copy of something. A globe shows what the land and water look like on Earth.

You can see a line around the widest part of the globe. This is the equator. The equator is an imaginary line. It separates north from south on Earth.

D. Hurst/Alamy Stock Photo

Explore Economics

The goods we buy can come from many different places. Some goods are produced locally such as fresh fruit we find at the farmer's market. Some goods come from other parts of the country such as orange juice produced in Florida. We can even purchase goods that were produced in other parts of the world such as clothes or toys made in other countries. The table below gives examples of food and where it is grown.

Food	Where it is Produced
Grapes	California
Potatoes	Idaho
Limes	Mexico

(t)StasKhom/iStock/Getty Images; (b)lynx/iconotec/Glowimages

PRIMARY SOURCE

135 B 1929 Advt. No. 9771

COFFEE

..is..

America's Favorite Drink

and practically three-fourths of all coffee consumed in the United States comes from

BRAZIL

COFFEE
★ AMERICA'S
favorite
DRINK
★ ★ ★ ★ ★ ★ ★

THE BRAZILIAN-AMERICAN COFFEE PROMOTION COMMITTEE
NEW YORK CITY

Talk About It

COLLABORATE

Look closely at the picture. Where do you think these goods were produced? What details in the picture support your ideas?

(l)©2017 Smithsonian, (r)lynx/iconotec.com/Glow Images

Explore Citizenship

You can make an impact by being a good citizen. The words below describe good citizens. They help us understand how to be good citizens in our home, neighborhood, school, community, country, and world.

Take Action!

You have learned to be a Social Studies Detective by investigating, finding evidence, and making connections. Then you practiced investigating geography, economics, and civics. Now it's time to explore and make an impact!

PRIMARY SOURCE

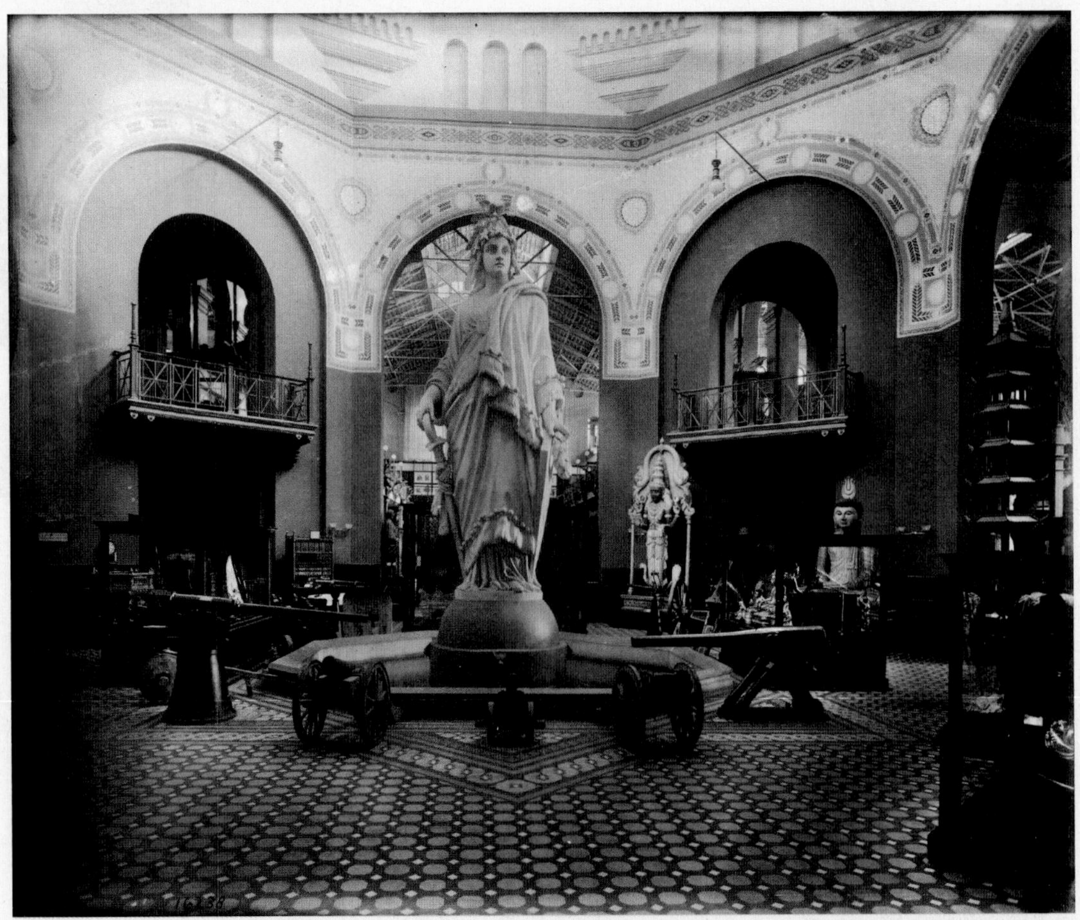

The Statue of Freedom sits atop the dome of the United States Capitol.

(t)StasKhom/iStock/Getty Images; (b)©2017 Smithsonian

Be a Good Citizen

COURAGE
Being brave in the face of difficulty

FREEDOM
Making choices and holding beliefs of one's own

HONESTY
Telling the truth

JUSTICE
Working toward fair treatment for everyone

LEADERSHIP
Showing good behavior worth following through example

LOYALTY
Showing support for people and one's country

RESPECT
Treating others as you would like to be treated

RESPONSIBILITY
Being worthy of trust

(bkgd)C Squared Studios/Photodisc/Getty Images; (inset)Daniel Kaesler/EyeEm/GettyImages

Chapter 1

Communities in California

Lesson 1
My California

Lesson 2
Features of the Land

Lesson 3
Living by the Sea

Lesson 4
Down in the Valley

Lesson 5
Desert Life

Lesson 6
Up in the Mountains

How Does Geography Impact California Communities?

A community's land, resources, and weather affect how people live and work. In this chapter, you will read about the different types of communities in California. You will explore where communities developed in California. You will also learn how people use California's land and resources. As you read, think about your own community. How do land, resources, and weather affect life in your community?

Rob Tilley/Blend Images LLC

The climate brings people from all over the country to California.

HSS.3.1.1, HSS.3.1.2, HSS.3.3.1

Why Do Communities Develop?

Communities come in many different shapes and sizes. Some are small and rural. Others are huge cities with millions of people. Many things can affect how communities develop.

California's valleys are perfect for farming. The soil is good for growing crops. The valleys get plenty of sunshine and rain. Small rural communities often developed around these farms. People came to the valleys to work on the farms.

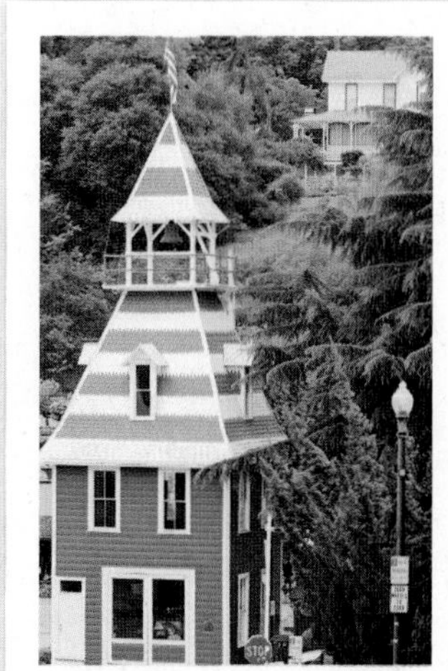

Many of California's communities grew because of the resources near them. People settled Auburn when gold was discovered in the area in 1848. Miners came to the town to get rich. Some mining towns disappeared once the gold was gone. However, many continued to grow as new businesses developed.

In 1850, Los Angeles was a small town with only about 1,500 people. The town began to grow when railroads were built in 1876 and 1885. People traveled by train to Los Angeles because of its warm climate. Many of them chose to stay. Los Angeles continued to grow in the 1930s and 1940s as people came to work in films or build airplanes. Today, nearly 4 million people live in Los Angeles.

(t)Ingram Publishing/SuperStock; (bl)compassandcamera/iStock/Getty Images; (br)David Sucsy/E+/Getty Images

Connect Through Literature

NATURE'S NOTE-TAKER

Nicole Groeneweg

John Muir loved nature and wrote about it almost every day. When he watched a swaying pine tree on a mountaintop, he jotted down that it looked like

"a magic wand in nature's hand"

He painted word pictures of the untamed West for others who could not visit those places. To share what he witnessed, Muir described sights, sounds, and smells in his notebooks. A rock hiding under a tree first inspired him to write,

"How beautiful the rock is
made by leaf shadows ...
still as if painted on stone,
now gliding softly as if
afraid of noise, now dancing
... jumping on and off
sunny rocks."

PHOTO:(b)George Grantham Bain Collection, Library of Congress, LC-DIG-ggbain-06861; (bkgd)McGraw-Hill Education;
TEXT:"Nature's Note-taker" by Nicole Grownewweg, Appleseeds March 2011, © by Carus Publishing Company, Reproduced with permission. All Cricket Media material is copyrighted by Carus Publishing Company,
d/b/a Cricket Media, and/or various authors and illustrators. Any commercial use or distribution of material without permission is strictly prohibited. Please visit http://www.cricketmedia.com/info/licensing2 for licensing
and http://www.cricketmedia.com for subscriptions.

Muir also loved storms. Once, after a storm had passed, he opened his journal and wrote,

"A few minutes ago, every tree was excited, bowing to the roaring storm, waving, swirling, tossing their branches."

To hear the "music of its topmost needles," he once climbed a 100-foot spruce tree during a winter windstorm. In his notes, he described the pine needles he'd heard as

"rising to a shrill, whistling hiss" then "falling to a silky murmur."

The minty scent of evergreens and the ocean mist on the wind also found their way into Muir's magazine articles and books. As he continued to explore the American wilderness, Muir sketched and wrote about each new discovery. His writings brought news of nature to people far away. Muir convinced city dwellers to hike in the mountains, because

"nature's peace will flow into you like sunshine flows into trees. The winds will blow their own freshness into you and the storms their energy."

Muir's words show his passion for nature. His writings changed the way Americans thought of the natural world and paved the way for our national parks.

Think About It

1. Why did John Muir write about nature?
2. What did John Muir mean when he described a swaying pine tree as "a magic wand in nature's hand"?
3. How is nature a part of our communities?

During his lifetime, Muir published more than **300** articles and **8** books. And **4** more books were published after his death.

(t)American Memory, Library of Congress, LC-USZ62-52000; (b)Prints and Photographs Collections, Library of Congress, LC-DIG-ppmsca-18943; (bkgd)McGraw-Hill Education

Lesson 1

Where Is My Community?

Communities in California

You live in a **community** in California. A community is a place where people live, work, and play. California is a large state with many different communities. What is your community like?

All communities are alike in some ways. Every community has homes where people live. Communities also have places where people work. Most communities have schools, libraries, and places of worship. Many communities have fire and police departments to help keep people safe. All communities have leaders elected by the people who live there. The leaders help decide what the laws should be and what kinds of services the community needs.

Communities can also be different from each other. Some communities have larger **populations** than others. Population is the number of people who live in one place. Some communities are crowded with many homes, businesses, and buildings. Other communities have fewer people and more open space. These kinds of differences make each community in California special.

Tara Wilsworth

HSS.3.1.1, HSS.3.1.2, HSS.3.3.1, HAS.CS.1, HAS.CS.2, HAS.CS.4, HAS.CS.5, HAS.HI.2

Matteo Colombo/DigitalVision/Getty Images

Van Ness Avenue in San Francisco

Urban, Suburban, and Rural Communities

There are three different kinds of communities in California: urban, suburban, and rural. Large cities, such as San Francisco and Los Angeles, are urban. An urban community has many people, busy streets, and buildings that are close together. More than 800,000 people live in San Francisco. Cities also offer people many ways to have fun. People enjoy going to parks, museums, and libraries.

A community just outside a city is called a suburb. Some suburban communities have more space between houses and buildings than in cities. The roads have less traffic than cities. Shopping malls and smaller businesses are often located in suburbs. Suburbs have schools and businesses just like cities, but there are fewer people. About 74,000 people live in San Ramon, a suburb of San Francisco. Some people who live in San Ramon travel into San Francisco to work.

Did You Know?

Los Angeles is the largest urban community in California. It has nearly 4 million people. Shoshone is one of the smallest communities. Fewer than 50 people live there.

A rural community

(t)SUNNYphotography.com/Alamy; (b)Suzanne Jamison/EyeEm/Getty Images

The third type of community is rural. Rural communities have small towns, farms, fields, and open land. Mendota is an example of a rural community. It is located in the San Joaquin Valley. Mendota is a small town with about 10,000 people. Rural towns like Mendota have only a few businesses.

Houses in Long Beach

Urban, suburban, and rural communities are very different. However, they depend on each other in many ways. Many people who live in the suburbs travel into urban areas for work. Farmers in rural areas grow food for people in all communities. Factories in cities make products that are sold everywhere.

People from all communities in California come together for fun. They might attend a baseball game in the city or visit a national park in the desert. Every summer, thousands of people from big cities and small towns attend the California State Fair in Sacramento. These events help connect all Californians.

COLLABORATE

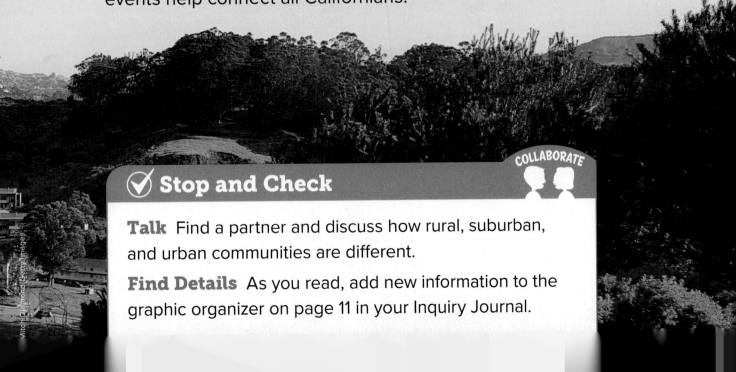

Stop and Check

Talk Find a partner and discuss how rural, suburban, and urban communities are different.

Find Details As you read, add new information to the graphic organizer on page 11 in your Inquiry Journal.

Mitch_Diamond/Getty Images

Locating My Community

If someone asks you where you live, how would you answer? Maybe you could start with the name of your community. Then you could describe it as urban, suburban, or rural. You also could use a map to show where your community is located in the state.

A map is a drawing of a place. Maps can show the entire world or a smaller area like a state, city, or town.

Look at the map on this page. It shows the state of California. Where is your community in the state? It may be in the middle of the state, near the water, or up in the mountains.

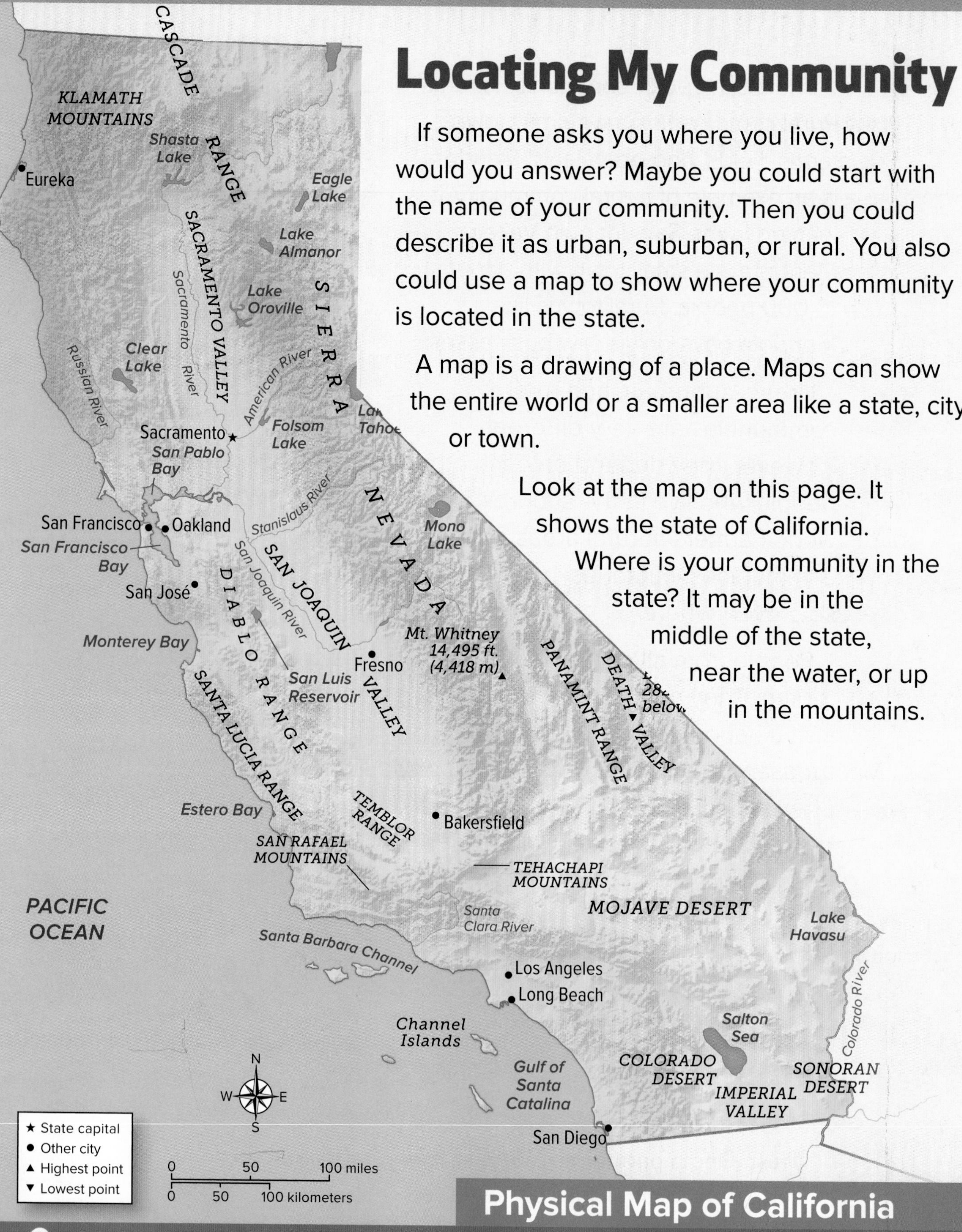

Physical Map of California

Map Skills Find the area where your community is on the map. What kinds of land and water are near your community?

Most maps have similar features. These features help us read and use maps. The map key, or legend, is a box that explains the symbols on the map.

Many maps also include a compass rose. A compass rose shows where north, south, east, and west are on the map. These are the *cardinal directions*. A compass rose might also show *intermediate directions*. These are in between the cardinal directions. For example, *northeast* is an intermediate direction. It is between north and east.

Maps are drawn using map scales. A map scale is a unit of measurement that stands for a real distance on Earth. On the map on this page, 1 inch stands for 10 miles on Earth. Each map has a different scale. The scale rule on this map has marks that represent actual distances.

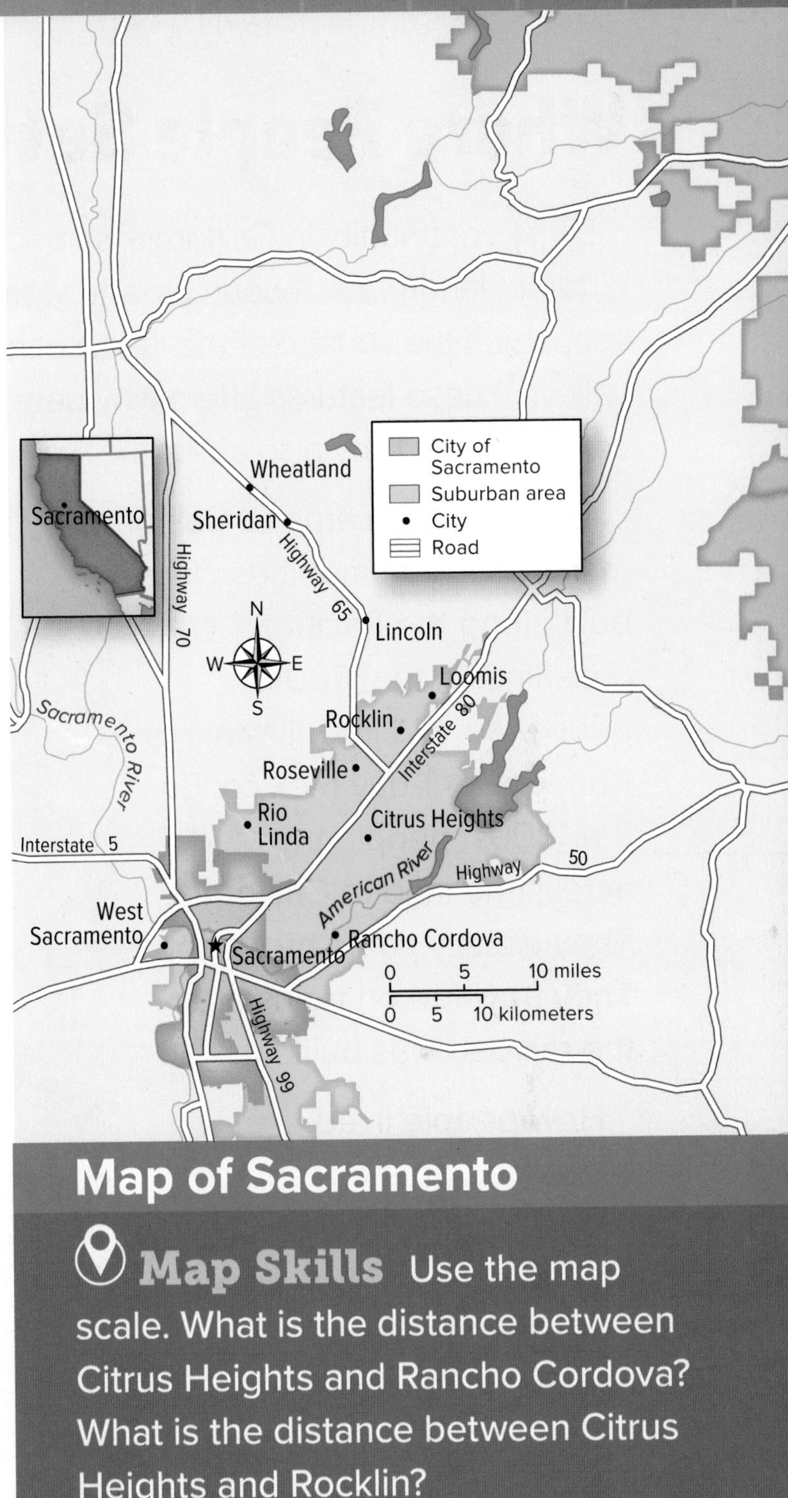

Map of Sacramento

Map Skills Use the map scale. What is the distance between Citrus Heights and Rancho Cordova? What is the distance between Citrus Heights and Rocklin?

Stop and Check

Think Use the map to identify two suburbs of Sacramento.

Where People Settle

Every community in California is special. Communities have different landforms, resources, and weather. Landforms are shapes on the surface of the land, such as mountains and valleys. These features affect why people settle in these communities. They also affect the way people live.

Many people came to California by ship. This is why many early communities were built along the Pacific coastline. In the 1700s, people arrived in California from present-day Mexico. By the 1800s, people traveled across the land to California. They usually came by wagon. They traveled on trains after the railroad was built.

How people lived depended on the resources in their community. The Sacramento and San Joaquin Valleys began as farming communities because the area had rich soil and plenty of water. San Francisco and Los Angeles were built along the coast. These cities shipped goods from ports. Miners built towns near the mountains where they searched for gold.

Sierra Nevada crossing, 1865

North Wind Picture Archives

The land, water, and climate continue to affect how people live in California's communities. **Climate** is the weather a place has over a long period of time. People who live in a place with a cold climate need different kinds of clothes and houses than people who live where it is warm. Climate also makes a difference to how people have fun. People who live along the coast might enjoy the beach. People who live in mountains might ski or hike. People who live in hot, dry desert communities might go rock climbing. Each community provides people with different ways to live, work, and play.

Stop and Check

COLLABORATE

Talk What are some ways the land and climate affect how people live?

What Do You Think? What is your community like? Is it urban, suburban, or rural? What kind of land and climate does it have?

Campers setting up tents.

Seth K. Hughes/Image Source/Getty Images

What Are Some Features of Each Region in California?

California's Regions

Think about where you live. Is it hilly or flat? Do you live near an ocean or a river? Is it cloudy, foggy, or sunny most of the time? Your answers will depend on the **region** where you live. A region is an area of land with certain features that make it different from other areas. Each region has its own type of landforms, bodies of water, and weather.

California has four main regions. These four regions are the valley, coast, mountains, and desert. Each region has different landforms and **climates**. The features of each region in California affect how people live.

Buck Forester/Moment/Getty Images

HSS.3.1.1, HSS.3.1.2, HAS.CS.1, HAS.CS.3, HAS.CS.4, HAS.HI.2

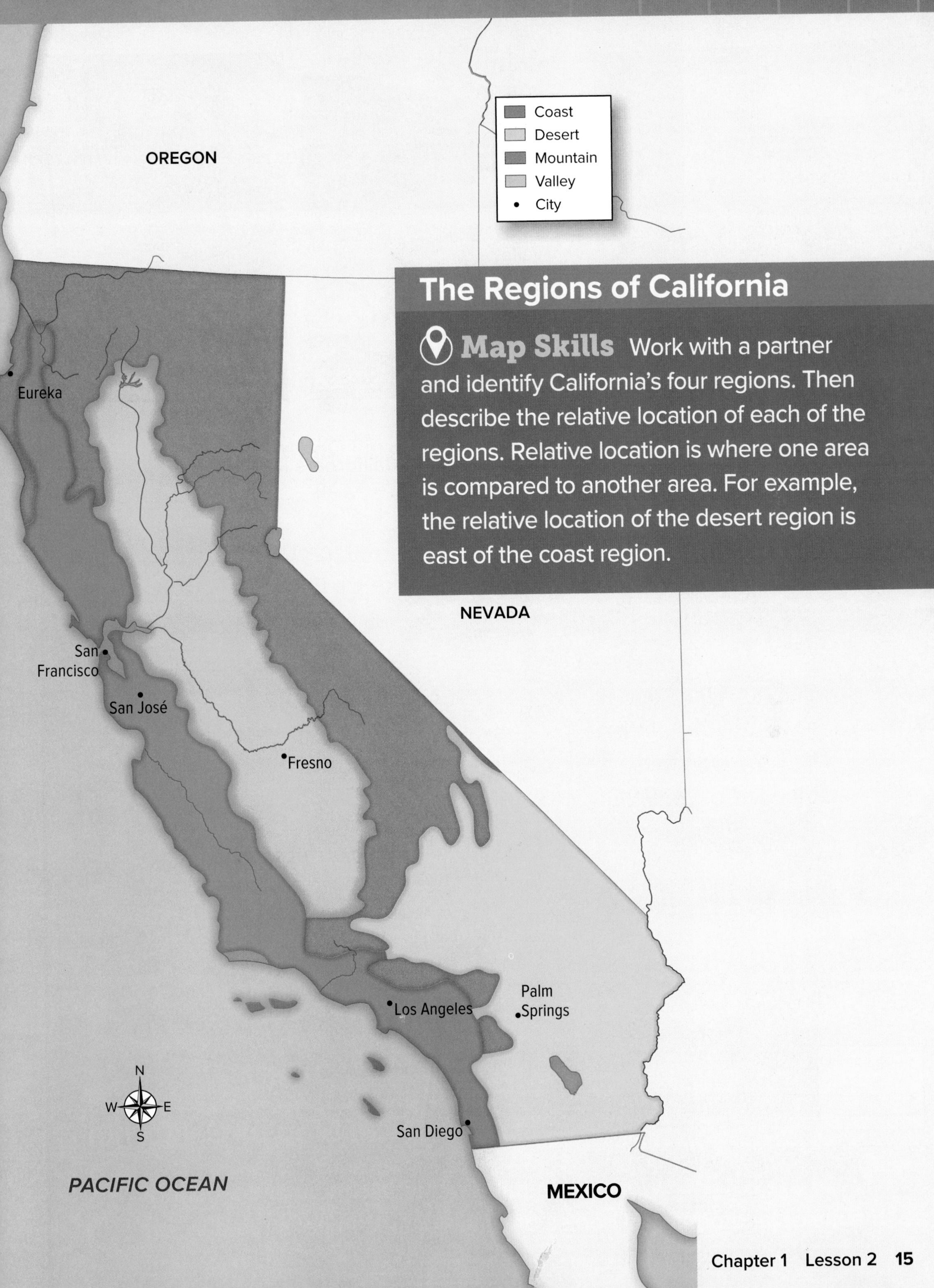

The Regions of California

Map Skills Work with a partner and identify California's four regions. Then describe the relative location of each of the regions. Relative location is where one area is compared to another area. For example, the relative location of the desert region is east of the coast region.

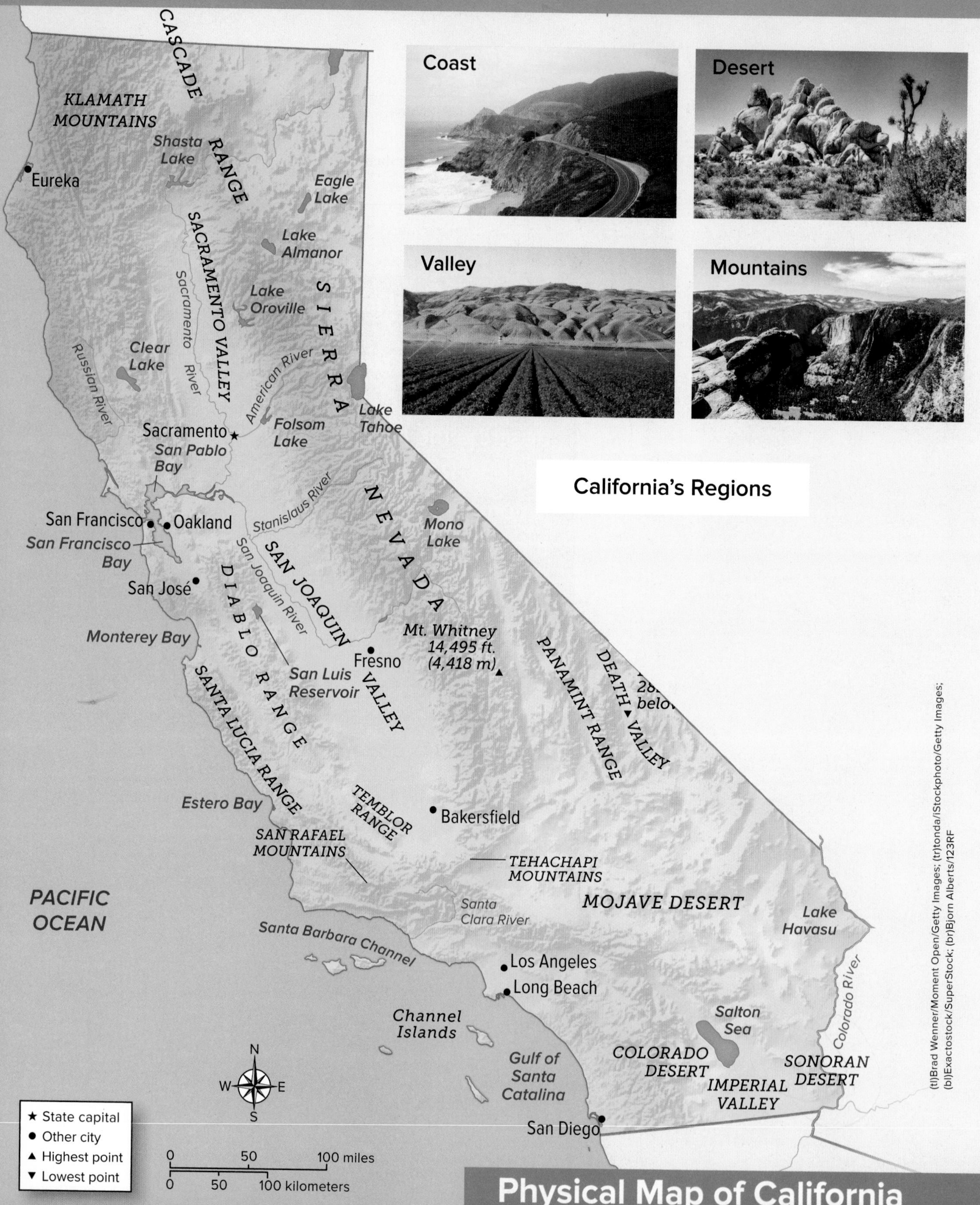

(tl)Brad Wenner/Moment Open/Getty Images; (tr)tonda/iStockphoto/Getty Images; (bl)Exactostock/SuperStock; (br)Bjorn Alberts/123RF

Map Skills Work with a partner and use the map to identify the major landforms and bodies of water located in each region.

California's valley region is found in the middle of the state and is called the Central Valley. This region includes the San Joaquin [hwah KEEN] Valley and Sacramento Valley. It is surrounded by mountains. The climate and soil in the valley are perfect for growing crops. Farmers in the Central Valley grow much of the nation's food, including tomatoes, carrots, lettuce, asparagus, grapes, almonds, pears, green beans, and more!

The coastal region runs along the shore of the Pacific Ocean. This region stretches more than 840 miles from the northern border of the state to the southern border. Many people live in this region. Most of the coast is lined with mountains that are close to the ocean.

There are two major mountain ranges, or rows of connected mountains, in California. These are the Coast Ranges and the Sierra Nevada. Mount Whitney, the highest peak in California, is in the Sierra Nevada. Some of California's mountains have many forests, but others are bare and rocky. Snow covers many of the mountains throughout the year, even in the summer!

The desert region is in the southern part of the state. This area includes the Mojave [mo HAH vay] Desert and the Colorado Desert. Some desert areas are 2,000 feet above sea level. The lowest is 282 feet below sea level in Death Valley. The plants and animals that live in the desert have adapted to its dry climate.

Stop and Check

Think How would you describe the land in your community? In which region do you live?

Find Details As you read, add new information to the graphic organizer on page 19 in your Inquiry Journal.

The Central Valley

California's Central Valley is more than 400 miles long. In most places, it is about 50 miles wide. Use the map on page 16 to find the Central Valley. As you can see, this region is bordered by mountain ranges. The Sierra Nevada is a mountain range to the east. The Coast Ranges are to the west. In the Coast Ranges, the Klamath Mountains are to the north, and the Tehachapi [tuh HA chuh pee] Mountains are to the south.

Rain and melting snow flow down the Sierra Nevada into the Central Valley. This mountain runoff creates streams that flow into the Sacramento and San Joaquin Rivers. Dams, canals, and pipelines have been built in this region to help farmers use the water for their crops.

Farmers in the Central Valley grow much of the country's vegetables, fruits, and nuts. Ranchers here also raise livestock such as cattle, sheep, and horses.

Exactostock/SuperStock

The Coast

Many of California's big cities—including San Francisco, Los Angeles, and San Diego—are in the coastal region. About one-half of California's **population** lives in these three busy areas along the coast. Long ago, settlers came to California in ships, and **communities** formed near the coast. Today, California's southern coast has the largest population in the state.

The climate in the northern part of the coastal region is rainy with cool winters. When the snow melts in the spring, the rivers may flood. Farther south, the temperature does not change much throughout the year. However, plants and grasses may dry up if there is not enough **precipitation**. This can lead to dangerous wildfires.

California's coast is a great place to enjoy ocean wildlife. People can fish, watch sea lions and seals at the harbor, or take boats out on the water. Animals such as coyotes and black bears also live in the mountains near the coast.

Brad Wenner/Moment Open/Getty Images

The Mountains

The Sierra Nevada is the largest mountain range in California. It stretches more than 250 miles from north to south. The mountains are rocky and tall. Some have snow on them all year round. The weather can be cold in the winters and warm in the summers.

The geography of the mountains made them difficult for early settlers. When they came to California in the 1800s, it took them a long time to travel across the high, rocky land. In the early 1860s, workers started to build a railroad that would link the east and west coasts of the United States. It was called the Transcontinental Railroad. Two railroad companies were involved in the project. The Central Pacific Railroad started in Sacramento, California. The Union Pacific started in Omaha, Nebraska. The two companies met in Promontory, Utah, in 1869. The Transcontinental Railroad helped move people and goods safely across the country. They could travel during any season, and it was safe. Today, highways make traveling through California's mountain region even easier.

California's mountains

Bjorn Alberts/123RF

The Desert

Much of California's land is desert. Some parts of this land can be high and rocky. It is low and flat in other places. Deserts have a very dry climate. Some parts of California's desert get only 2 to 6 inches of rain each year. That's just enough for some plants and animals to survive.

Joshua Tree National Park in the Mojave

The Mojave Desert is one of the largest deserts in California. The Mojave Desert alone is larger than the state of West Virginia! An area in the northern part of the Mojave Desert is called Death Valley. Death Valley is the lowest, driest, and hottest place in the United States.

Then and Now

For more than 10,000 years, people have lived in and moved through the Mojave Trails area in the Mojave Desert. This is an area of mountains, lava flows, and sand dunes. Over time, a highway was built through the land. However, people did not build homes here. Instead, they traveled to the area to see its natural beauty. In February 2016, President Barack Obama named the Mojave Trails a national monument.

 Stop and Check

Talk In which region is it easiest for people to survive? In which is it most difficult? Use evidence from the lesson to support your answers.

(t)tonda/iStockphoto/Getty Images; (b)Bob Wick/U.S. Bureau Of Land Management

California's Water

You might think that a state that borders the ocean has an unlimited supply of water. However, the ocean is saltwater. People, plants, and animals need freshwater from rain, melting snow, and rivers to survive. In California, getting this water can be difficult. The southern part of the state and the large deserts have a very dry **environment**. Other areas receive too much rain or water from melting snow all at once. This can cause dangerous floods and mudslides.

So how do people get the water they need? Long ago, people settled near rivers. Today, people move water from rivers to places where it is needed. Engineers design dams, canals, and pipelines to move water. These changes affect the land. This helps some areas but can hurt others.

The Oroville Dam on the Feather River is 770 feet high. It is the highest dam in the United States.

alacatr/E+/Getty Images

Conserving Water

Water is a valuable resource. All living things need it to survive. Think of the ways people use water: drinking, bathing, cooking, playing, and more. We must be careful to **conserve** what we have. To conserve water means to use it without wasting it. It also means keeping our water sources clean. Today, people work to find solutions to use water in a fair and responsible way.

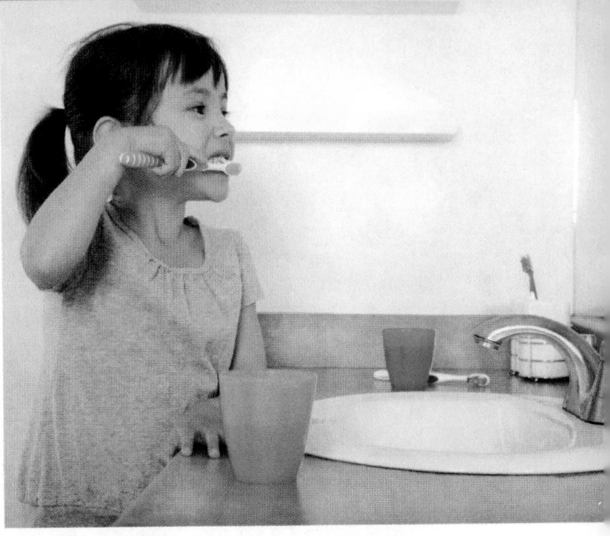

You can save water while you brush your teeth.

Did You Know?

How can you make simple changes to help conserve water? Here are some tips.

- **Only run water while you are using it.** Turn off the faucet while you brush your teeth. Turn off the hose after you wash off your muddy shoes.
- **Use less water.** Wait until your clothes are dirty to wash them. Wait until the dishwasher is full to run it. Take a short shower instead of a bath.
- **Reuse water.** Instead of pouring out used water from a vase, pour it on other plants. Collect rainwater to fill your dog's bowl or water a garden.

Stop and Check

COLLABORATE

Talk With a partner, discuss what you can do to conserve water.

What Do You Think? In your opinion, where is the best region to live in California? Why?

Chris Bernard/E+/Getty Images

What Are the Features of a Coastal Community?

Physical Features of California's Coast

What do you imagine when you hear the word *coast*? You might think of playing on a sandy beach or swimming in the ocean. You also may picture towering cliffs and giant redwood trees. Both are correct if you are in California.

A coast is an area of land along water. Have you ever been to the coast of California? California's coast stretches about 840 miles along the Pacific Ocean. Much of the land along the coast is mountainous. This is because the coastal **region** is part of the Coast Ranges. These mountains start in the state of Washington. They extend south through Oregon and into California. The land is rocky and the seawater is cold along the northern coast. The southern coast has sandy beaches and warm water.

In general, California's coast has a mild **climate**. In the north, summers are cool and dry. Winters are wet and cold. As you travel south, it is dry and warm all year long. People who live in a coastal **community** enjoy good weather much of the year.

Jon Bilous/Shutterstock.com

HSS.3.1.1, HSS.3.1.2, HSS.3.3.1, HAS.CS.1, HAS.CS.3, HAS.CS.5, HAS.HI.2

Inspiration Point in Corona del Mar, California

Coastal Resources

Northern California coastline

California's coastal communities have many **natural resources**. The Pacific Ocean is one of the region's major resources. Fishing in the Pacific Ocean is an important **industry** and provides food for millions of people. An industry is a group of businesses that do the same type of work. Ships cross the Pacific Ocean to transport goods between countries.

The coast is also home to many types of animals and plants. Blue whales, the world's largest animal, swim off the coast. Plants such as giant kelp grow in the water. They form forests in the water where other plants and animals live. The land is unusual, too. The coast is very rocky. In some places, the land has worn away over time. This is called erosion. Erosion happens when waves break apart and move the rocks and sand. Erosion changes the land and can wash away beaches.

A diver finds an octopus off the California coast.

(t)Robert Schwemmer, NOAA, NOS, CINMS/Department of Commerce; (b)Ashley Wiley/E+/Getty Images

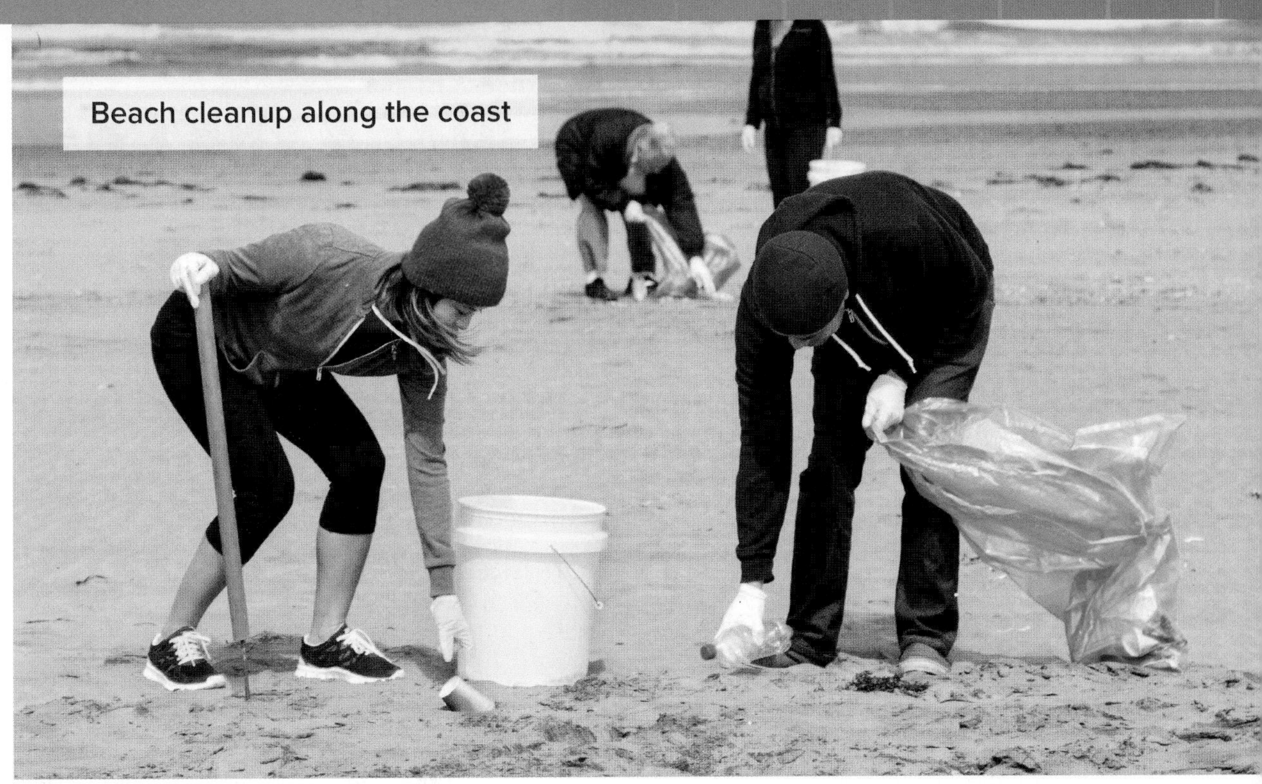
Beach cleanup along the coast

Protecting the coast is very important to many Californians. People in coastal communities such as Long Beach have worked to protect their **environment**. Long Beach is located between two rivers. This causes a problem for the community. Trash gets into these rivers. The rivers move the trash into the ocean. Then the waves push the trash back onto the beach. This leaves trash on the beach with nowhere to go.

A community group called the 30-Minute Beach Cleanup works to clean the beaches. Once a month, people pick up trash and other debris. The community has collected thousands of bags of trash. The people of Long Beach work together to keep their community clean.

Talk With a partner, discuss the types of resources that are found in California's coastal region.

Find Details As you read, add new information to the graphic organizer on page 27 in your Inquiry Journal.

Jason Doiy/iStock/Getty Images

Making a Living Along the Coast

Many people who live along the coast work in the fishing and shipping industries. These industries rely on the resources the ocean provides.

There are many fishing communities along California's coast. Crescent City, Shelter Cove, and Albion are towns that are located in Northern California. People in these communities fish for salmon from the rivers and ocean. Moss Landing and Morro Bay are located along the Central Coast. People here catch sardines and squid. Farther south, people in San Pedro, Dana Point, and Mission Bay catch spiny lobster and red sea urchin. These communities all work in the same industry, but they depend on different types of ocean resources.

Fishermen off the Sausalito waterfront

Did You Know?

People in the armed forces work at military bases along California's coast. The Presidio of Monterey is an Army base. Vandenberg Air Force Base is located near Lompoc. People make and test equipment used for space missions. Camp Pendleton is the major West Coast Marine base and is located along the coast of Southern California. North Island Naval Complex is located in San Diego. The Navy SEALs train there for missions around the world.

Chad Ehlers/Alamy Stock Photo

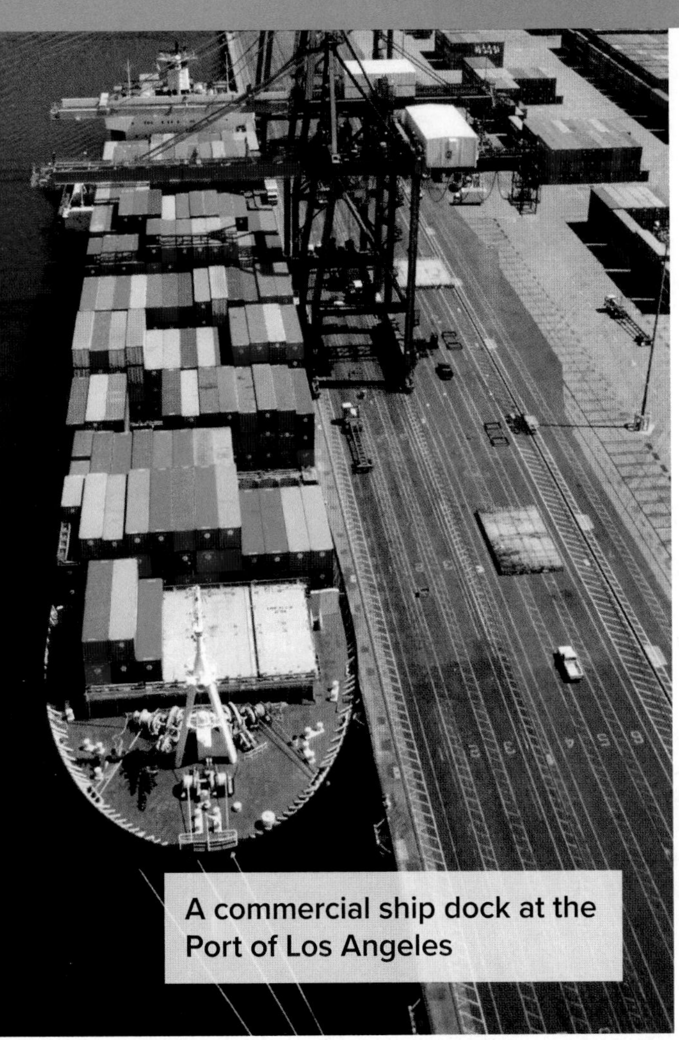

A commercial ship dock at the Port of Los Angeles

Containers are taken off ships and loaded onto trucks at the port.

A port is a place where ships and boats can load and unload. Los Angeles and Oakland are two port cities on the Pacific Coast. These ports are very busy. Ships from around the world come to the ports. The ships carry goods that will be sold in California and throughout the United States. Ports provide jobs for many people.

The people of Los Angeles and Oakland built docks for the ships. A dock is a flat surface where boats or ships are tied up to be loaded and unloaded. The Port of Oakland has several miles of shoreline where ships can dock. This makes it easy to ship goods.

Stop and Check

Think How do people in coastal communities use the Pacific Ocean?

(l)Tom Paiva Photography/Blend Images/Getty; (r)Glowimages/Getty Images

Coastal Communities at Play

How do people who live in California's coastal communities have fun? The environment offers a lot of choices. Many people like to go to the beach. Others enjoy surfing. People also play volleyball or build sandcastles along the beaches of Southern California. At Mission Bay in San Diego, people travel across the bay in sailboats and kayaks, or on paddleboards.

People who live on California's coast do more than just go to the beach. The beaches in Northern California are rocky, and the ocean is colder than it is in Southern California. Many people enjoy hiking and exploring the coast there. Watching the many animals in a tidepool is a great way to learn about life in the ocean.

People enjoy the beach in many California communities.

Erik Isakson/Getty Images

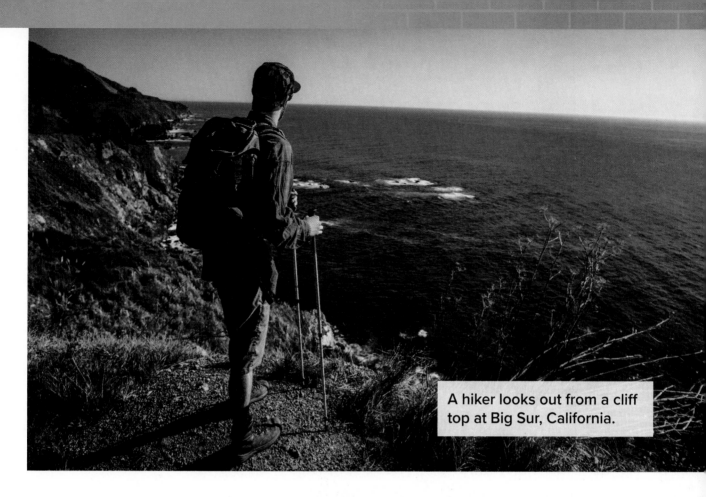

A hiker looks out from a cliff top at Big Sur, California.

People who live along the coast also enjoy nature. Many people visit an area called Big Sur, on the Central Coast. There, people can drive on a winding road along the coast. They can also enjoy beautiful views of the Pacific Ocean and visit areas of nearby Los Padres National Forest.

In Northern California, people hike in redwood forests and national parks. These contain some of the world's tallest and oldest trees!

Stop and Check

COLLABORATE

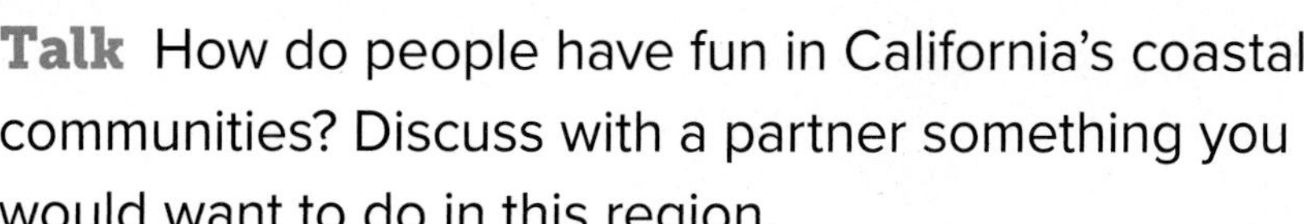

Talk How do people have fun in California's coastal communities? Discuss with a partner something you would want to do in this region.

What Do You Think? You have read about the features of California's coastal community. Which features do you think make this region special?

Corey Jenkins/Alamy Stock Photo

How Did Valley Communities Develop?

California's Valleys

A valley is low land between hills or mountains. Valleys are long but not very wide. Many valleys have rivers flowing through them. A valley forms when water from glaciers or rivers flows through an area of land and wears it down. It takes many, many years for a valley to form. Valleys are usually good places for farming because the soil has many minerals. These minerals help plants to grow.

slobo/iStock/Getty Images

HSS.3.1.1, HSS.3.1.2, HSS.3.2.1, HAS.CS.1, HAS.CS.2, HAS.CS.5

There are many valleys in California. The largest is the Central Valley, which runs for more than 400 miles down the center of the state. It is made up of the Sacramento Valley in the north and the San Joaquin Valley in the south. The Sierra Nevada mountain range is on the eastern side of the Central Valley. This **region** has most of California's farms. The state capital, Sacramento, is also in the Central Valley.

Farmland in the Central Valley, near Sacramento

Settling in the Valleys

California Indians were the first people to live in the valleys. They lived in valley areas for thousands of years. Their way of life was shaped by the **natural resources** around them.

The Miwok [MEE wahk] lived in the Central Valley. The men hunted deer and caught fish in the rivers and lakes. The women gathered acorns from oak trees and ground them into flour. California Indians in the northern valleys also found plenty to eat. Women and girls gathered berries and nuts. Men and boys hunted for deer and elk. They made nets to catch salmon and trout. They built houses from cedar wood.

The first settlers from Europe began exploring California's valleys in the early 1800s. During the Gold Rush of 1849, people raced to California from many parts of the world to look for gold. Some of these people stayed to begin farming in the valley regions.

Yosemite Valley, California: "The Bridal Veil" Fall
Currier & Ives (1866)

Yale University Art Gallery

The flat lands and rich soil of the valleys were ideal for farming. The **climate** also helped. The winters were cool with a lot of rainfall. The hot, dry summers were good for many crops. At first, most California farmers planted wheat and barley. Later, many started growing vegetables and fruits.

Soon, farmers in the California valleys were producing more than their families needed. Their farms became larger. People started growing crops to sell outside of California. California quickly became one of the largest producers of fruits and vegetables in the country.

A farmer and his sons harvest corn near Manteca, California, around 1938.

U.S. Farm Security Administration; Library of Congress, LC-USF34-018767-C

Stop and Check

Talk How did California Indians and early European settlers use the land differently?

Find Details As you read, add new information to the graphic organizer on page 35 in your Inquiry Journal.

Cattle grazing in valley fields.

Life in the Central Valley

Today, farming remains important to the people who live in the valley region. The Central Valley continues to provide more than half of the fruits, vegetables, and nuts grown in the United States. Valleys are also good **environments** for raising livestock. Many farms in the Central Valley raise cattle, goats, chickens, and hogs.

Did You Know?

Almonds are a popular and healthy food. California produces almost 90 percent of the world's almonds! Almonds grow on trees. A machine shakes the trees and the almonds fall to the ground. Then the almonds dry on the ground in the sun for about a week. Finally, a machine called a sweeper gathers the almonds.

(t)Tami Sojka/Alamy Stock Photo; (b)John Crowe/Alamy Stock Photo

Farming in the Central Valley can be difficult. The northern part of the valley sometimes gets too much rain. The southern part of the valley sometimes receives too little rain. Californians have worked to find ways to solve this problem. The Central Valley Project was formed in 1935 to find a way to move water to farmers. Today, it is one of the largest water transport systems in the world. It uses a system of dams, canals, and pipelines to move water throughout the valley. This allows everyone in the region to have water for drinking and farming.

Sprinklers water rows of green lettuce in the Central Valley.

Pgiam/E+/Getty Images

 **Stop and Check**

Talk Why can farming be difficult in the Central Valley?

At Work and Play

The Central Valley is home to many large cities. Fresno is a large city in the middle of the San Joaquin Valley. It has many shops, parks, and a zoo for people to visit. Bakersfield is in the southern part of the valley. It is famous for its music. Many artists and musicians live there. Visitors can go to concerts and art shows.

The state capitol in Sacramento

Many other areas of the valley region are popular for tourists, too. People travel there to enjoy the outdoors. They hike through the valleys. They go fishing and whitewater rafting on the rivers. They also visit the area's state and national parks.

Spondylolithesis/iStock/Getty Images

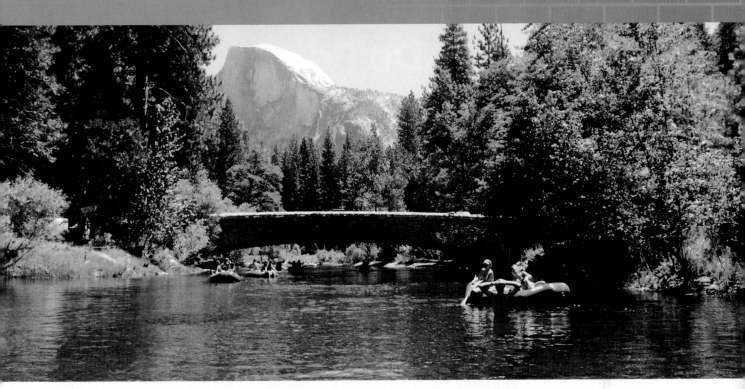

People enjoy rafting on the Merced River in Yosemite National Park.

The Yosemite Valley in the western Sierra Nevada mountains contains Yosemite National Park. Thousands of people travel there every year for camping, hiking, fishing, and many other activities. It has beautiful waterfalls, large valleys, and giant sequoia trees. Scientists also do studies in the area to learn about protecting the land as it changes.

Another area people visit is Napa Valley. This area is northeast of San Francisco. People can taste many kinds of food and enjoy scenic farms. There are hundreds of vineyards for people to visit as well.

Stop and Check

Talk How does the geography of California's valleys affect tourism?

What Do You Think? What are the most important reasons why people settled in the valleys of California?

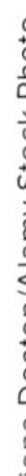

How Do People Live in a Desert Community?

Exploring a Desert Environment

When you hear the word *desert*, what comes to mind? Many people think of deserts as hot, dry, sandy areas with few plants and animals. That is almost correct. A desert is an area of land that is very dry. It gets less than 10 inches of **precipitation** each year. Because a desert gets very little water, many animals or plants cannot survive there.

A desert can be hot or cold. California's Great Basin Desert is an example of a cold desert. The precipitation it does get is snow, not rain. Only a small amount falls in the winter. On the other hand, the Mojave Desert is very hot. It can reach temperatures of 120°F in the summer!

California's deserts can have very different kinds of land. Some areas are mountainous. Some are large valleys with small changes in height. Some are rocky. Some have miles of sand dunes. More than 20 percent of California's land in the southeast is covered by the desert. That would be almost 32,000 square miles!

HSS.3.1.1, HSS.3.1.2, HSS.3.3.1, HAS.CS.1, HAS.HR.2

Ronnie Kaufman/Larry Hirshowitz/Blend Images/Getty Images

Friends play in the California desert.

To survive in the desert, plants have had to adapt. Some plants have developed very large roots. This allows the plant to hold as much water as possible. Their large root systems also allow them to live in extremely dry areas. The Joshua tree is a very successful desert plant. It has deep and shallow roots. Shallow roots gather rain from any rainfall. A Joshua tree can live for more than a hundred years. Unfortunately, as the climate has gotten warmer in recent years, even Joshua trees are finding it hard to survive in California's deserts.

The saguaro cactus stores water in its arms.

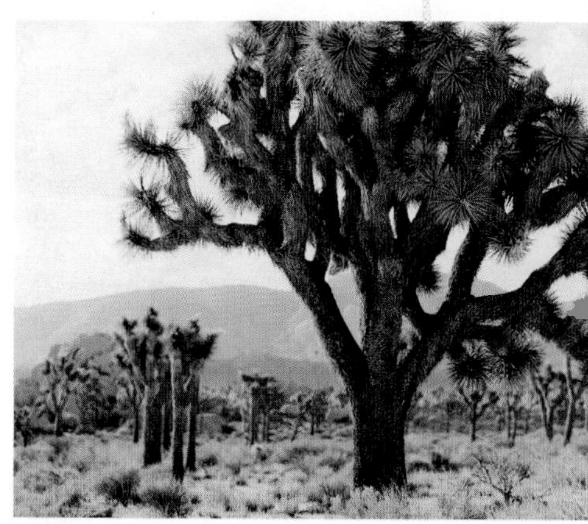

Joshua trees can live 150 years.

Only some animals can survive the harsh desert **environment**. Bighorn sheep live in higher areas of the desert. They eat small brushy plants to survive there. Coyotes roam the desert in search of small mammals and reptiles. Both of these animals have changed their diet to live in a desert environment. The long ears of black-tailed jackrabbits help them keep cool in the desert's hot **climate**. A desert tortoise can survive for a year in the desert without water.

Did You Know?

In 2013, a new reptile was discovered in California's Mojave Desert. Its official name is the yellow-bellied *Anniella campi*. It looks like a snake. However, it is actually a legless lizard because it has ears and eyelids. It eats insects and spends nearly its entire life underground.

(t)Lucky-photographer/Shutterstock.com; (c)trentonmichael/RooM/Getty Images; (b)Stuart Wilson/Science Source

A dry lake bed in Death Valley

One unusual area in California's Mojave Desert is called Death Valley. It is the lowest, driest, and hottest area in North America. Death Valley gets less than 2 inches of rain each year. Its air temperature can get higher than 120°F. The ground temperature has reached an amazing 201°F.

PRIMARY SOURCE

In Their Words... William Lewis Manly

"North and west was a level plain, fully one hundred miles wide it seemed, and from anything I could see it would not afford a traveler a single drink in the whole distance or give a poor ox many mouthfuls of grass."

—William Lewis Manly, *Death Valley in '49*

Stop and Check

Talk What can you conclude about life in the desert?

Find Details As you read, add new information to the graphic organizer on page 43 in your Inquiry Journal.

PHOTO: fotoVoyager/E+/Getty Images
TEXT: Manly, William Lewis. Death Valley in '49: Important Chapter of California Pioneer History. San Jose, CA: The Pacific Tree and Vine Co., 1894.

When enough rain falls in Death Valley in the spring, wildflowers spread across the valley. These flowers remain seeds underground until the right amount of rain falls and they bloom. Many animals live there, too. These include red-spotted toads, desert kangaroo rats, and mountain lions.

Using Desert Resources

People might think that deserts are not very useful. But deserts have many valuable **natural resources**. Precious metals such as gold and silver have been mined there for years. Some deserts have been a source of minerals such as salt and borax. Borax is used to make glass, ceramics, and detergent. The town of Boron was founded because people mined borax there.

The desert's plants also are a very important resource. Sheep and cattle have grazed in the Mojave and Colorado Deserts for centuries. There is growing concern, however, that this grazing is bad for the environment. It can lead to erosion and the loss of desert plants.

The deserts themselves have become a natural resource as well. Some areas have become national parks. These include Death Valley National Park, Joshua Tree National Park, and Mojave National Preserve. Visitors to these parks can explore the natural beauty of California's desert **region**.

Bringing Water to the Desert

Water is hard to find in the desert. For people to be able to live and work there, water must be brought in. The farms in the Coachella and Imperial Valleys exist only because of the water that is brought in and used to irrigate the vegetable and fruit crops. Irrigate means to supply land and crops with water.

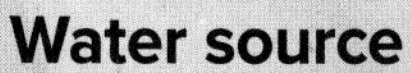

1 Water source

A major water source, such as the Colorado River, provides the water.

2 Canals

Hundreds of miles of canals transport the water to locations in the desert.

3 Pipes

Pipes lead from the canals to the farmers' fields.

4 Irrigation

Drip and sprinkler irrigation systems water the vegetables and fruit trees.

Stop and Check

Think How has irrigation changed life for people who live in the desert region?

(bkgd)McGraw-Hill Education

Making a Living in the Desert

The desert can be a tough place to live. But it has become easier because people now bring water there. People can make a living like those who live in less harsh environments.

People who live in the desert usually live in small towns. They are farmers, office workers, and business owners. They often provide services along major highways. For example, the small town of Baker is located along a highway in the Mojave Desert. It is one of the few places travelers crossing the desert can stop to get gas, food, and a place to rest. Some desert towns, like Palm Springs, host tourists.

Biking in the foothills of the Sierra Nevada Mountains

Greg Epperson/Shutterstock.com

Anza-Borrego Desert State Park is California's largest state park at more than 600,000 acres.

Tourism is one of the region's most important **industries**. The unusual geography attracts people to the area. Many local Californians provide the services these visitors need. Some give hiking tours. Some work as guides for overnight camping. Others work as park rangers at the many national and state parks. Some people work at resorts where visitors can enjoy the weather while they relax.

Scientists also work in California's deserts. Biologists are scientists who study the plants and animals to learn how they survive in this environment. Archaeologists are scientists who study the desert to learn about its ancient history. They can learn about who lived there by studying fossils and artifacts. Some scientists study the environment to see what is changing and what is causing these changes.

Stop and Check

Talk What attracts tourists to the deserts of California? Discuss with a partner why you would want to visit this region.

What Do You Think?

What is it like to live in a desert community?

David H. Carriere/Stockbyte/Getty Images

What Makes a Mountain Community Unique?

California's Mountains

A mountain is a high landform with steep sides. It is much higher and larger than a hill. Mountains rarely exist alone. They are usually grouped together in what is known as a range. California is a large state, so it is not surprising that it contains several mountain ranges.

The Cascade Mountains are part of a range that extends from Canada into Northern California. This mountain range was created by volcanic activity. Lassen Peak is located in the Cascade Mountains. It is one of six active volcanoes in California, including Mount Shasta and Coso Peak. Lassen Peak rises to an **elevation** of over 10,000 feet into the air. Elevation is how high an area of land is above sea level. Sea level is 0 feet. Lassen Peak is very, very tall!

LACMA - Los Angeles County Museum of Art

HSS.3.1.1, HSS.3.1.2, HSS.3.3.1, HAS.CS.1, HAS.HR.2

Running along the western part of the state is a series of ranges called the Coast Ranges. The elevation of these ranges is fairly low. They have an average elevation of only about 3,000 feet. However, some peaks reach an elevation of over 6,000 feet.

California Pines, 1878
Painted by William Keith

Most of the mountain ranges in California run north to south. However, the Transverse Ranges in Southern California run east to west. These mountains start north of Los Angeles and spread southeast into the desert **region**. Their elevations range from 3,000 feet to 11,000 feet.

The Sierra Nevada spans more than 400 miles along the state's eastern border. It is a very dramatic mountain range. It was created millions of years ago by an up, down, and tilted movement of the Earth's crust. As a result, the western side slowly slopes down into the valley. However, the slope on the eastern side sometimes drops off from as high as 10,000 feet!

Mount Whitney is the highest peak in the Sierra Nevada. At 14,494 feet tall, it is one of the highest points in the United States. The peak of Mount Whitney has almost no plant life and is often covered in snow. The elevation and seasons also affect the temperature and climate of mountain **communities**.

Did You Know?

herreid/iStock/Getty Images

Glaciers are large chunks of ice that have been on Earth for hundreds of thousands of years. As they melted over time, their weight, movement, and melting water changed the land. This created mountains, valleys, and lakes. Today, glaciers are found in the polar regions of Antarctica, Greenland, and Canada. There are also small glaciers in California, including on Mount Shasta and in the Sierra Nevada.

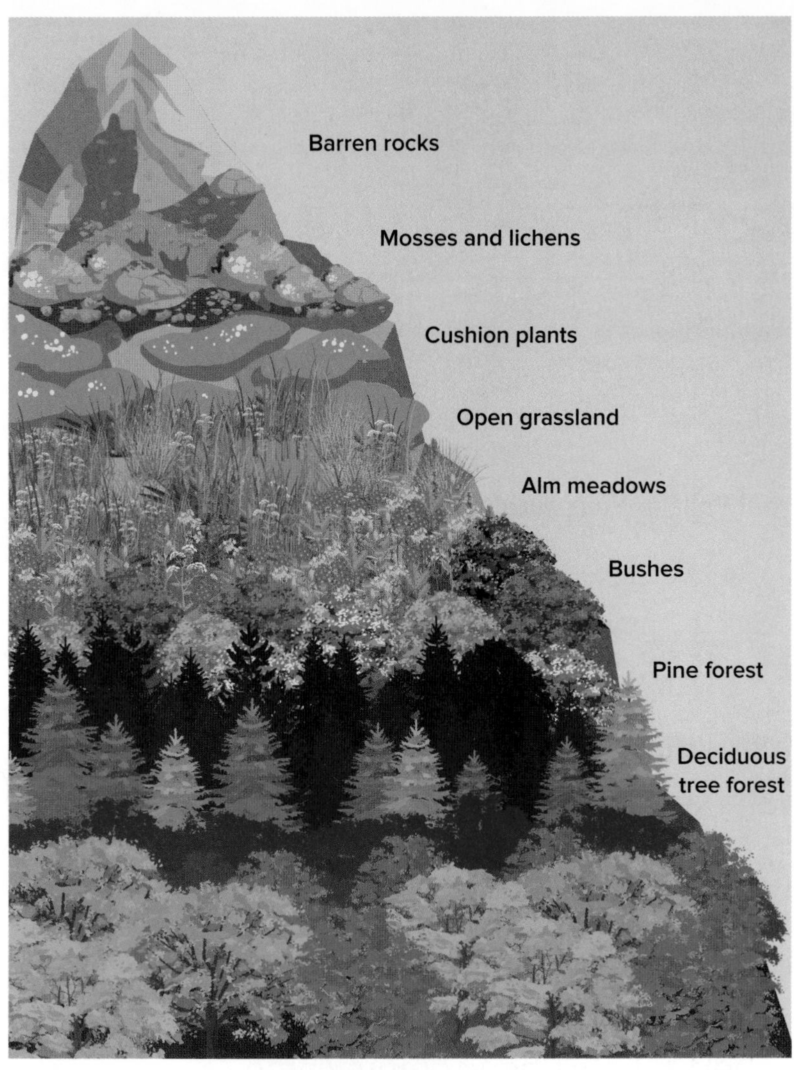

The effects of elevation on plants and trees

Melting snow and rainwater flow down a mountainside. The amount of water increases as it flows down the mountain. Sometimes the water creates small streams. Other times it flows over the edge of the mountain in a waterfall. Eventually the water flows into rivers that carry this water, known as mountain runoff, across the valley below. The Sierra Nevada runoff drains through a system of rivers in the Central Valley. This water eventually empties into the Pacific Ocean.

PRIMARY SOURCE

In Their Words... John Muir

"The whole landscape showed design, like man's noblest sculptures. How wonderful the power of its beauty!"

—from *My First Summer in the Sierra*

Muir, John. My First Summer in the Sierra. Boston, MA: Houghton Mifflin Company, 1911.

Stop and Check

Write Write a paragraph to discuss the similarities and differences among the mountain ranges you have learned about. How are they similar to each other? How are they different?

Find Details As you read, add new information to the graphic organizer on page 51 in your Inquiry Journal.

Rainbow over Mist Trail at Vernal Falls in Yosemite National Park

Using Mountain Resources

There are many **natural resources** in this region. Plants, animals, minerals, and water are all important parts of California's mountains. Before Europeans and Americans arrived, several California Indian groups lived and traveled through the Sierra Nevada. The Yokut [YOH kuht] and Sierra Miwok Indians used the resources in the streams and forests for food and shelter. Later, newcomers came to the region. They too hunted animals for their fur. They traded these resources to people in other areas.

Did You Know?

The giant sequoia [suh KOI uh] is only found in the Sierra Nevada. It grows at elevations between 3,000 and 8,500 feet. It is considered to be the world's largest tree. It can grow to be about 300 feet tall and almost 100 feet wide! Giant sequoias can live for more than 3,000 years.

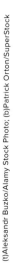

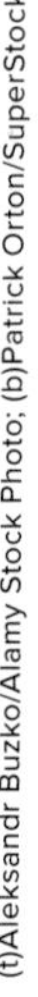
(t)Aleksandr Buzko/Alamy Stock Photo; (b)Patrick Orton/SuperStock

Bodie is an abandoned gold-mining town that once had a population of 10,000 people.

When gold and silver were discovered in California's mountains, the land was changed forever. Miners from around the world arrived in California in the mid-1800s. To get to the metals, miners cut holes into the mountains. These holes remain today. Trees were cut down for lumber. Settlements developed as well. Roads, houses, stores, and railroads all brought lasting changes to the area. Some of the mining settlements have become tourist attractions. Today, visitors from all over travel to the mountains to learn about California's past.

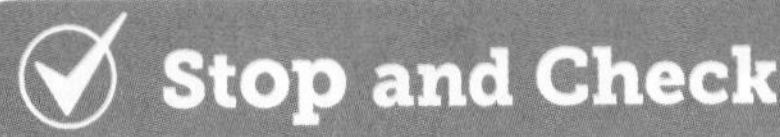

Stop and Check

Think What natural resources are available in a mountain region?

Jon B. Lovelace Collection of California Photographs in Carol M. Highsmith's America Project, Library of Congress, LC-DIG-highsm-22427

Life in Mountain Communities

Where people live in the mountains can determine how they live. For example, people who live in the higher elevations may have to travel farther to reach a town than people who live in lower elevations. Transportation can be difficult in the winter. Heavy snows sometimes block roads completely. This can make living in the mountains challenging.

However, there are many things to do in the mountains. Tourism is an important business in mountain communities. In the winter, skiers and snowboarders travel there for sport. In the summer, people enjoy rock climbing, hiking, canoeing, and camping in the mountains. These activities bring money into the region. This allows the people who live in the region to earn a living.

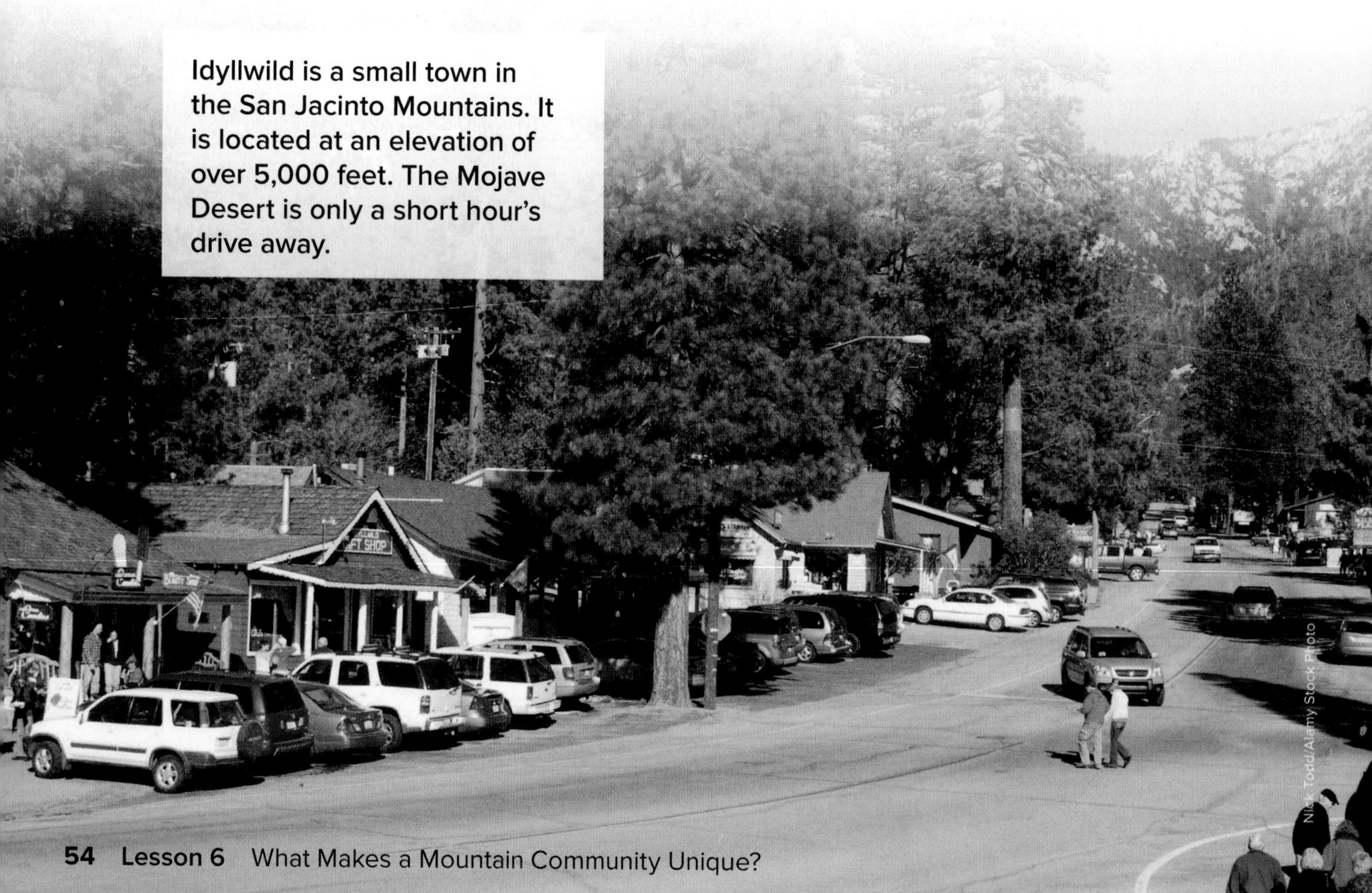

Idyllwild is a small town in the San Jacinto Mountains. It is located at an elevation of over 5,000 feet. The Mojave Desert is only a short hour's drive away.

Nick Todd/Alamy Stock Photo

The national park system of the United States has protected many areas in the mountains of California. There are several national and state parks throughout the state. These parks were created to preserve the natural beauty of the mountains. Yosemite National Park was one of the first national parks created. In the 1800s and early 1900s, Californians took action to make sure this area was protected. Today, visitors can explore nearly 1,200 miles of unchanged wilderness in Yosemite.

Skiing at Lake Tahoe

People can also explore the hot springs at Lassen Volcanic National Park. They can view the giant trees in Sequoia National Park. Campers can enjoy the wilderness of the Klamath National Forest. Mountain communities support the protection of the state's mountain ranges. They work with state and local governments to follow the laws to protect the land. This makes sure that their beauty will be preserved for years to come.

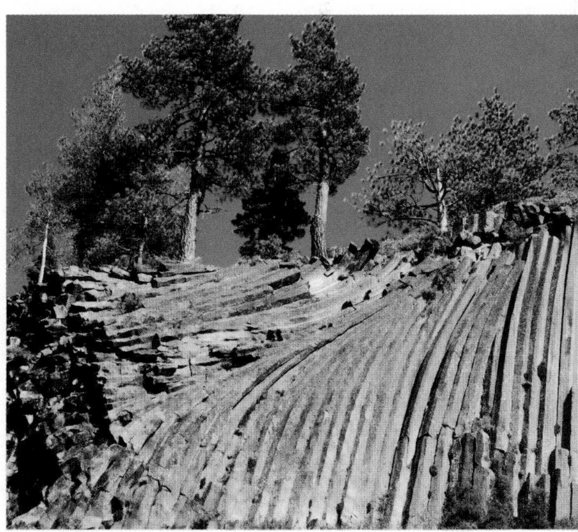

Devils Postpile National Monument

COLLABORATE

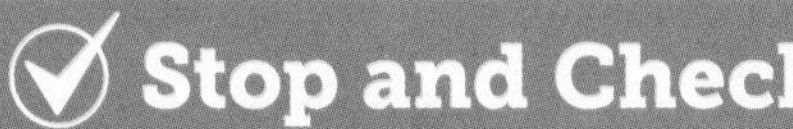

Stop and Check

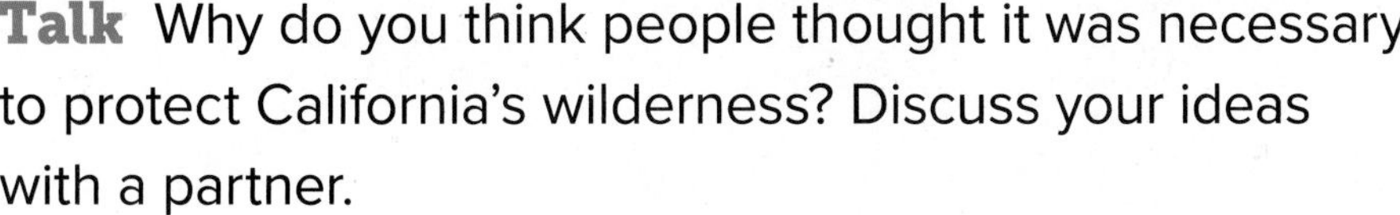

Talk Why do you think people thought it was necessary to protect California's wilderness? Discuss your ideas with a partner.

What Do You Think? What do you think is most appealing about living in a mountain community?

(t)Purestock/Getty Images; (b)Lucyna Koch/E+/Getty Images

Connections in Action

Back to the EQ

Think about the chapter EQ, **"How does geography impact California communities?"**

- **Talk** with a partner about how geography shaped your community. What feature of your community's land, resources, or climate do you think had the most influence on your community? Why do you think so?
- **Share** your opinions with the class.

(tl)Yale University Art Gallery; (tr)Aleksandr Buzko/Alamy Stock Photo; (b)trentonmichael/RooM/Getty Images

More to Explore

How can you make an IMPACT?

Brainstorm Synonyms

Look at the chapter vocabulary words. With a partner, take turns coming up with synonyms, or words that mean the same thing, for each word. Keep track of the number of synonyms you both come up with for each word. The one who comes up with the most wins!

Create a Television Ad

The mayor has asked you to write a television ad to encourage people to visit your town. Choose four things that you think visitors would want to see or do in your community. Use these to write a 30-second script that will encourage people to visit. Think about pictures you could use in the ad.

Compose a Song

Imagine you have been asked to write and perform a song about why you love your community. Think about your community. What do you like about it? What do you enjoy doing there? Try to use some of the vocabulary from the chapter in your song.

Chapter 2 American Indians of the Local Region

ESSENTIAL QUESTION EQ

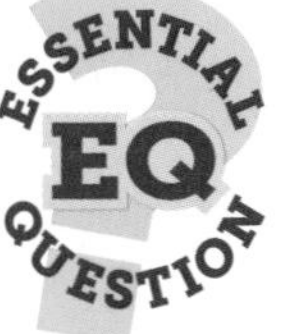

How Have California Indians Influenced the Local Region?

American Indian groups have lived in California for thousands of years. In this chapter, you will read about where and how they lived. You will also explore what they used to meet their needs. As you read about these groups, think about the ways in which California Indians continue to play an important role in our communities.

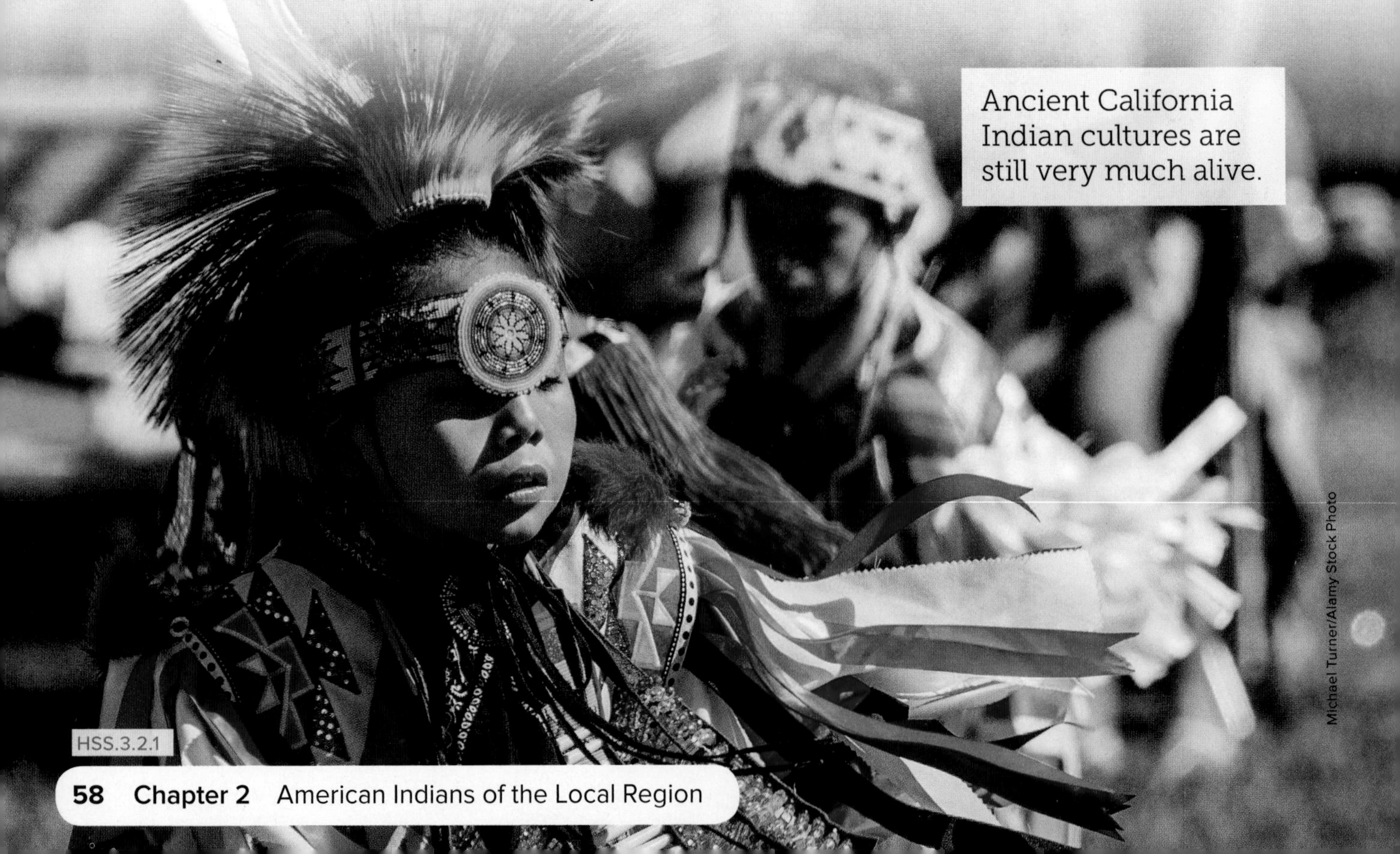

Ancient California Indian cultures are still very much alive.

Michael Turner/Alamy Stock Photo

HSS.3.2.1

Where Do You See California Indian Influence Today?

There are many ways that California Indians help shape your community.

The ancient California Indian groups changed their environment for many reasons. Many of these changes lasted only a short time. However, you can still see some of these changes today.

California Indians created beautiful baskets and pottery. They often used patterns or symbols that represented a local resource or animal. You may find similar designs in the buildings and art in your community today.

American Indians are members of our communities. They own businesses. They work in stores, offices, and government. But their culture is still a part of their lives. They are proud of their traditions and work to keep them alive.

(t)SumikoPhoto/iStock/Getty Images; (bl)Paul Marcus/Shutterstock.com; (br)Spencer Weiner/Los Angeles Times/Getty Images

Connect Through Literature

THE BASKET WEAVER

by Jacque Summers
Art by Felicia Hoshino

Thousands of years ago, the Chumash People lived on the beautiful shores of California. And in the valley Aw'hay, there was a young girl named Yo'ee. Yo'ee was very, very shy. She never spoke to anyone, except her mother, father, or grandmother. No one knew why Yo'ee was so shy, and neither did she. But every day she would play alone.

One morning, Yo'ee's grandmother was sitting on the ground before the fire, weaving a basket. She saw Yo'ee playing. Yo'ee smiled as Grandmother waved her over to join her.

"Would you like to learn to make baskets?" her grandmother asked.

Yo'ee nodded. "I love baskets," she whispered.

Grandmother showed Yo'ee how to start the basket by wrapping juncus rushes with split reeds and stitching them into a beautiful, coiled base. After that she sewed more rows of reeds to the base. Her hands moved gracefully, like the wings of a bird. Yo'ee loved to watch her grandmother weave baskets.

Yo'ee and Grandmother began to weave baskets together every day. Yo'ee helped her grandmother gather and prepare the reeds. They went down to the river and pulled bundles of slim, green stalks. Some they would dry in the sun until they turned brown.

(bkgd)McGraw-Hill Education

The others they would soak in mud, turning them black as night before setting them out to dry. Then Yo'ee and Grandmother dipped the stiff reeds in water to soften them, and wove them into baskets.

One day, as Yo'ee came back from the river with an armful of reeds, she heard the chief telling a story to the village children. The chief was not only a wise leader—he was a great storyteller. He spoke in a strong, clear voice that rose and fell like the river's song.

The children listened as he told a story Yo'ee knew well. Coyote, Lizard, and Eagle, the first creatures of the earth, decided to make a new creature called man. But they could not decide on his hands.

"Proud Coyote wanted man to have hands like his," the chief said. He held up his own hands and curled them as if they were sharply clawed. "Lizard and Eagle didn't argue, though Lizard knew Coyote was unwise.

"The next day, Coyote led the others to a white rock. If he stamped his paw on the rock, it would be final—humans would have hands just like the coyote.

"Lizard had to do something! He quickly crawled to the rock while Coyote wasn't looking and pressed his own tiny hand into the rock. Coyote was furious! But thanks to clever Lizard, we have useful hands with five fingers, just like him!" The children looked at their hands and laughed.

The Basket Weaver by Jacque Summers ill. by Felicia Hoshino; Ladybug, October 2012. Copyright © by Carus Publishing Company. Reproduced with permission. All Cricket Media material is copyrighted by Carus Publishing Company, d/b/a Cricket Media, and/or various authors and illustrators. Any commercial use or distribution of material without permission is strictly prohibited. Please visit http://www.cricketmedia.com/info/licensing2 for licensing and http://www.cricketmedia.com for subscriptions; (bkgd)McGraw-Hill Education.

Yo'ee saw how the children loved to listen to the chief. She wished she could tell stories, too, to make others happy. But she was afraid. She thought her voice was too quiet to be heard. Still, she wanted to share the stories of her people.

Then one day, as she was playing with a blue feather, she had an idea. She ran to tell her plan to Grandmother, who thought it was a wonderful idea. That minute they sat down and began working on a very special basket.

Soon it was time for the Acorn Harvest. Everyone in the village came together for the festival, eating, singing, and dancing. Yo'ee brought her new basket along.

After the feast, the chief asked if there were any who would like to tell a story. Yo'ee stood up, clutching her basket. Everyone was surprised. The chief nodded to her and sat down, ready to listen. Yo'ee took a deep breath and held up her basket for all to see.

On the first side of the basket, Yo'ee had woven a scrub jay. He was black and featherless, with his head cast down in sadness. The people murmured, impressed by her handiwork. When everyone had seen the scrub jay, she turned the basket.

On the next side, the black jay was flying up to the basket's blue-feathered rim, as if asking the sky for some of its color.

(bkgd)McGraw-Hill Education

Yo'ee then turned the basket again. Now the sky dropped its blue feathers down to the jay. She turned the basket once more.

On the last side of the basket was the beautiful blue scrub jay, finally dressed in his sky-colored feathers. Yo'ee stood very still to show her story was over, then went back to sit by her grandmother.

Everyone cheered at Yo'ee's tale. The chief stood and said, "Our village has another great storyteller. Next festival we look forward to another story from Yo'ee."

Yo'ee's family hugged her proudly. Her grandmother's eyes twinkled. "You've found a way to tell a story without speaking a word," she said to Yo'ee. "Your story was in the weaving of the basket."

And Yo'ee knew there would be plenty more stories to tell.

Think About It

1. What does Yo'ee's grandmother teach her to do?
2. How does Yo'ee find her voice?
3. What lesson does Yo'ee teach us?

(bkgd)McGraw-Hill Education

Who Lived in Early California?

The First Californians Arrive

How and when did people first arrive in North America? There are many ways people could have **migrated** to North America. To migrate means to move to a new area. Some scientists believe people traveled by boat from Asia northwest to North America. Other scientists think people traveled to North America by foot. During the last ice age, which began about 30,000 years ago, water levels in the oceans were very low. This uncovered a piece of land between Asia and North America. People could have walked across this land to reach North America.

Once people reached North America, they migrated across the land. Some went east, some went south, and some stayed in the north. Many people moved into the land that is now California. Their descendants still live there today.

HSS.3.1.2, HSS.3.2.1, HSS.3.2.2, HSS.3.2.4, HSS.3.3.1, HAS.CS.1, HAS.CS.2, HAS.CS.5, HAS.HR.2, HAS.HI.3

Edward Sheriff Curtis/LACMA - Los Angeles County Museum of Art

This photograph of California Indians launching a boat was taken around 1927.

Learning About the Past

The people who stayed in the California area settled all across the region. More than 100 different groups lived in California. Some lived in permanent settlements. Others were **nomads**. This means they traveled from place to place to hunt and gather food. In most groups, the men were responsible for hunting and the women did most of the gathering. The different environments around each California Indian group affected how each group lived.

The Chumash [CHOO mash] Indians settled along the California coast. They lived in small villages. They built dome-shaped houses out of the local trees and grasses. The ocean was their main source of food. The Chumash fished and hunted sea mammals from canoes made out of trees. They used whalebones to make tools such as knives. They also gathered plants and seeds in baskets made from grasses.

The Yokut Indians settled in the Central Valley region. Their homes were built with mats made from grasses. Many families lived in each home. The Yokuts also made traps to hunt small animals such as rabbits. They used bows and arrows to hunt deer and other large animals. They also fished in the rivers and gathered seeds, fruit, and plants in this fertile region.

A Chumash Indian home provided protection from the weather.

Chuck Place/Alamy Stock Photo

The Southern Paiute [peye YOOT] Indians were also nomads. They traveled from the Colorado River to the Mojave Desert. They settled in different regions during different seasons. They built homes using the plants around them. They hunted small animals and gathered seeds, nuts, and plants for food.

Another group, the Sierra Miwok Indians, lived in the Sierra Nevada. During the summer, the Sierra Miwok lived higher up in the mountains. They built houses out of tree bark and branches. During the winter, they moved down to the base of the mountains. Their homes there were made from dirt, trees, and plants. They hunted, fished, and ate fruits and nuts gathered from the region.

A Miwok Indian fishing in a river.

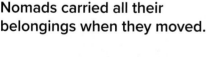

Nomads carried all their belongings when they moved.

 Stop and Check

Write Think about where you live. Write two to three sentences to describe the type of home a California Indian who lived in your region had.

Find Details As you read, add new information to the graphic organizer on page 71 in your Inquiry Journal.

(t)Edward S. Curtis Collection, Library of Congress, LC-USZ62-120024; (b)North Wind Picture Archives/Alamy Stock Photo

Europeans Bring Change

In the 1500s, European **explorers** began to explore the land of California. An explorer is a person who travels to learn more about other places. Juan Rodriguez Cabrillo [kah BREE yoh] and his crew landed in what is now San Diego in 1542. They claimed the region for Spain. Soon many other Europeans came to the region.

In the 1700s, Spain wanted to control California. In 1769, a group of Spanish settlers traveled to San Diego. They built a presidio, or fort. This was the first European settlement on the West Coast of North America. This presidio became the Spanish settlers' home.

The Spanish wanted to convert the California Indians to the Christian faith. One way they did this was to build **missions** near the presidios. A mission was a settlement built around a church. California Indians were brought to the missions to live, work, and learn about Christianity. Over time, 21 missions were built throughout California.

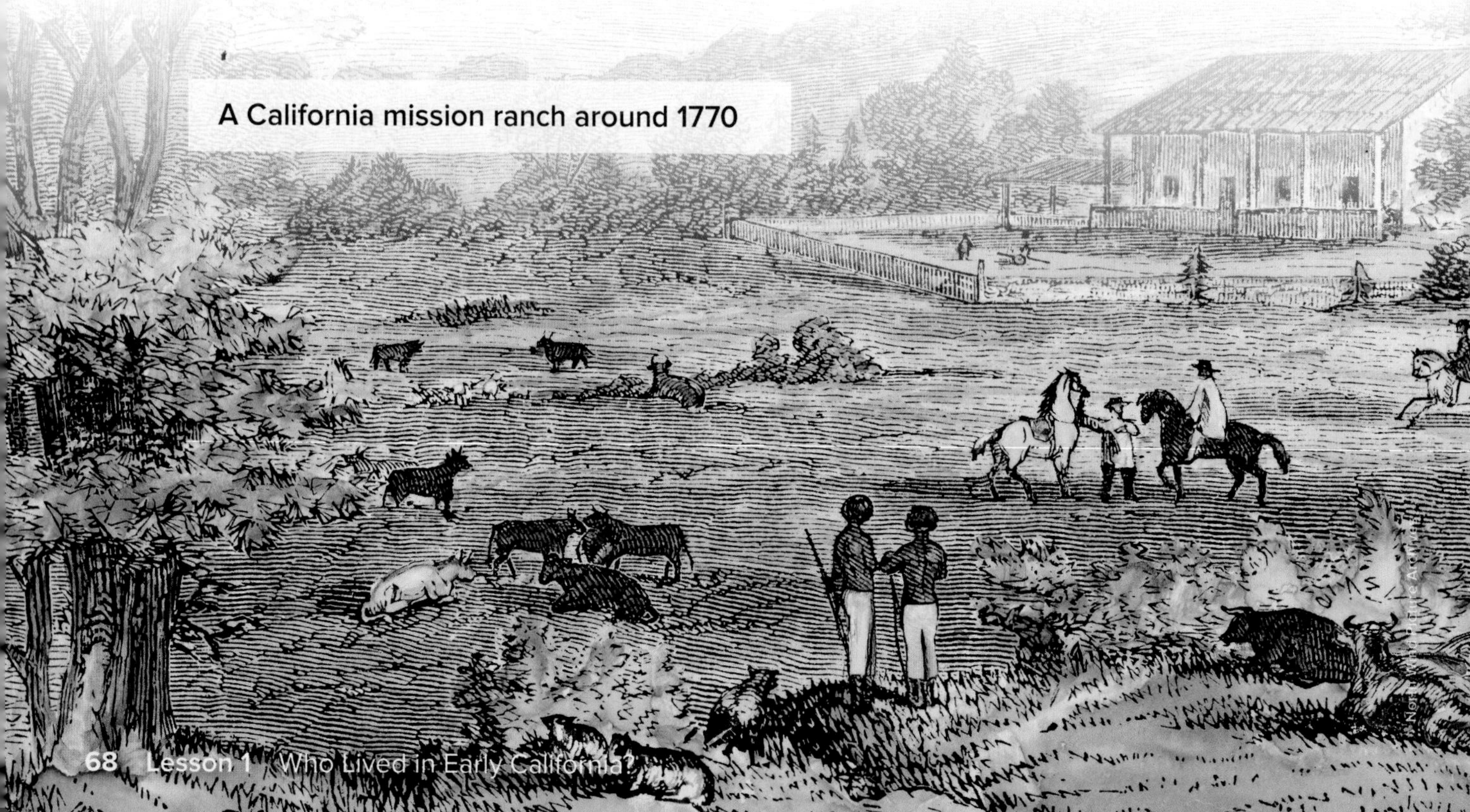

A California mission ranch around 1770

California Indians living at the missions were required to work and practice the Catholic religion. They were no longer free. They were forced to farm the land to support the mission. They also had to help build the missions. The Spanish did not pay them for their work. The California Indians had to adapt to the Spanish ways of life. They had to follow rules the Spanish made. Many were punished for breaking the rules or trying to escape. It was a very different and difficult life for them.

Many California Indians also became very sick during this time. The Europeans brought new diseases to the region. These diseases, such as smallpox, were deadly. Thousands of California Indians died. As a result, some California Indian groups were almost completely destroyed. There were around 300,000 California Indians before the Spanish arrived. By the mid-1800s, the population was below 50,000.

California Indians and Spaniards at Mission San Gabriel

Stop and Check

Think How did the Spanish explorers affect California Indian groups?

The New York Public Library.

Keeping the Past Alive

Explorers and settlers changed the lives of California Indian groups forever. However, California Indians continue to be an important part of California today. They work to keep their **traditions** alive. Many traditions are passed down through the stories, songs, and dances that adults teach to children. Traditional art forms such as basket weaving and beaded jewelry are still created. Some words, such as *Mojave* and *Yosemite,* are California Indian words. The counties of Mono [MAH noh] and Modoc [MOH dahk] are named after California Indian groups, too.

A Yurok boy performs a traditional dance for a powwow.

Eyal Nahmias/Alamy Stock Photo

Did You Know?

Most California Indian history was never written down. Instead, it was shared through spoken stories. These stories, known as oral traditions, were a way to pass down a group's history and beliefs from one generation to another. Many California Indian groups continue storytelling today.

More than 360,000 American Indians live in California today. In fact, California has the largest population of American Indians in the United States. Los Angeles and San Diego are among the nation's top cities with the largest American Indian populations. In these cities and other places across the United States, you can learn about the histories and traditions of American Indians. Some groups hold special festivals to teach others about their past. There are many museums you can visit to learn about American Indians, too. Think about your community. What influence from California Indians do you see around you?

Stop and Check

Write How do California Indians keep their traditions alive?

What Do You Think? What was life like for California Indians before the Spanish arrived? Give examples from the text to support your answer.

Bryan Chan/Los Angeles Times/Getty Images

How Did the Land Affect California Indians?

California Indians and Their Environment

As you have read, California Indians lived in different areas across what we now call California. Each region had a different environment. Each group adapted to its environment and used the resources that were available to them. The climate determined the types of clothes they wore. They used the natural resources around them to build homes and make tools. The rivers, forests, fields, and deserts provided food for them to eat. The land of each region also affected how each group lived.

HSS.3.1.1, HSS.3.1.2, HSS.3.2.1, HSS.3.2.2

California Indians harvesting corn.

Adapting to California's Regions

The Hupa [HOO pah] Indians lived in a mild climate along the Trinity River in northwest California. This valley had many natural resources. The Hupa used the land around them in many ways. The river was used for water and for travel and trade between villages. It was also a source of food. The Hupa fished for salmon and trout in the river. They learned how to preserve the fish so they would have food to eat in the winter.

Hupa medicine woman

The Hupa built houses using planks from nearby cedar trees. The houses had walls and slanted roofs. This allowed water and snow to slide off. These strong homes kept the Hupa warm and dry.

Women gathered acorns and berries from the forests. They dug up tree roots and wove them into baskets. The Hupa also used tree branches to make tools such as bows and arrows. The men used these tools to hunt elk and deer. The animals were used for food, clothes, and tools.

PRIMARY SOURCE

In Their Words... The Miwok

"If you look closely at the ground in the woods you will see how the top is leaves and bark and pine needles and cones, and how a little below the top these are matted together, and a little deeper are rotting and breaking up into earth. This is the way the world grew—and it is growing still."

—Miwok myth, "How the World Grew"

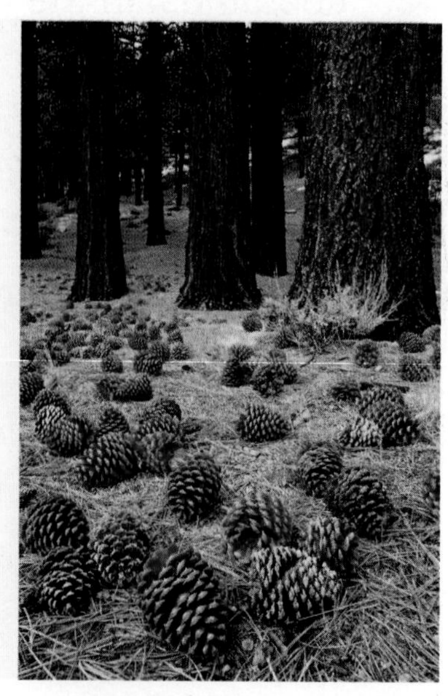

PHOTO: (t)Library of Congress, Prints & Photographs Division, Edward S. Curtis Collection, LC-USZ62-110505, (b)Michael Orton/Getty Images
TEXT: "How the World Grew." In The Dawn Of the World: Myths and Weird Tales Told by the Mewan Indians of California, edited by C. Hart Merriam, 225. Cleveland, OH: The Arthur H. Clark Company, 1910.

The Ohlone [oh LOH nee] Indians lived in California's coastal region. They lived in an area that stretched from present-day San Francisco Bay to Point Sur. The ocean, shoreline, and rivers influenced their daily lives.

The Ohlone used the area's **vegetation** in many ways. Reeds, or tall grasses, found along the beaches were used for boats. The boats were used for fishing in the oceans or rivers. Women used the reeds, beach grasses, and plant roots to weave baskets. The shoreline vegetation was also used to build houses. The Ohlone wove the leaves together. The leaves were put onto wooden poles. The domed houses were held together with willow branches.

The ocean provided the Ohlone with fish, clams, and oysters. They used the land around them for food, too. The forests had seeds, nuts, roots, and berries. They also hunted bear, deer, and small animals. The rivers provided the Ohlone with fish, duck, and geese. They used feathers for clothing. In the winter, the feathers helped to keep them warm. They also used feathers for ceremonial costumes. In the warmer weather, the Ohlone wore clothing made from grasses and animal skins.

A California Indian boat made of cattails

Bobbi Onia/Underwood Archives/Getty Images

Stop and Check

Write What effect did the climate have on what the Hupa and Ohlone wore?

Find Details As you read, add new information to the graphic organizer on page 79 in your Inquiry Journal.

The Maidu [MAHY doo] Indians lived in the Sierra Nevada. They fished in the streams. They hunted elk and deer in the forests. Their lives were influenced by the seasons and climate. In the winter, they lived near the bottom of the mountains. In the summer, they traveled up into the mountains to hunt and gather food. They gathered as much food as possible to help them through the winter.

The homes the Maidu lived in during the winter were almost completely underground. First they dug a deep, round pit. Then they used trees to make a frame. Finally, they covered the tree frame with bark and dirt. These homes protected them from wind and snow. During the summer, they built temporary shelters when they moved up into the mountains.

Since the summers were hot, the Maidu wore few clothes and no shoes. However, in the winter, they wore a lot of clothes to stay warm. They wore deerskin pants and fur wraps around their shoulders. They wore moccasins stuffed with grass to protect their feet from the cold and snow.

California Indian mother and child

Did You Know?

Like many other California Indians, the Maidu used bows and arrows to hunt. The Maidu used obsidian rocks to make their arrowheads. Obsidian is a type of rock found in California. It can be chipped to make a sharp point. This made it a good choice for arrowheads.

(t)Library of Congress, Prints & Photographs Division, Edward S. Curtis Collection, LC-USZ62-112235, (b)Ingram Publishing/SuperStock

The Chemehuevi [cheh meh WAY vee] Indians lived in the Mojave Desert. The desert was a difficult place to live because it was hot and dry. To protect themselves from the sun, they built homes with roofs made of brush. Sometimes they lived in caves in the mountains.

The Chemehuevi were **nomads** because resources in the desert were hard to find. The Chemehuevi traveled in small groups in search of food and water. As they moved from place to place, they gathered seeds and nuts. They also looked for agave. The Chemehuevi used this cactus plant for food. They also made rope from the fibers in the leaves. The ropes were used to make nets for hunting. The Chemehuevi trapped small animals. They also ate lizards.

The Chemehuevi used plants and animals for clothes, too. They wore animal skins. They also made hats to protect them from the desert sun.

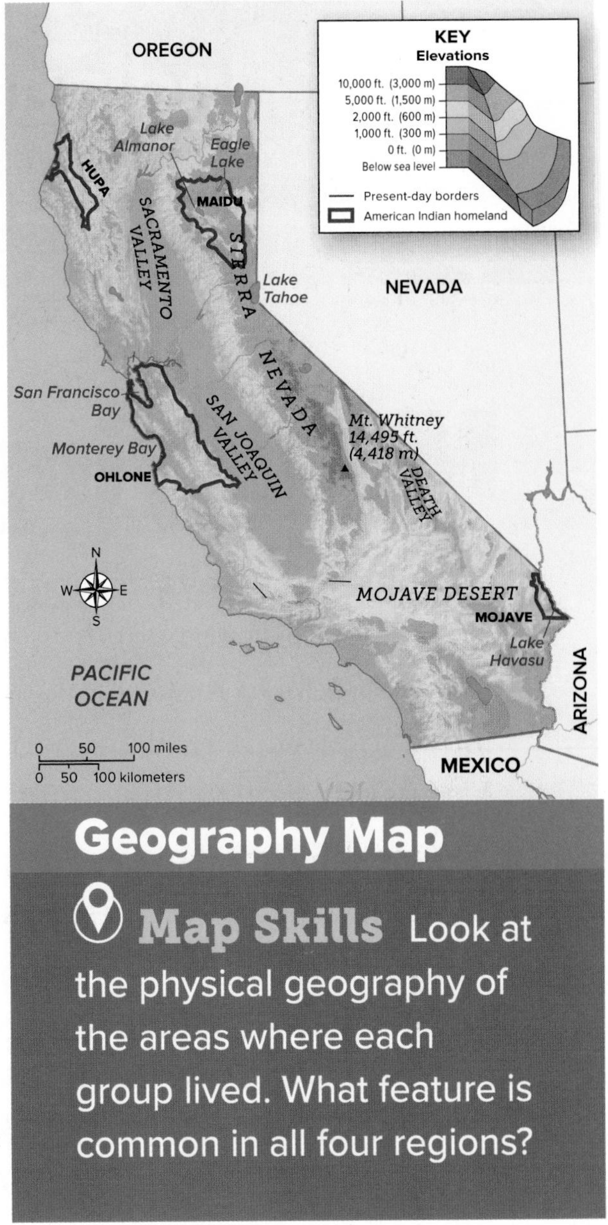

Geography Map

Map Skills Look at the physical geography of the areas where each group lived. What feature is common in all four regions?

Stop and Check

Think How were the homes of the Maidu and Chemehuevi similar?

What Do You Think?

What resources in your community do you think would be useful to California Indians? How would they use these resources?

How Did California Indians Change the Land?

Modifying the Land

People are always making changes to their environment. Today we blast through mountains to build roads. We cut down forests to make lumber to build houses. We create farms to provide us with food. We build wind farms to harness energy to power our cities and towns.

In the past, California Indians also changed their environments to meet their needs. They used fires to clear land for farming. They grew food. They built dams in rivers to catch fish more easily. The environment had an effect on the lives of California Indians. The California Indians also had an effect on their environments.

HSS.3.1.2, HSS.3.2.2

A California Indian community sits beside a river.
Nets are used to catch fish.

Using Fire

Groups such as the Maidu, Miwok, and Ohlone used fire in many ways. Fires kept them warm. Fires were used to cook food. Fire was also an important tool that California Indians used to change the land.

Fires were set to burn grass and brush on the ground. These controlled fires helped the groups make sure they had the food they needed. First, these controlled fires removed weeds. This created space for new seeds and plants to grow. Animals were attracted to these plants. This made animals easier to hunt. Controlled fires helped to keep insects away, too. Fires also controlled the spread of disease. By changing the land through the use of controlled fires, California Indians were able to control their food supply and stay healthy.

PRIMARY SOURCE

In Their Words... The Hupa

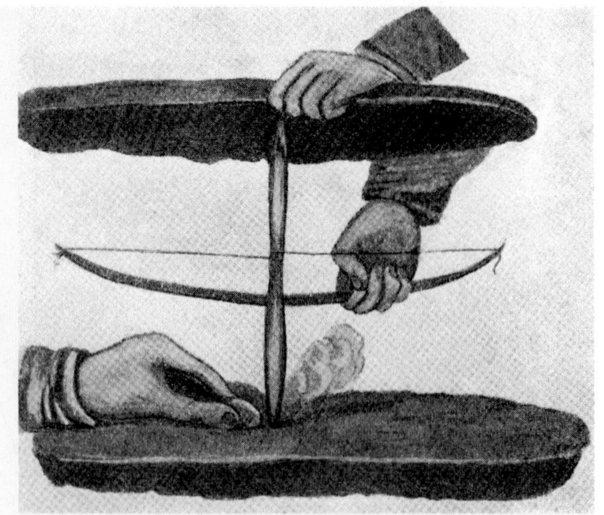

"It was the Old-man-across-the-ocean. He picked up stones and struck them together. Nothing happened. Then he picked up a willow root and whittled it down to the dry part. He bored holes in it and then setting another stick in one of the holes, rolled it, between his hands. He was surprised to see smoke come out. Soon fire rolled out. That was the way it happened."

—Hupa myth

PHOTO: North Wind Picture Archives/Alamy Stock Photo
TEXT: "Origin of Fire." In American Archaeology and Ethnology, edited by Frederic Ward Putnam, 197. Berkeley, CA: Berkeley University Press, 1903-1904.

Did You Know?

Acorns were an important food for many California Indians. However, the nuts needed to be ground and soaked before they were eaten. Women would grind the acorns on a rock. Over time, this created a permanent pit in the rock. Many of these pitted grinding rocks can be found in California today.

Using Water

California Indians changed the land around them by building fishing traps, called weirs. These traps were built across a river with poles and branches. The traps let water flow but blocked fish. The Hupa and Yurok [YOR ahk] used weirs to make fishing easier. They threw nets into the water to catch many fish at one time. Weirs did not block all the fish. Some fish kept swimming so there would always be fish to catch.

A Hupa fishing weir

California Indian groups found other ways to modify their land, too. The Chemehuevi and Mojave dug ditches for water. This early form of irrigation allowed new crops to grow. Beans, corn, and wheat became important food sources.

Stop and Check

Talk Why did California Indians change the land?

Find Details As you read, add new information to the graphic organizer on page 87 in your Inquiry Journal.

(t)phleum/iStock/Getty Images; (b)Edward S. Curtis Collection, Library of Congress, LC-USZ62-98669

How California Indian Children Lived

From an early age, California Indian children began learning important skills. Boys learned how to track animals and to hunt and fish. Girls learned which plants were good to eat, how to weave baskets, and how to make flour from acorns. They learned to cook with their mothers, too. Both boys and girls enjoyed learning stories, music, and songs on special days.

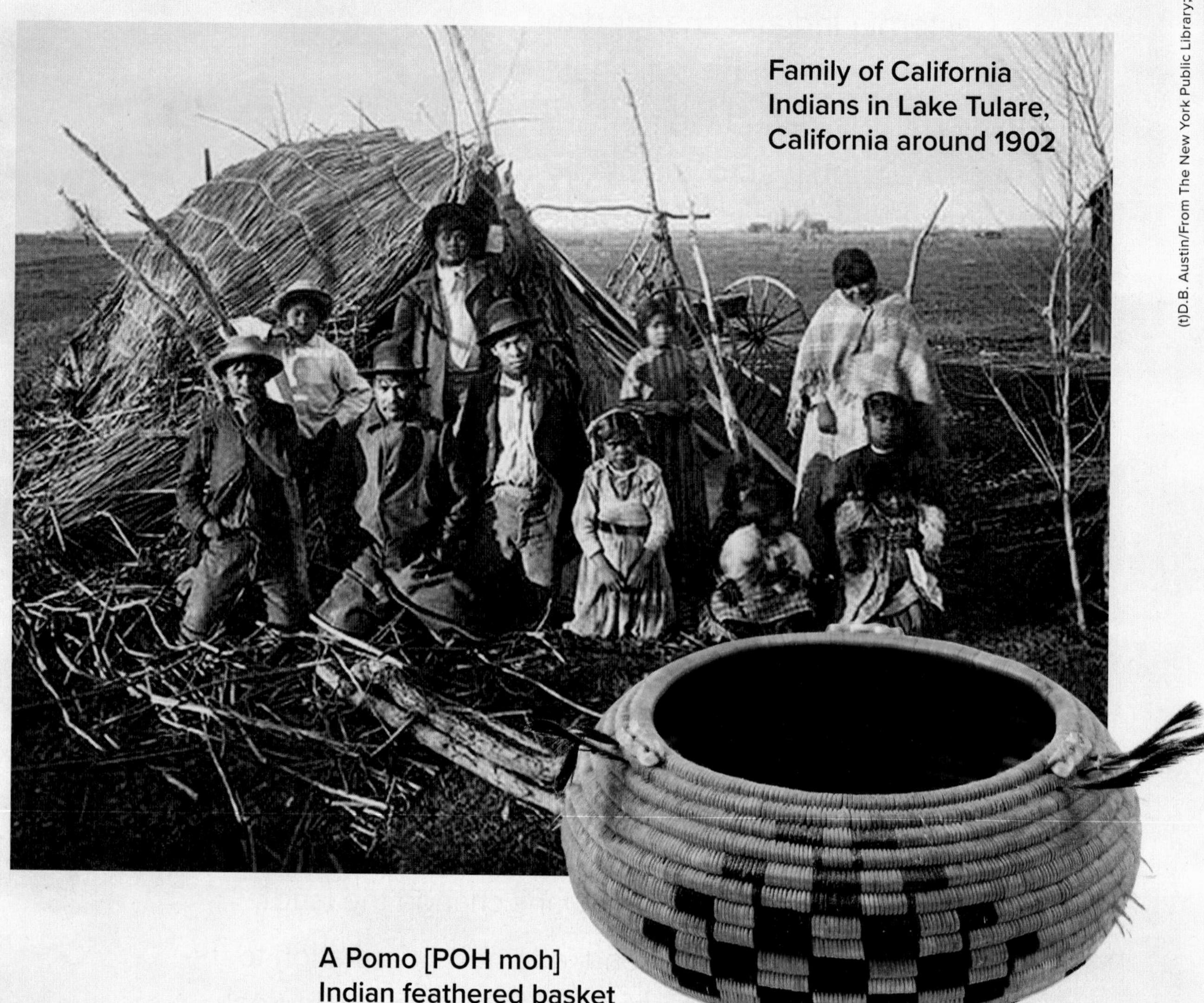

Family of California Indians in Lake Tulare, California around 1902

A Pomo [POH moh] Indian feathered basket

(t)D.B. Austin/From The New York Public Library; (b)Paul Marcus/Shutterstock.com

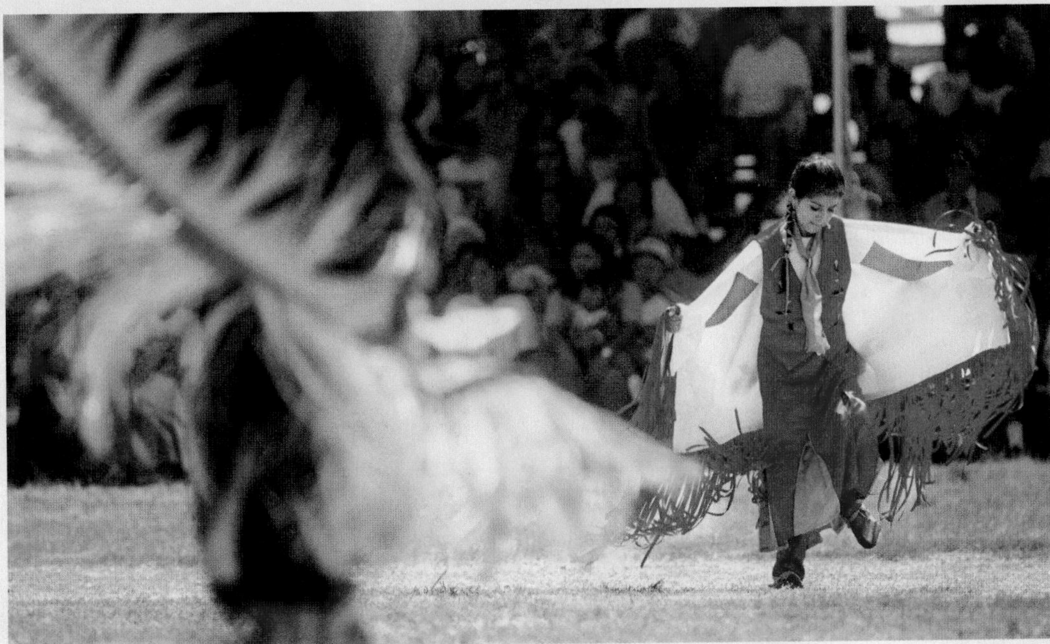

A young girl dances at a powwow in Costa Mesa, California.

Stop and Check

COLLABORATE

Talk How were early California Indian children's lives similar to yours? How were they different?

What Do You Think?

How did California Indian groups change the land? Why were these changes important?

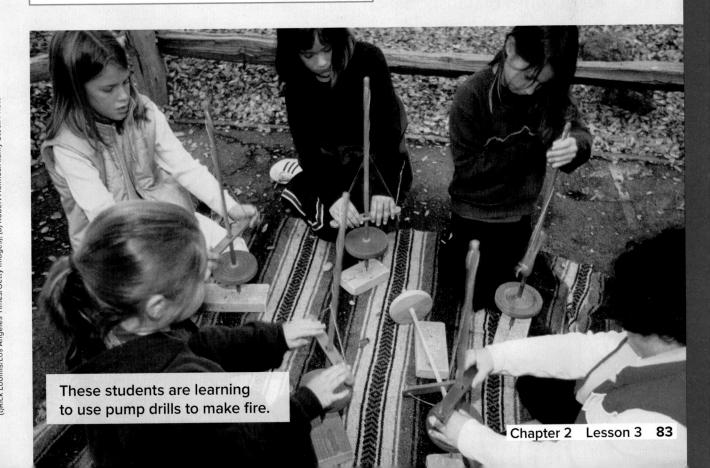

These students are learning to use pump drills to make fire.

(t)Rick Loomis/Los Angeles Times/Getty Images; (b) Robert Holmes/Alamy Stock Photo

How Did California Indians Use Natural Resources?

Using California's Resources

The environment of California shaped the **culture** of its native people. Culture is the way of life shared by a group of people. This includes their food, language, arts, and beliefs. Each group of California Indians used the resources around them in different ways. They found ways to change their natural resources into food, clothing, shelter, forms of transportation, and even art!

HSS.3.1.2, HSS.3.2.1, HSS.3.2.2

A Pomo woman weaves a basket.

Ingo Brede/Alamy Stock Photo

The Miwok Indians lived in the Central Valley. They were surrounded by oak trees. The Miwok used the acorns from these trees to make stew and bread. The acorn was such an important part of Miwok culture that they had a festival each year to celebrate it. Each fall they **harvested**, or gathered, acorns and stored them for use throughout the year. The people hoped for a harvest large enough to last the winter.

The Chumash Indians lived in villages along the southern coast. They got much of their food from the ocean. They used trees to build large canoes. These canoes, called tomols, were used for fishing. A tomol could be up to 30 feet long, but light enough for two people to carry.

Did You Know?

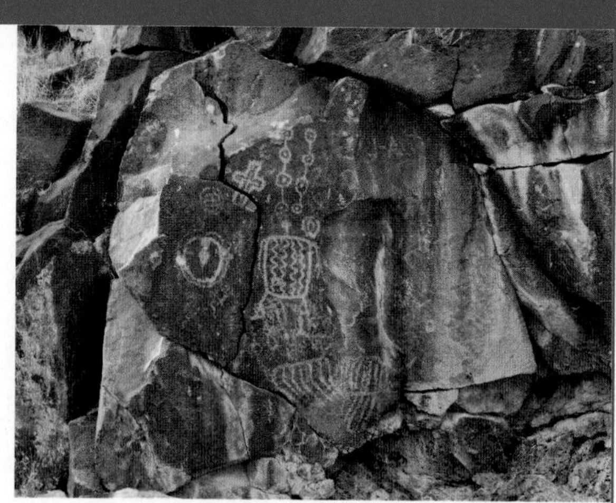

Rock art was an important part of California Indian culture. Some artists painted on rock walls. They used paints made from minerals and brushes made from plant stems. Other artists carved pictures into the rock. These pictures had different meanings. They may also have marked important events, including a solar eclipse in 1677. Some of this art is still visible today.

Witold Skrypczak/Alamy Stock Photo

The Kawaiisu [KOO wah zoo] Indians lived in a different region depending on the time of year. In the winter, they lived in Mojave Desert valleys. In the summer, they moved up into the mountains. They learned to use the natural resources from both regions. In the valley, they built shelters of branches and bark to protect themselves from spring rains. On cold nights, they warmed their homes with rocks from the cooking fire. In the mountains, the Kawaiisu built grass-covered shelters to protect them from the sun. If a food source became low in one region, they moved where the food was more plentiful.

Hupa white deerskin dance costume

Ancient American Indian baskets

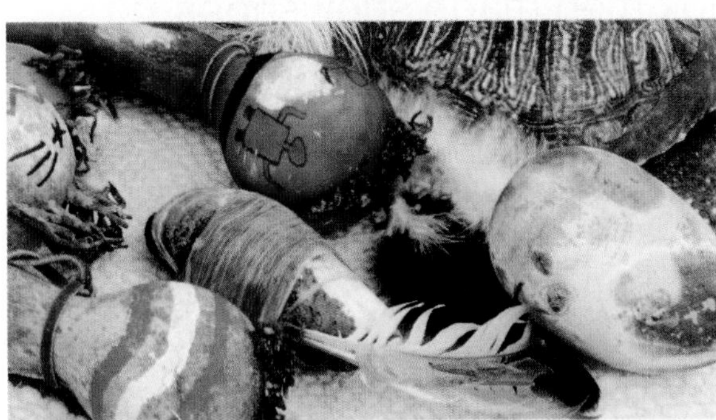

Chumash Indian rattles

Chumash boys paddling a tomol

Stop and Check

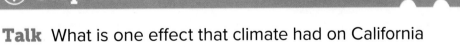

Talk What is one effect that climate had on California Indians?

Find Details As you read, add new information to the graphic organizer on page 95 in your Inquiry Journal.

(tl)Edward S. Curtis Collection, Library of Congress, LC-USZ62-101260; (tr)Michael DeFreitas North America/Alamy Stock Photo; (bl)Chuck Place/Alamy Stock Photo; (br)Spencer Weiner/Los Angeles Times/Getty Images

Using Plants and Animals

California Indians used many plants in their environment for food. In the spring, the Miwok gathered fresh green plants. In the summer, they gathered seeds, roots, and mushrooms they found in the mountains. The amole, or soap plant, was a favorite food of the Chumash. They roasted the bulb and ate it. They also used the plant to make soap. They even made brushes from the plant's husks.

Granite mortar with pestle

Like the Chumash, the Kumeyaay's [KOO mee yigh] homeland was in Southern California. They learned which plants were good to eat. They also knew which plants, such as willow, could be used to make tools, baskets, and medicine. They used agave for both food and medicine.

California Indian groups also made clothes from animal skins and plant parts. The Miwok men made snowshoes from branches and grapevines when they hunted in the hills during winter. Other groups used plant materials, such as bark, to make skirts and reeds to weave hats. Women often decorated their dresses with shells and seeds.

Miwok snowshoes

(t)New-bold-pics/iStock/Getty Images; (b)duncan1890/iStock/Getty Images

Meat was important for many California Indian groups, too. They hunted large animals, such as bear and elk. They also hunted small animals, such as rabbits, squirrels, and birds. Sometimes they used traps made from plants to catch animals. They usually used bows and arrows made from willow branches to hunt. They made arrowheads from sharp stones. They used these arrows to hunt large animals.

Seafood was another important food source. The Chumash ate fish and shellfish such as clams. Groups such as the Miwok caught and cooked fish from mountain streams. The Hupa caught salmon from the Trinity River each spring and fall. They caught enough fish to last for months.

Salmon smoking on sticks next to a fire.

Andrew Ferguson/Shutterstock.com

Stop and Check

Think How did California Indians use plants and animals?

InfoGraphic

How California Indians Used Their Environments

California Indians used the land and resources around them in different ways. They used these resources to build homes. They also used them for clothing, tools, and transportation. Let's look at the ways California Indians used their environments.

Hupa winter house

The Hupa needed to build houses that would protect them from rain and snow. They dug a pit and placed stones around it to hold up the wooden walls and roof. This type of shelter kept water out.

Chemehuevi shelter

The Chemehuevi lived in the hot desert. Unlike the Hupa, they needed protection only from the sun. They built shelters out of brush to make areas of shade.

Yurok canoes

The Yurok lived near the forest, so they built their canoes out of logs. They used fire or a shell to hollow out a log. This made a place for them to sit and paddle to move along their local rivers.

Ohlone canoes

The Ohlone lived on the coast. They used reeds found along the beaches to build things. They tied the reeds together to build their canoes.

(bkgd)McGraw-Hill Education

Miwok clothing

The Sierra Miwok hunted deer in the forests. They used deer skins to make clothing. Women wrapped them around their bodies to form dresses. Men wore them around their waists and hips.

Mohave clothing

The Mojave Indians lived in the desert. Women wore skirts of pounded bark or woven grass. Men wore waistcloths also made from bark or grass.

Stop and Check

COLLABORATE

Talk What is one way that two California Indian groups lived differently because of where they lived?

What Do You Think?

How did California Indians use the resources around them for food, clothing, and shelter?

What Defines a California Indian Community?

California Indian Communities

Life has changed over time for the Indian communities in California. However, they have kept many of their **traditions.** A tradition is a belief or custom handed down from one generation to the next. Different communities often have different traditions. Traditions, such as the powwow, help to hold communities together. A powwow is a festival where people perform and share drumming, dances, and crafts.

One common value among California's Indian communities is the importance of family. Lines of kinship, or family relationships, often connect members of a community. These bonds are important in a community.

HSS.3.2.1, HSS.3.2.3

Michael Turner/Alamy Stock Photo

A young California Indian dancer performs at a powwow in Anderson, California.

Traditions and Folklore

California Indian groups formed their own **culture** over time. Today, California Indian groups still hold on to and preserve their culture and traditions. They also take part in new traditions.

BALL-PLAYING ON THE PRAIRIES.

One way California Indians preserve their culture is by learning their native language. They also learn to play traditional Indian instruments. Today, young people learn the language and music of their tribe. This helps connect them to older members of the tribe and it helps them learn more about their culture.

Biography

Traditionally, the American Indian flute was an instrument played only by men. It was unusual for a woman to play the Indian flute. **Mary Youngblood** changed that.

From an early age, Mary showed a talent for music. She learned to play the piano at six years old and the violin at age eight. At ten, she learned classical flute and guitar.

When Mary Youngblood grew up, she began to explore her American Indian past. When she discovered the American Indian flute, she loved it. She learned how to play the instrument, and now she performs professionally. Mary has recorded six albums and has earned two Grammy Awards for her music.

(t)North Wind Picture Archives/Alamy; (b)Roger Bacon/Alamy Stock Photo

Sharing stories, or folklore, is another important part of native culture. Folklore includes stories and beliefs that are shared from one generation to the next. Storytelling keeps folklore alive. Most of today's California Indians have a rich tradition of storytelling. Folklore often includes stories about how Earth, humans, and animals were created. Today, some California Indians continue to share their stories at festivals. The annual California Indian Storytelling Festivals are held in different areas throughout the state.

The coyote is a favorite character in California Indian myths and legends.

COLLABORATE

Stop and Check

Talk Why do you think it is important for California Indian groups to share stories?

Find Details As you read, add new information to the graphic organizer on page 103 in your Inquiry Journal.

Living in Two Worlds

Many California Indians today split their time between cities and their tribe's **reservations**. A reservation is land set aside for American Indians by the United States government. There are about 100 reservations in California. These areas are spread across the state.

One group of California Indians that lives on a reservation is the Hupa Valley Tribe. They live a life very similar to other Californians. The tribe runs several businesses. For example, Hupa Forest Industries cuts down and sells logs from surrounding forests. The company also has a mill on the reservation to turn the logs into lumber. Another company builds homes for people in the area. Both of these businesses employ many members of the tribe.

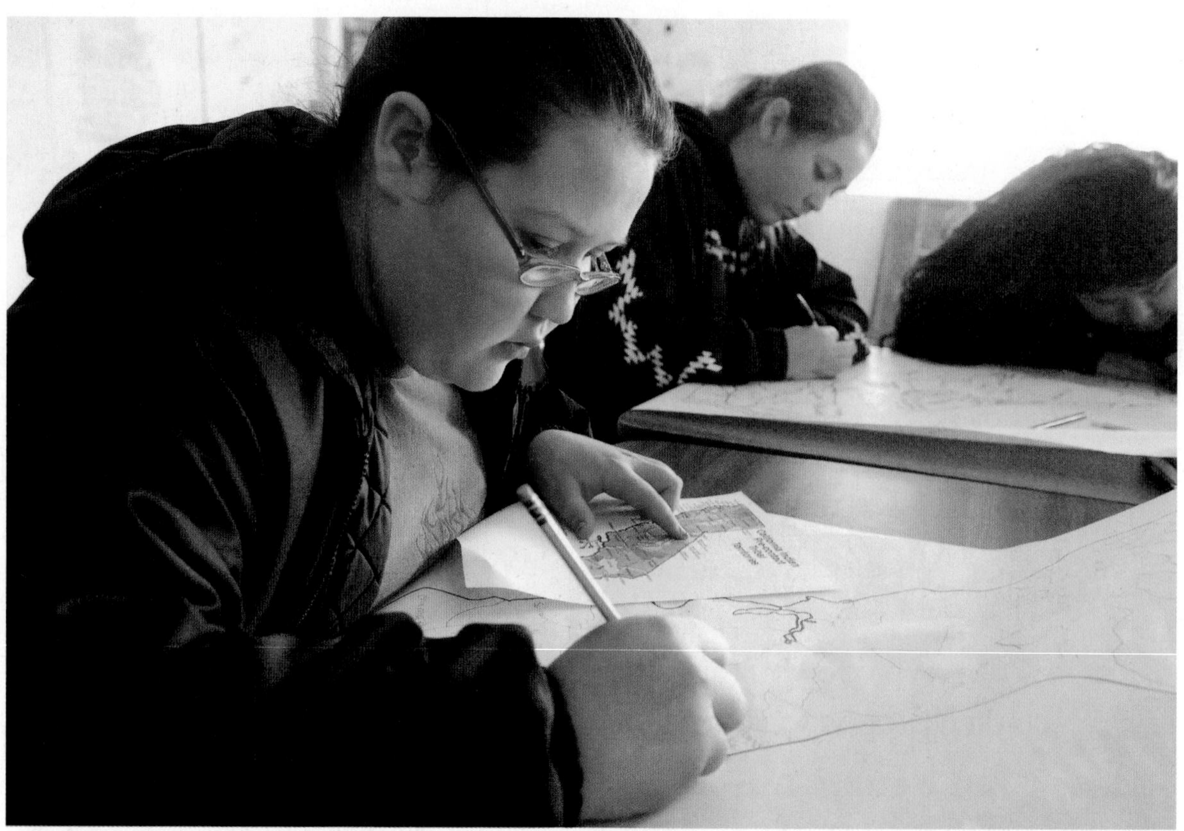

Amber Gensaw works on a lesson at Klamath River Early College of the Redwoods, a school on the Yurok Indian Reservation.

ZUMA Press, Inc./Alamy Stock Photo

Perspective

American Indians have lived in California for thousands of years. How can you learn about the cultures of California Indians from your community? You could start with a search on the Internet. Is there a local museum, park, or visitor's center you could visit? Ask your teacher and friends for information, too. Through these investigations, you can learn about the daily life and culture of many California Indians. For example, the Kumeyaay people share Bird Songs to tell about how different animals came to be. These songs are long and difficult. They take many years of practice to learn them.

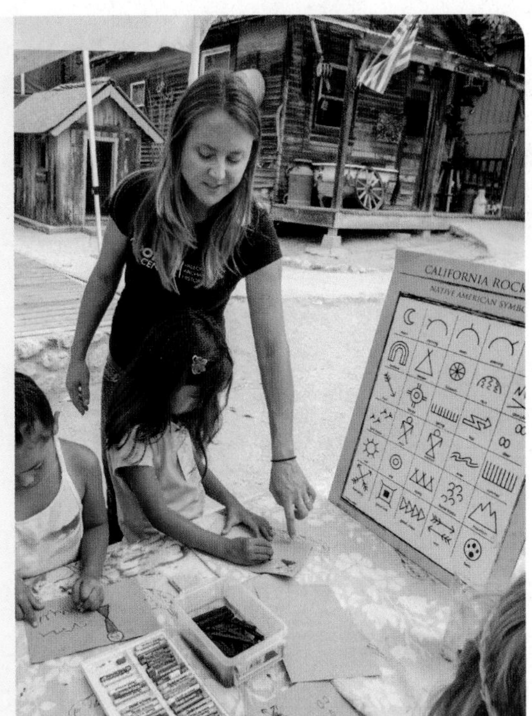

The tribe has employees who take care of everyday needs on the reservation. These jobs include managing a budget and managing elections. Natural resources departments take care of the forests and waterways. The reservation has its own police department as well.

The tribe holds festivals throughout the year. These events are a way for visitors to learn more about the Hupa. They help to keep traditions alive, and they are fun! People show off their horse-riding skills during the Hupa Rodeo. The Stick Game Tournament brings kids together for exercise and fun.

Stop and Check

Think How is life on a reservation the same as life in your community? How is it different?

What Do You Think? Why is it important for California Indians to keep their traditions alive?

Marmaduke St. John/Alamy Stock Photo

Lesson 6

How Do California Indian Communities Work?

Money and Trade

In the past, California Indian groups traded with each other to get the things they needed. They shared their goods and resources with groups from different areas. They traded the goods they made, such as canoes and clothes, for goods and resources they needed. They used shell beads as a form of money. Larger shells were worth more than small shells. Shells that were hard to find were worth more. Longer strands of beads were worth more than shorter strands of beads. Traders would measure the value of a strand of beads by its length.

The ways California Indian groups buy and sell goods are different today. California Indians use money, just like everyone else. They sell items they make to people who need them. They buy goods they need from people who have them. They own businesses such as banks and construction companies. They also provide services to people across the country.

HSS.3.2.1, HSS.3.2.3

Sophie James/Alamy Stock Photo

The National Museum of the American Indian in Washington, D.C.

California Indian Governments

Just as the California Indians had their own economies, they had their own governments. A government is a group of people in charge of leading a community, state, or nation. Tribes made their own laws. They had their own businesses. The tribal governments made important decisions to keep the tribes safe. They often voted for their leaders. Sometimes leaders were members of the same family.

Many California Indian governments still work in the same way today. They also work with the local, state, and federal governments. Most of today's tribal governments are based on a **constitution**. A constitution is a written plan of government. This document makes rules for how the government works. It also lists the rights and duties of members. It includes the powers of the government. These include collecting taxes, passing and enforcing laws, and making decisions for the tribe.

PRIMARY SOURCE

Tribal Constitutions

Most California Indian tribes have constitutions. Below is the introduction from the constitution of the Tule [TOO lee] River Indian Tribe. It was approved in 1936.

UNITED STATES
DEPARTMENT OF THE INTERIOR
OFFICE OF INDIAN AFFAIRS

CONSTITUTION AND BYLAWS
OF THE TULE RIVER
INDIAN TRIBE
CALIFORNIA

APPROVED JANUARY 15, 1936

UNITED STATES
GOVERNMENT PRINTING OFFICE
WASHINGTON : 1936

A tribal constitution helps the tribe govern its members.

Preamble

We, the members of the Tule River Bands of the Tule River Indian Reservation in the State of California, in order to establish our tribal organization, to conserve our tribal property, to develop our community resources, to administer justice, and to promote the welfare of ourselves and our descendants, do hereby ordain and establish this constitution and bylaws of the Tule River Indian Tribe, to serve as a guide for the deliberations of our tribal council in its administration of tribal affairs.

Stop and Check

COLLABORATE

Talk Why do you think many California Indian tribes wanted to have a written constitution?

Find Details As you read, add new information to the graphic organizer on page 111 in your Inquiry Journal.

IMAGE: US Department of Interior Office of Indian Affairs
TEXT: Constitution and Bylaws of the Tule River Indian Tribe California. Washington DC: United States Government Printing Office, 1936.

Citizens of Two Nations

California became part of the United States in 1848. It became a state in 1850. As the country grew and settlers moved west, California Indians lost their land and homes. The United States government created **reservations** over the years. Many American Indian groups were forced to live on reservations.

However, the government treated American Indian tribes as their own nations. California Indians are citizens of two nations. They are citizens of the United States, and they are citizens of their own tribe. Tribes have relationships with the federal and state governments. They are also very independent.

Tribes continue to have their own governments, make laws, collect taxes, and control what happens on reservations. There are many ways California Indians can work for their government. In this way, they work to keep their communities safe.

Member of the Chumash tribe speaks at a city board meeting.

Spencer Weiner/Los Angeles Times/Getty Images

California Indians serve in many levels of the United States government, too. Some work in local governments to help build strong communities. Some work in state government to help solve problems that affect all Californians. And some work for the federal government.

Biography

Dr. Joely Proudfit

Joely Proudfit is a descendant of the Pechanga Band of Luiseño [loo ee SEN yo] Mission Indians, and she is of the Ngeesikat clan. She owns Naqmayam Communications, a public relations, marketing, and advertising firm dedicated to preserving and protecting tribal sovereignty. She is a three-time tenured professor. Dr. Proudfit works with tribal leaders and government legislators to create new legislation that benefits American Indians.

In 2016, Dr. Proudfit was appointed to the National Advisory Council on Indian Education. In this role, she works on programs with the United States government to help American Indians throughout the country.

Dr. Joely Proudfit, PH.D., member of the National Advisory Council on Indian Education

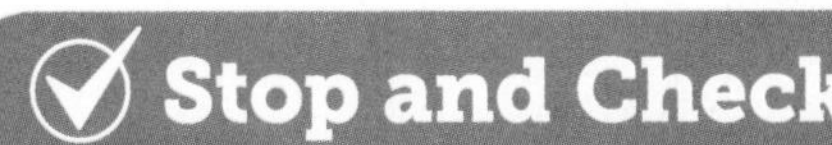

Stop and Check

Talk Discuss why you think some people want to serve in government. What are some of the advantages and disadvantages of doing so?

What Do You Think? Why are American Indians considered citizens of two nations? How does this work?

California State University San Marcos

Field Trip!

The National Museum of the American Indian

One place in Washington, D.C., looks like no other place in the city. It is the National Museum of the American Indian. It is the perfect place for a field trip!

Walk up to the museum and notice its shape. The museum has smooth, curved walls that look like the large rocks found in the desert. Some American Indian groups, such as the Ancestral Puebloans [PWEB loh ins], or Anasazi [ah nuh SAH zee], lived among rocks like these in the Southwest region of the United States.

Next, look at the land that surrounds the museum. Many kinds of plants and animals live there. You can see a small forest with more than 30 kinds of trees. You can also see a wetland that is home to ducks and dragonflies. Wildflowers and plants that can be used as medicine grow in a meadow.

Inside, the museum has one of the largest collections of American Indian artifacts in the world. These artifacts tell stories of the American Indians from across North America. They help us learn about life in the past. We can also use them to understand the **cultures** of today.

Bert Hoferichter/Alamy Stock Photo

The museum is called a “living museum.” The land that surrounds the museum is living and is always changing. Visitors can see performances, listen to talks, and watch videos. These activities are lively and fun. The museum celebrates the different cultures of American Indians who lived both long ago and today.

(t)Mira/Alamy Stock Photo; (b)Alex Wong/Getty Images News/Getty Images

Stop and Check

COLLABORATE

Write Plan a field trip for your classmates! Working in a group, choose a location that is educational, such as a museum. Begin by writing the goal of the trip. Next, write the plan as a series of steps. Include details about transportation, locations, snacks, and so on.

Connections in Action

Back to the EQ

Think about the chapter EQ, **"How have California Indians influenced the local region?"**

- **Talk** with a partner about the California Indians in your community. Make a list of examples of where you see their influence in your region.
- **Share** your list with the class.

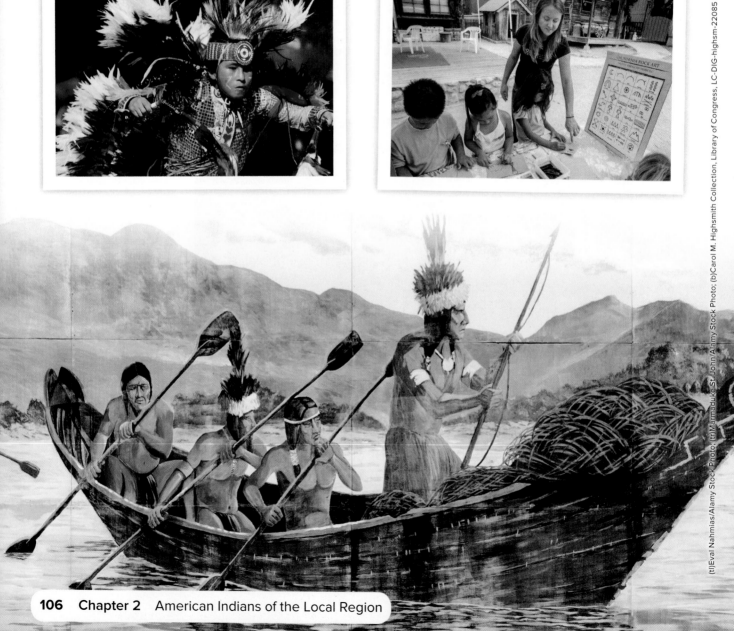

(tl)Eyal Nahmias/Alamy Stock Photo; (tr)Marmaduke St. John/Alamy Stock Photo; (b)Carol M. Highsmith Collection, Library of Congress, LC-DIG-highsm-22085

More to Explore

How can you make an IMPACT?

Make Connections Across Time

What are some ways in which we change our environment today? How are these similar to the changes California Indians have made? How are they different?

Organize a Cultural Event

You would like to invite a local California Indian group to talk to your school. Write a letter to the local tribal leaders to ask them to visit. Tell them what you would like to learn about. Explain why you think learning about their heritage is important to your school community.

Create a Design

Choose a landform, plant, or animal that represents your community. Create a design that stands for that landform, plant, or animal. Then draw a picture of a basket, pot, or piece of clothing you would make that includes this design.

Chapter 3 How and Why Communities Change Over Time

How Has Life Changed for People in My Community Over Time?

Communities grow and change over time. In this chapter, you will read about the ways some communities in California have changed. You will also explore what makes the many different communities in California special. As you read, think about how people have helped your community grow. Think about how your community has changed over time.

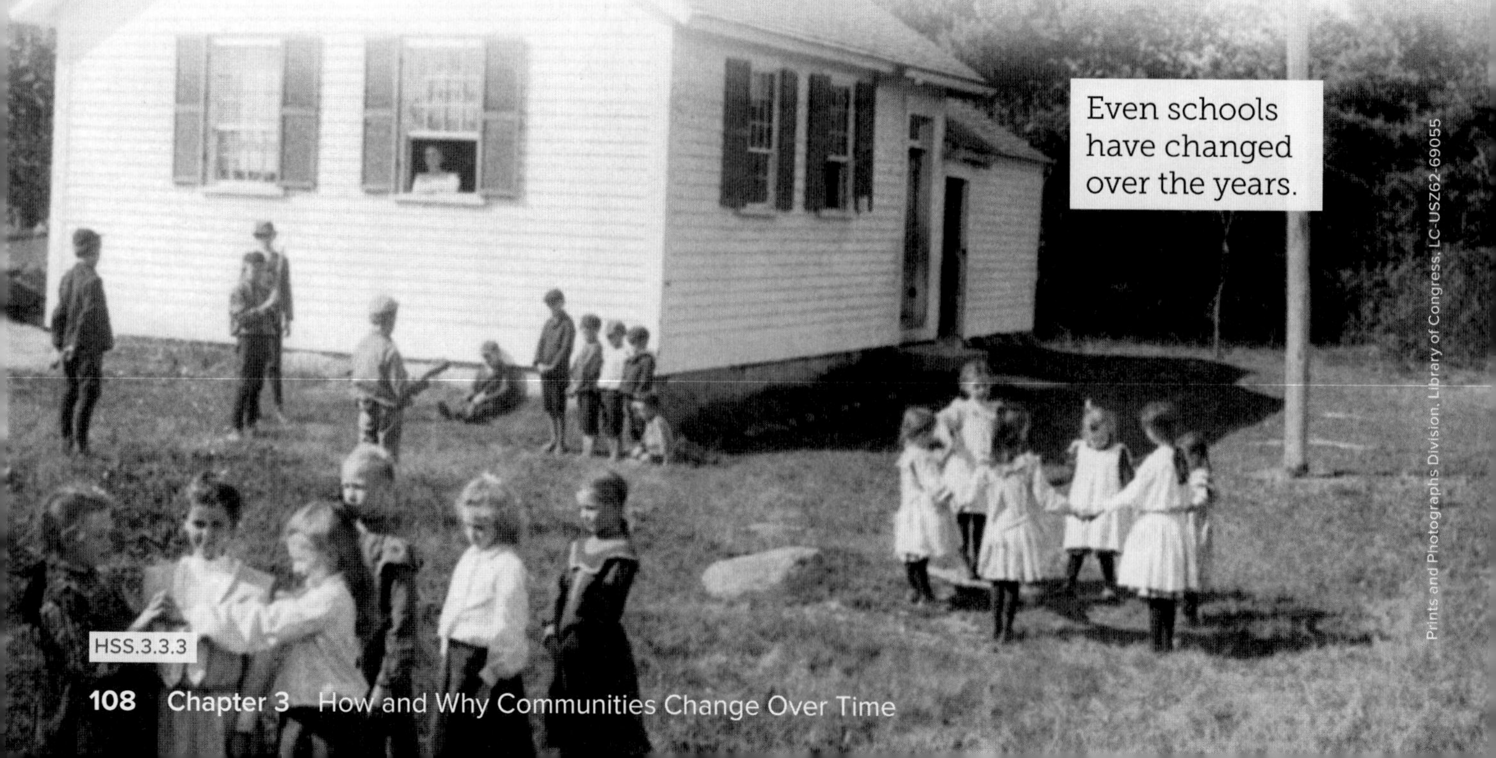

Even schools have changed over the years.

Prints and Photographs Division, Library of Congress, LC-USZ62-69055

HSS.3.3.3

How Has Life in Communities Changed?

Communities are always changing. New inventions and people from many cultures have played a role in these changes.

Life in the 1800s was very different from today. It was slower and dirtier. People could travel only as fast as their horse. News and letters took weeks to reach a community. Roads were made of dirt. Without the steel we use today, buildings could be only several stories high.

Water is important to communities. Most places are built near a body of water. Early settlers were happy when they could use a hand-powered pump to pump water directly into their houses. They did not have to carry water in a bucket from a well any more.

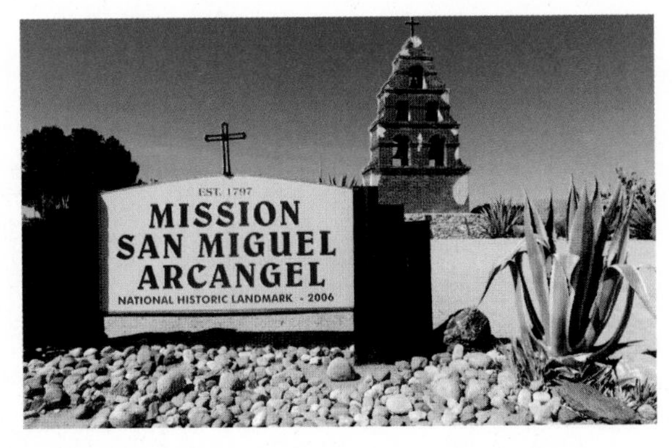

When Spanish settlers arrived, they changed the landscape. They farmed the land using European methods. They built buildings using European technology. When the Spanish came to California, they changed the California Indian communities forever.

(t)Lawrence and Houseworth Collection, Library of Congress, LC-DIG-ds-04481; (bl)jpbcpa/E+/Getty Images; (br)Carol M. Highsmith Collection, Library of Congress, LC-DIG-highsm-21627

Connect Through Literature

Visions of URBAN CALIFORNIA

by Harvey Jones

California's early painters liked to paint landscapes showing the state's spectacular natural beauty. In the 1800s, many settlers came to California. They were attracted by this beauty, and by the promise of gold, rich farmland, or a new life. Cities sprang up, and urban growth changed California's landscape forever. California artists have painted the urban landscape in many ways. They show its excitement, its harsh realities, its promise, and its human-made beauty.

California Pines, painted by William Keith in 1878

PHOTO:(b)LACMA - Los Angeles County Museum of Art; (bkgd)McGraw-Hill Education
TEXT: "Visions of Urban California" by Harvey Jones from California Chronicles, May 1999. Copyright © by Carus Publishing Company. Reproduced with permission. All Cricket Media material is copyrighted by Carus Publishing Company, d/b/a Cricket Media, and/or various authors and illustrators. Any commercial use or distribution of material without permission is strictly prohibited. Please visit http://www.cricketmedia.com/info/licensing2 for licensing and http://www.cricketmedia.com for subscriptions.; LACMA - Los Angeles County Museum of Art

William Hahn's *Sacramento Railroad Station* shows a busy railroad station in 1870s Sacramento. Hahn was a master of a type of painting called "genre." Genre paintings show people doing everyday things. These paintings reveal something about life in a particular time and place. They are similar to today's candid (unposed) photographs. In this genre painting, Hahn is not trying to present a beautiful and flattering view of Sacramento. He wants to show city life as realistically as possible.

Sacramento Railroad Station, painted by William Hahn in 1874

(b)taviphoto/iStockphoto/Getty Images; (inset)Archivart/Alamy Stock Photo; (bkgd)McGraw-Hill Education

Newcomers streamed into the Los Angeles area during the Great Depression of the 1930s. At this time, many artists turned away from pretty landscapes. They began painting scenes of everyday urban life, or the "American Scene." Millard Sheets was a leader of this style of painting in California. His 1934 painting *Tenement Flats* shows people living in a crowded Los Angeles apartment building. The people in Sheets's painting live in cramped, uncomfortable conditions. But Sheets shows more than just the difficult side of their lives. We see them enjoying the warm morning sunshine that lights up crisp white laundry blowing in the breeze. Sheets's painting is lively and colorful. It's not dark and sad.

The Great Depression was a time of hardship and poverty for people all over the world. It began in 1929 and lasted through the 1930s.

Tenement is a word for cheap, overcrowded, and often unsafe apartment buildings. *Flats* means "apartments."

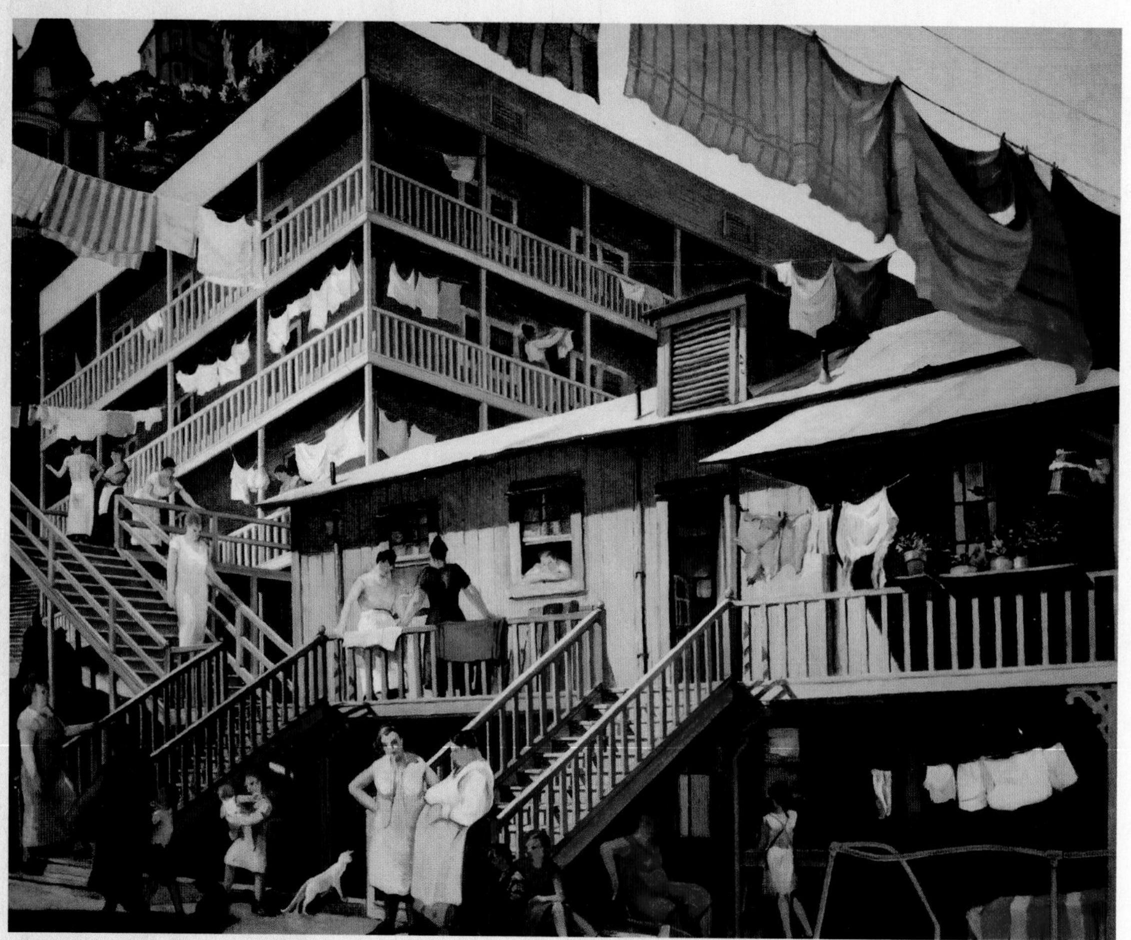

Tenement Flats, painted by Millard Sheets in 1934

(b)Niday Picture Library/Alamy Stock Photo; (bkgd)McGraw-Hill Education

As cities have grown bigger, they have also grown taller. Skyscrapers give shape to today's cities. Wayne Thiebaud's *San Francisco West Side Ridge*, painted in 1992, captures the character of modern San Francisco. It shows the city's steep hills covered with high-rise apartments and office buildings. Thiebaud has bathed his imaginary view of the city in brilliant sunlight and deep shadows. His special painting style also celebrates the rich, vibrant colors and creamy textures of the paint itself.

Think About It

1. What is "genre" painting?
2. Why did the subject of paintings of California change?
3. How can paintings help us understand how life has changed for people in a community?

San Francisco West Side Ridge, painted by Wayne Thiebaud in 1992

(b)C Squared Studios/Photodisc/Getty Images; (inset)B Christopher/Alamy Stock Photo; (bkgd)McGraw-Hill Education

Why Do People Move to a New Region?

Why People Move to New Places

Have you or a friend ever moved from one place to another? There are many reasons why people move. Some people move to find a better job. Others may choose to move to a place because of the weather. They want to live somewhere with a nice climate. Still others may move to be closer to their friends and families or to get away from a bad situation. Other people may need to find a new home after a natural disaster, such as an earthquake or a **drought**. People migrate from one place to another for many reasons.

Read on to learn more about why people have migrated to California over the years.

HSS.3.3.1, HSS.3.3.2, HAS.CS.1, HAS.CS.2

U.S. Farm Security Administration, Library of Congress, LOC_LC-USF34-019420-E

Building a new house in Salinas

People have migrated to California for many reasons. Some communities formed near water. Ships could dock, and people and goods could travel to and from the community. Other communities were built in valleys, where the soil was good for growing crops and raising animals. Farmers and ranchers moved to this area because of the land. Some people came looking for gold in the mountains or other precious minerals or oil deep in the earth.

Did You Know?

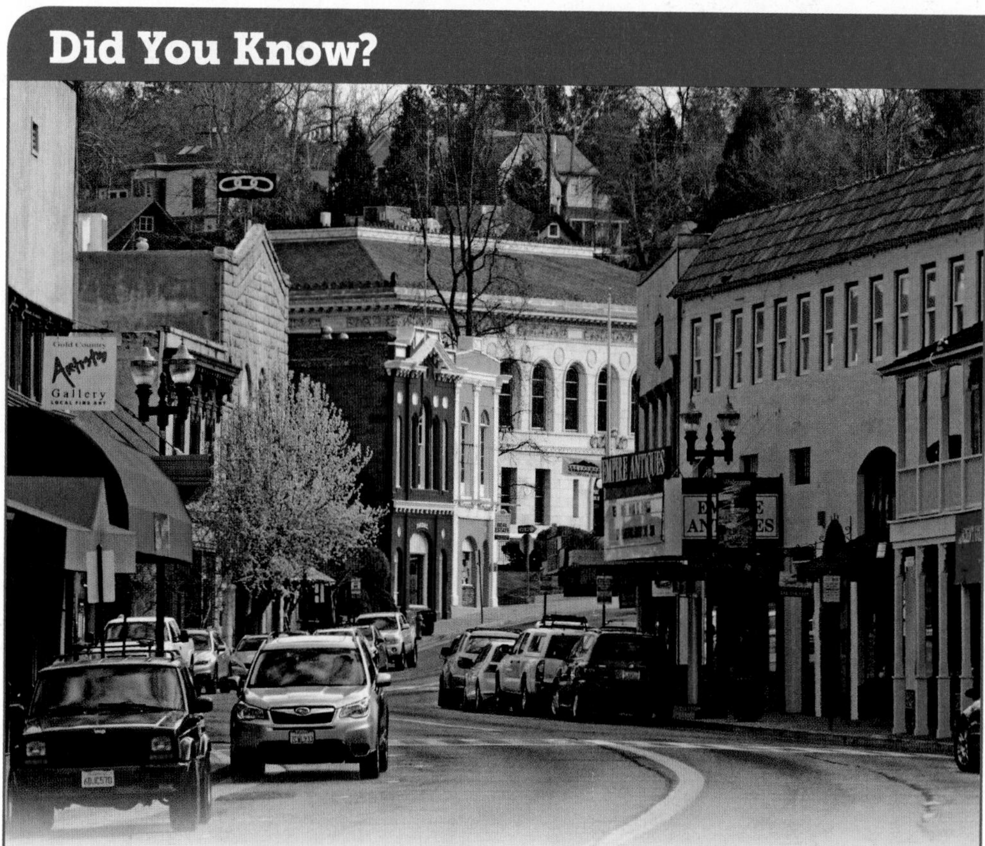

Gold miners settled in what is now called Placerville in 1848. They named this mountain town near Sacramento "Dry Diggins." This is because the river where they dug for gold dried up during the summer. "Placer" comes from a Spanish word for a place near a sandy stream bank where gold can be found. Today, Placerville is a modern community. Visitors to the town can learn about the history of gold mining in California.

johnrandallalves/iStock/Getty Images

Oklahoma migrants moving to California during the Great Depression

During the Great Depression of the 1930s, many people in America lost their jobs. Thousands of migrants moved to California from other parts of the country looking for work. They found jobs working on farms. A **decade** later, in the 1940s, people took jobs building planes, tanks, and other goods during World War II. Many stayed and many more moved into the state to work in the growing aircraft and technology industries. Today, people continue to move to California to work in these and other industries.

Stop and Check

COLLABORATE

Think Give two reasons people move to new places and explain why they move. If you could move somewhere new, where would you want to go? Why?

Find Details As you read, add new information to the graphic organizer on page 125 in your Inquiry Journal.

Farm Security Administration, Library of Congress, LOC_LC-USF34-009871-E

Communities Grow and Change

Most communities begin as small settlements and grow slowly. As businesses open in a community, more people will move there to find jobs. As more people come to the community, new homes, stores, schools, and roads are built. The community becomes larger.

Then and Now

San Francisco

San Francisco is one community that has changed over time. It started as a tiny settlement near the coast. But San Francisco grew quickly during the mid-1800s. Gold seekers from all over the world came to try to strike it rich. Other people came to San Francisco to start businesses that sold tools and other things to the miners. San Francisco is now one of California's largest cities. Today, as in the past, San Francisco is a city of many different people and cultures.

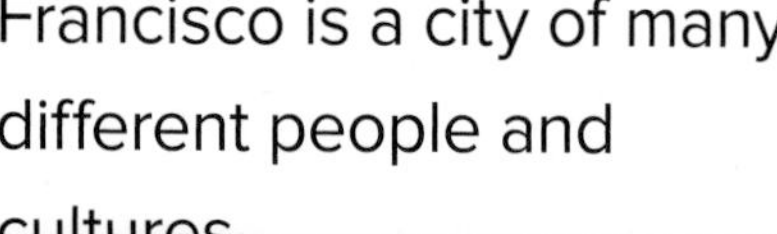

(t)Jan Hanus/Alamy Stock Photo; (b)Digital image courtesy of the Getty's Open Content Program

San Bernardino is another example of a town that has grown and changed over time. The Serrano Indians created hunting trails through the San Bernardino Valley. The Spanish later used these trails when they explored California. By the mid-1800s, **settlers** were coming to the valley.

In 1862, gold was discovered in the valley. San Bernardino grew quickly and became an important mining town. But the gold soon ran out and people left. San Bernardino could have become another ghost town, but it did not.

In 1883, the Southern Pacific Railroad reached San Bernardino. A few years later, the Sante Fe Railroad laid tracks through the city. San Bernardino had become a center of trade and transportation. The city's population doubled in the decade between 1900 and 1910.

The invention of the automobile kept San Bernardino growing. In 1926, a new road called Route 66 was built, stretching from the Midwest into California. Route 66 ran through San Bernardino and brought more people to the city. Business and industry grew. More jobs made it easier for people to have things they wanted and needed.

Not all of these changes were good. People and factories polluted the water. The land was changed when roads and buildings were built. The people of California have had to work hard to expand their communities without causing more problems.

Stop and Check

Talk Discuss with a partner how communities grow and change.

What Do You Think? When people move to new places today, how are their reasons for moving similar to those of people who moved long ago?

FiledIMAGE/iStock/Getty Images

How Did Settlers and California Indians Interact?

Spanish Explorers Arrive in the Americas

In 1492, Christopher Columbus sailed from Spain to find a way to travel to Asia across the Atlantic Ocean. Columbus did not find a way to Asia, but he did reach islands in the Caribbean Sea and, on later trips, South America. Europeans did not know about this land. When Columbus arrived, he claimed the land for Spain. By 1535, Spain had gained control of the region and called it New Spain.

As time went by, the Spanish explored the continent of South America. By the mid-1500s, they began to explore North America. Eventually, they arrived in what today is California. They met Indians who had lived there for thousands of years.

Underwood Archives/age fotostock

HSS.3.2.4, HSS.3.3.1, HAS.CS.1

The first meeting of Juan Rodríguez Cabrillo and California Indians

Most of the early explorers of California came from Spain. This is why many places in the state have Spanish names. Some of these explorers wanted to find safe places for Spanish ships to land as they traveled west to Asia. Other explorers wanted to know more about the new land. The Spanish sent an **expedition** to southern California. An expedition is a journey for a specific purpose. Juan Rodríguez Cabrillo led this expedition. Then the Spanish sent several expeditions north along the coast. Sebastián Vizcaíno led one of these journeys.

In 1602, Vizcaíno left New Spain and headed north. He traveled along the California coast. He marked areas on a map that showed where ships could land safely. He also named some of the land and water features in the region. He named the Santa Barbara Channel Islands, the Santa Lucia Mountains, and Monterey Bay. We still use these names today.

Spanish explorer Sebastián Vizcaíno

taviphoto/iStockphoto/Getty Images

Biography

Juan Rodríguez Cabrillo

Juan Rodríguez Cabrillo was a Spanish soldier. He led an expedition to explore the coast of California for Spain. In 1542, he and his crew traveled north to what is now Monterey Bay. Bad storms forced the expedition to return to New Spain. On the trip, Cabrillo fell and broke a bone during a battle with California Indians. He ended up dying from his injury. Today, there is a monument of Cabrillo in San Diego honoring his exploration of the coast of California.

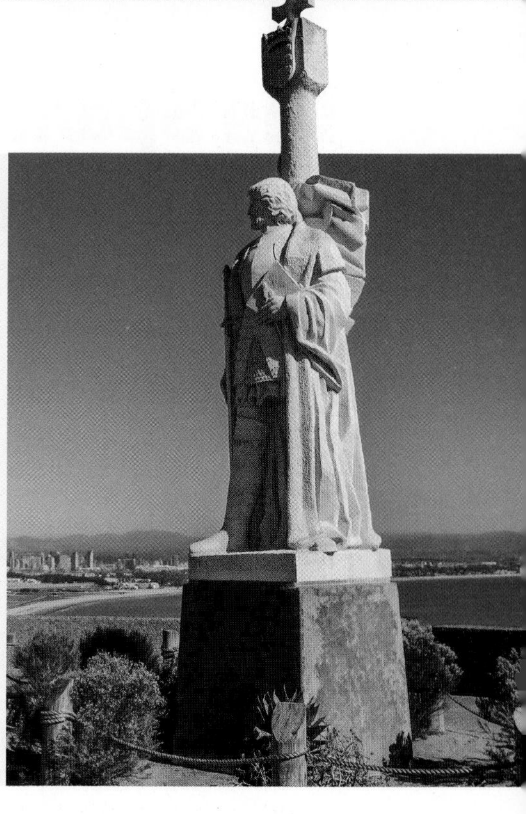

During these voyages along the coast, the explorers met several California Indian groups. They met the Coast Miwoks, Kumeyaay, and Ohlone. Sometimes the California Indians traded goods with the Spanish. Sometimes they helped the Spanish repair their ships. Often, the California Indians and the Spanish fought. The Indians did not want these strangers taking over their land.

At first, very little changed for the California Indians because of these explorers. However, their lives began to change during the 1700s when the Spanish began to build settlements in California.

Stop and Check

Think Why did the Spanish send explorers along the California coast?

Find Details As you read, add new information to the graphic organizer on page 133 in your Inquiry Journal.

maislam/iStock/Getty Images

The Spanish Settle in California

In 1769, Spain ordered Gaspar de Portolá to build several presidios, or forts, in California. Spain used these forts to defend its claim over the region. A Catholic priest named Father Junipero Serra joined Portolá. Serra was a missionary, not an explorer. He was interested in the people who lived in this new land. Serra believed that the California Indians would live better lives if they changed their religion and learned Spanish ways of life. He worked hard to build missions that would serve to convert the Indians to Christianity.

The first presidio and mission were built in San Diego in 1769. The Spanish built a total of five presidios along the California coast by 1782. A total of 21 missions were built by 1823. Missions at San Diego, San Francisco, and Santa Barbara were all founded during this time. These were connected by a series of roads called El Camino Real. In English, this means "the royal road."

Did You Know?

The early missionaries who settled in California often named their communities after Christian saints. In Spanish, the word for saint is *San*, *Santo*, or *Santa*. You can find many cities throughout California that begin with these words. San Francisco, for example, is Spanish for Saint Francis.

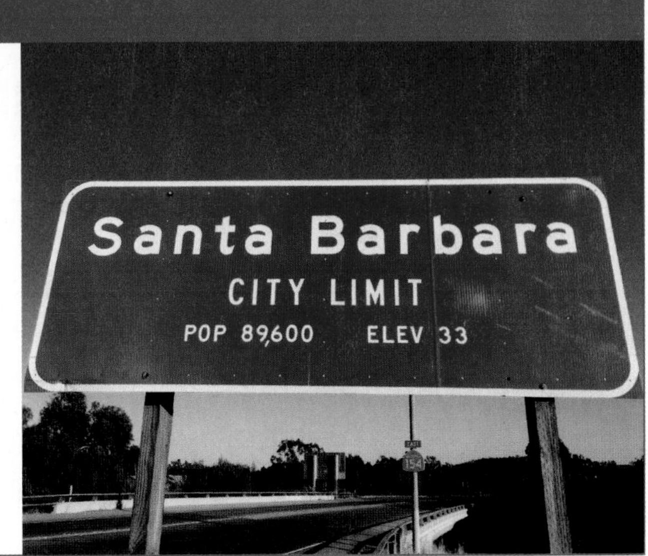

Santa Barbara
CITY LIMIT
POP 89,600 ELEV 33

Spanish **settlers** lived at missions. However, most of the population at a mission was made up of California Indians. These Indians came from many different tribes. California Indians had to live and work at the mission.

The Spanish forced California Indians to change their religion and become Roman Catholic. The Spanish also forced them to give up their lands. Then the Spanish taught them how to farm the land Spanish style. The California Indians also learned how to care for horses and cattle.

Life at the missions was very different for the California Indians, and they struggled to survive. They were exposed to European diseases such as smallpox. Many were not able to recover from these illnesses. Thousands of California Indians died from the harsh working conditions, diet changes, and diseases.

Geri Lavrov/Moment Open/Getty Images

 Stop and Check

Write Explain why the Spanish built the presidios and missions in California.

American Settlers Impact California Indians

The arrival of the Spanish greatly changed the lives of the California Indians. But their lives changed even more with the arrival of American settlers. In 1848, after a war, the United States won a large amount of land from Mexico, including California. American farmers began to settle in California. Then gold was discovered. News of this discovery spread across the country. Even more people moved into California during the "rush" for gold in 1849.

The populations of farming and mining communities grew quickly. The farmers and miners needed many things, such as food and clothing. In a short time, towns developed to support them. These American settlers had taken over the California Indians' homelands. Americans settlers believed they had the right to the land. They forced the California Indians off their homelands. This caused conflict between the California Indians and settlers.

PRIMARY SOURCE

In Their Words... Chief Joseph

"We gave up some of our country to the white men, thinking that then we could have peace. We were mistaken."

—Chief Joseph of the Nez Perce, speech in Washington, D.C., 1879

PHOTO:Edward S. Curtis Collection, Library of Congress, LC-DIG-ppmsca-39872
TEXT:Joseph, Young, Chief of the Nez Perces. "An Indian's View of Indian Affairs." The North American Review Volume 0128 Issue 269, April 1879.

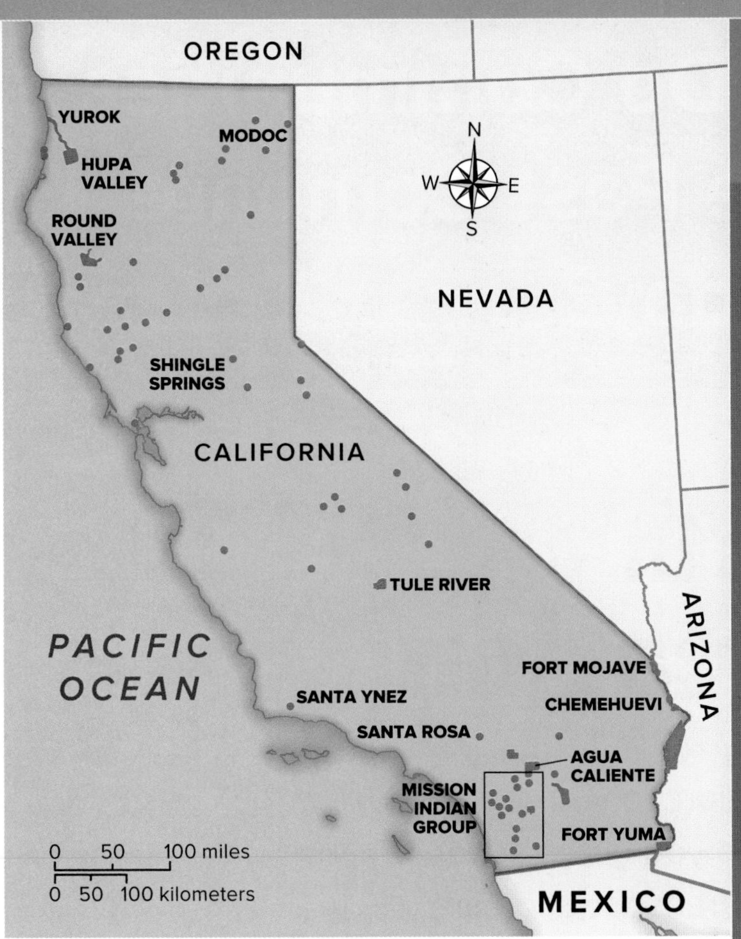

California Indian Reservations Today

Map Skills In the 1850s, the United States government started to form reservations in California. In many cases, the land chosen for these reservations was very poor. American settlers did not want to live there. This map shows the reservations in California today. What do you notice?

Many settlers wanted California Indian groups to become more like them. Some California Indian children were forced to attend special schools. There they were expected to learn how to look and talk like the children of American settlers. California Indians were taught to change their ways of living. This separated them from their traditions and culture. This loss of freedom nearly destroyed the cultures of the California Indians.

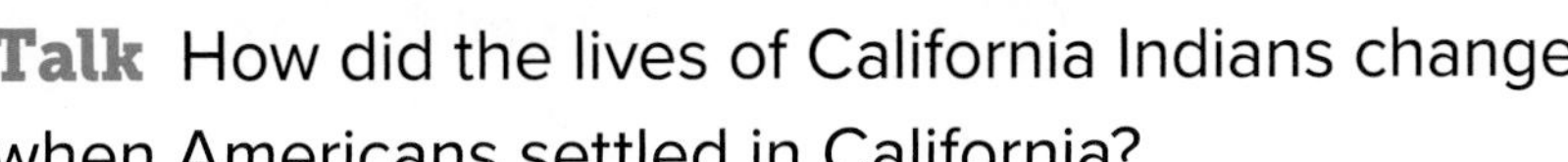

Stop and Check

COLLABORATE

Talk How did the lives of California Indians change when Americans settled in California?

What Do You Think? What did settlers and California Indians learn from each other?

How Do Communities of the Past Compare to Today?

Innovations in Transportation

What types of transportation do you use each day? Do you ride a bike? Do you get to school by bus or car? These types of transportation are common today. But they were not so common in the nineteenth **century**.

Think about how long it takes you to walk to a store or to a friend's house. Now imagine how long it would take you to travel by car to a different part of the state. You could probably get to your destination in the same day, even if it was hundreds of miles away. **Settlers** coming to California were not as lucky. Many traveled in covered wagons that were pulled by oxen. There were no paved roads, and a wagon could only travel between eight and twenty miles a day. Some people walked beside the wagon. It was a long, slow trip.

netopaek/iStockphoto/Getty Images

HSS.3.1.2, HSS.3.3.3, HAS.CS.2, HAS.CS.3, HAS.HI.2

Transportation got better in the 1800s. This was a time of **innovation** in technology. New machines changed the way people lived and traveled. After the invention of the steam locomotive, trains could move along at an amazing twenty miles an hour. Trips that used to take a month could now take just a few days. Steam engines also made travel across the ocean faster. People and goods traveling on a steamship reached their destination much more quickly than before.

Traveling by covered wagon through a California mountain pass

Library of Congress, Prints and Photographs Division [LC-DIG-ppmsca-02887]

In 1869, Americans celebrated when the final tracks in the nation's first transcontinental railroad were joined together. This new railroad connected California with the eastern part of the United States. It moved goods and people from one part of the nation to another. For the first time ever, farmers and ranchers could sell their fruits and vegetables across the nation. Goods made in California's factories could be sold in new places. This helped the state's economy grow.

In communities across America, trolleys and cable cars had been pulled by horses. In the late 1800s, electricity provided the power. The electric trolley car made traveling around a community easier, cleaner, and faster.

Automobiles made the greatest change in the way people traveled. By 1900, inventors used the new technologies of steam, electricity, and gasoline engines to create "horseless carriages."

In 1913, Henry Ford developed the assembly line. On an assembly line, the car moves down the line and each worker has a job to do to build the car. This shortened the time it took to make a car. It cost less to make a car because it took less time. Cars became much cheaper to buy. More people could afford to buy a car.

PRIMARY SOURCE

In Their Words... Henry T. Williams

"In no part of the world is travel made so easy and comfortable as on the Pacific Railroad. To travelers from the East it is a constant delight, and to ladies and families it is accompanied with absolutely no fatigue or discomfort."

—*The Pacific Tourist*, 1876

PHOTO: Prints and Photographs Division, Library of Congress, LC-USZ62-100217
TEXT: Williams, Henry T. The Pacific Tourist. New York:Adams & Bishop, Publishers, 1879.

PRIMARY SOURCE

In Their Words... Henry Ford

"I will build a motor car for the great multitude. ... But it will be so low in price that no man making a good salary will be unable to own one."

—Henry Ford and Samuel Crowther, *My Life and Work,* 1922

As more people drove cars, new roads and highways were built. People could get to more places easily. Cars gave Americans new freedom. They could travel anywhere.

A modern Ford car

By the 1950s, the airplane became the fastest way to travel. You could travel across the country on the same day. The makers of airplanes have made many innovations since then. Airplane travel is even faster today. A flight from San Francisco to San Diego takes just 90 minutes. You can fly from Los Angeles to New York City in about five hours.

Stop and Check

Write What innovations in transportation were developed over the last hundred years? What were their benefits?

Find Details As you read, add new information to the graphic organizer on page 141 in your Inquiry Journal.

(t)Mfotophile/iStockphoto/Getty Images; (b)Oleksiy Maksymenko Photography/Alamy Stock Photo
TEXT: Ford, Henry. My Life and Work. Garden City, New York: Garden City Publishing Co., Inc., 1922.

Communities Develop and Grow

Towns began to form across the state. People opened stores that sold tools for miners and farmers. They also sold items for people's homes. Farmers bought goods in town, and they sold their fruits and vegetables there. Most towns had a hotel, a blacksmith, and a doctor.

As more people moved into towns, new businesses opened. These included grocery stores, lumberyards, and hardware stores. People also looked for entertainment. They went to theaters to see plays. Newspapers told people what was happening in their own town and around the country. Parks gave people new places to play and enjoy the outdoors.

As towns and cities grew, so did the need for public services. Towns built schools and hired teachers. Police and fire departments helped keep the people in the community safe. Over time, towns provided water, sewage, and electricity services. Communities formed local governments to pay for and manage these public services.

Early fire wagon

Prints and Photographs Division, Library of Congress, LC-USZ62-101290

How are the towns and cities of California the same today as in the past? How are they different? General stores that sold goods to early settlers have almost disappeared. Other types of stores have changed because people today have different needs. Local governments still provide public services.

Electrical lines bring power to a city.

Many jobs are still the same. People farm and mine for minerals. However, people use improved tools today. Doctors, lawyers, and teachers still work in our communities. Technology has created new careers such as computer programmers and graphic designers.

Both in the past and in the present, a community is created by the people who live there. People of many different races and **ethnic groups** live in California. Different cultures help define a community, just as a region's geography and resources help define it.

Did You Know?

The population of Southern California is the largest in the state. Due to the lack of rainfall, water is brought into the region. One source is the Colorado River. The State Water Project moves this water across the state through a series of canals and pipes. This provides water to millions of Californians.

(t)Historic American Buildings Survey, Library of Congress, HAER CAL,19-PASA.V, 1–2; (b)Ron Chapple Photography, Inc./Alamy Stock Photo

Stop and Check

Think Why do towns and cities grow? What do you think would cause a town to disappear?

InfoGraphic

Communities in California: Then and Now

In some ways, life in California communities has not changed much since the 1800s. Towns and cities continue to provide the supplies and services people need. People work to earn a living. However, modern innovations have made our lives easier.

Shopping Then

The general store was the only place settlers could buy many of the items they needed. People bought tools, shoes, cloth to make clothes, and other supplies.

Shopping Now

Today, we have many choices when we go shopping. We can go to different stores to buy what we need. We can go to a mall to buy clothes. We can go to the local hardware store to find just the right tool. We can also shop on the Internet.

Farming Then

In the 1800s, farmers worked mostly by hand. They also used metal plows pulled by livestock. It could take days to plow and harvest a field. A farmer's life was difficult.

Farming Now

Today, farmers use many types of equipment to plant and harvest their crops. This speeds up the process. Farmers can also grow more because they can plant and tend larger fields.

(bkgd spread)McGraw-Hill Education, (t)Harris & Ewing Photographs, Library of Congress, LC-DIG-hec-09174, (tc)In Green/Shutterstock.com, (bc)

Transportation Then

In the 1800s, people often rode horses when they traveled. Sometimes they rode in a wagon pulled by horses or oxen. Wagons were slow, and long-distance travel took months.

Transportation Now

Cars, buses, and trains make it easy to get to towns and cities. We can now travel longer distances much faster. We can live much farther away from our workplace.

Technology Then

The newspaper was the main source of news and information in the 1800s and early 1900s. Newspapers told people about the issues and events of the day. It could be difficult to get newspapers to people, so the news could be weeks old before people read about it.

Technology Now

Today, we are able to find out instantly what has happened anywhere in the world. With the touch of a finger, we can hear what the weather will be like tomorrow. We can find out what our friend just ate. We can learn what happened in a country far away.

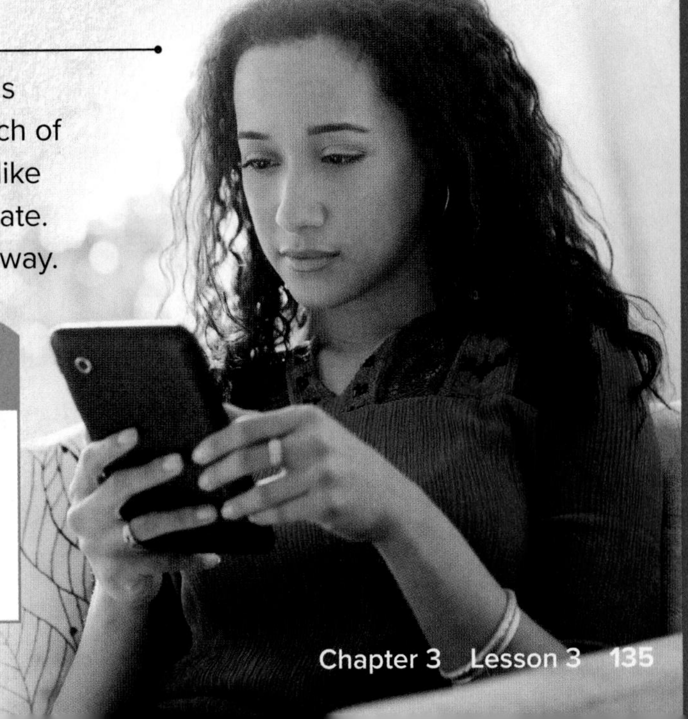

Stop and Check

COLLABORATE

Talk How are our lives similar to and different from the lives of early Californian settlers?

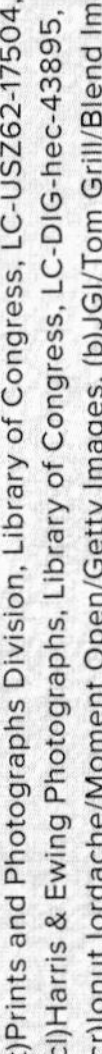

(t)Prints and Photographs Division, Library of Congress, LC-USZ62-17504, (cl)Harris & Ewing Photographs, Library of Congress, LC-DIG-hec-43895, (cr)Ionut Iordache/Moment Open/Getty Images, (b)JGI/Tom Grill/Blend Images LLC

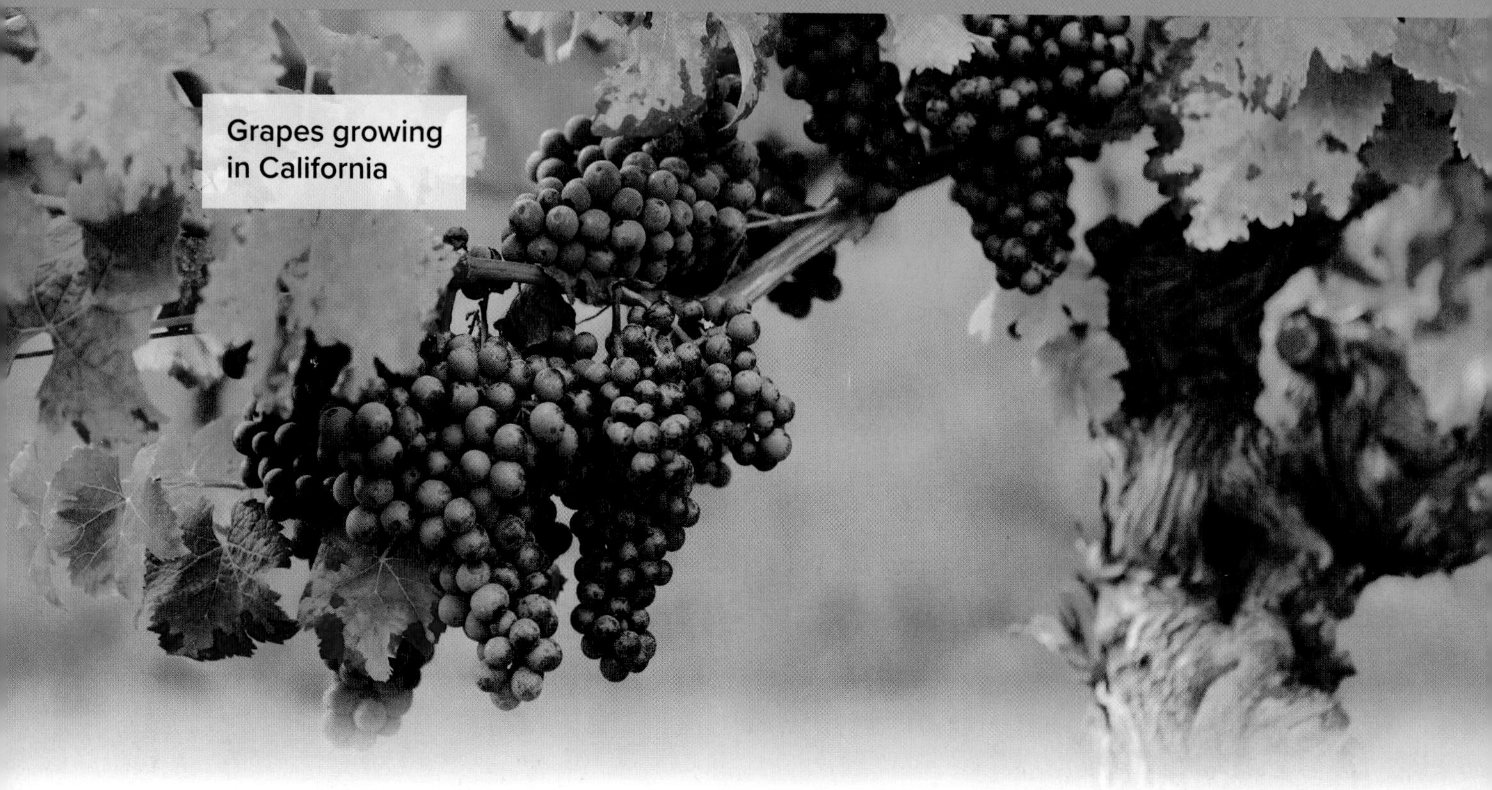

Grapes growing in California

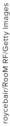

Physical Geography of California Communities

California's physical geography has played an important role in the state's history. People settled in places because of the land, water, and climate there. The geography continues to impact why people come to the state and where they live.

Many settlers came to California because of its fertile soil. The flat, rich land in the Central Valley was perfect for farming. As more farmers settled here, towns formed. Farmers sold their goods in places such as Sacramento and Fresno. Both cities had railroads. These allowed farmers to ship their goods around the country. Today, most of our nation's fruit, nuts, and vegetables come from this region. The fertile soil in Napa Valley also brought settlers to California. This valley region is known for growing many crops such as grapes, olives, peaches, pears, and walnuts.

roycebair/RooM RF/Getty Images

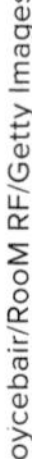

In the mid-1800s, gold was discovered in California's mountains. Miners from all over the world came here. They hoped to get rich quickly. Small communities were built around these mines. When the mountains ran out of gold and silver, people moved away from the communities they had built. These empty towns were called "ghost towns." Today, tourists visit old mining communities to learn about the past.

California's coastal region also became a popular location for people to live. Areas with busy shipping ports often developed into large cities. This is because they were perfect locations for trade. The shipping industry moves goods to and from California. People also chose to live along the coast because of the warm climate and the beautiful beaches. The people who live in San Diego, Santa Monica, and Malibu enjoy both the surf and sun.

Stop and Check

Think How did the physical geography of California influence the growth of communities?

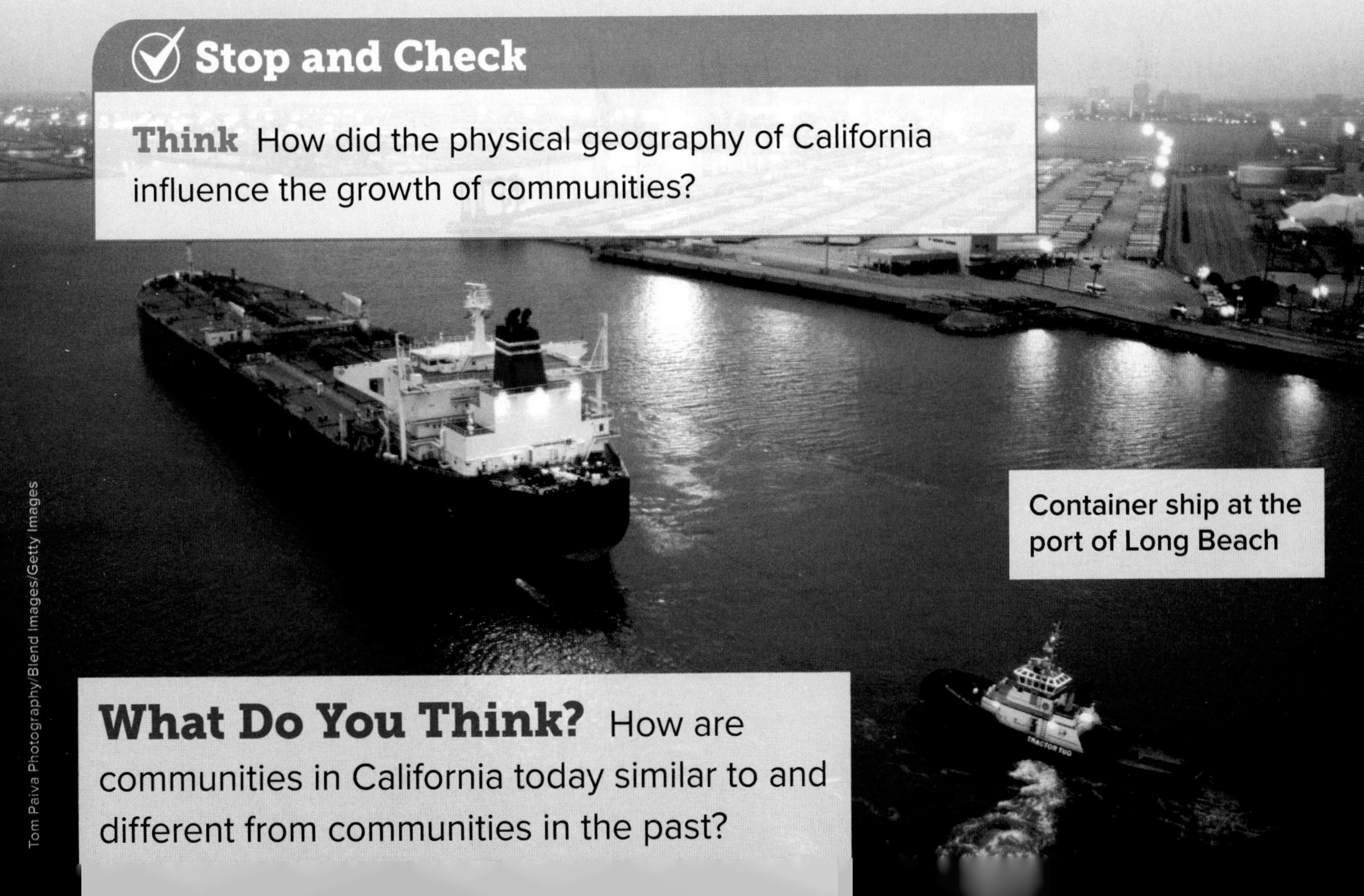

Container ship at the port of Long Beach

Tom Paiva Photography/Blend Images/Getty Images

What Do You Think? How are communities in California today similar to and different from communities in the past?

Lesson 4 How Have People Changed the Land?

How People Use the Land

Where does the food at the grocery store come from? Where does the water you drink come from? Where does the wood, brick, or stone used to build your school come from? "The land" will probably be part of your answers to all of these questions. People everywhere need food, water, and a home to live in. People have used the land for thousands of years to meet these needs.

The land has always been a source of food. Long ago, people traveled across the land to hunt animals and gather food. Later they learned how to farm the land to grow crops and raise animals.

Water is another important resource. We cannot survive without it. Many people settled near streams, rivers, or lakes. If water was far away, people dug ditches to bring the water to them. In some places, they dug wells to reach water under the ground. People also built dams in rivers to collect and store water.

Royce Bair/Moment/Getty Images

HSS.3.1.2, HSS.3.3.3, HAS.CS.2

Long ago, people built homes out of trees, branches, and dirt. Over time, we have learned other ways to use nature's resources for building. Today, we make boards out of wood and bricks out of clay. We also use stone. Sometimes people dig into the earth for these huge pieces of stone. This creates a large hole in the ground called a quarry. The rocks and sand from quarries are used in cement and concrete. People use these materials for buildings such as schools and libraries.

A mountaintop quarry

Changing the Land

People change the land when they build dams for water and dig quarries for stone. Another way they change the land is by building roads.

Sometimes the shortest distance from one place to another is directly through a mountain instead of over it. People have to change the landscape to make this shortcut. We blast into a mountain to make a tunnel. Or we use machines that cut into the surface of a mountain and create a shelf. This shelf allows cars and trains to travel along the side of a mountain. If a mountain is low enough, we can flatten the land to create a pass for a road. The Cahuenga Pass is one example of this method. The pass now connects one valley directly to another.

Then and Now

The Cahuenga Pass

Early photo of the Pass

Today's Pass

The Santa Monica Mountains separate the Los Angeles Basin from the San Fernando Valley. The lowest point in this mountain range is an area called the Cahuenga Pass. It was once a hilly path through the mountains. In 1940, the shortcut was turned into a highway. Today it is a major freeway used daily by thousands of drivers.

(l)CH Collection/Alamy Stock Photo; (r)ZUMA Press Inc/Alamy Stock Photo

An irrigated farm in the California desert

Moving Water

People have also used technology to grow food in places where it would not grow before. For example, the Mojave Desert is a very dry place. It is difficult to grow crops there. However, farmers now grow crops such as cotton and alfalfa in the Mojave Desert. Irrigation makes this possible. Water is transported from miles away or from underground. Then it is pumped through sprinklers or drip systems to water desert areas to grow crops.

Farmers in the Central Valley also use irrigation. Water is collected from streams and rivers in the Sierra Nevada. It is moved to Southern California through an **aqueduct**. This aqueduct is a series of reservoirs, pipes, and canals that bring water from as far north as Sacramento. As a result, there is more farmland in the southern part of the Central Valley. This increases the food supply and helps the economy of the local region.

COLLABORATE

Stop and Check

Talk How have people changed the land to meet their needs?

Find Details As you read, add new information to the chart on page 149 in your Inquiry Journal.

Glowimages/Getty Images

Effects on the Environment

You have just read about the benefits of changing the land. However, changing the land can also harm the environment. Often these problems affect people, too.

Water

Dams and aqueducts move water from its natural locations to cities and farms. However, moving water to a different place can permanently change the ecosystem of a region. An ecosystem is all of the plants and animals in an area. When water is taken for cities and farms, the amount of water in rivers and streams can get dangerously low. This lowers fish populations. The land becomes dry. Plants and animals may not survive. Some of California's ecosystems, such as Owens Valley in eastern California, have been deeply affected by moving water away from the region.

Did You Know?

California has hundreds of dams. They help provide water to people. They help control flooding. They also provide electricity. Water has a lot of power. Its movement is used to create electricity. Many of California's dams are connected to hydroelectric plants. These plants produce electricity for communities throughout the state.

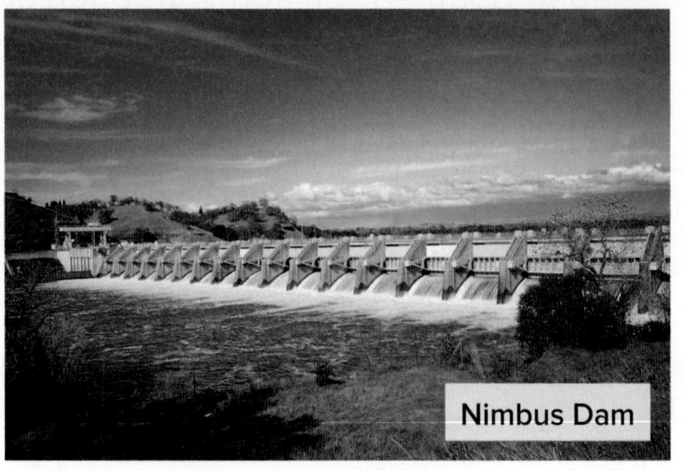
Nimbus Dam

Dale Kolke/California Department of Water Resources

Urban sprawl in San Francisco

Urban Sprawl

Urban sprawl is a major problem created by California's growing population. As the population grows, communities become crowded and more land is used. People build more houses, roads, and businesses on land that surrounds the city. Trees are cut down. Open fields are turned into neighborhoods. Urban sprawl also increases the need for water in these areas. This means that more water must be moved from communities in one part of the state to another.

Stop and Check

Talk What is urban sprawl? What effects does it have on the environment?

Carol M. Highsmith Archive, Library of Congress, LC-DIG-highsm-12748

Did You Know?

Earthquakes are measured on the Richter scale. This measures the power of an earthquake in numbers from 0 to 10. In 2014, a 6.0 earthquake was measured in the San Francisco Bay Area. It injured more than 200 people and caused nearly $1 billion in damage.

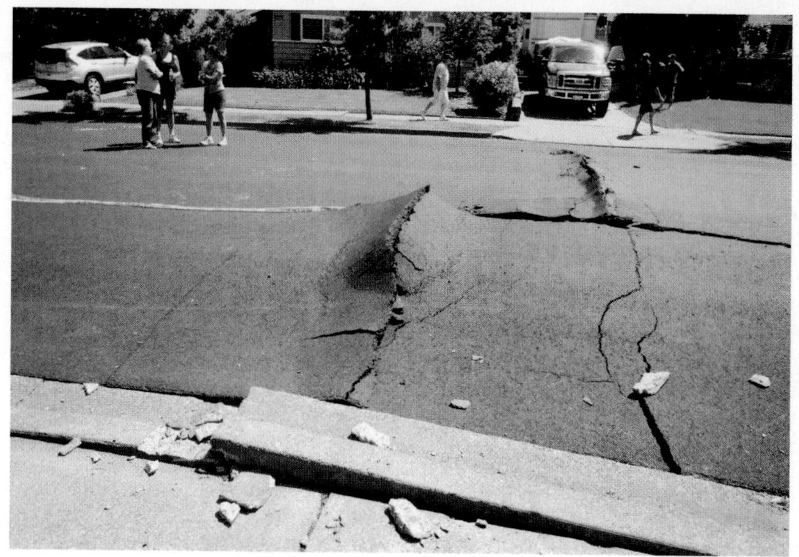

Earthquakes

People have not caused all of the problems in California's environment. Faults, or breaks in the land, stretch across California. These faults have existed for thousands of years. The land along these faults is always moving. Usually the movements are very small. Sometimes, the movements are so large that we experience an earthquake. This force of nature affects all regions in California.

People cannot stop earthquakes from happening. However, there are things we can do to help survive them. Your family may have a safety plan so each of you knows what to do during an earthquake. You probably have had safety drills at school for earthquakes. Buildings are built in ways to help them survive earthquakes, too.

EPA/Alamy Stock Photo

Pollution

Air **pollution** is another problem in California. California's warm climate and geography trap the polluted air. This trapped air causes smog, which is a cloud of dirty air. Sometimes a city like Los Angeles is completely hidden by smog. California now has laws to help reduce air pollution.

Wildfires can cause air pollution, too. Wildfires are a major problem in California. Sometimes there is not enough rain in an area. A lack of rain and a warming climate can cause a **drought**. A drought increases the risk of wildfires. Wildfires can spread quickly and destroy huge areas of land, damaging homes and businesses. They also make the air dirty. The wind can blow smoke and ash to areas far away from the fire. This affects the air we breathe. The dirty air also harms animals and plants. People can help prevent wildfires by being careful with fire in open areas.

Los Angeles covered in smog

A forest fire in California

Stop and Check

COLLABORATE

Talk What causes air pollution in California? What changes can people make to help prevent air pollution?

What Do You Think? How have people changed the land to meet their needs for food, water, and homes? What effects on the environment have these changes caused?

(t)Daniel Stein/E+/Getty Images; (b)Natural Selection David Ponton/PunchStock

How Do Communities Develop?

Community Focus: Santa Clara, California

Like all communities, Santa Clara has grown and changed over the years. Let's take a look at the history of Santa Clara. Looking at this history can help us understand why it's important to find out how communities grow and change.

HSS.3.2.1, HSS.3.3.1; HSS.3.3.2, HAS.CS.2

Ellen Isaacs/Alamy Stock Photo

Santa Clara today

Why People Moved to Santa Clara

The city of Santa Clara is in the Santa Clara Valley. This valley begins at the southern end of San Francisco Bay and extends southeast.

People have lived in Santa Clara for thousands of years. The Ohlone Indians were the first people to live in this area. In the late 1700s, the Spanish settled in the area. The Spanish called the Ohlone *los Costanos*, which means "the coast people." The Spanish built a mission in 1777. They named it Mission Santa Clara. As the town grew, it was called Santa Clara.

The Spanish stayed in this area because the valley had good soil for farming and the climate was pleasant. This made the valley a good place to build a community.

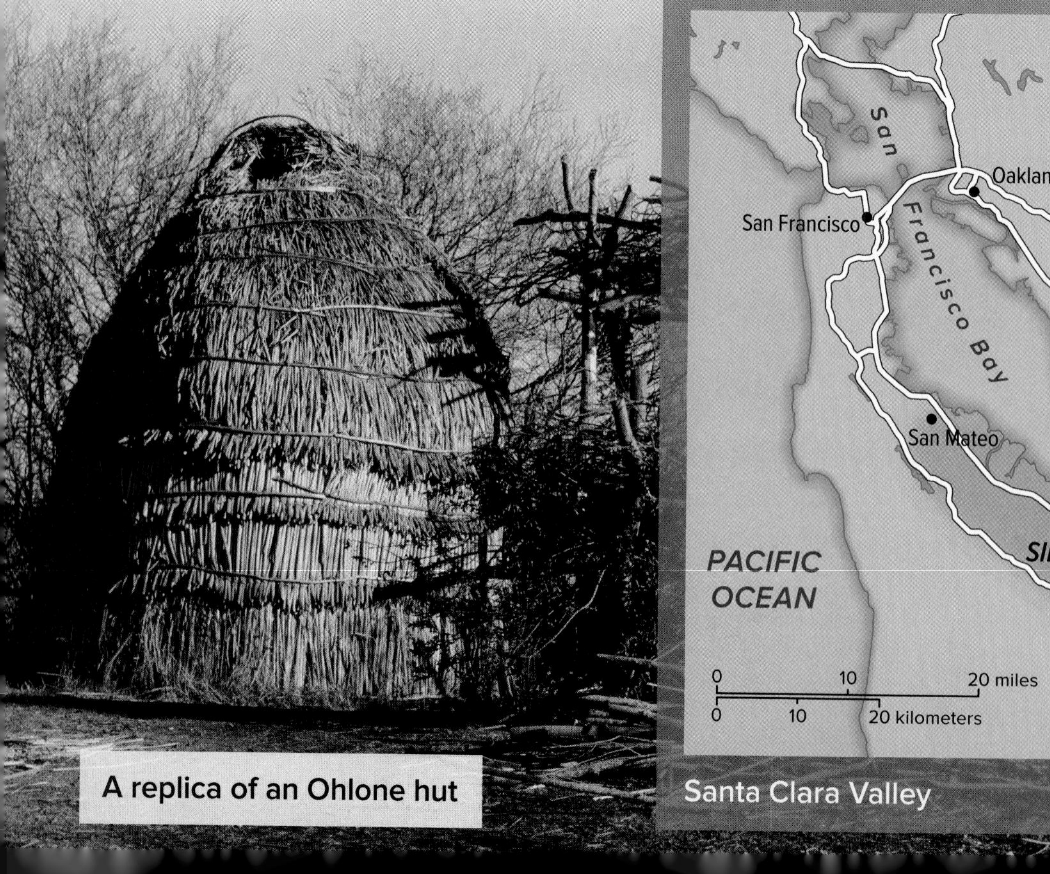

A replica of an Ohlone hut

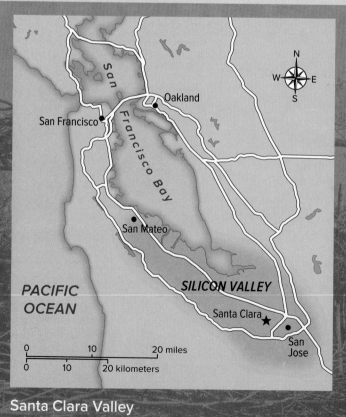

Santa Clara Valley

Robert Clay/Alamy Stock Photo

PRIMARY SOURCE

Photograph of Santa Clara in about 1909

In the 1800s, more people started to move to Santa Clara. Many of them first came to look for gold and other minerals that were discovered in the nearby mountains. They were hoping to earn a lot of money quickly, but very few people got rich from mining gold. People liked the area, though. Many settled on farms and ranches in the valley. Santa Clara was beginning to grow into a real town.

COLLABORATE

Stop and Check

Talk What do you think the area around Santa Clara was like when the new settlers arrived? What might they have said about the land?

Find Details As you read, add new information to the graphic organizer on page 157 in your Inquiry Journal.

Moving to California by covered wagon

(t)Prints and Photographs Division, Library of Congress, LC-USZ62-127217; (b)Prints and Photographs Division, Library of Congress, LC-USZ62-16867

Businesses in Santa Clara

Santa Clara became an official town in 1852. Over the next one hundred years, the town grew. People built schools, churches, and businesses. The main industry in the area around Santa Clara was farming. The area had many orchards and plants for packing the fruit that grew there. In the 1940s and 1950s, the town grew very quickly. Santa Clara outgrew the original city limits. Houses and other buildings were built on what used to be farmland. Today, there is very little farmland around Santa Clara.

One reason so many people moved to Santa Clara in the 1950s was because of the new computer industry. The community changed from a farming area to a city.

Today, there are many technology companies located in the area. Santa Clara is part of the world-famous Silicon Valley.

Then and Now

Did you know computers were being used more than 50 years ago? Back then only big businesses and governments used them. They were not small. Some of them filled entire rooms! One computer, the ENIAC, was called a "Giant Brain." It weighed 54,000 pounds.

(t)Archive Holdings Inc./Archive Photos/Getty Images; (b)U. S. Army Photo

Santa Clara is in the heart of Silicon Valley. In recent years, many people have come to this area to start new technology businesses. These people are called **entrepreneurs** (ahn truh pruh NURZ). An entrepreneur takes a risk to start a new business. Some of these new businesses develop computer software. Others develop new energy technology, such as solar panels. All of these new ideas are considered private property, and California has laws to protect them. Owners understand that their designs, products, and ideas will not be used without their permission. As these businesses grow, the economy of the community grows too.

Aerial view of present-day Silicon Valley

Santa Clara is an exciting community with an interesting history. You might like to find out about the history of your community. Here are some resources to help you do that:

- Check out the local library. The librarian can help you find books and other resources about your town's history.
- Pay a visit to your town's history museum, if it has one.
- Stop in at the local newspaper office. It might have news stories and photos from your town's past.
- Go online and visit your town's website.

Stop and Check

Think How are entrepreneurs similar to settlers who came to the region in the 1800s?

What Do You Think? How does what you've learned about the history of Santa Clara help you understand how communities develop over time?

Aerial Archives/Alamy Stock Photo

Citizenship

Saving California's LANDMARKS

California's landmarks remind us of the past. Landmarks are important to our history. They can be buildings or places that played a role in history. It is important to protect landmarks in order to remember our history. Saving a landmark means working with many different groups of people. The owners of the property, local government officials, and local neighborhood groups all must work together.

The Los Angeles Central Library was built in 1926. It was saved by the work of the Los Angeles Conservancy.

The Mission Santa Clara de Asis was rebuilt after a fire destroyed the church in 1926. Today, it is the chapel of Santa Clara College.

(t)Carol M. Highsmith Collection, Library of Congress, LC-DIG-highsm-24465; (b)Peter Gridley/Stockbyte/Getty Images, (bkgd)McGraw-Hill

Many groups across California help preserve the past. In Santa Clara, the Historical and Landmarks Commission works to preserve important buildings. The California Preservation Foundation works across the state to save landmarks that are important to our history. The L.A. Conservancy is a local group. It works to save historic buildings around Los Angeles. Groups like these make sure California preserves some of its landmarks for the future.

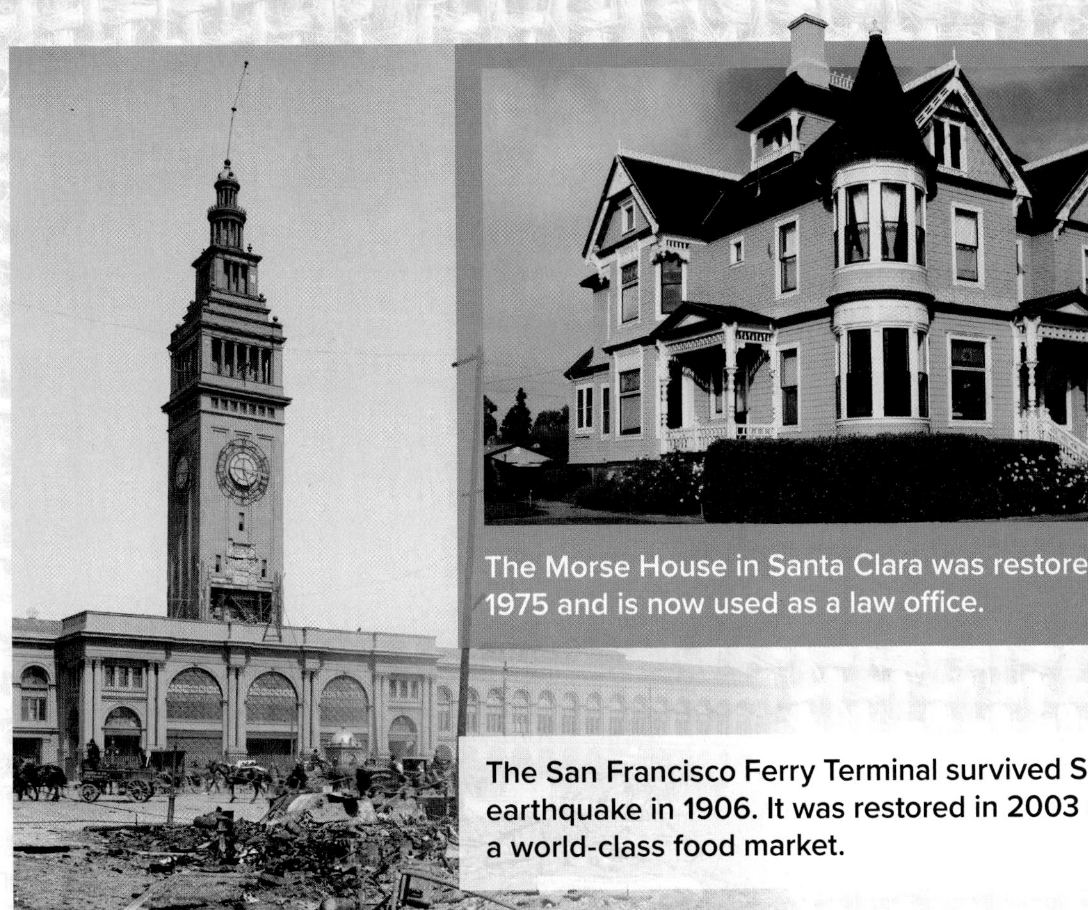

The Morse House in Santa Clara was restored around 1975 and is now used as a law office.

The San Francisco Ferry Terminal survived San Francisco's earthquake in 1906. It was restored in 2003 and made into a world-class food market.

(l)Circa Images/Alamy Stock Photo; (r)Jason O. Watson/historical-markers.org/Alamy Stock Photo

Stop and Check

Write Choose one old building in your city or town. Write a letter to the editor of your local newspaper explaining why you think the building should be saved. Give at least three reasons for your opinion.

What Makes My Community Special?

The Past Affects the Present

Look around your community. What do you see? Are there old buildings or old roads? What are the names on the street signs? What languages do you hear? What types of restaurants do you see? The answers help you understand what makes every community special. We have all been affected by people and events of the past.

In some neighborhoods, the names of streets give us clues about a community's history. Telegraph Avenue in Oakland got its name from the telegraph line that was built along the original road in 1859.

Telegraph Avenue in Oakland

Ian Dagnall/Alamy Stock Photo

HSS.3.1.2, HSS.3.3.1, HSS.3.3.3

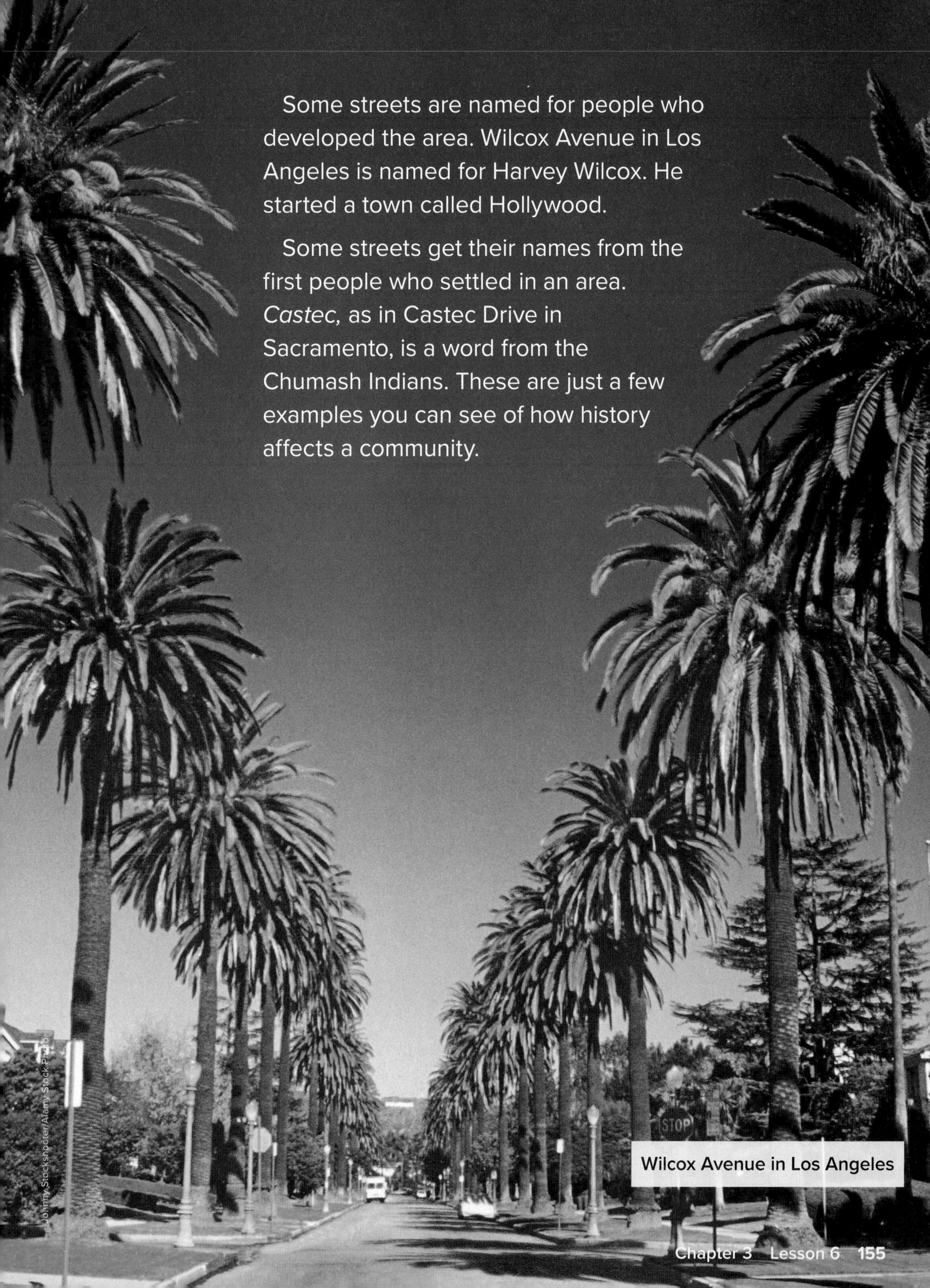

Some streets are named for people who developed the area. Wilcox Avenue in Los Angeles is named for Harvey Wilcox. He started a town called Hollywood.

Some streets get their names from the first people who settled in an area. *Castec,* as in Castec Drive in Sacramento, is a word from the Chumash Indians. These are just a few examples you can see of how history affects a community.

Wilcox Avenue in Los Angeles

Johnny Stockshooter/Alamy Stock Photo

Communities Change Over Time

The geography of California communities has changed over time. People have changed the land in communities to meet their needs.

In San Francisco, parts of the bay were filled in to create dry land. This is called landfill. Today, some of San Francisco's tallest buildings stand on land that was once part of San Francisco Bay. Other communities have built dams on rivers to create lakes. Shasta Lake was created when a dam was built on the Shasta River. Communities near the ocean have built walls called breakwaters to prevent towns from flooding. When a breakwater was built at Redondo Beach, the city grew into a beach resort.

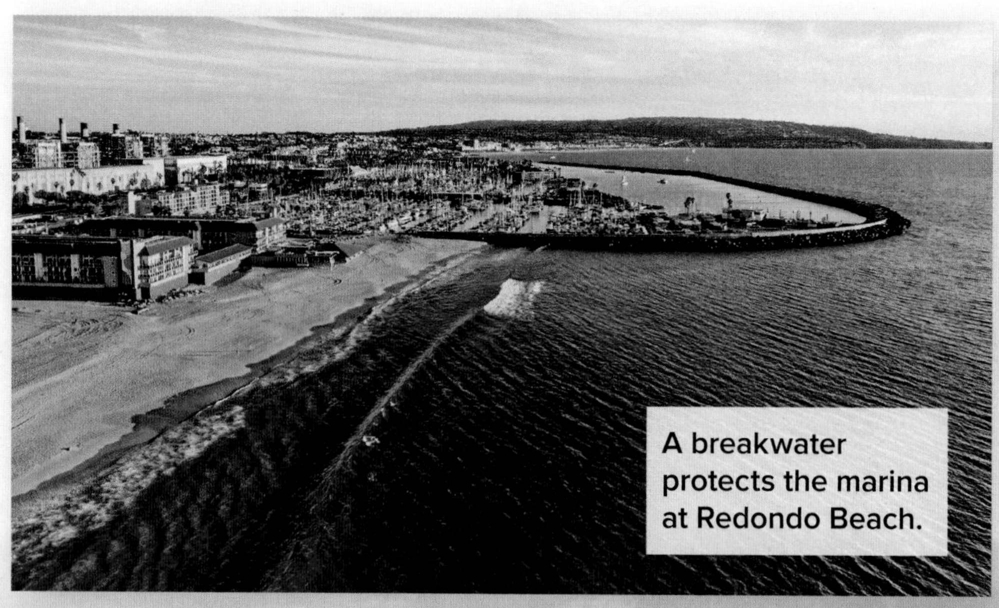
A breakwater protects the marina at Redondo Beach.

San Francisco

(t)hermosawave/iStock/Getty Images; (b)kropic1/Shutterstock.com

Streets and buildings in communities can help us remember the past. In earlier times, many streets in California towns were paved with bricks. As communities grew, these streets were widened and then paved over. Sometimes the original bricks appear when a street is being repaved.

Old Sacramento is the oldest part of California's state capital. This city neighborhood looks the way it did long ago. Today, the old downtown area features historic buildings. Other buildings were rebuilt to look much like they did long ago. The Eagle Theatre, which was originally built from wood and canvas, was rebuilt on its original location.

Buildings in some cities remind us who the early **settlers** were. In many California cities, buildings are built in a Spanish style. This reminds us that the Spanish were early settlers in California.

COLLABORATE

Stop and Check

Talk About It Discuss with a partner how you can see the past in communities today.

Find Details As you read, add new information to the graphic organizer on page 165 in your Inquiry Journal.

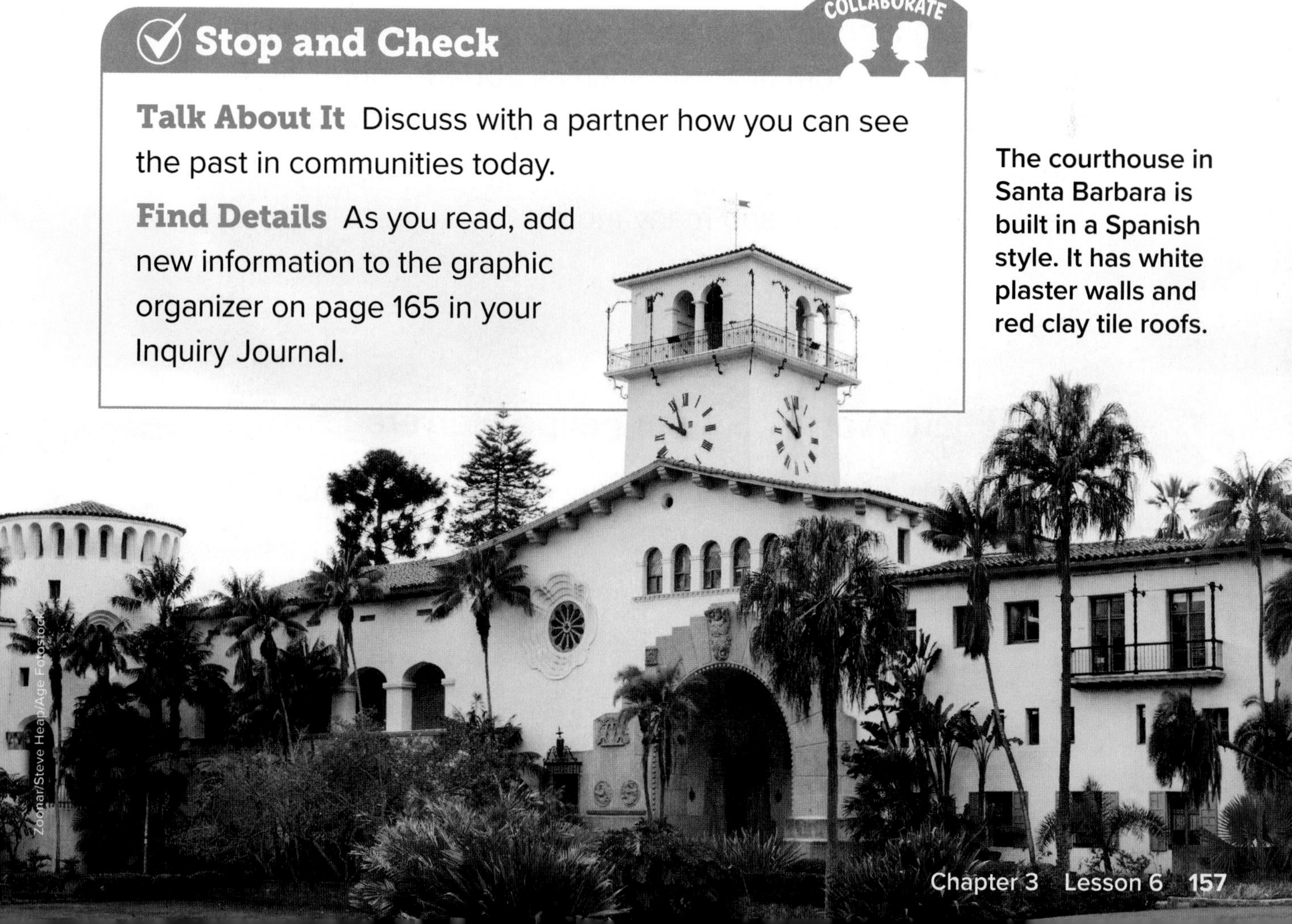

The courthouse in Santa Barbara is built in a Spanish style. It has white plaster walls and red clay tile roofs.

Zoonar/Steve Heap/Age Fotostock

A Mix of Cultures

California communities have always welcomed people from around the world. There are many different **ethnic groups** in California. An ethnic group is a group of people who share the same culture. Today, people from all around the world live and work in our state.

As people have moved to California over the years, they have brought their cultures with them. These include different languages, customs, foods, and music. Sometimes, these cultures have blended together. One way this has happened is through language. For example, people who speak English often use words from Spanish, such as *bodega, patio,* and *canyon*. Many different languages are spoken in California. These include Spanish, Chinese, Tagalog, Persian, Russian, Vietnamese, and many more.

PRIMARY SOURCE

In Their Words... Juan Felipe Herrera

"Diversity really means becoming complete as human beings—all of us. We learn from each other."

—U.S. Poet Laureate Juan Felipe Herrera, 2015 interview

PHOTO:Maureen P Sullivan/Moment Open/Getty Images
TEXT:Herrera, Juan Felipe. "U.S. Poet Laurette Juan Felipe Herrera Signs with Candlewick." Publishers Weekly, September 29, 2015

Another way cultures are shared is through food. All cultures in California are represented by their foods. These are shared in homes, restaurants, and at festivals. Think about some of your favorite foods. Were they brought to the United States from other countries?

Chinese New Year celebration in San Francisco

Californians also celebrate holidays that are unique to their heritage. Some people celebrate Christmas. Other people celebrate Rosh Hashanah, Ramadan, or Kwanzaa. Diwali is a major holiday in India, and it is celebrated in cities and towns throughout California. San Francisco holds one of the largest celebrations for the Chinese New Year. People celebrate with a parade and fireworks.

Did You Know?

Cinco de Mayo is a Mexican holiday. It honors a Mexican victory in a battle with France. Today Cinco de Mayo is a time to celebrate Mexican culture. California communities celebrate the day with special activities. Los Angeles has one of the largest Cinco de Mayo celebrations in the United States.

Stop and Check

Talk What cultures are represented in your community? What has each culture contributed to the community?

What Do You Think? What are some things that make your community special?

David R. Frazier Photolibrary, Inc./Alamy Stock Photo

Field Trip

Downtown Los Angeles

Los Angeles is the largest city in California. Nearly four million people live there. The city has many neighborhoods, and people from all over the world live in those neighborhoods. Let's take a trip downtown to see some of the old and new places in Los Angeles.

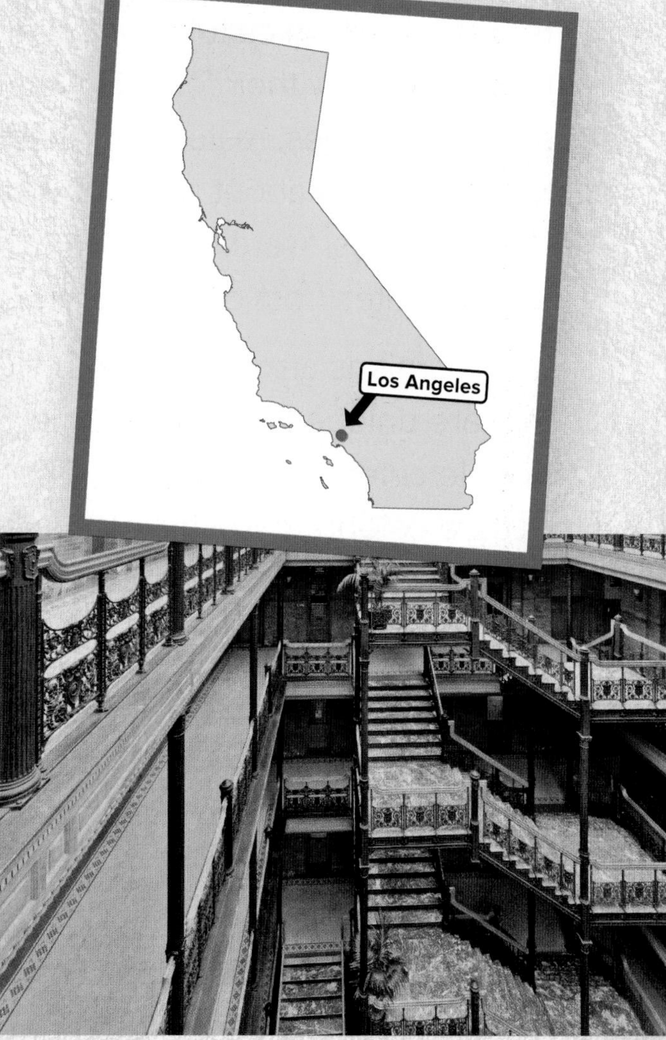

1. Bradbury Building

The Bradbury Building is an office building that was built in 1893. It's a National Historic Landmark. Because it has old-fashioned iron railings and cage-like elevators, it's a popular place to film movies.

2. Grand Central Market

The Grand Central Market is the oldest and largest public market in Los Angeles. The types of food available in the market show the diverse population of Los Angeles. You can buy food from all over the United States and the world.

(t)Curt Teich Postcard Archives/Alamy Stock Photo; (tr)compassandcamera/iStock/Getty Images; (b)P. Eoche/Photolibrary/Getty Images; (bkgd)McGraw-Hill Education

3. Walt Disney Concert Hall

The Walt Disney Concert Hall opened in 2003. It was designed by the famous architect Frank Gehry. The outside of the building is made of huge pieces of curved steel.

4. El Pueblo

El Pueblo is where Los Angeles began in 1781, when Spanish settlers founded the city. The old pueblo has been preserved as a 44-acre historic park. Olvera Street is a busy Mexican marketplace.

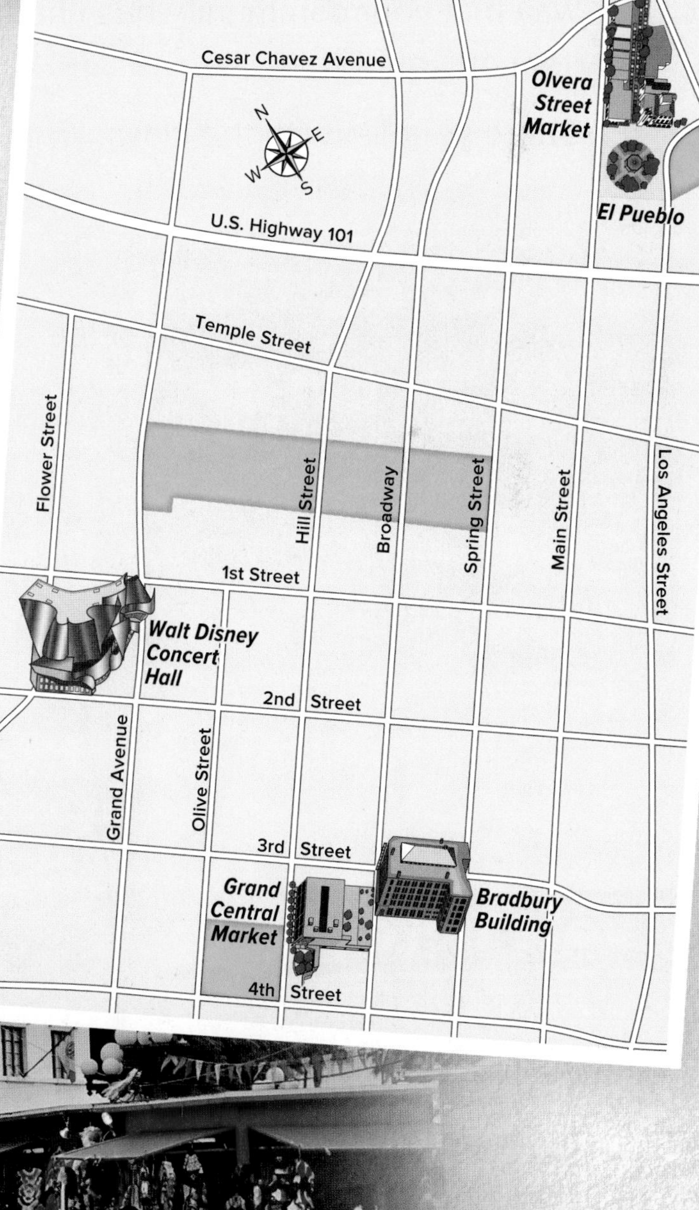

(t)Carol M. Highsmith Archive, Library of Congress, LC-HS503-428; (b)Robert Rosenblum/Alamy Stock Photo, (bkgd)McGraw-Hill Education

Connections in Action

Back to the EQ

Think about the chapter EQ, **"How has life changed for people in my community over time?"**

- **Talk** with a partner about how life in your community has changed over the years. Make a list of what causes a community to grow and change. Then write at least one way that your community has changed because of each item on your list.
- **Share** your list with the class.

(t)U.S. Farm Security Administration, Library of Congress, LC-USF34-016489-E; (r)JGI/Tom Grill/Blend Images LLC; (bl)Maureen P Sullivan/Moment Open/Getty Images

More to Explore

How can you make an IMPACT?

A Special Community

You have read that communities are special. Think about what makes your community special. Then write a letter to a person who lives in another state explaining why that person should visit your community. What places should that person visit? What activities can that person do?

Finish My Sentence

Choose three of the vocabulary words from this chapter. For each word, write a sentence that tells about your community. For example, you could write, "Settlers founded my community in the mid-1800s." Then read each sentence to a partner without saying the vocabulary word. Have your classmate say the missing word to complete the sentence.

My Community Then and Now

Think about what your community might have looked like in the past. Then think about what your community looks like today. Draw two images that show what your community looked like when it first began and what it looks like today. Share your drawings with a partner and talk about what they show.

Chapter 4 American Citizens, Symbols, and Government

ESSENTIAL QUESTION EQ

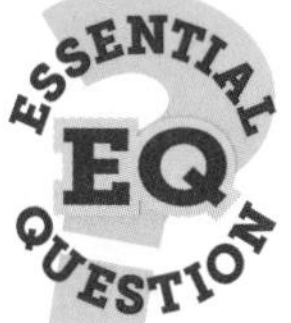

How Do Our Government and Its Citizens Work Together?

We are responsible for making our community, state, and country fair and safe places to live. In this chapter, you will read about how our government was created and how it works today. You will learn why laws are important. You also will explore what it means to be a good citizen. As you read, think about what you can do to be a good citizen.

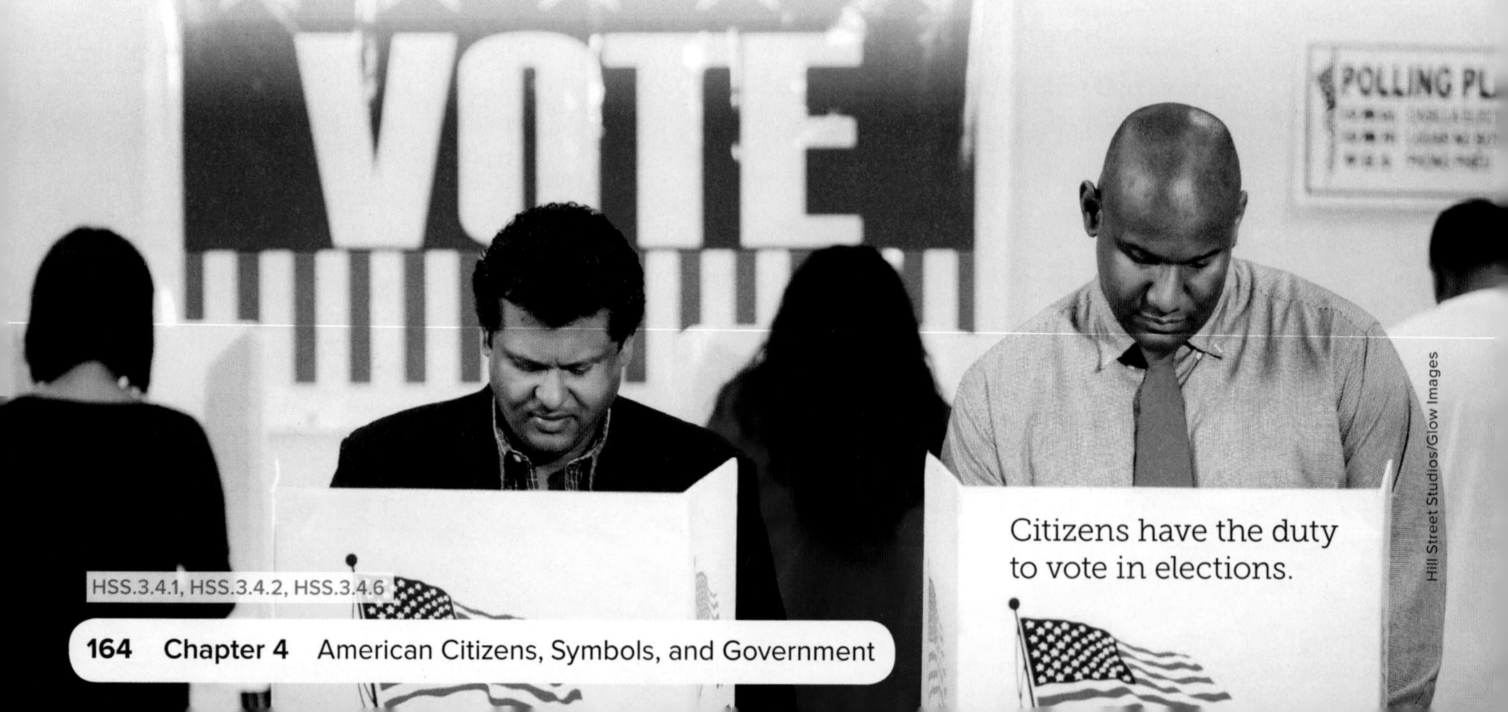

Citizens have the duty to vote in elections.

Hill Street Studios/Glow Images

HSS.3.4.1, HSS.3.4.2, HSS.3.4.6

What Does It Mean to Be a Good Citizen?

A good citizen is part of the community, the state, and the country. What does it take to be a good citizen?

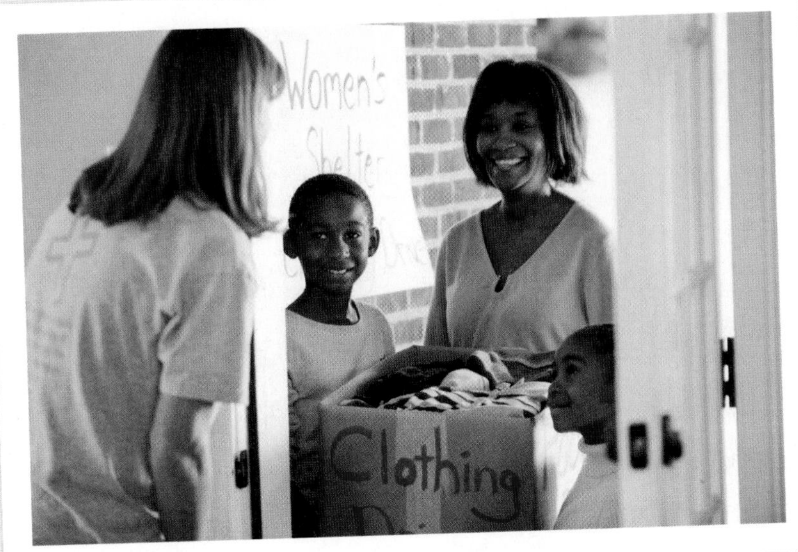

Good citizens are honest, polite, and kind. You can be a good citizen by doing simple tasks. A good citizen could hold the door open for someone or carry groceries for a neighbor. Behaving like a good citizen every day is easy.

Good citizens take part in government. They can help someone run for office or sign up people to vote. They can run for office themselves. They make sure they know about the people who are running for office before they vote. In a democracy, your vote is your voice in government.

Many citizens work for the common good. Some volunteer their time and energy to help others. A good citizen can make a community a better place by volunteering to lend a hand.

(t)Design Pics Inc./Alamy Stock Photo; (bl)Ariel Skelley/Blend Images/Getty Images; (br)Leland Bobbé/Fuse/Getty Images

Connect Through Literature

A VOICE *from Paris*

By Joy Dueland

Thomas Jefferson

Patsy Jefferson lifted up her long skirts and picked her way between the cartons of books spilling out of her father's study. What would the French servants think if she fell on her nose! A twelve-year-old daughter of an American diplomat had to mind her dignity. Since her mother's death two years ago she had tried to run her father's household, but it wasn't easy with servants who spoke only French. Patsy missed America.

Here in France to arrange trade treaties for the new United States, her father had made himself at home with his books as usual. He liked France far more than the old enemy, England. In Paris, he said to Patsy, a man could live his life without finding any rudeness.

But Thomas Jefferson missed America as much as his daughter did. He was in France because his country needed him here; the United States needed trade to grow strong. But Patsy knew how he longed right now to be in Philadelphia, where Americans would soon be framing their new Constitution.

Patsy stubbed her toe on a pile of books, and as they tumbled down the noise made her father look up. He smiled at her.

"Patsy, these are books for Mr. Madison. Have care, my child. He asked me to send him a few books to help him plan our new Constitution."

PHOTO:(t)Popular Graphic Arts Collection, Library of Congress, LC-USZC4-3254, (bkgd)McGraw-Hill Education;
TEXT: "A Voice from Paris" by Joy Dueland, Cobblestone, May 1999, © by Carus Publishing Company. Reproduced with permission. All Cricket Media material is copyrighted by Carus Publishing Company, d/b/a Cricket Media, and/or various authors and illustrators. Any commercial use or distribution of material without permission is strictly prohibited. Please visit http://www.cricketmedia.com/info/licensing2 for licensing and http://www.cricketmedia.com for subscriptions.

"A few books! Papa, these will fill several crates. How can he possibly read them before he goes to Philadelphia?"

"These books will give him direction," Patsy's father said. "He must convince the other delegates that protection of the people's rights is essential to the new Constitution."

Patsy's father had discussed with her his deep fears that the powerful and rich Americans back home would not care enough to protect the rights of the common people. It was obvious that here in France the ordinary people had few rights under the law. The king and his nobles could even throw a person in jail without a trial.

Jefferson believed the common people in America would make their wishes heard. He was speaking aloud as his goose quill scratched on a letter to be mailed to Madison.

"The only security of all is in a free press. The force of public opinion cannot be resisted."

Patsy listened as she bent down to put some volumes in their crates. Poor Mr. Madison. All this reading!

Weeks and months passed. The boats carrying mail between America and France were slow. Thomas Jefferson could guess at what was going on in Philadelphia, but any news he received was already many weeks old.

(t)galdzer/iStockphoto/Getty Images; (b)Photos.com/Getty Images; (bkgd)McGraw-Hill Education

Patsy, who attended a French school where they called her "Jeffy," was home the day her father received a copy of the Constitution from John Adams, the United States ambassador in London. She saw the dismay on his face as he swiftly leafed through the document, then let it fall onto his desk.

"There's not one mention of a bill protecting the rights of the people! The American public must be in an uproar over this! How could James Madison and General Washington have allowed this! And there's no limit put to the number of terms the president can serve. He could become a king!" He banged his fist on the desk and Patsy jumped. "I hope this Constitution is not ratified by the thirteen states!"

Patsy had not seen her gentle father so upset since her mother's death. He strode from the room, leaving the pages of the document scattered on the floor. With a heavy heart, she picked them up. Perhaps Mr. Madison would be writing soon to convince her father of the worth of this Constitution. But she wondered if there was anything that could overcome her father's bitterness.

When at last Madison did write, he sent a draft of the proposed Constitution along with twenty-five pages of explanations. How much Mr. Madison must have wanted Thomas Jefferson's approval! Patsy watched anxiously as her father read swiftly through Madison's letter. He would occasionally turn from it to refer to some part of the Constitution. He rubbed a hand over his mouth at one point as if trying to keep himself from speaking aloud. Finally Patsy ventured a question.

McGraw-Hill Education

Think About It

1. Why were Thomas Jefferson and James Madison writing to each other?
2. How did Jefferson's time in France help him realize the importance of a Bill of Rights?
3. In your opinion, is it important to have laws that protect the rights of the individual? Why or why not?

"Father, does Mr. Madison's letter change your mind? Can you now accept the Constitution?"

Jefferson ran his long fingers through his hair. "Mr. Madison has made me more sympathetic to it. I have to admit there are things here I must approve, such as the two houses of Congress. It is a good method of balance."

"But, Papa, what about your Bill of Rights?"

Jefferson shook his head, sadly. "Madison tells me there was no chance of getting it through the Convention, and I trust Madison's judgment."

"Do you still want the Constitution not to be ratified?"

Jefferson stretched his long legs and sighed. "I have spent hours thinking it over, Patsy. Two-thirds of the states must vote approval to ratify the Constitution and make it the law of the land. Out of thirteen states, nine are needed for passage. I hope that nine will indeed pass it, so that we do not have chaos in our country. But if the remaining four will insist on proper changes, we may yet have a Bill of Rights. I have hopes, Patsy, I have hopes."

The ratification process turned out very much as Jefferson had hoped. Nine states ratified, and the remaining four insisted on the ten amendments, which we today call the Bill of Rights.

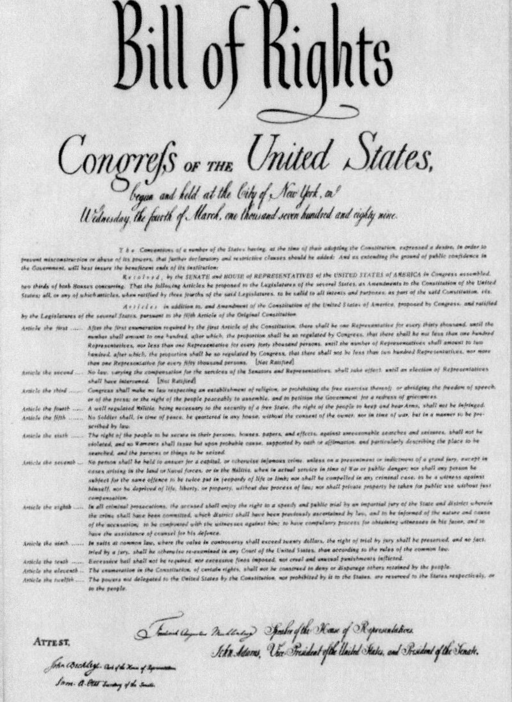
Bill of Rights

Congress of the United States,
begun and held at the City of New-York, on
Wednesday, the fourth of March, one thousand seven hundred and eighty nine.

(r)leezsnow/iStockphoto.com; (bkgd)McGraw-Hill Education

People You Should Know

Alexander Hamilton

Alexander Hamilton was one of the founders of the United States. In 1787, he attended the Constitutional Convention. The people there helped create the U.S. Constitution. Hamilton believed the country should have a strong national government. He wrote essays that encouraged the states to approve the Constitution. His ideas helped shape the new government.

Cesar Chavez

Cesar Chavez was a Mexican American farm worker. The pay was low, and workers lived in crowded camps with no running water or electricity. Chavez wanted farm workers to be treated better. He formed the National Farm Workers Association. This group helped farm workers work for better treatment. Chavez has become a symbol for the rights of workers.

(l)Popular Graphic Arts, Library of Congress, LC-USZC4-6423; (r)Tim Graham/Hulton Archive/Getty Images

Thurgood Marshall

Thurgood Marshall was a lawyer who fought for the rights of African Americans. In the court case *Brown* v. *Board of Education*, Marshall argued that segregated schools were unfair. The Supreme Court agreed. The government made segregation against the law. Later, Marshall became the first African American judge to serve on the Supreme Court.

Sally Ride

Sally Ride was born in Los Angeles and studied physics at Stanford University. In 1978, she successfully applied for a job at NASA. A few years later she became the first lesbian American woman to travel in space. After her time at NASA, Ride worked as a professor of physics. Then, in 2001, she founded Sally Ride Science to inspire young people to study science and math.

(l)Prints & Photographs Division, Library of Congress, LC-USZ62-60139; (r)National Aeronautics and Space Administration (NASA)

Why Is the Constitution of the United States Important?

The History of the Constitution

Have you ever had to make a plan? A plan is a set of directions. It helps people figure out how to do something. Your family may have a plan for emergencies, such as what to do when the electricity goes out.

The United States government also has a plan. This plan for how to run the government is called the U.S. Constitution. Why does our country need a written constitution? To answer this question, we need to go back in time.

More than 200 years ago, people from Europe formed thirteen colonies in North America. A colony is an area that is controlled by another country. The American colonies were controlled by Great Britain. Many people living in the colonies were unhappy about this. They did not like the high **taxes** that they were forced to pay. They wanted to rule themselves. To win their freedom, the American colonists fought a war with Great Britain. We call this war the Revolutionary War. It began on April 19, 1775.

Revolutionary War soldiers

(b)taviphoto/iStockphoto/Getty Images, (inset)Popular Graphic Arts Collection, Library of Congress, LC-USZC2-2572

HSS.3.4.1, HSS.3.4.3, HAS.CS.1

Timeline

July 4
The 13 colonies declare their independence from Great Britain.

1776 1777

November 15
The Articles of Confederation are approved.

1788

June 21
The U.S. Constitution becomes law.

1791

December 15
The Bill of Rights is added to the Constitution.

Dwight Nadig/E+/Getty Images

The United States Capitol in Washington, DC

The Articles of Confederation

While they were fighting the British, the American colonies needed to band together and form a government. In 1776, leaders from each colony met in Philadelphia, Pennsylvania. They talked about the best way to set up their new government.

Many Americans wanted a weak national government. They believed that the king of Great Britain had too much power. They did not want to give one person or group too much power in their new country. So in 1777, American leaders approved a set of laws called the Articles of Confederation. This became the first plan of government for the new nation. The articles created a weak national government.

Eventually, many Americans came to believe that the U.S. government was too weak. When the Revolutionary War ended in 1783, they realized that the United States needed a stronger national government.

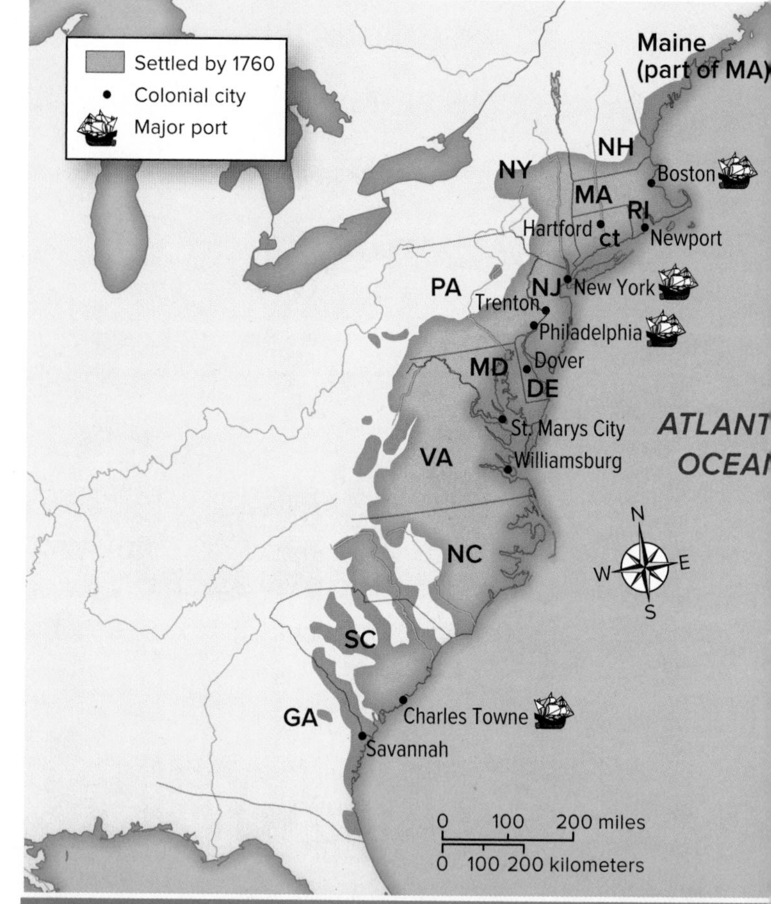

Colonial Settlement by 1760

Map Skills Thirteen colonies became the first U.S. states. Discuss with a partner which colony was located farthest north. Which colony was located farthest south?

The Constitutional Convention

In 1787, the leaders met again in Philadelphia. They called this meeting the Constitutional Convention. At this meeting, they discussed how to set up the government. How much power should each state have? Should the national government be more powerful than the states? Finally, they came to an agreement. They signed the United States Constitution into law on June 21, 1788. This written document states the duties of the government.

Biography

Benjamin Franklin

Benjamin Franklin worked on the writing of both the Declaration of Independence and the Constitution. He was 81 years old during the Constitutional Convention. He gave the other leaders advice on how to write the Constitution. A year later, he wrote to a French friend:

"Our new Constitution is now established, and has an appearance that promises permanency; but in this world nothing can be said to be certain, except death and taxes."

PHOTO: Popular Graphic Arts Collection, Library of Congress, LC-USZC2-2004
TEXT: Franklin, Benjamin. The Works of Benjamin Franklin Volume VI. Philadelphia: William Duane, 1809.

Stop and Check

COLLABORATE

Talk Discuss with a partner why the U.S. Constitution was written.

Find Details As you read, add new information to the graphic organizer on page 185 in your Inquiry Journal.

The Constitution Is Written

The 55 men who wrote the U.S. Constitution are called the founders. These founders each have an important place in our country's history. George Washington led the meetings at the Constitutional Convention. He was our nation's first president. James Madison took careful notes during the meetings. He became our fourth president. Benjamin Franklin gave valuable advice. Alexander Hamilton suggested many new ideas. These representatives and others worked together to create a system of government that would work best for our country.

When the meetings ended, 39 of the representatives signed the Constitution. It was then approved by each state. Today, the U.S. Constitution is the oldest national constitution that is still in use. Many other countries around the world have used it as a model for their own written constitutions. Today, you can see our ideas for government in the constitutions of other countries.

Did You Know?

Today, the original Constitution of the United States is on display in the Rotunda of the National Archives Museum in Washington, D.C. This important place is the home of the Constitution, the Declaration of Independence, and the Bill of Rights. Together, these three documents are called the Charters of Freedom. About one million people visit the National Archives every year to view these important documents.

The Constitution on display in the National Archives Museum

Carol M. Highsmith Archive, Library of Congress, LC-DIG-highsm-15688

The founders argued for a long time about how the states would be represented in the new system of government. Some believed that states with more people should have more representatives than states with fewer people. Others believed that each state should have the same number of representatives, regardless of how many people lived in the state.

The founders solved this disagreement with a **compromise**. They decided that Congress would have two parts. The Senate would have the same number of representatives from each state. It did not matter how many people lived in each state. The number of representatives a state could send to the House of Representatives would be based on state population. This is the system we still use today.

The Constitution was debated and signed in Independence Hall.

Comstock/Stockbyte/Getty Images

Stop and Check

Talk Discuss with a partner why the founders decided that Congress would have two parts.

The preamble to the Constitution of the United States

How the Constitution Works

The Constitution sets up how our government works. It unites all the states under a national government. The introduction, called the preamble, tells the purpose for the Constitution. It begins with the words "We the People." These three words are important because they make it clear that the people of the United States control our government.

The Articles in the Constitution explain how the government is organized. They explain the responsibilities of the three branches of government. The Articles also explain how changes to the Constitution can be made. These changes are called **amendments**. The founders understood that, over time, some changes might be needed to the Constitution.

The first ten amendments were made in 1791. This was when the Bill of Rights was added to the Constitution. These amendments explain the **rights** that all people in the United States have. These rights include freedom of speech, freedom of the press, and freedom of religion. Today, the Constitution has 27 total amendments. The last amendment was made in 1992.

Scukrov/iStock/Getty Images

FEDERAL POWERS

- Maintain armed forces
- Declare war
- Set up a postal system
- Set standard weights and measures
- Protect copyrights and patents

SHARED POWERS

- Collect taxes
- Establish courts
- Make and enforce laws
- Regulate banks
- Borrow money
- Provide for the common good

STATE POWERS

- Establish local governments
- Set up schools
- Regulate state businesses
- Make laws for marriage
- Establish and regulate corporations

Federal and state governments share some powers.

The Constitution separates the power of the government across three parts, or branches. The **legislative branch** is Congress. It makes our laws. The **executive branch**, led by the president, carries out the laws. The **judicial branch** is our court system. This branch interprets the laws and decides whether the laws follow the Constitution. Each branch has its own duties, but the three branches must work together.

The Constitution lists the powers of the **federal**, or national, government. It also lists the powers of state governments. The chart on this page shows how these powers are divided. It also shows the powers that the federal and state governments share.

The U.S. Constitution is a very important document. It has guided our leaders for more than 200 years.

Stop and Check

Talk Discuss with a partner why the founders created three branches of government.

What Do You Think? Why is the Constitution important to the people of the United States?

How Do the Branches of Government Work Together?

The Constitution Guides Our Government

You have learned that the Constitution explains how our government is organized. But who works in our government? In the United States, the government is elected by the people. Members of the government come from all over the country. They work in Washington, D.C., our nation's capital.

The people who work in our government promise to obey the Constitution. That means they cannot pass a law or act in any way that goes against the laws in the Constitution. They have to follow the laws that are written in the Constitution.

HSS.3.4.1, HSS.3.4.2, HSS.3.4.3, HSS.3.4.4, HAS.CS.2

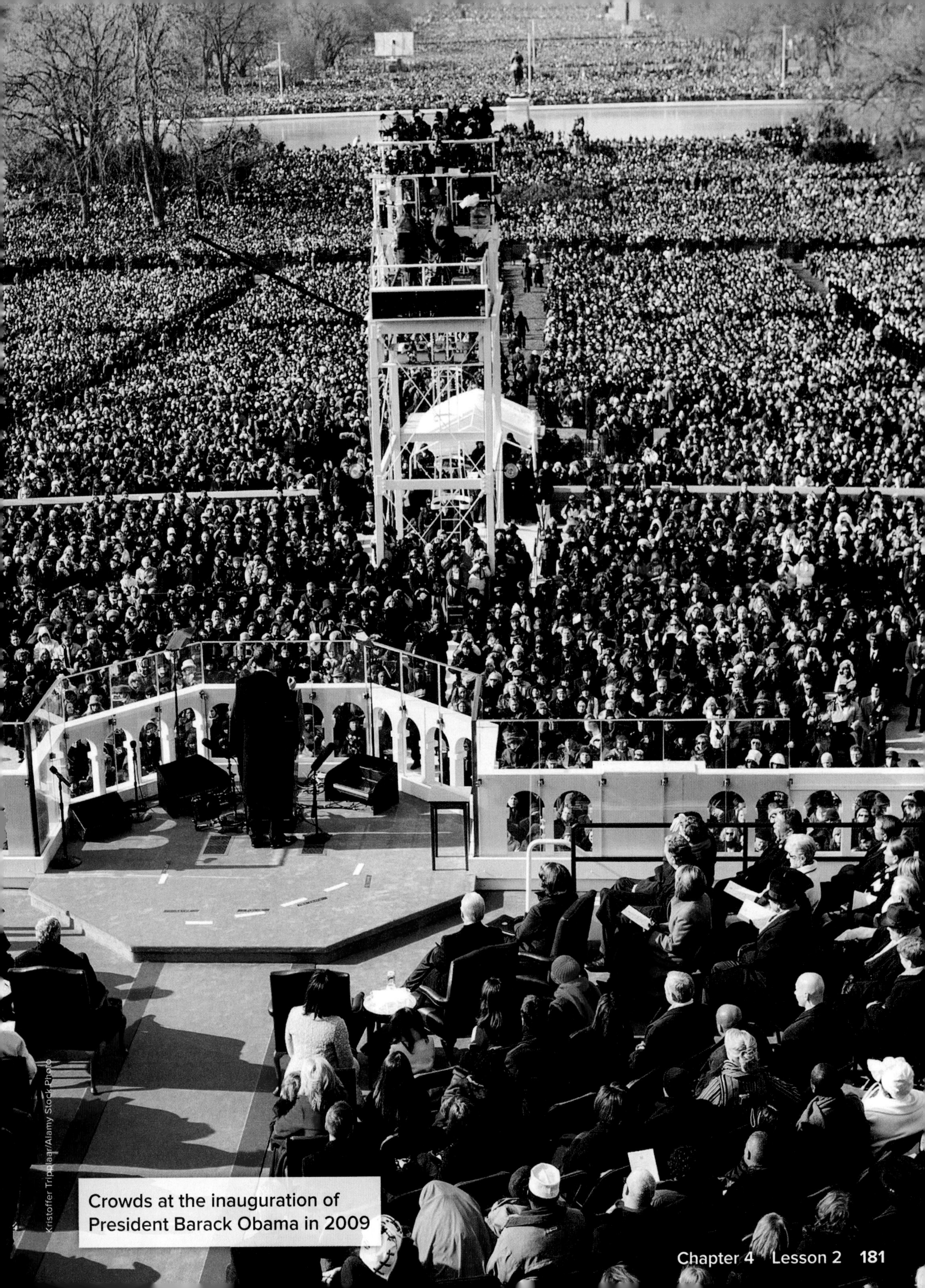
Kristoffer Tripplaar/Alamy Stock Photo
Crowds at the inauguration of President Barack Obama in 2009

The Branches of the Government

As you have learned, there are three branches of government. Each branch has its own responsibilities. All three branches work together to make sure our country runs smoothly.

Executive Branch

The **executive branch** is the part of government that carries out laws. The president of the United States is the head of the executive branch. The president leads our country. The president's main job is to make sure that the laws passed by Congress are being followed. The vice president supports the president. The vice president also leads the Senate. The president and vice president are elected to serve for four years.

Several people lead different departments of the executive branch. They are part of the president's cabinet. They are known as cabinet members. Part of their job is to give advice to the president.

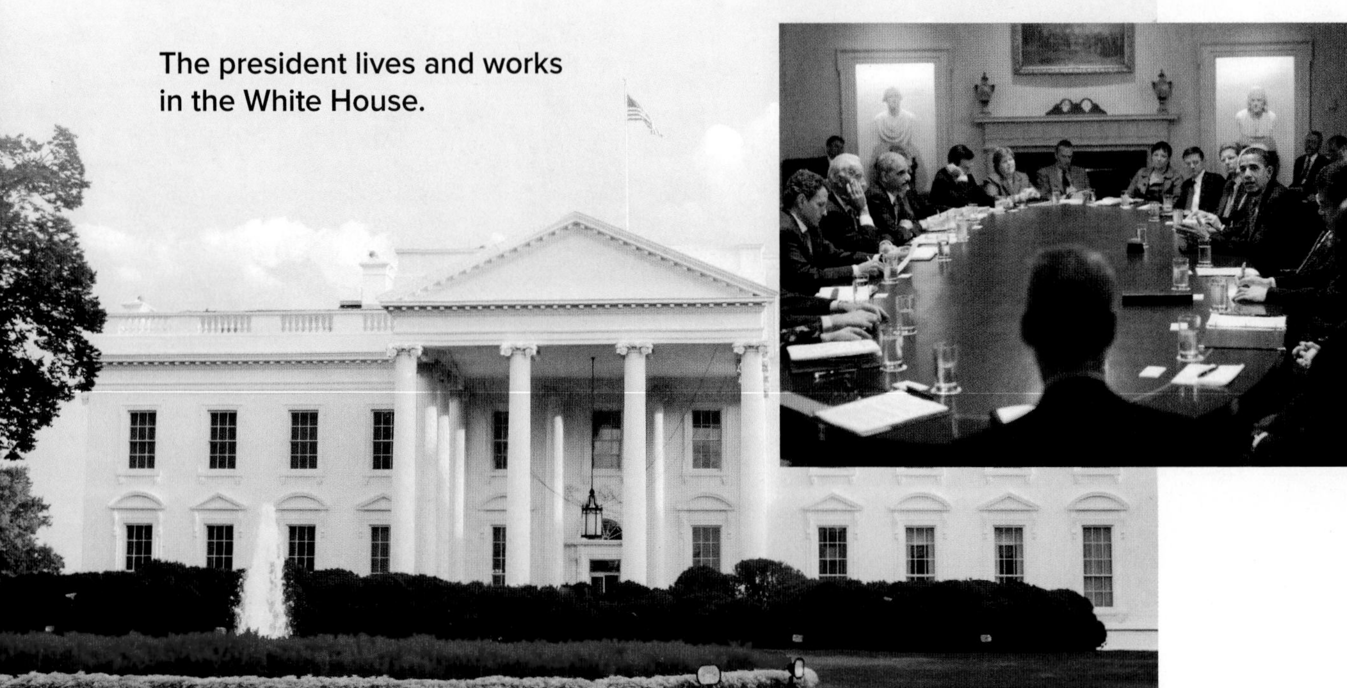

The president lives and works in the White House.

(t)Pete Souza/Official White House Photo; (b)solomonjee/iStockphoto/Getty Images

Legislative Branch

The **legislative branch** makes laws for everyone to follow. In the **federal** government, Congress makes laws for the entire country. Congress is made up of two parts—the Senate and the House of Representatives. Citizens elect members of Congress. Senators are elected every six years. Representatives are elected every two years.

Each state has two senators, so there are 100 senators in the Senate. The House of Representatives is much bigger than the Senate. It has 435 members. The number of representatives from each state is based on the size of its population. California elects the most representatives to the House of Representatives. Why? Because it has the largest population of any state!

Members of Congress work in the Capitol Building.

Stop and Check

Think What is the main difference between the executive branch and the legislative branch of our government?

Find Details As you read, add new information to the graphic organizer on page 193 in your Inquiry Journal.

Glow Images

Judicial Branch

The **judicial branch** is made up of federal courts and judges. They decide what the laws mean. They also make sure that laws agree with the Constitution.

The Supreme Court is our country's most important court. Supreme Court judges, called justices, are nominated by the president. Justices must be approved by the Senate. There are nine justices on the Supreme Court. Justices serve until they resign, retire, or are removed from office.

Justices of the U.S. Supreme Court make sure that our laws follow the Constitution. They hear important legal cases. Justices review cases from state courts and decide which ones to hear. Supreme Court decisions are final.

Supreme Court building

The Supreme Court justices in 2015

(l)Joe Ravi/iStockphoto/Getty Images; (r)ZUMA Press/Alamy Stock Photo

Sharing Power

The Executive Branch

The president is the head of the executive branch. The president's main job is to make sure laws passed by Congress are carried out. The president can veto, or say no to, a law.

The Judicial Branch

The judicial branch is made up of federal courts and judges. The country's most powerful court is the Supreme Court. The Supreme Court makes sure that laws passed by Congress follow the Constitution.

The Legislative Branch

The legislative branch, called Congress, makes laws. Congress sometimes can overrule the president if the president vetoes a law. Congress also approves the members of the Supreme Court.

The Constitution limits the power of each branch. The branches must share power to make the government work. Each branch also has some power over the other branches. For example, the president can reject laws that Congress makes. The Supreme Court can decide that a law is not permitted under the U.S. Constitution. This keeps Congress from having too much power. Congress can refuse to pass a law that the president wants. This limits the power of the president.

Stop and Check

Think Why does the Constitution limit the power of each branch of government?

(l)Joe Ravi/iStockphoto/Getty Images; (c)solomonjee/iStockphoto/Getty Images; (r)Glow Images

Symbols and Holidays

The leaders of our government have passed laws over the years about national and state symbols. They have also passed laws to make certain days holidays.

How do you feel when you see the United States flag? The flag is a symbol of our country. Did you know that the stars and stripes on the flag are also symbols? The stars stand for the fifty states. The stripes represent the thirteen original colonies. The original flag of our country only had thirteen stars. As states were added to our country, stars were also added to the flag.

U.S. flag

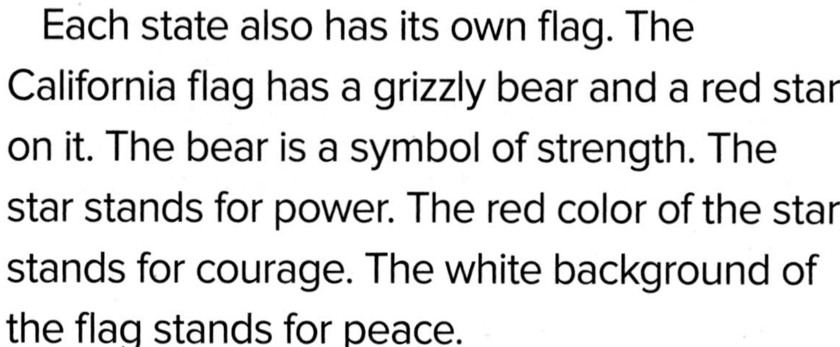

Each state also has its own flag. The California flag has a grizzly bear and a red star on it. The bear is a symbol of strength. The star stands for power. The red color of the star stands for courage. The white background of the flag stands for peace.

California flag

The Statue of Liberty is another symbol of our nation. The statue is on an island in New York Harbor. It stands for freedom. Millions of people have come to the United States to be free.

Statue of Liberty

Did You Know?

The bald eagle is our national bird. It is a symbol of beauty, strength, and freedom. A popular story says that Benjamin Franklin wanted the wild turkey to be our national bird! He considered the turkey to be a "bird of courage."

(t)Jan Hanus/iStockphoto/Getty Images; (c)YangYin/E+/Getty Images; (b)TongRo Image Stock/Alamy Stock Photo

Holidays

Holidays are one way we celebrate our country and state. We celebrate Independence Day every year on the Fourth of July. This honors the day Congress approved the Declaration of Independence in 1776. This is the day the United States became a country. Communities celebrate with parades, picnics, and fireworks.

Memorial Day is another important national holiday. On this day we remember the military men and women who have died for our country.

We also celebrate the men and women who served in the military on Veterans Day. This holiday falls on November 11.

In California, March 31 is Cesar Chavez Day. This day celebrates the birth and work of Cesar Chavez. Chavez worked to improve the lives of farm workers. He helped to get better pay and treatment for them. Schools and government offices are closed to honor this holiday.

Stop and Check

Perspectives In your opinion, what is the best symbol of our country? Why?

Citizens Give Back Through Public Service

Mimi Walters is a United States representative.

Why do people choose to work in the government? Many people want to help make a difference in other people's lives. Mimi Walters is a U.S. representative from California. Here is what she says about working in government: "As a mother of four, I was inspired to run for higher public office to help ensure a better future for my children and their generation."

You do not have to work in government to make a difference. There are many different public service jobs. Firefighters, emergency medical technicians, and police officers help to protect our communities. Public school teachers help kids learn.

President Barack Obama

President Barack Obama once said of public service, "Public service is a calling which has meant so much to so many. It . . . reflects our drive to serve a cause beyond our own—to give back to our Nation, leave our mark, and nudge history forward. There is no greater opportunity to help more people or to make a bigger difference."

PHOTO: (t)Tom Williams/CQ-Roll Call Group/Getty Images; (b)Pete Souza/Official White House Photo; (bkgd)McGraw-Hill Education
TEXT: Walters, Mimi. "We Must Be the Solution-Oriented Congress." Washington D.C., January 30, 2015.,
Obama, Barack. "Presidential Proclamation -- Public Service Recognition Week, 2015." Washington, D.C., May 02, 2015.

How can you help make your school a better place? One way is by being involved in your school government. You can help bring about changes right where you learn!

You can continue to be involved in government when you grow up. People in local government work every day for better schools and medical care. They work for better transportation and for a cleaner environment. They work so all the people in their community can have better lives.

Remember to vote in your school elections!

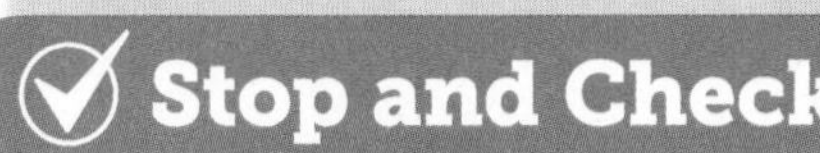

Stop and Check

Connect to Now What is a reason to choose a career in public service? Discuss your reason with a classmate.

What Do You Think? Describe the three branches of our government. How do the branches work together?

Harry Choi/Alamy Stock Photo

Why Do Communities Need Governments?

State Government

Every state, including California, has its own government and its own constitution. California's government is similar to the **federal** government. The state government has three branches, just like the national government. All three branches work together to help California run smoothly.

The **legislative branch** makes the laws in California. It is made up of two parts. They are the State Assembly and the State Senate. Both groups meet in Sacramento, the state capital. The head of California's **executive branch** is called the governor. The **judicial branch** reviews state laws to see if they are fair. The judicial branch includes all of the state courts.

HSS.3.2.3, HSS.3.4.3, HSS.3.4.4, HSS.3.4.5, HAS.HR.2

California Governor Jerry Brown signs a bill into law.

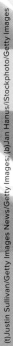

(t)Justin Sullivan/Getty Images News/Getty Images; (b)Jan Hanus/iStockphoto/Getty Images

State and local governments hire police officers, pave the streets, and set speed limits.

The state government meets different needs than the federal government. The state government takes care of state roads and parks. It also helps to decide what you learn in school. State laws say how old you must be to drive a car and get married. Lawyers and other professionals have to pass state tests before they can work in the state. The state also sets up elections for its **citizens**. These are issues that directly affect people every day.

Not all states have the same laws. For example, in California, you can get a provisional permit to drive when you are 15 years and 6 months old. In Iowa, you can get a learner's permit when you are 14.

Where does the state get the money to pay for things like roads, parks, and schools? It comes from taxes. A **tax** is money that people must pay to support the government. People pay a sales tax when they buy certain items. They pay an income tax on the money they earn from a job. Taxes are used to pay for things that everyone in the state needs.

(l)Hill Street Studios/Blend Images LLC; (c)Dennis MacDonald/Alamy Stock Photo; (r)McGraw-Hill Education

Biography

Governor Jerry Brown

Edmund Gerald "Jerry" Brown was first elected governor of California in 1974. Governor Brown tried to use tax money wisely. While he was governor, he drove an old car. He lived in a small apartment. He worked hard to bring jobs to California and to clean up pollution.

During most of the 1980s, Brown worked as a lawyer. In 1998, he was elected mayor of Oakland. In 2010 and 2014, he was elected governor of California again. In 2018, he will become California's longest-serving governor—16 years in all.

The U.S. Constitution divides power between the federal and state governments. Only the federal government can do certain things, such as declare war and print money. State governments control everything the Constitution does not give to the federal government. Both federal and state governments can pass laws, raise taxes, and borrow money. Sometimes the federal government directs all states to follow the same rule, such as to reduce air pollution. State governments work together with local governments to provide services. Local governments are created by the state. They must follow the state constitution and all state laws.

Stop and Check

COLLABORATE

Talk What are some services provided by the state government? Discuss your ideas with a partner.

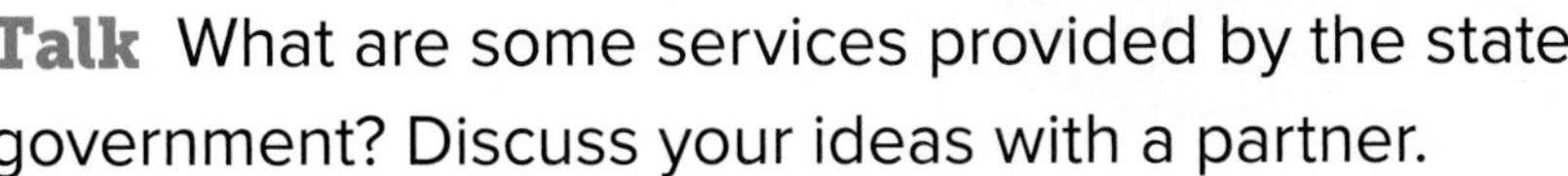

Find Details As you read, add new information to the graphic organizer on page 201 in your Inquiry Journal.

Alex Wong/Getty Images News/Getty Images

Field Trip

California State Capitol Building

The California State Capitol building is in Sacramento. This building is home to California's state government. The State Assembly and Senate meet in this building to make laws. The governor also has an office there.

Visitors can take guided tours of the state capitol building. Tour guides share information about the building's history. They also explain how California state government works.

The California State Capitol building

California State Legislature

When you visit the state capitol building, you can watch the State Assembly and Senate debate issues and vote on bills. Visitors must be quiet and not interrupt the legislators. Cheering and clapping are not allowed! But watching the legislators at work can help you understand how ideas turn into laws.

(t)Spondylolithesis/iStockphoto/Getty Images; (b)Ken James/Bloomberg/Getty Images

Fun Facts

- California's state capitol building was designed to look like the U.S. Capitol in Washington, D.C.
- The state capitol building has a large round room called a *rotunda*. The rotunda is covered by a domed roof.
- The California Senate Chamber is decorated in red. It is located in the north end of the state capitol building. The Assembly Chamber is decorated in green. It is located in the south end of the state capitol building.

Many people also enjoy visiting Capitol Park. The park is located next to the state capitol building. The park has gardens with flowers, plants, and trees from around the world. In Capitol Park, people can see statues that honor important people and events in California history. For example, the California Veterans Memorial helps people remember the state's soldiers.

Capitol Park in Sacramento

photo.ua/Shutterstock.com

Stop and Check

Think Why did the people in charge of building the state capitol building want it to look important?

Local Governments

Who hires firefighters and police officers? Who decides if a street corner needs a traffic light? Your local government does! Local governments affect our everyday lives.

Local city governments have executive and legislative branches, just like our federal and state governments. The legislative branch of a local government is usually called a city council. The city council makes laws for the city. The mayor is the head of the city council. Citizens vote for the mayor and city council members.

In most California cities, the executive branch is headed by a city manager. The city manager carries out the city council's plans. In some larger California cities, like Los Angeles, the mayor is the head of the executive branch.

Most cities don't have their own court system. They use the county courts. Many minor crimes, such as traffic tickets, are judged in local courts. A judge listens to the issues brought before him or her and follows the law to make a fair decision.

A city council meeting

Matthew S. Masaschi/USCG

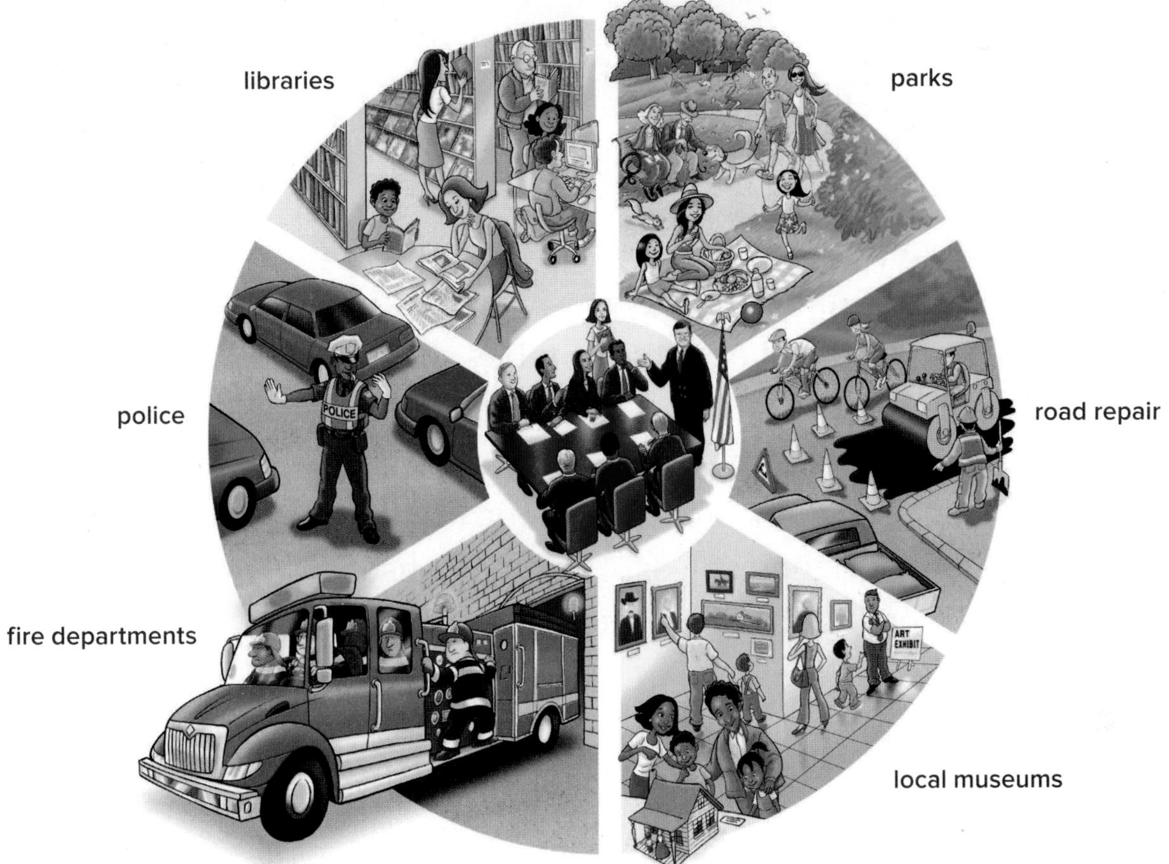

Local governments provide many services.

Most local city councils meet every week at the city hall. Citizens can attend city council meetings. At each meeting, the council listens to the concerns of citizens. Then the council decides what actions to take. In some locations, citizens can watch city council meetings on television.

Like state government, local governments provide important services to people. One major difference between state and local government is in the sharing of power. Local governments have only the power that the state gives to them.

Stop and Check

Think Why do you think some California cities put their city council meetings on television?

Governments of California Indian Nations

When European settlers came to America hundreds of years ago, they treated American Indian tribes as independent nations. They often signed treaties with the tribes. A treaty is a formal agreement between nations. The United States made many promises in the treaties it signed with American Indians. In one treaty, the United States promised tribes that they could continue to govern themselves. The U.S. Constitution recognizes that tribal nations have the right to govern themselves.

American Indians are citizens of the United States. They are also citizens of their own tribes. As American citizens, they are citizens of the state where they live. They vote in national, state, and local elections. American Indians also follow local, state, and national laws.

American Indian tribes also have their own governments. Tribal members choose leaders and make laws. States cannot tell tribal governments what to do. However, the national government can pass laws that affect tribal affairs.

A tribal chairman speaking at a Santa Barbara County meeting

Spencer Weiner/Los Angeles Times/Getty Images

Tribal governments work like other local and state governments. They provide community services to members of the tribe on their reservation.

Tribal governments also encourage businesses to come to the community. And they work to preserve their own cultures and to support education.

Point of View

The Agua Caliente Indian Reservation is in Southern California, in and around Palm Springs. In 1951, the last spiritual leader of the Agua Caliente died. The next year, members of the tribe wrote a constitution and formed a tribal government. Palm Springs had been a quiet town, but it was beginning to grow. Federal laws controlled what reservations could do with their land. The new five-member tribal council went to Washington, D.C. They won the right to rent their land at better terms. Now they could rent their land to people who wanted to build homes, hotels, and restaurants in Palm Springs. Life became better for the Agua Caliente people.

Stop and Check

Talk What are some ways tribal governments are the same as state governments?

What Do You Think? Why do we need state and local governments?

What Are Some Rules That We Must Follow?

Obeying Rules and Laws

When you ride your bike, you must stop at a light. Before you can speak in class, you must raise your hand. Do you know which of these examples is a rule and which is a law?

Rules are set by people like your parents or your teacher. Rules help people get along well and work together. They help teach you right from wrong. Rules can also help you learn to respect one another.

Laws are set by the government. They are the rules that you and all the members of your community must follow. Laws help keep people safe. They also make sure people are treated equally.

HSS.3.4.1, HSS.3.4.2

Rules help make sure that everyone in the class is heard.

Digital Vision/Getty Images

Rules help people get along and treat each other fairly.

Rules are important because they teach people how to behave and how to treat others. Your classroom rules help you learn about fairness and honesty. You do not cut in line because it is unfair. You do not copy another student's homework because it is dishonest. There are rules also against bullying. People who follow the rules try to do what is best at all times.

The laws of your community are created to protect people's safety. It is against the law to drive faster than the speed limit. This law protects walkers and other drivers. Restaurant workers must wash their hands. This protects the health of their customers. Laws also protect our property. For example, it is against the law to break into a house and take something without permission.

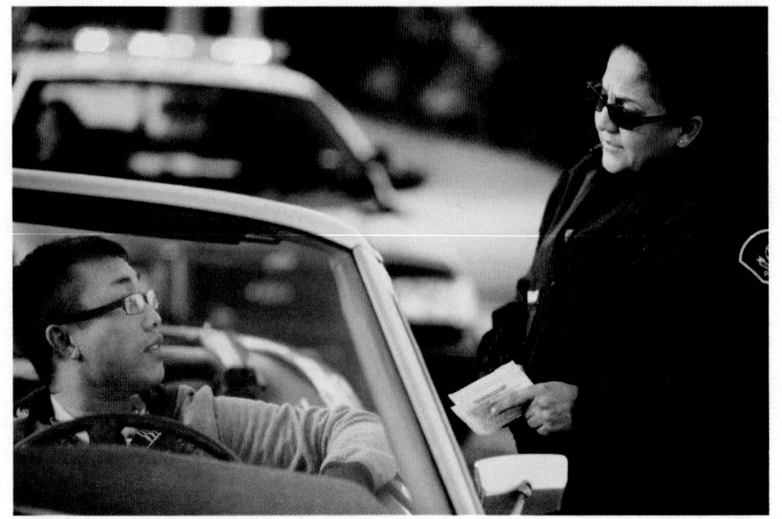

A driver who speeds is breaking a law. He or she may have to pay a fine.

What keeps people from breaking a rule or law? All rules and laws have consequences. A consequence is something that happens as a result of something else. If you know what the consequence will be, you might not break a rule. Your family may have a rule that you must do your homework or you cannot watch your favorite show. You know the consequence for breaking the rule is that you cannot watch your favorite show. This means that you will probably do your homework. People who break laws are punished. They may have to pay money or go to jail.

Did You Know?

In California, there are many laws about bicycles. Your bike must have a brake. You cannot leave your bicycle lying down on a sidewalk. Also, you must wear a helmet whenever you ride a bike. If you are caught without a helmet, you might have to pay a fine of $25.

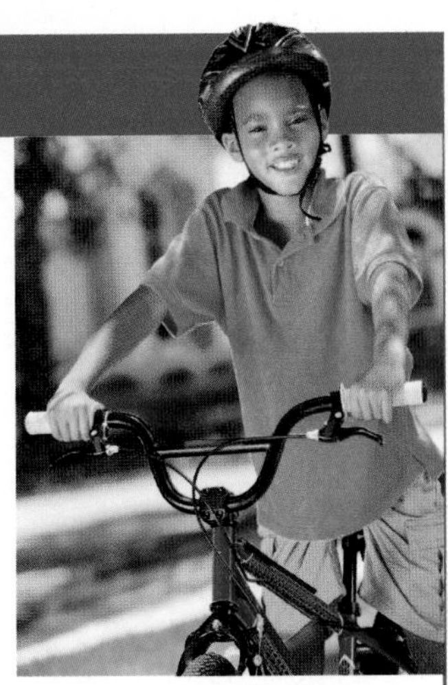

Obeying bike laws

Stop and Check

COLLABORATE

Talk With a partner, discuss how a law is different from a rule. What are the consequences of breaking a law?

Find Details As you read, add new information to the graphic organizer on page 209 in your Inquiry Journal.

Spotmatik/iStock/Getty Images

PRIMARY SOURCE

In Their Words... Theodore Roosevelt

"Not only should there be complete liberty in matters of religion and opinion, but complete liberty for each man to lead his life as he desires, provided only that in so doing he does not wrong his neighbor."

—speech at the Sorbonne, Paris, France, 1910

Protecting Our Rights and Keeping Us Safe

The Bill of Rights

- *The right to practice any religion.*
- *The right to meet peacefully in groups.*
- *The right to say what we think.*
- *The right to write what we think.*
- *The right to be treated fairly under the law.*

The United States Constitution sets forth the laws our government must follow. It also lists the **rights** of American **citizens**, which the government must protect. For example, the Constitution protects people from discrimination because of their race, gender, or disability. This protection makes sure all Americans are treated equally. No one can take away any of these rights.

California also has a constitution. It is the highest law in the state. It lists the same rights as the ones in the U.S. Constitution. However, it describes those rights in more detail. It also includes different rights, such as the rights of crime victims.

PHOTO: (t)Prints and Photographs Division, Library of Congress, LC-USZ62-13026
TEXT: Roosevelt, Theodore, Speech at the Sorbonne, 1910, quoted in Battling For the Right: The Life-Story of Theodore Roosevelt by Charles Morris. Princeton, 1910.

A Day in the Life

Members of the California National Guard might go to work at a regular job during the week. On weekends, they take part in military training. At any time, they can be called to serve the state of California. They help and protect people when there is an emergency. Sometimes they are sent to protect people in other states or other countries.

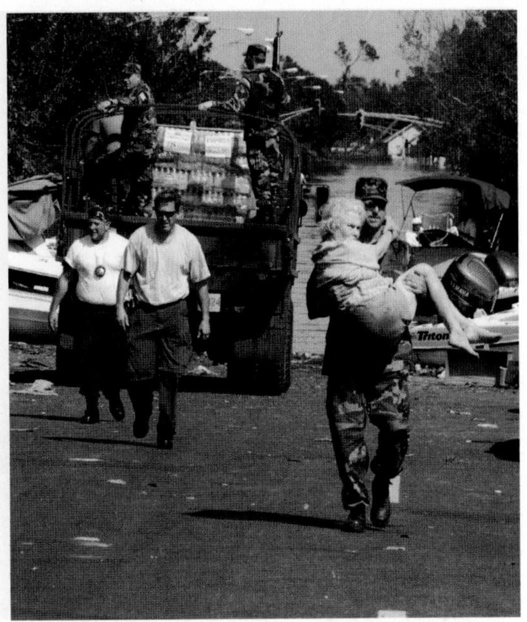

California's laws are listed in a series of codes. Many of these codes protect our safety and security. One code created California's National Guard. Members of the Guard help Californians after a natural disaster, such as an earthquake.

California's Health and Safety Code sets rules for how food is handled. It also sets rules that doctors, nurses, and hospitals must follow. These laws make sure the food we eat is safe. They also make sure that we get good medical care.

The California Vehicle Code lists traffic laws and the consequences of breaking these laws. For example, every driver and passenger must wear seat belts to keep them safe. If they break the law, they could pay a fine.

Stop and Check

Draw Choose one of the laws listed in the text. Make a drawing that shows how that law protects your safety.

What Do You Think? What are some rules that we must follow? Why is it important to follow these rules?

Liz Roll/FEMA

How Has Citizenship Changed Over Time?

American Citizenship

What does it mean to be a **citizen**? A citizen is a person who lives in a community. A citizen also has certain rights and duties. You are a citizen of the community where you live. You can also be a citizen of your country.

How does a person become a citizen of the United States? You are a citizen if you were born here. But what if you were born in another country? You can become a citizen if one of your parents is a citizen. If neither of your parents is a citizen, you can become a citizen through naturalization.

Naturalization is a way for a person to become a citizen of a country. Naturalization in the United States has several steps. First you fill out papers saying that you want to become a citizen. Next you are interviewed. Then you have to pass a test about U.S. history and government. Finally, you take an oath of allegiance to the United States. This means you promise to be a loyal and good citizen.

Anke Van wyk/Hemera/Getty Images

HSS.3.4.2, HSS.3.4.6

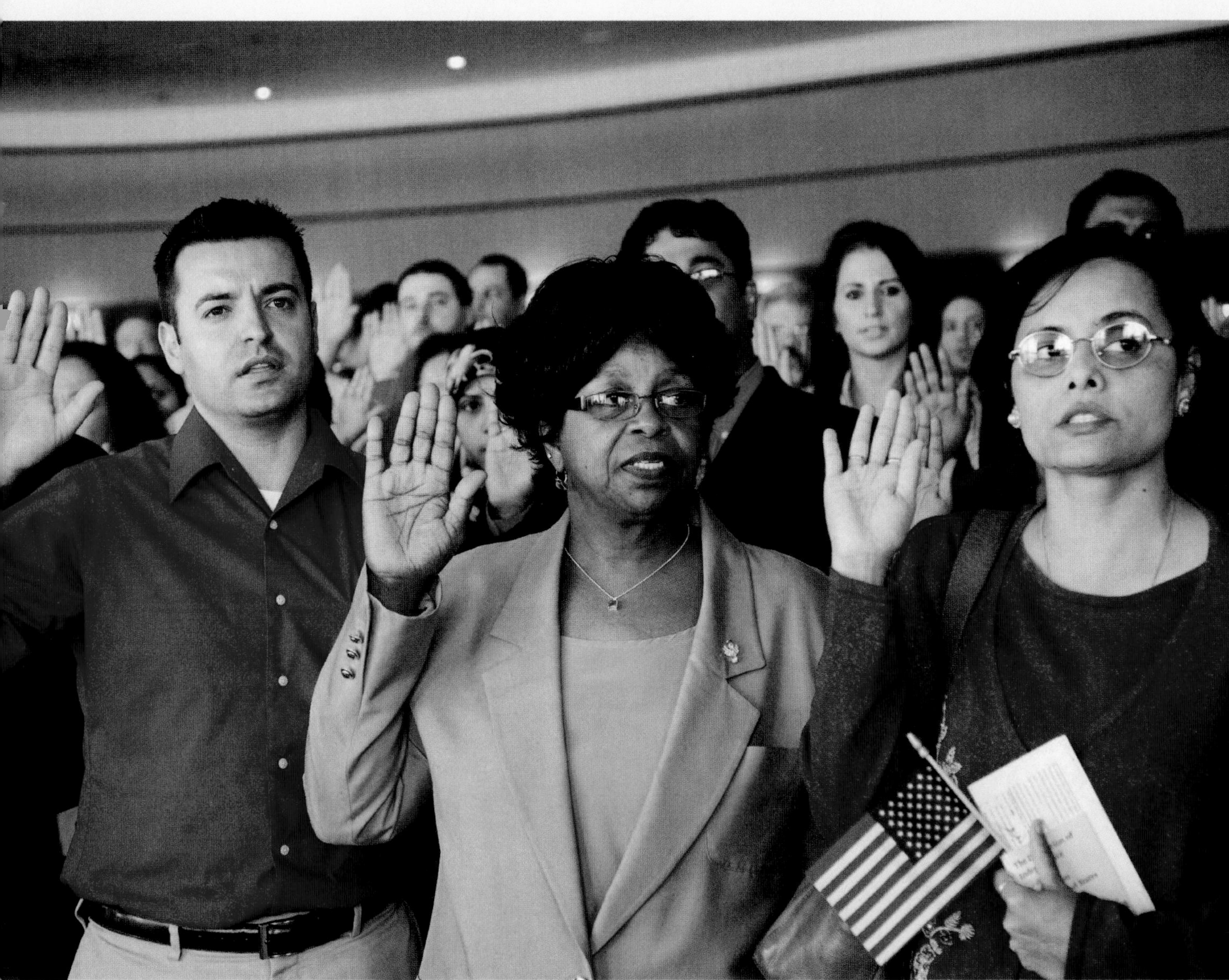

Taking the Oath of Allegiance at a naturalization ceremony

Jim West/Alamy Stock Photo

Being a Good Citizen

How can you be a good citizen? Good citizens follow the rules and laws of their community. They know that rules and laws protect everyone. They respect the **rights** and opinions of others. They also are honest and trustworthy.

Good citizens believe in the common good. This means that they do what is best for their community. They might serve as a government leader. They might volunteer to help clean up their local park. They do what they can to make their community a better place to live.

Most importantly, citizens support the rules and laws of the United States. Good citizens know that every American has the right to worship as they wish. Every American has the right to an opinion. Every American has the right to be treated fairly. Good citizens follow the laws to protect everyone's rights and differences.

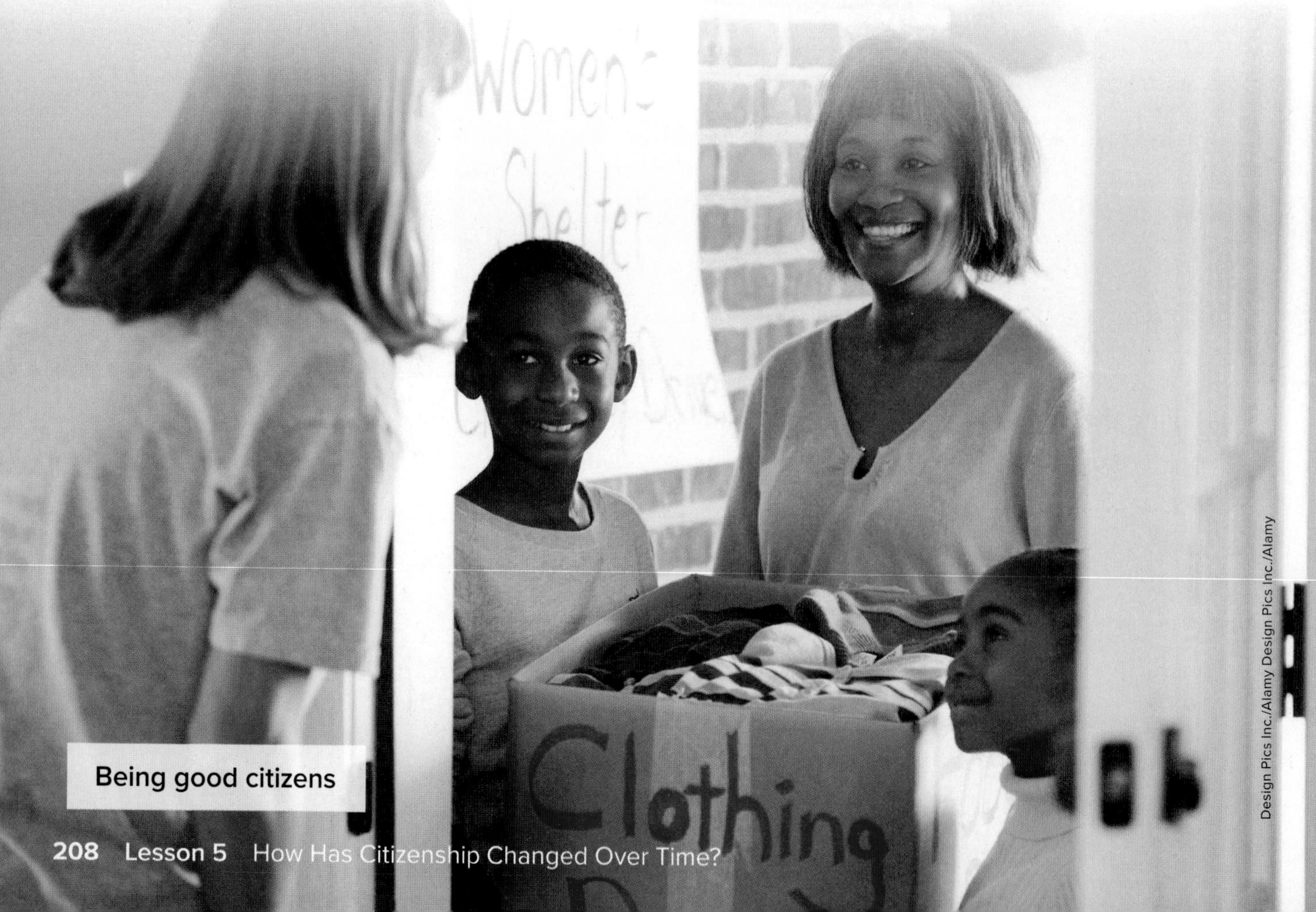

Being good citizens

Design Pics Inc./Alamy Design Pics Inc./Alamy

Citizens serving on a jury

American citizens have certain responsibilities. A responsibility is a duty or job.

All American citizens have the responsibility to vote. When citizens vote, they choose the people who will make and enforce the laws. Good citizens are informed about the issues that affect their community. This helps them make good choices about what their community needs. They stay informed by reading newspapers and watching the news.

American citizens are required to serve on a **jury** if they are asked. A jury is a group of citizens who are chosen to decide a legal case. A jury helps make sure that a person who is accused of a crime has a fair trial.

A good citizen pays **taxes**. Taxes help to pay for the services in your community. Taxes pay for services such as schools, libraries, and police and fire departments.

Stop and Check

Talk What does it mean to be a good citizen? Discuss your answer with a partner.

Find Details As you read, add new information to the graphic organizer on page 217 in your Inquiry Journal.

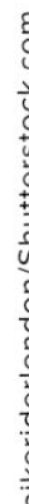

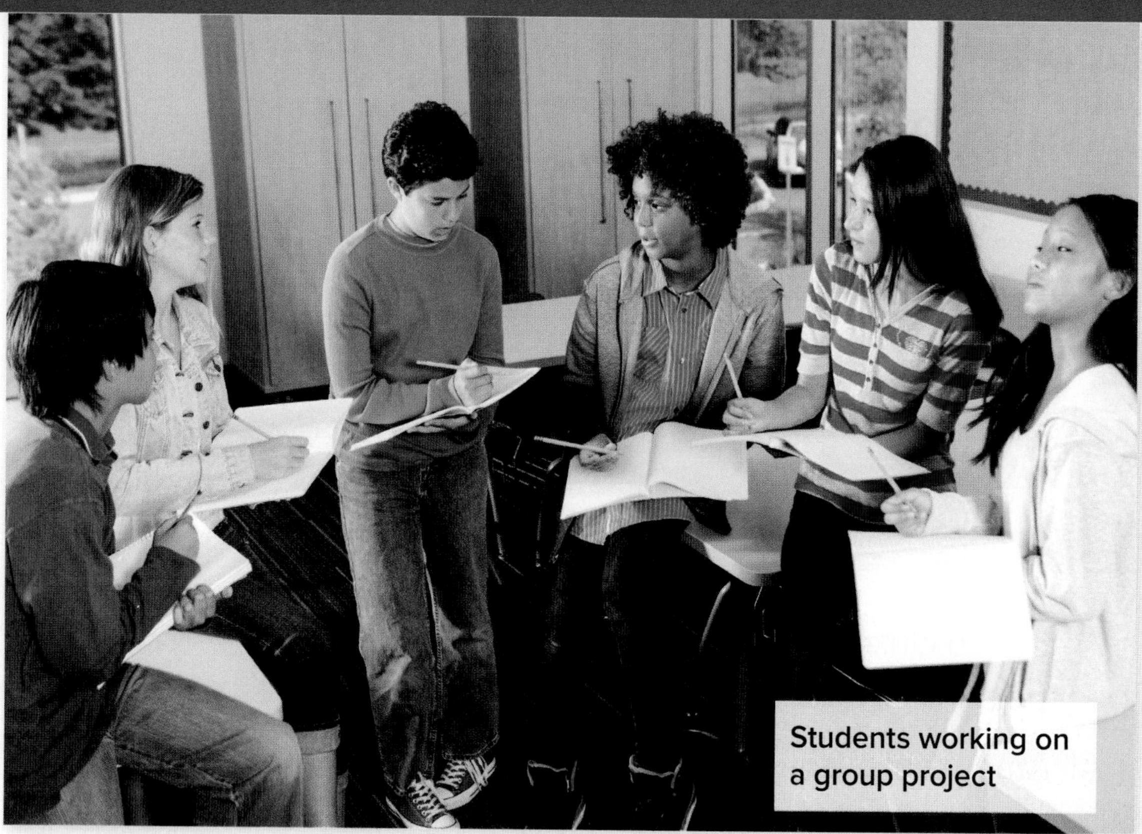
Students working on a group project

Learning how to become a good citizen starts at school. Your classroom is your community, and you are one of its citizens. As its citizen, you are expected to follow the rules. Before you speak, you must raise your hand. You form a line before going to recess. You are expected to listen when your teacher speaks.

Your teacher may ask you to work with other classmates in a group. You get to share ideas and listen to your classmates' ideas when you work in a group. You learn to cooperate by working together.

You also learn how to **compromise** when your group has many opinions. A compromise is an agreement that people make when they have different ideas. Each person or group gives up something they wanted to make the agreement. For example, imagine your group has three ideas for a project, but the group can create only one project. Your group has to work together to find a compromise. This could include combining some of the ideas into one project.

Kali Nine LLC/iStockphoto/Getty Images

Pledging allegiance

Your classroom teaches you to be responsible for how you behave. To be a good citizen in your classroom, you should be honest, trustworthy, and loyal. You should respect your classmates' things. You also should keep your desk and classroom clean.

Your classroom also teaches you to care about our country. You show that you care when you say the Pledge of Allegiance. When you say the Pledge of Allegiance, you promise to support and defend the values of the United States.

You may be too young to vote for issues in your community, but you may be able to vote for class leaders. Before you vote, you should think about the qualities you want in a leader. Do you want a leader who listens to other people's ideas? Do you want a leader who makes all of the decisions? You can use that information to make an informed choice.

Andersen Ross/Stockbyte/Getty Images

Stop and Check

Think What do you think is the most important characteristic of a good citizen in your classroom?

Then and Now

An American Citizen

The responsibilities of an American citizen have not changed much since our country was founded. Citizens have always been expected to obey the laws, pay taxes, and stay informed about issues. They also have been expected to vote. But not all people had the rights of citizenship.

For a time, only white men who owned land had all of the rights of citizenship. Women were citizens, but they did not have the right to vote or to own land. For many years, most African Americans were enslaved. They were not considered citizens. American Indians were not considered citizens either. All three groups fought hard for equality. Eventually, they gained the rights of citizenship.

Today, an American citizen can be a man or a woman. A citizen can be from any race or ethnic group.

Only half of the citizens in this photo could vote before August 1920.

(b)Imagesbybarbara/E+/Getty Images; (bkgd)McGraw-Hill Education

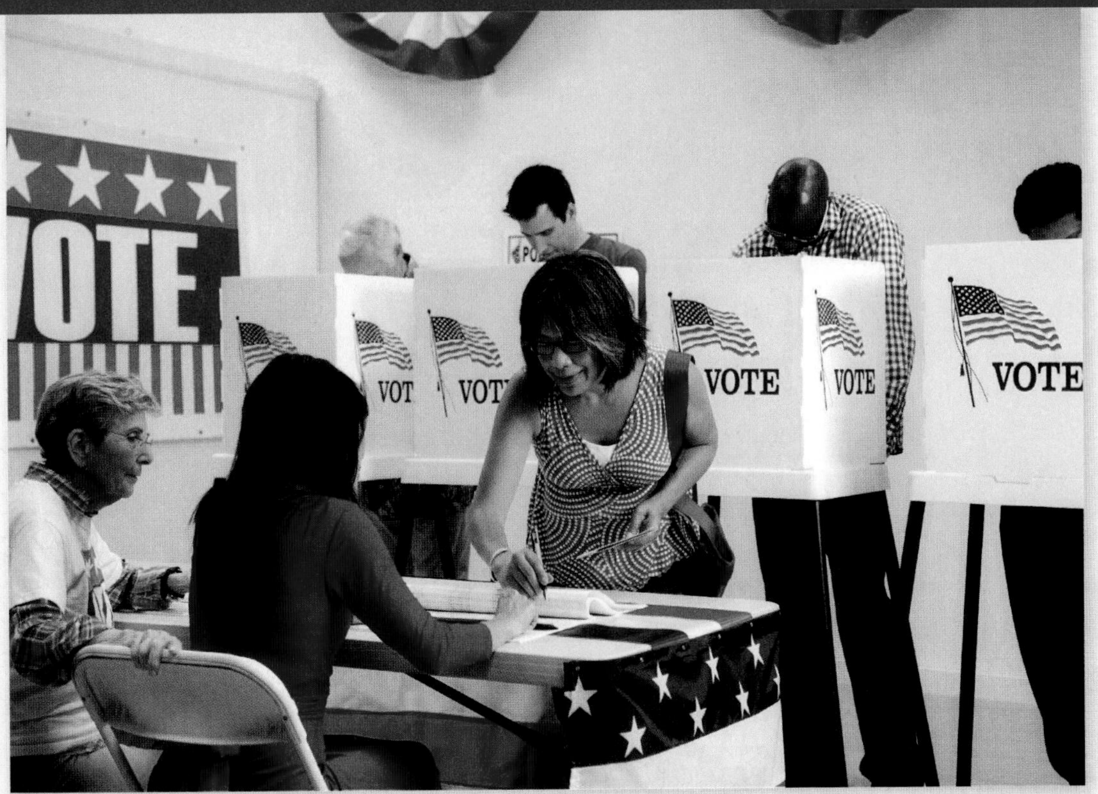

Today, all American citizens who are 18 or over can register and legally vote.

Citizens have always worked for the common good. They try to make our country a better place to live. Sometimes making the country better means fighting for what is right. Many citizens in the past worked to make the country a fair place to live for all citizens. Harriet Tubman helped African Americans escape from slavery. Martin Luther King Jr. fought for equality and rights for all African Americans. Susan B. Anthony fought for women's rights.

Today, citizens still work to make their communities better. Some citizens work to protect the environment. Others help people in need. A good American citizen is not only concerned about our country, but the entire world.

Stop and Check

Think What did Martin Luther King Jr. and Susan B. Anthony have in common? Would you consider Martin Luther King Jr. and Susan B. Anthony good citizens? Why or why not?

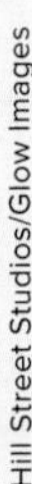
Hill Street Studios/Glow Images

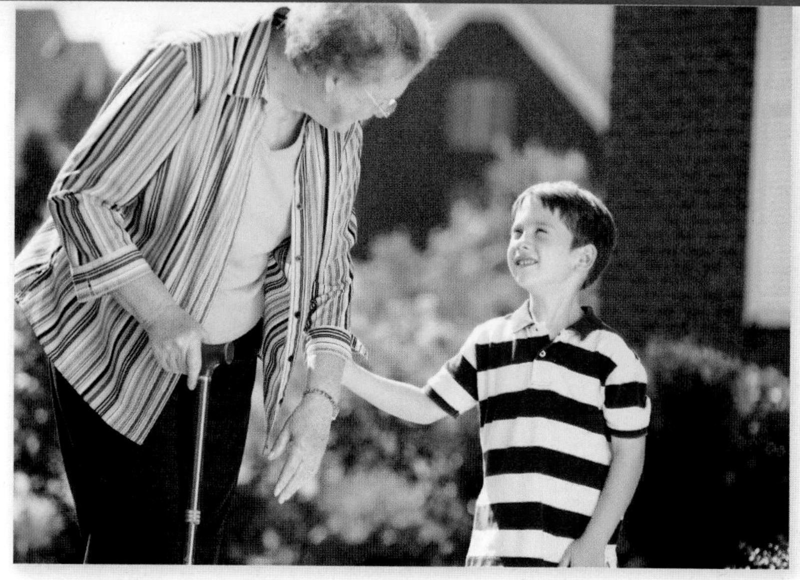

Volunteering in your community

What Can I Do For My Community?

Have you ever volunteered? To volunteer means to offer help without being paid. Many Americans believe that volunteering is an important responsibility of all citizens.

There are many ways to volunteer. You can volunteer to clean up a local park or beach. You can plant trees in a community garden. You can visit people in a nursing home. You can work with your school to gather money, food, and clothing for those in need. You can even volunteer to help animals in a local shelter. You make your community stronger when you volunteer and help others.

Did You Know?

Earth Day takes place every year on April 22. On Earth Day, millions of people participate in activities to celebrate Earth. These include festivals, planting trees, and volunteering to clean up trash. Will you celebrate Earth Day this year?

(t)Design Pics Inc./Alamy Sotck Photo; (b)KidStock/Blend Images/Getty Images

PRIMARY SOURCE

In Their Words... John F. Kennedy

"Ask not what your country can do for you—ask what you can do for your country."

—President Kennedy, Inaugural Address, 1961

Some people have paid jobs that allow them to help their community. Some work with homeless families. Others help people who need food, jobs, and resources. Others work with people who have served in the military. Do you know anyone who has a job helping the community?

Volunteers at a soup kitchen

 **Stop and Check**

COLLABORATE

Talk Why is volunteering a responsibility of a good citizen? What type of volunteer work would you want to do? Discuss your answers in a small group.

What Do You Think? In your opinion, why is it important that we work for the common good?

(t)NASA Headquarters - GReatest Images of NASA (NASA-HQ-GRIN); (b)Ariel Skelley/Blend Images/Getty Images
TEXT: Kennedy, John F. Inaugural Address of President John F. Kennedy. Washington D.C., January 20, 1961.

How Have Heroes Helped Their Communities?

What Is a Hero?

Heroes are people who have done great things or behaved with great honor. Heroes can be young or old, boys or girls. We see superheroes with amazing powers in movies or on television shows. Everyday people can be heroes, too. Teachers, firefighters, police officers, nurses, and others in your community are heroes. The person who smiles and makes you feel better when you're having a bad day is a hero. Think about some of your everyday heroes.

A firefighter can be a hero.

Rick Rhay/E+/Getty Images

HSS.3.4.2, HSS.3.4.6

Our nation's history is filled with heroes. Women and men fought for the freedoms we enjoy every day. They fought for freedom of speech, the right to vote, and the right to attend school. They fought so that all Americans would have equality, or equal **rights**.

In this lesson you will read about some of our nation's heroes. All of them risked their lives to change their communities. They also changed our nation. The stories of their lives will help you understand how people can solve problems and create positive changes.

Martin Luther King Jr.

Thomas Jefferson

(l)Comstock Production Department/Alamy Stock Photo; (r)U.S. News & World Report Magazine Photograph Collection, Library of Congress, LC-DIG-ppmsc-01269, (inset)John Parrot/Stocktrek Images/Getty Images

American Heroes

Thomas Jefferson and Benjamin Franklin are heroes who helped create our country. They worked together with others to write the Declaration of Independence. This document is dated July 4, 1776, and it lists the reasons why Americans wanted to be free from Great Britain. Jefferson was a skilled writer who wrote most of the document.

Franklin and Jefferson working on the Declaration of Independence

Benjamin Franklin was also important because of work he did to form our government. Franklin was a member of the Constitutional Convention. He worked with other leaders to organize the government of our new nation. Franklin asked Congress to end slavery in our new nation, but Congress refused. It took more than 70 years for another American hero named Abraham Lincoln to bring an end to slavery in the United States.

On January 1, 1863, President Abraham Lincoln issued the Emancipation Proclamation. This was an executive order that freed our country's enslaved people. Lincoln spoke out against slavery and worked to end it.

(t)kittimages/iStockphoto/Getty Images (inset)John Parrot/Stocktrek Images/Getty Images

PRIMARY SOURCE

In Their Words... Abraham Lincoln

"I do order and declare that all persons held as slaves within said designated States, and parts of States, are, and henceforward shall be free; and that the executive government of the United States, including the military and naval authorities thereof, will recognize and maintain the freedom of said persons."

—from the Emancipation Proclamation

Abraham Lincoln

Harriet Tubman and Frederick Douglass also worked to end slavery. Both were born into slavery. They were able to escape and then worked to free others. Tubman risked her life leading enslaved people to freedom. The routes she followed and the houses where people could hide were known as the Underground Railroad. Tubman helped many people to freedom.

Frederick Douglass taught himself to read and write. He started a newspaper to speak out against slavery. He gave speeches to tell how he suffered in slavery. Even after slavery became illegal, African Americans were not given the same rights as other people. Douglass continued to work for equality for all people.

COLLABORATE

Stop and Check

Talk How were Tubman and Douglass similar?

Find Details As you read, add new information to the graphic organizer on page 225 in your Inquiry Journal.

PHOTO: Popular Graphic Arts Collection, Library of Congress, LC-USZ62-2070
TEXT: Lincoln, Abraham. The Emancipation Proclamation. Washington, D.C., January 1, 1863.

As you have read, African Americans were not treated equally even after slavery ended. It took another 100 years and the work of heroes such as Dr. Martin Luther King Jr. to bring equality to African Americans. Dr. King was an African American minister who spoke out against segregation. Segregation is the separation of people by the color of their skin. Dr. King asked government leaders to change segregation laws. He led peaceful protest marches. He refused to use violence to meet his goals. Dr. King was killed in 1968 while working for civil rights. The country celebrates his birthday each January.

Many other American heroes risked their lives to bring equality to people. Before 1920, women were not allowed to vote in the United States. Elizabeth Cady Stanton and Susan B. Anthony worked to change that. They worked to bring equal rights to all women.

Another American hero, Dennis Banks, helped found the American Indian Movement. The goal of this organization was to bring civil rights to American Indians. Banks fought for fair and equal treatment for American Indians.

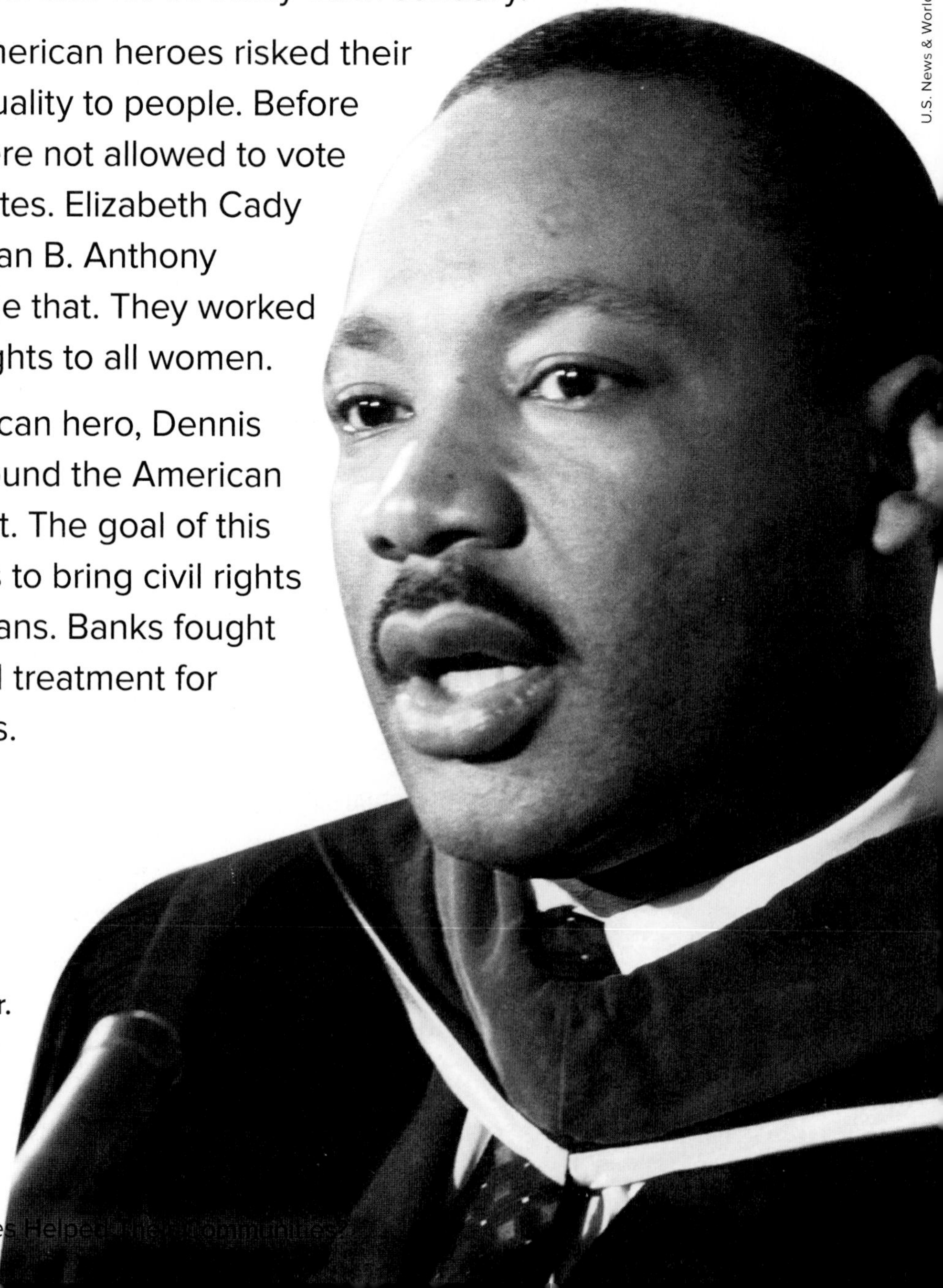

Martin Luther King Jr.

U.S. News & World Report Magazine Photograph Collection, Library of

Humanitarian Heroes

Some heroes work to make the world a better, safer place to live. These people are called humanitarian heroes. Clara Barton was a humanitarian hero. She helped get medicine and supplies to soldiers who were sick and hurt during the Civil War. She earned the nickname "angel of the battlefield." When a war started in Europe, Barton helped provide supplies for people there. Barton also convinced people in the government to sign the Geneva Convention, an agreement on how to treat sick and wounded soldiers. In 1881, she started the organization that is now known as the American Red Cross.

Clara Barton, a pioneer in nursing

Around the World

The American Red Cross is part of an international group. The Red Cross helps people around the world during war and natural disasters. When there are earthquakes, floods, hurricanes, or tornadoes, the Red Cross brings food and medical supplies. It also helps provide places for people to stay and helps them find loved ones who are missing.

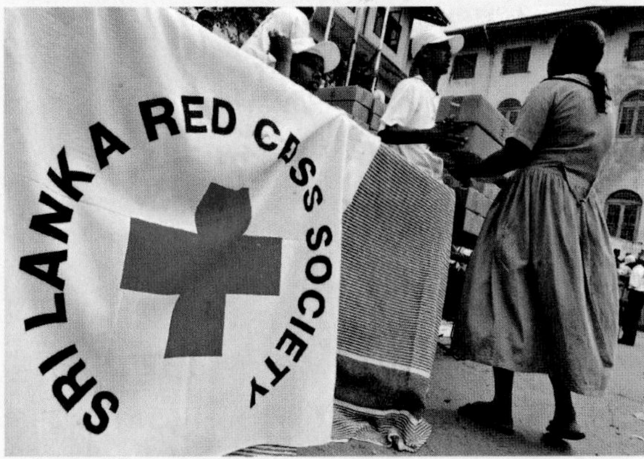

The Red Cross in action

Stop and Check

Think Why do you think equality is important? How did the actions of these heroes make a difference?

(t)taviphoto/iStockphoto/Getty Images; (b)JIMIN LAI/AFP/Getty Images; (inset)U.S. Farm Security Administration/Office of War Information/Office of Emergency Management/Resettlement Administration Black & White Photographs, Library of Congress, LC-USW33-042483-ZC

Biography

Eleanor Roosevelt

Eleanor Roosevelt was born in New York in 1884. In 1905, she married Franklin D. Roosevelt. Her husband began working in politics. She helped him with his work. Franklin Roosevelt became governor of New York in 1929. He was elected president in 1932.

Eleanor Roosevelt changed the role of First Lady. She often traveled around the country for President Roosevelt. This was because Franklin had a disease called polio. This made it hard for him to walk and to travel. When she returned from her trips, she told the president what she had seen. She also wrote a newspaper column and spoke at meetings. As First Lady, Mrs. Roosevelt worked for the rights of women, African Americans, and other groups.

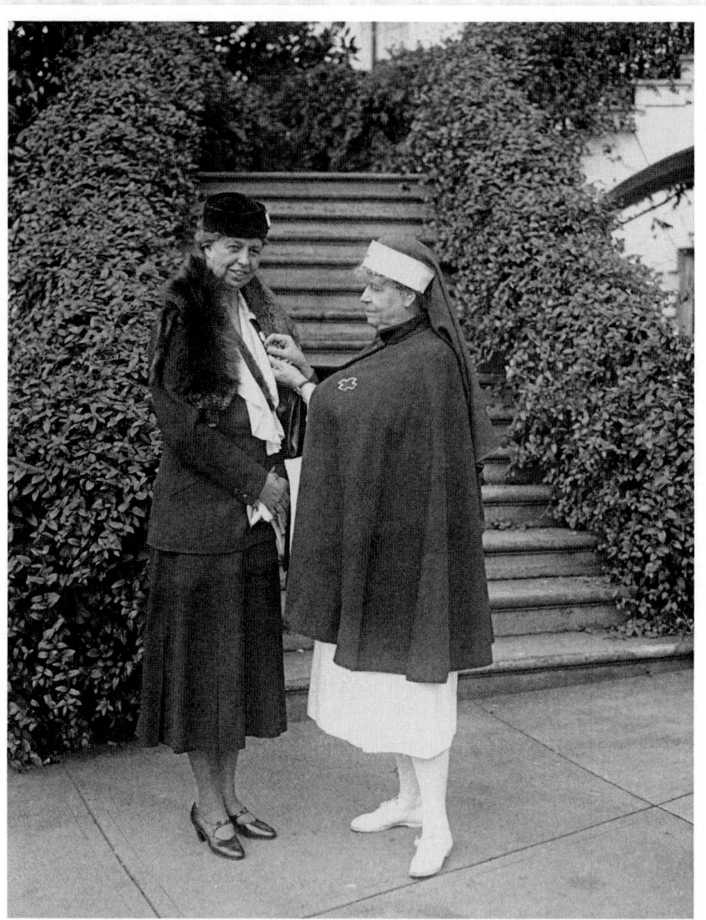

Eleanor Roosevelt receiving a pin from the Red Cross

Harris & Ewing Photographs, Library of Congress, LC-DIG-hec-46973; (bkgd)McGraw-Hill Education

Eleanor Roosevelt continued to work for Americans even after she was no longer the First Lady. She worked at the United Nations and helped write the Universal Declaration of Human Rights. This document lists basic rights that all people should have. It says that all people have the right to life, liberty, and security. Many of the rights listed in this document are also found in the U.S. Bill of Rights. Eleanor Roosevelt spent her life helping others. The work she did helped to bring equality to many people.

PRIMARY SOURCE

In Their Words... Eleanor Roosevelt

"It is not a treaty; it is not an international agreement. It is not and does not purport to be a statement of law or of legal obligation. It is a Declaration of basic principles of human rights and freedoms, to be stamped with the approval of the General Assembly by formal vote of its members, and to serve as a common standard of achievement for all peoples of all nations."

—A speech on the adoption of the Universal Declaration of Human Rights (1948)

Mrs. Roosevelt holding a large copy of the Universal Declaration of Human Rights in 1947

Stop and Check

Talk Why is the Universal Declaration of Human Rights important?

PHOTO:Fotosearch/Archive Photos/Getty Images
TEXT: The Department of State Bulletin, Volume XIX: Numbers 470-495. Washington, D.C.:U.S. Government Printing Office, July-December 1948

Heroes Today

Heroes are found everywhere. Some heroes fought for equality in education. Before the 1950s, black students and white students in many states were not allowed to go to school together. They were segregated, or legally separated. In 1954, the U.S. Supreme Court heard the case of a third grade African American girl named Linda Brown. The case was called *Brown* v. *Board of Education*. The Supreme Court ruled that in education, separate can never be equal. It ended the legal segregation of schools.

Linda Brown answering questions from the press in 1984

Did You Know?

Linda Brown lived in Topeka, Kansas. She had to attend school a mile from her home, even though there was one much closer. The school near her home was for white children only. She was not allowed to go there. She had to attend a school for African American students. Her court case changed segregation laws. As an adult, Linda Brown continued to speak against segregation.

Don Hogan Charles/Archive Photos/Getty Images

Heroes are people who take action when they see a problem in their communities. They may clean trash from the side of a road or the local park, or shovel mud out of flooded homes. Some heroes visit the elderly and help them with chores. Other heroes plant new seeds on hillsides after a large fire. All of these people do what they can to make their communities better places to live. Sometimes they do big things and become famous. Sometimes only a few people know what they have done. They are all heroes.

Helping someone who needs assistance

Stop and Check

Think What can you do to be a local hero?

What Do You Think? Who do you think is a hero in your community?

Datacraft Co Ltd/imagenavi/Getty Images

How Can Citizens Build Strong Communities?

What Makes a Strong Community?

A community is a group of people who live in the same area. Families shop at the same stores and go to the same parks. The children in a community often go to the same schools. To make a community strong, people need to work together. Leaders serve the community. They listen to **citizens** and work to improve life for everyone. The people in the community trust them to make good decisions.

Citizens help their leaders by giving their opinions and volunteering their time. People in communities work with community leaders to have good schools for their children. They work together to build businesses and provide jobs for people. People in communities work with their leaders and each other to take care of the environment. They also respect each other and make sure everyone is treated fairly.

Sean D/Shutterstock.com

HSS.3.4.2

Recycling is good for our environment.

JGI/Jamie Grill/Blend Images LLC

Building a Stronger California

How have some Californians helped make their communities even stronger? Read about how ordinary people are working to make their state extraordinary.

Colin and Karen Archipley own a farming business called Archi's Acres. It is located in Escondido. They have an organic greenhouse business that uses the natural resources in their area. They grow basil, kale, and other herbs and produce. They give back to their community by producing healthy foods in ways that help the environment. They also help their community by training others to grow crops in this way.

An organic greenhouse at Archi's Acres

Did You Know?

California has been in a drought. Warmer winters reduce the amount of snow in the mountains. This means less water and drier soil for the rest of the state. The governor asked people to reduce their use of water. In just a few short months, Californians saved enough water to give millions of people water for a year! Citizens are now working to make water conservation a way of life.

Sandy Huffaker/Corbis Historical/Getty Images

Besma Coda works with people who have come to California from Middle Eastern countries. She is part of a program in El Cajon that helps people settle into their new communities. It helps people find health care, schools, and other services they need. Coda works to help people find a better way of life.

Besma Coda

Anna Cuevas works for the National Urban League. This organization helps people living in cities. Cuevas writes a blog that gives people free information on how to manage their money.

Teresa Cheng works for people's **rights**. Her work began as a student at the University of Southern California. Teresa led a group that helped people learn about the rights of factory workers. Workers need to be paid fairly. They also need safe factories. Her work has forced companies to treat their workers better.

Stop and Check

COLLABORATE

Talk How have these people made California stronger? Why is it important for us to help people in our community?

Find Details As you read, add new information to the graphic organizer on page 233 in your Inquiry Journal.

ZUMA/Alamy Stock Photo

What Makes a Good Leader?

It takes a good leader to help communities grow. Let's read about some qualities a leader needs.

Good leaders who want their communities to grow work hard with everyone else. Good leaders are honest. They say what they mean, and they keep their promises.

Good leaders understand the needs of others. They can help the community make sure it meets everyone's needs.

Good leaders think about what the community needs. They work with citizens and other leaders to find solutions to problems.

Good leaders know how to communicate their ideas. They encourage people to work together to develop ideas that are good for the community.

Good leaders know they cannot do everything by themselves. They ask people in the community to help because they know a strong team is important.

How can you be a good leader in your community?

Leaders in your community

(t)CSA Plastock/CSA Images/Getty Images; (bl)Neil Setchfield/Alamy Stock Photo; (br)arsenik/E+/Getty Images

Biography

Patricia Castellanos

In 2013, Patricia Castellanos brought together different organizations to clean up ports and docks in Los Angeles. Ships and trucks created pollution. This caused diseases such as asthma and cancer. Because of Patricia's work, the Harbor Commission started a Clean Truck Program. Now ships and trucks create much less pollution. People in the area have better air to breathe. They are able to lead healthier lives.

PRIMARY SOURCE

In Their Words... Dr. Karen Smith

"Health begins in our homes, schools, workplaces, neighborhoods, and communities. To have healthy people and healthy communities, we have to create the social and physical environments that give every Californian the opportunities we need to be healthy."

—Dr. Smith is the Director of the California Department of Public Health.

Stop and Check

Think How did Patricia Castellanos show that she was a good leader?

PHOTO: 1996-98 AccuSoft Inc/Glow Images, TEXT: Smith, Karen. Health Leaders Invite Innovation to Improve California's Health. Sacramento, CA. September 14, 2016.

Ways to Make a Difference

How can you make a difference in your community? First you should do research to find out about good things and things that need to be better. Then think about ways you can help make things better. There are many ways you can make a difference.

You can write a letter to the editor of your local newspaper to let more people know about a problem. You can also write a letter to one of your community or state leaders. Your letter should clearly explain the problem. It should also give ideas for possible solutions. Include any research you have done when you send your letter.

If you like to talk, you can ask to speak at a town meeting. A town meeting is a time when members of a community come together to talk about issues that face the community. A town meeting is a good place to talk directly to the leaders of your community. It is also a good place to ask questions.

People raising issues at a town meeting

Don Hammond/Design Pics

Another way to make a difference is by organizing people. You can organize a rally to tell your community about a problem. You can talk with business owners about ways to make the community better. You can organize a group that collects trash one day a week in the public areas of your neighborhood.

You can also find out about groups in your community that are already doing something to make a difference. There are groups that build houses for people, run food pantries, and collect used clothing. Other groups collect toys for children in the hospital. Look for a group that is doing something to fix a problem you see. Ask them how you can participate.

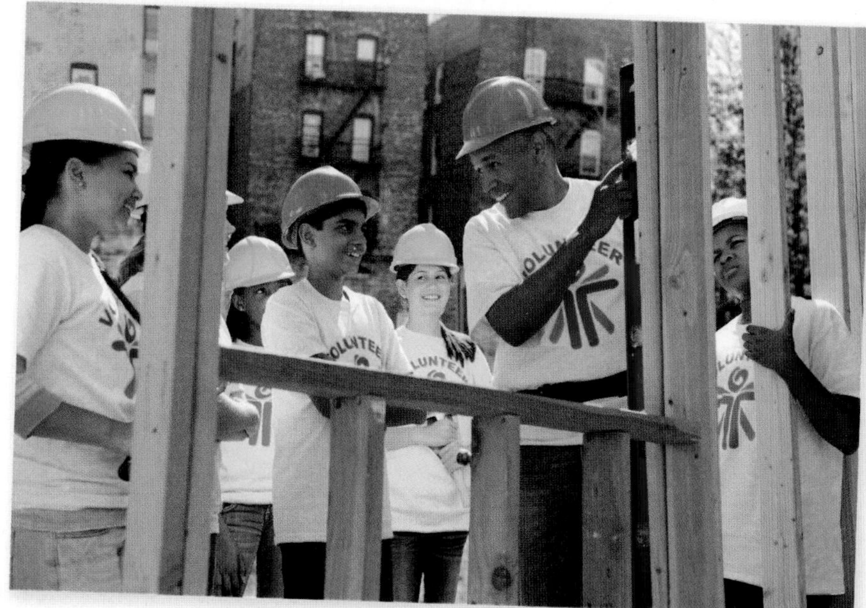

Students building houses for others in the community

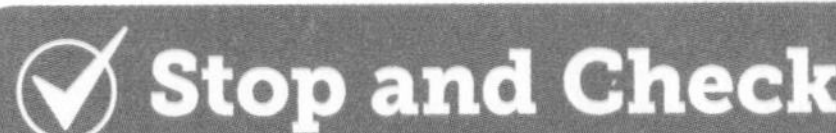

Stop and Check

Talk What skills do you have? How can you use your skills to help your community make a change for the better?

What Do You Think? Can you have a strong community without good leaders? Why or why not?

Kidstock/Image Source

Connections in Action

Back to the EQ

Think about the chapter EQ, **"How do our government and its citizens work together?"**

- **Talk** with a partner about the ways American citizens and the government work together. List ways that students your age could work with your community's government. What could government leaders learn from working with students? What could students learn from working with government leaders?
- **Share** your list with the class.

(tl)Tom Williams/CQ-Roll Call Group/Getty Images; (r)U.S. News & World Report Magazine Photograph Collection, Library of Congress, LC-DIG-ppmsca-49864; (bl)Don Hammond/Design Pics

More to Explore

How can you make an IMPACT?

Write a Letter to the Mayor

Think about how your community could be a better place to live. Write a letter to the mayor describing your ideas. Begin your letter with a short summary of your ideas. Then tell why you think your ideas will improve your community. Use at least one vocabulary word in your letter.

Citizenship in Action

Think of ways that you and your classmates can be good citizens. Then work with a partner or small group to create a skit that shows how to be a good citizen. Write a script and make sure that each of you has a role. Perform the skit for the class.

Create a National Symbol

You have read about some symbols that have meaning to all Americans. These include our flag and the Statue of Liberty. Imagine that you have been asked to create a new national symbol. Create a sketch of your symbol. Write a short paragraph that tells what the symbol represents and why you chose the design.

Chapter 5 Economics of the Local Region

How Do People in a Community Meet Their Needs?

People work to earn money. This allows them to buy the things they need and want. In this chapter, you will read about the goods and services provided by California businesses. You will learn how people and businesses make and spend money. You will also explore how trade-offs affect our spending choices. As you read, think about how you can make good choices when you spend your money.

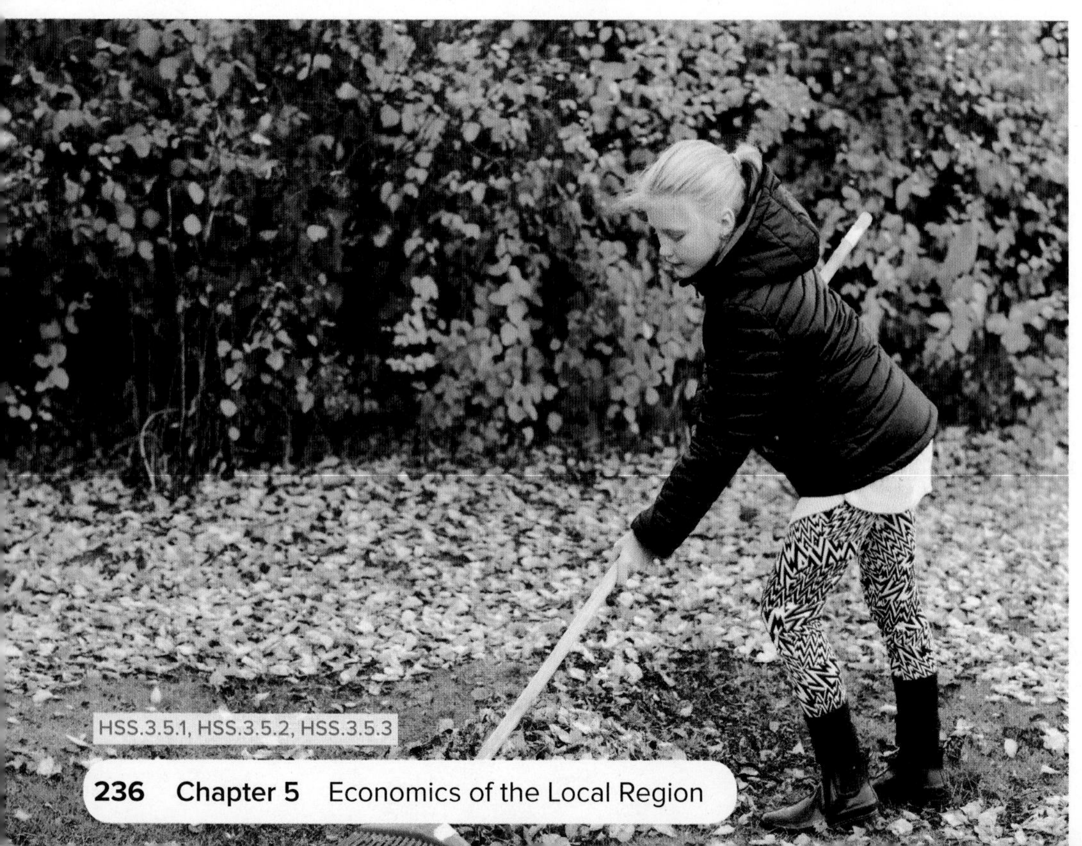

Even you can earn money selling goods or services.

Jdandanell/iStock/Getty Images

HSS.3.5.1, HSS.3.5.2, HSS.3.5.3

How Do People Meet Their Needs?

Today people buy many of the things they need. But first they must have money to do so.

Spending money at local stores helps people in your community. The money you spend provides an income for the business owners and their employees. The money they earn can be spent on items that they need or want. In this way, everybody in your community can meet their needs.

Earning money takes time and effort. You may wish to spend your money as soon as you get it. But you should think before you buy. You may need money later to buy something that you really need. Sometimes, saving money rather than spending it is how people can best meet their needs.

Importing goods helps people get items that their country can't make or grow. This helps both the business that exports the goods and the people buying them. The business makes money and the buyers get the goods they need.

(t)Steve Hix/Corbis/Getty Images; (bl)Chris Ryan/age fotostock; (br)barmalini/iStock/Getty Images

Connect Through Literature

Clothes with an IQ

by Meg Moss

Art by Dave Clark

Smarty Pants

Some new fabrics can track your body's motions and functions. These e-textiles don't look much different from ordinary clothing, even though they have electronic components and electrical circuits woven right in. Some monitor heart rate and blood pressure. This is great for people with heart problems. Runners may someday wear pants that measure their speed, distance, and gait. Or how about a backpack that knows what you've forgotten? These work with computer chips that can be programmed to identify all the stuff you want to carry and alert you when something is missing.

Super Suits

In space, one tiny hole in your suit can be deadly. Astronauts working outside their spacecraft depend on their suits. Space suits help keep their bodies properly pressurized. Some researchers have developed a suit layered with high-tech fabrics and gel. If a smidge of space debris punctures the suit, the gel oozes into the hole to seal it up. If a larger hole opens up, tiny computers in the fabric alert the astronaut to head for the nearest space capsule.

(bkgd)McGraw-Hill Education

Plug It In

Ever want a piece of toast on the beach or a hair dryer on the ski slope? We aren't there yet, but some companies are developing jackets that can charge your electronic toys. Just strap on a solar panel and plug in your phone or iPod. Another jacket charges batteries and powers devices by turning the vibrations of your body into electrical energy.

Better Than Skin

For superheroes and ski racers, it's all about speed. The developers of this new fabric studied the skin of sharks and the dimples on golf balls. They wanted to find out what kind of surface helps an object move the fastest. The result is a stretchy, skintight material that is carefully woven in a special pattern to lower wind resistance. For clumsy superheroes and ski racers, the fabric can be made with remarkable padding that hardens on impact and then softens up again.

Think About It

1. What are some ways "clothes with an IQ" can help keep us safe?
2. Why do you think it's dangerous for an astronaut's suit to have a hole in it?
3. Which of the "clothes with an IQ" do you think is most useful? Use details from the text to explain your choice.

"Clothes with an IQ" by Meg Moss, art by Dave Clark from ASK, February 2008, © by Carus Publishing Company. Reproduced with permission. All Cricket Media material is copyrighted by Carus Publishing Company, d/b/a Cricket Media, and/or various authors and illustrators. Any commercial use or distribution of material without permission is strictly prohibited. Please visit http://www.cricketmedia.com/info/licensing2 for licensing and http://www.cricketmedia.com for subscriptions.

How Do Businesses Use Resources?

What Is Economics?

Alex walks his neighbor's dog to earn money. What will he do with the money? His parents pay for the things he needs. Needs are things you cannot live without, like food and clothing. So Alex can spend the money on things he wants. Wants are things that you do not really need but that are nice to have. Maybe he will buy goods or services. Goods are something you can use, like comic books. Services are something a person does for you. For example, a person might give you a guitar lesson.

The study of how people use money, goods, resources, and services is called economics. Sellers provide goods and services to buyers. Buyers use money to pay for these goods and services. Buyers and sellers work together so people can get what they want and need.

FineArtCraig/iStock/Getty Images

HSS.3.5.1, HSS.3.5.2

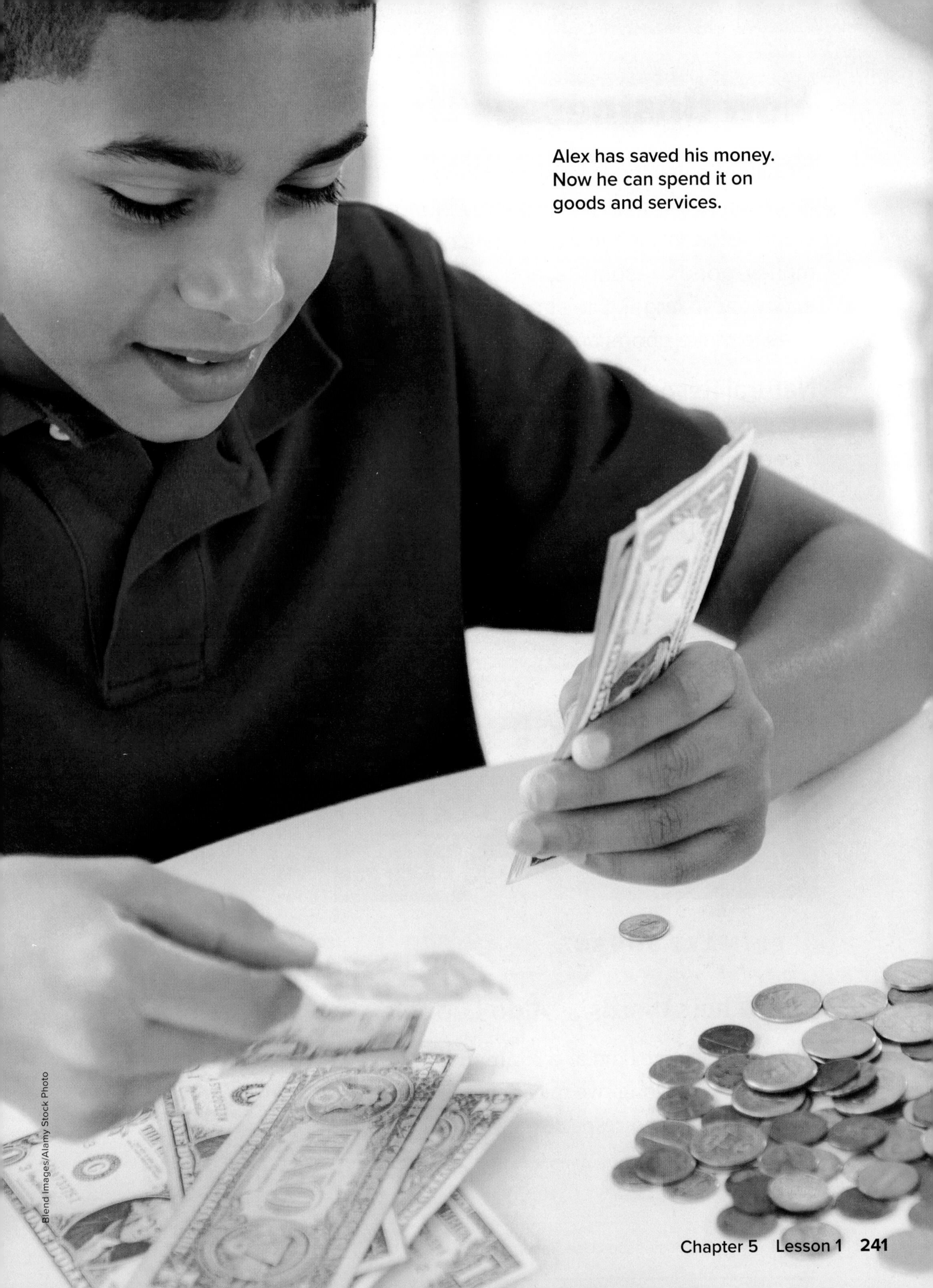

Alex has saved his money. Now he can spend it on goods and services.

Blend Images/Alamy Stock Photo

How Businesses Use Resources

California has the largest **economy** in the United States. It is even larger than the economy of most countries in the world! Economy is the way a state or country uses its money, goods, resources, and services. Why is California's economy so large? The state has many resources that it uses to make goods and provide services.

Natural Resources

California has many natural resources. Natural resources come from nature. In California, many goods come from the land. Fruits, vegetables, and livestock are grown and raised on farms. Farmers sell these goods to people all across the world.

PRIMARY SOURCE

In Their Words... Aldo Leopold

"When we see land as a community to which we belong, we may begin to use it with love and respect."

—from *A Sand Country Almanac*, 1949

TEXT: Leopold, Aldo. *A Sand County Almanac and Sketches Here and There.* New York: Oxford University Press, 1949.
PHOTO: (t)Everett Collection Historical/Alamy Stock Photo; (b)Thomas Arbour/iStock/Getty Images

California also has other natural resources. Lumber comes from the northern forests. Seafood is caught off the coast. Minerals are mined in the desert region. Energy resources are also important to California's economy. Water power and wind energy help to create electricity. Solar panels collect sunlight and turn the energy into electricity, too. Electricity powers homes and businesses so they can create goods and services.

Water, wind, and sun are renewable resources. These are resources that can be replaced over time. Other energy resources are nonrenewable resources. These natural resources cannot be replaced. Petroleum is a nonrenewable resource. Oil refining plants in San Francisco and Los Angeles turn petroleum into gasoline. Companies sell the gasoline to make money.

COLLABORATE

Stop and Check

Talk Discuss with a partner the kinds of natural resources that California has. How do people use these resources?

Find Details As you read, add new information to the graphic organizer on page 247 in your Inquiry Journal.

Ted Mead/Gary Weathers/Brand X/Getty Images

Solar panels in the California desert

Human Resources

California has many **human resources**. Human resources are the people who work for a business or person. People with ideas and skills provide services. Engineers design airplanes. Programmers write computer software. Factory workers turn cotton into clothing. Actors and directors create movies. These workers are all important resources.

Tourism is a big part of California's economy. The money that tourists spend helps our economy. The tourist industry uses human resources, too. Park rangers and tour guides help visitors learn about California's environment. Staff members at amusement parks and zoos answer questions from tourists. Bus drivers, hotel clerks, and other people who provide services help tourists as well.

Human Capital

Businesses look for people with the skills, knowledge, and experience to do a job well. These characteristics are known as **human capital**. A person's human capital can add value to a business. If a person lacks skills or experience, it can take away value. As we learn, we gain skills, knowledge, and experience. This helps us develop our human capital.

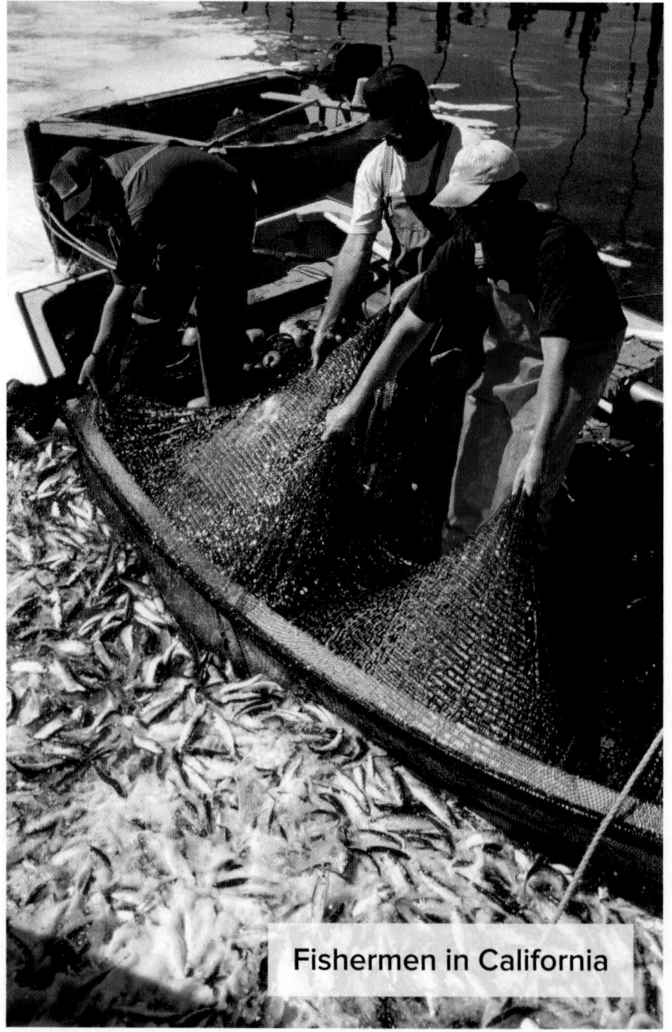
Fishermen in California

Brian Atkinson/Alamy Stock Photo

Capital Resources

The fishing industry is important to California. For example, men and women who work in the fishing industry catch many pounds of tuna. But how does the tuna get from the boat into the can? Factories use special machines to process the fish. A factory is a place that makes goods. The machines put the fish into cans. People who work in the factory operate the machines. They also load the cans onto trucks to deliver them to stores.

Canning machines are an example of a **capital resource**. Capital resources are the tools and machines that people use to make other goods. People in California build airplanes, make bread, and create movies. Each of these businesses uses capital resources to make goods.

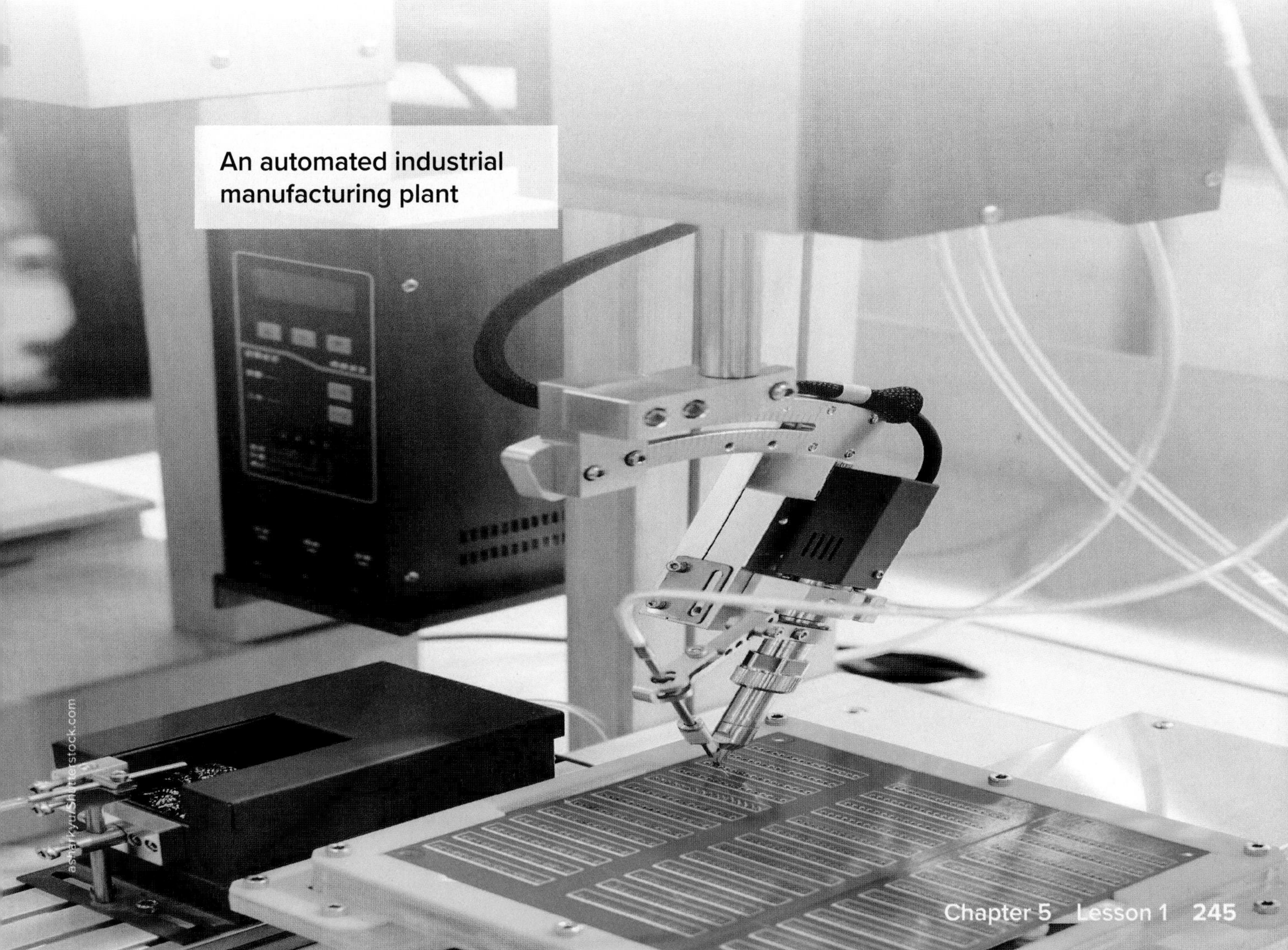

An automated industrial manufacturing plant

asharkyu/Shutterstock.com

A Day in the Life

A RESTAURANT OWNER

Camilla owns a restaurant. She needs resources to run it. She uses natural resources to make the food. Camilla buys avocados at a farmers' market. When she goes to the market, she is the buyer. She uses the avocados to make guacamole. In the kitchen, Camilla turns on the lights and washes her hands at a faucet. Her mixer makes it easy to make large batches of guacamole. She uses these capital resources and tools to make meals for her customers.

Camilla helps her community when she buys goods from local farmers.

slobo/iStock/Getty Images; (bkgd)McGraw-Hill Education

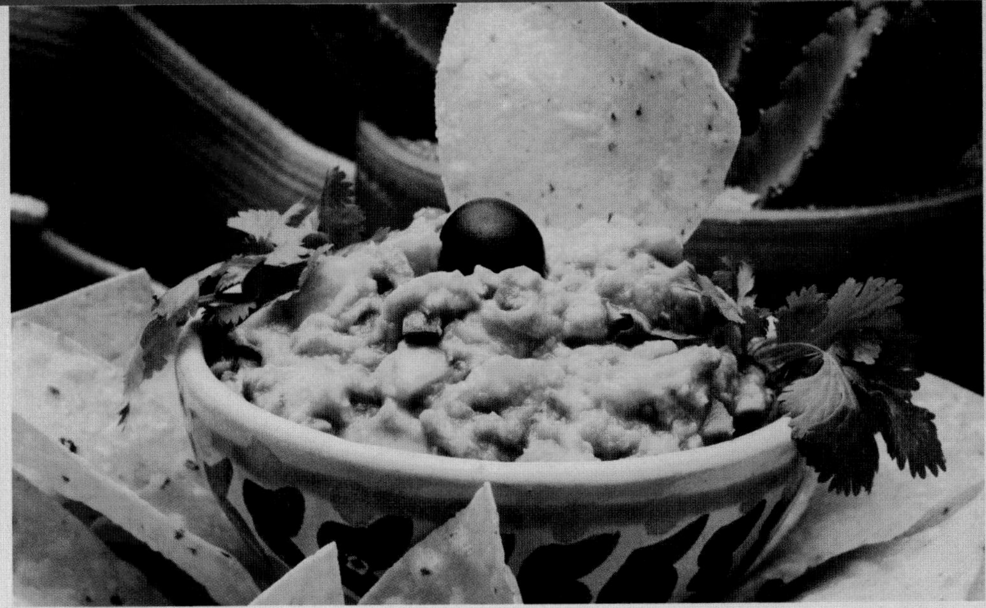

Camilla uses many resources to provide her customers with meals.

People love to go to Camilla's restaurant. When she is working, Camilla is the seller. She gives her customers food and they pay her for it. But Camilla needs help. The workers she hires are the human resources she needs. The workers provide services, such as making food, waiting on tables, and washing dishes. Camilla is also an employer.

At the end of the day, the restaurant has earned money. Camilla uses some of the money to pay workers. She saves some money to buy more avocados and to pay taxes to the government. She keeps some for herself. She can spend this money on things she wants and needs. Camilla has had a busy day!

Stop and Check

COLLABORATE

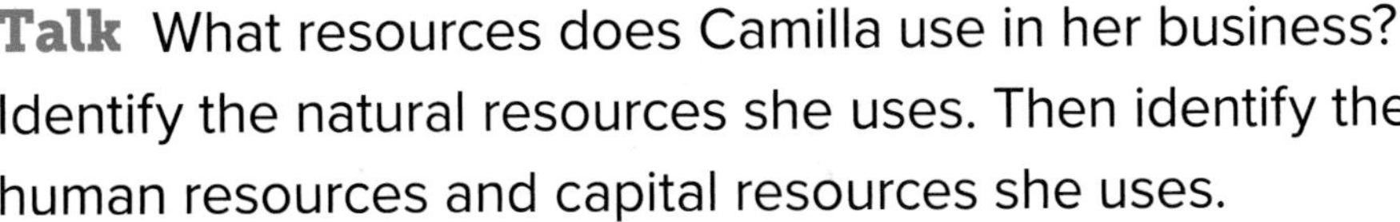

Talk What resources does Camilla use in her business? Identify the natural resources she uses. Then identify the human resources and capital resources she uses.

What Do You Think? Businesses use natural, human, and capital resources. Which are most expensive? Which are most important?

PureStock/Getty Images; (bkgd)McGraw-Hill Education

How Have Goods and Services Changed Over Time?

Goods and Services in California

California's **economy** has changed over time. Many people came to the state looking for gold in the 1800s. Others became storekeepers and sold goods to gold seekers. Some hired workers to work in their stores. Farmers also came to California. California was the perfect place to grow wheat, fruits, and vegetables. In the early 1800s, farmers began growing citrus fruits, such as oranges and lemons. By the early 1900s, there were more than 4 million citrus trees. Today, California produces more than half of the country's fruits and vegetables!

In the early 1900s, California also produced more petroleum than any other state. The oil industry helped many other businesses grow. In the 1940s, aircraft plants and shipyards grew. Universities and colleges also grew in the mid-1900s. Many people came to California to work in these industries.

A pickaxe is used to look for gold.

wawritto/iStock/Getty Images

HSS.3.5.2, HAS.CS.1

California oil fields, Los Angeles, 1906

Stereographs, Library of Congress, LC-USZ62-72117

California's four main regions all have strong economies.

The Central Valley continues to be California's main farming region. About one-third of all the farm-produced food in the United States comes from here.

Today, however, crops are also grown in California's desert region. Water is brought from other regions. Dates and grapefruit are grown in Coachella Valley. Farmers in the Colorado Desert grow alfalfa, sugar beets, and cotton.

Shipping and fishing are important industries for the coastal region. Cities along the coast have other major industries today, too. The modern technology and film industries developed there over the past hundred years.

California's mountain region produces lumber. In the 1800s, animals helped move heavy logs. By the 1930s, loggers used tractors and trucks to move logs. Today, technology helps produce more useable lumber from each tree. This protects the environment by using fewer trees.

Grapes were first grown in California in the late 1700s.

Tetra Images/Alamy Stock Photo

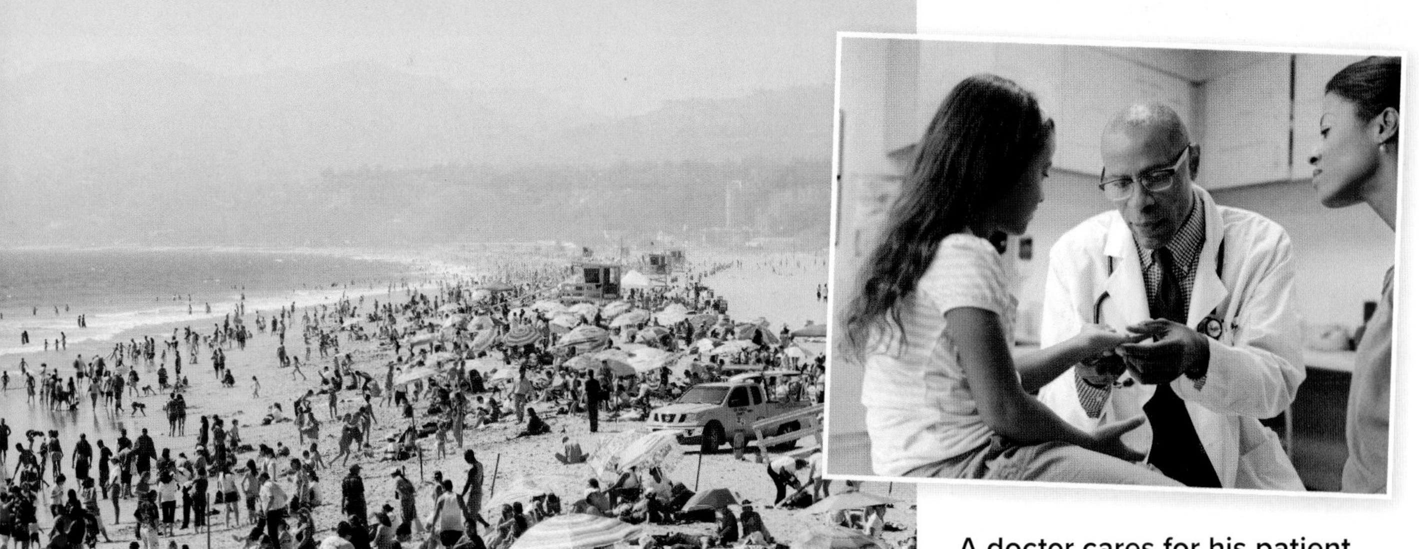

A doctor cares for his patient.

Tourists enjoy the beaches of California.

The tourism and service industries are important in all regions of California. Visitors love the natural beauty of the state's parks, mountains, deserts, and beaches. Theme parks like Disneyland, SeaWorld, and Universal Studios attract millions of tourists each year. Cities such as Los Angeles and San Francisco offer sightseeing, shopping, dining, and entertainment. The tourism industry needs lots of service workers. Hotel rooms need to be cleaned. Meals need to be cooked and served. Tourism is one of the largest industries in the state. Doctors, nurses, dentists, and teachers are also part of the service industry.

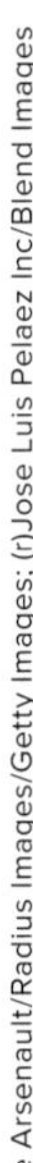

(l)Pierre Arsenault/Radius Images/Getty Images; (r)Jose Luis Pelaez Inc/Blend Images

Stop and Check

COLLABORATE

Talk Which industries are linked to specific regions in California? Why?

Find Details As you read, add new information to the graphic organizer on page 255 in your Inquiry Journal.

What Do You Think? What goods or services do you think are most important to California's economy? Why?

Then and Now

CALIFORNIA'S RAILROADS OVER TIME

California's first settlers from the East had a difficult journey. Crossing the mountains on foot or in wagons was hard. When gold was discovered in 1848, more settlers made the journey.

In 1863, two railroad companies began connecting rail lines. One began laying track from Sacramento heading east. The other started in Omaha, Nebraska, heading west. After more than six years, the rail lines met in Utah. California was now connected to the rest of the nation. More railroads were built in the following years, using new and better machines. Travel was faster, easier, and cheaper. A cross-country rail journey once cost $1,000 or more and could take four weeks. Today it costs less than $500 and takes only a little over three days.

Building the Western Pacific Railroad around 1906, using a steam shovel.

Prints and Photographs Division, Library of Congress, LC-USZ62-72117; (bkgd)McGraw-Hill Education.

The railroads transported goods and people to and from the state. They also provided new jobs. Many Chinese immigrants worked to build the railroads. Workers were hired to load goods onto the trains.

New towns popped up along rail lines. Towns grew because they were better connected. When the town of Los Angeles got a direct rail line to the East, its population quickly grew four times larger.

Today, Californians have many ways to travel and move goods. The railroad is not as popular as it once was. However, many cities have newer rail lines. Subways and transit systems help people travel quickly and easily.

Urban transit railroad system

A modern-day train in California

Stop and Check

Think Why did California need railroads? Why are they less important today?

PRIMARY SOURCE

In Their Words... John Moody

"The close relationship between railroad expansion and the general development and prosperity of the country is nowhere brought more distinctly into relief than in connection with the construction of the Pacific Railroads."

—from *The Railroad Builders*, 1919

PHOTO: (t)Medioimages/Superstock; (b)Meinzahn/iStockphoto/Getty Images
TEXT: Moody, John. The Railroad Builders: A Chronicle of the Welding of the States. New Haven:Yale University Press, 1919.

How Do Businesses Make Money?

How Goods Are Made

You've learned that businesses in California provide many goods and services. In this lesson, you'll look more closely at how businesses make money.

Some businesses **manufacture** goods. To manufacture means to make goods using machinery. California factories manufacture computers, clothes, airplane parts, electronics, and many other things.

Let's look at how a company manufactures blue jeans. The company uses cotton to make cloth. Cotton is a natural resource. The company uses machines and other tools to turn the cloth into blue jeans. Machines and tools are **capital resources**. The factory building is also a capital resource. People design the blue jeans and run the machines that make them. These **human resources** are also necessary to make blue jeans.

HSS.3.5.2

andresr/E+/Getty Images

It takes natural resources, capital resources, and human resources to make a pair of blue jeans.

Where Goods Come From

In the past, people made or grew most of the things they needed in their communities. Today, most people buy the goods they need. Some of these goods are manufactured locally. But many of them are made in other places. Countries **import** goods that they cannot grow or make. To import means to bring in goods from another country.

California imports goods such as oil, electronic parts, cars, and clothing. These goods come from countries such as China, Vietnam, Mexico, and Canada. Some of the clothing you wear was imported.

Many goods are imported and exported on huge cargo ships.

Evren Kalinbacak/iStockphoto/Getty Images

The United States **exports** many goods as well. To export means to send goods to another country to sell them. For example, California is one of the world's top producers of almonds. The state grows more almonds than our country needs. California growers export the extra almonds to other countries to be sold.

California imports clothing from other countries.

Goods are moved around the world in many ways. Airplanes move some goods. But most goods are moved to and from the United States on cargo ships. California has several ports that are used by cargo ships. There are large ports in the cities of Oakland, Los Angeles, and Long Beach. Once the goods arrive at the port, they are transported to a factory or store.

Countries all over the world depend on trade to get the goods they need and to make money. Trade is the exchange of goods. This exchange allows countries to sell goods they make and buy goods they cannot make. Exporting goods is one way that businesses make money.

Stop and Check

Talk How does exporting goods help companies? How does importing goods help communities?

Find Details As you read, add new information to the chart on page 263 in your Inquiry Journal.

hadynyah/iStock/Getty Images

Making Money from Imports

California businesses import goods so they can make money. Let's look at a T-shirt as an example. A business might buy the shirt from a factory in Bangladesh and sell it in the United States at a higher price. After paying for the shirt and transportation costs, the money that remains is called a **profit**.

Businesses decide how they want to use these profits. They can build more factories or plant more crops. They can pay their workers higher wages or they can hire new workers. Businesses use profits to continue to grow.

Making and selling goods makes the **economy** stronger. A strong economy means people have jobs and money to spend. Trade helps the economies of California and the United States grow.

Airplane manufacturing plant

California imports cell phones.

(l)Monty Rakusen/Cultura/Getty Images, (r) koya979/Shutterstock.com

Where Does Your T-shirt Come From?

Where do you think your T-shirt was made? Chances are, the tag in it says "Made in Bangladesh" or "Made in Honduras." But that's only part of the story. The trip a T-shirt makes from cotton to a store near you is a long journey.

Cotton grows in Mississippi.

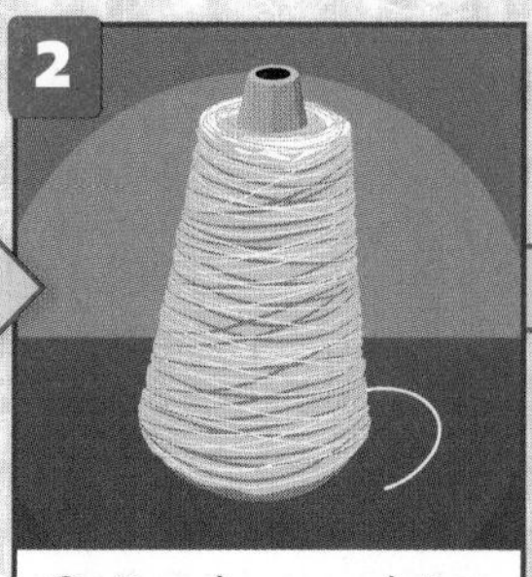

Cotton is spun into yarn in Indonesia.

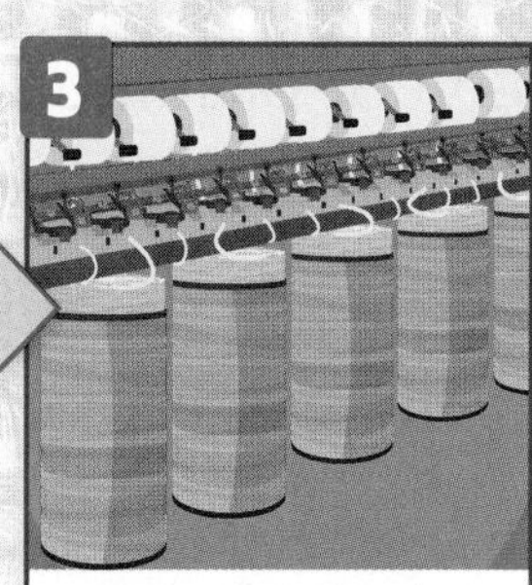

Yarn is knit into cloth in Bangladesh.

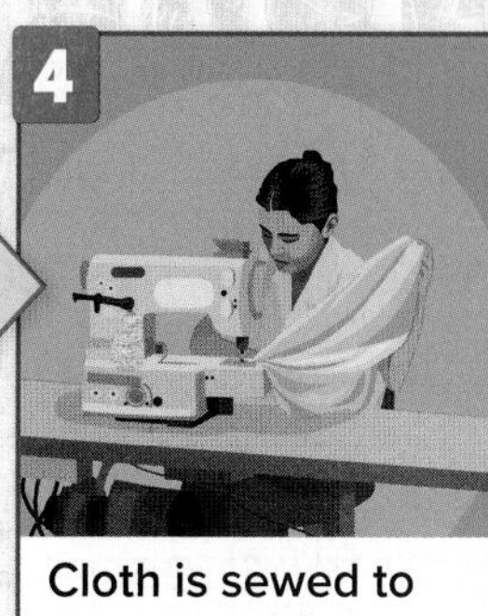

Cloth is sewed to make a T-shirt.

The T-shirt travels to California.

A truck takes the shirt to a store.

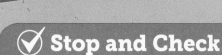

CALIFORNIA
6
MISSISSIPPI
1
5
PACIFIC OCEAN
3 4 BANGLADESH
2
INDONESIA

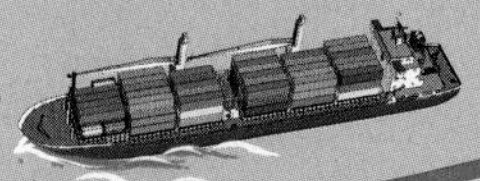

Stop and Check

Perspectives How does a business make a profit when importing goods?

McGraw-Hill Education

Providing Services

You have read that businesses sell goods. Businesses also sell services. Businesses provide many kinds of services. Some businesses have people who teach different skills, like how to dance or ride a horse. Workers at a restaurant provide a service, too. When you go out to dinner, servers take your order, bring your food, and clear the table. Transportation is another service. A taxi driver takes you from one place to another. Doctors and nurses take care of your health. A barber or hair stylist provides a service when he or she gives you a haircut. When people pay for these services, the businesses make money.

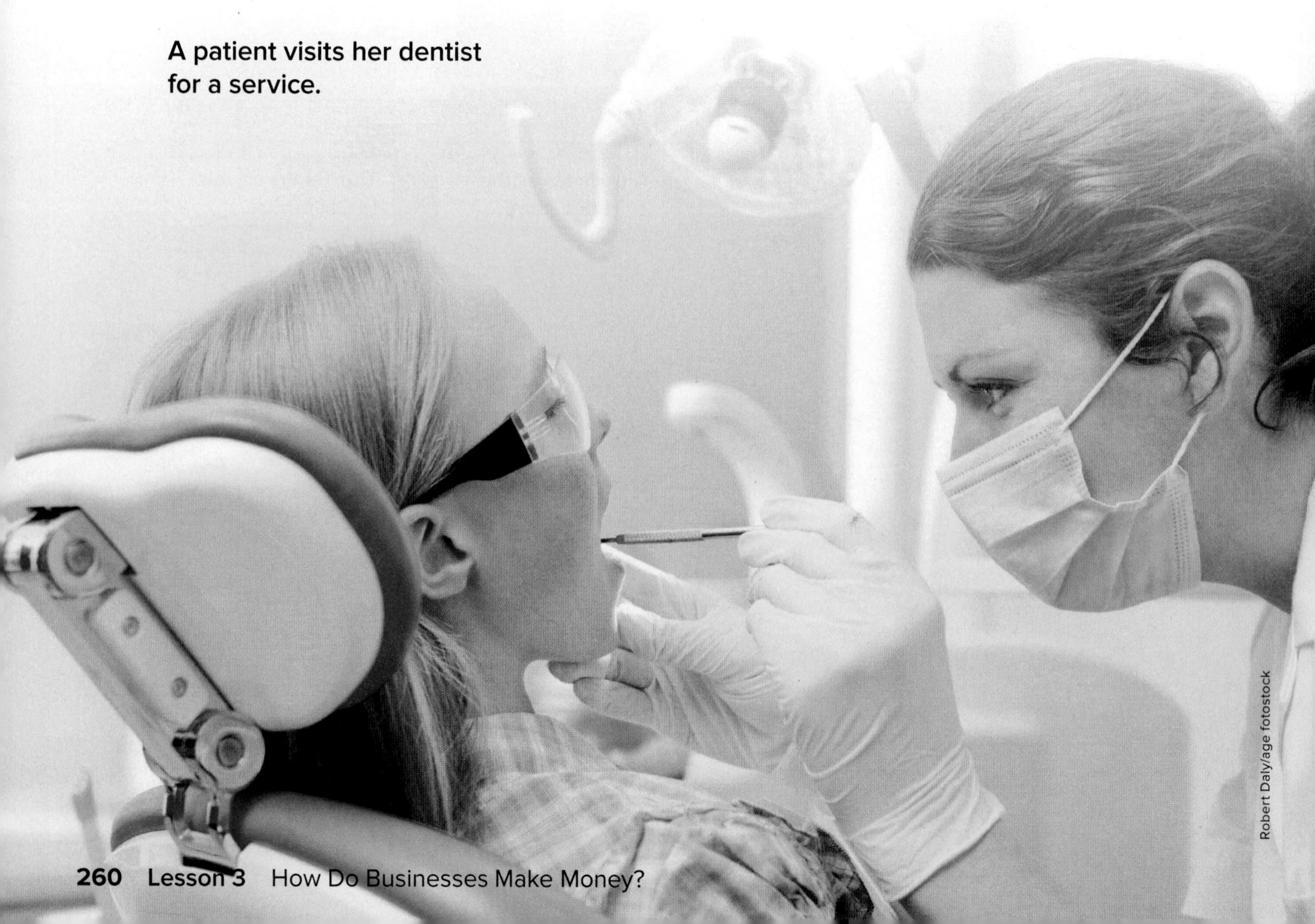

A patient visits her dentist for a service.

Robert Daly/age fotostock

Points of View

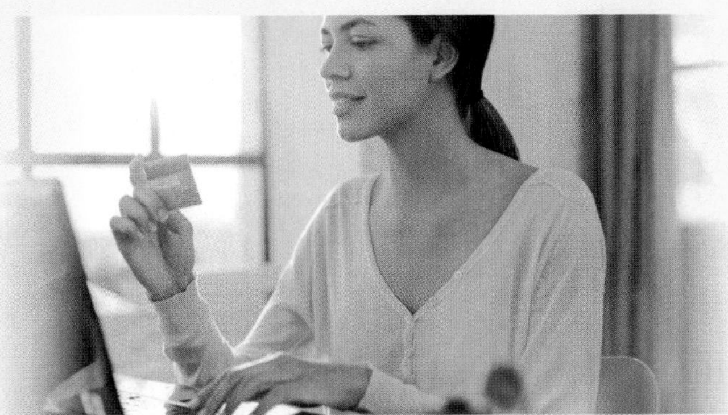

Some businesses like to sell their services online. It does not cost much to get started. It is easy to set up a website. Consumers can visit the website any time, day or night. And the business can sell its services to people all over the country and around the world.

Some businesses find it hard to sell their services online. There may be other businesses selling the same service. Also, some consumers do not like to buy services online. This can make it harder for a business to earn a profit.

Just like businesses that produce goods, people provide services to make money. They set a price that covers how much they spend to provide the service. Then they charge a little more to make a profit. This profit allows people to grow their businesses.

A chef at his restaurant

(t)Caia Images/Glow Images; (b)Monty Rakusen/Cultura RF/Getty Images

 **Stop and Check**

Talk What is a service? With a partner, list examples of service businesses in your community.

Businesses Around the World

Businesses exist all over the world. Everywhere you go, you will find stores, offices, restaurants, and factories. An entrepreneur is a person who starts and runs a business. Entrepreneurs run businesses all over the world.

A "mom and pop" store in India

Many businesses are small stores such as grocery stores and hair salons. They are sometimes called "mom and pop" shops. This is because a family started the business. There may be a local deli or grocery store on a corner near your house. In India, "mom and pop" grocery stores are common. These businesses sell fruit and vegetables to people who can walk to the store. This means that people do not have to drive to larger stores to buy food.

Rice farming in the Philippines

In the Philippines, farmers found that consumers wanted to eat organic food. This is food that is grown without chemicals. Because these farmers do not use chemicals, they protect the soil from harm. The farmers protect the environment and sell healthy products to their customers.

(t)SIBSA Digital Pvt. Ltd./Alamy Stock Photo; (b)Glowimages/Glowimages RF/Getty Images; (bkgd)McGraw-Hill Education

Where in the World?

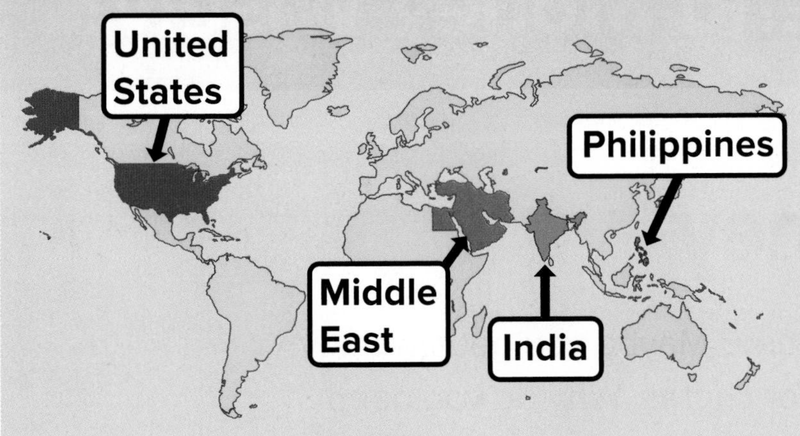

This map shows the regions described on these pages.

Many people today use the Internet to provide services. The Internet allows people to work anywhere in the world. Entrepreneurs create websites and sell products they make themselves. People can work from home and run a business such as computer support. Some women in the Middle East have created online businesses. They can earn money while they care for their families at home.

An entrepreneur presents her ideas to potential customers.

Stop and Check

Write In a short paragraph, tell what an entrepreneur is. Then describe an idea you have for a product or service you could sell.

JohnnyGreig/E+/Getty Images

What Do You Think? How do businesses make money? Describe several ways that businesses make money selling goods and services.

How Can People Spend Money Wisely?

Using Money

How do you earn money? Maybe you get a weekly allowance or get paid for chores. Why do you need money? Money is something we use to buy goods and services. It has a value.

Perhaps you have traded a book or a game with a friend. You traded because the items had the same value. Would you trade a video game for a baseball cap? Probably not. They have very different values. We use money because it is an easy way to exchange things of equal value. If a video game costs $50, you exchange that amount of money for the game. It is an equal exchange.

People use money to buy things they need, such as food and clothing. They also use money to buy things they want.

(l)Lev Kropotov/Alamy Stock Photo; (r)forest_strider/iStockphoto/Getty Images

HSS.3.5.3, HSS.3.5.4

Montgomery Martin/Alamy Stock Photo

People buy many things every week. They buy things they need, such as food. They buy things they want, such as computer games and toys.

To get money, people need to work to earn it. You may earn money by doing chores. Adults earn it by working at jobs. There are many types of jobs, such as construction workers, bankers, teachers, or truck drivers. People have jobs to earn an **income**. An income is the money a person receives for work.

Earning income in an office

By earning an income, people have money to spend. Most money is spent on needs such as a place to live, food, or electricity. But sometimes there is money left over. This can be spent on something that is nice to have, or it can be saved. When people choose to save their money, they can buy things in the future.

A forklift operator

(t)Ingram Publishing; (b)Sigrid Gombert/Cultura RF/Getty Images

Earning Money to Help Others

A good citizen tries to help people in need. Sometimes this means helping communities in other countries. Students in San Anselmo, California, created the Ross Valley Free the Children Club. Its members volunteer and raise money to help other people nearby and around the world.

The group learned that some communities in Ecuador could not get clean water. The club decided to raise money to buy equipment that would provide clean water to those communities. Students organized many events to raise funds. They made and sold bracelets, held bake sales, and conducted a Walk for Water. In the end, the club raised over $20,000 for the clean water systems.

People can help make a difference by giving money for a good reason. Would you make the choice to give some of your money to help others?

A walk to raise money for charity

Stop and Check

Think Why is it sometimes good to save money rather than spend it right away?

Find Details As you read, add new information to the graphic organizer on page 271 in your Inquiry Journal.

asiseeit/E+/Getty Images

Making Economic Choices

Before you buy something, you need to think about the costs and **benefits** of your choices. Every buying choice involves a trade-off. You give up something you want when you buy something else.

Look at Jamie's choices. Which should Jamie buy? First, look at the cost of each item. Jamie has enough to buy either one. If Jamie buys the tablet, he would have to spend all of his savings. Now, what are the benefits of each item? Jamie could use the tablet to do research and play games. Jamie could use the bike to get to school and to soccer practice. Buying choices are not always simple. Jamie must decide what is more important to him.

Jamie got $125 for his birthday. He has $25 in his savings account. What should Jamie buy?
What can I buy with my savings?
Do I buy this? I can do my homework on it. I can also play games.
$150
Or should I get this? I can ride to school. I can ride to soccer practice.
$120

(l)Samuel Borges Photography/Shutterstock.com; (tr)Robert Mora/Alamy Stock Photo; (br)Rudy Umans/Shutterstock.com

Another way to help make buying decisions is to keep a budget. A budget is a plan for using money. It shows all the income expected in a month. It also shows all the expenses that must be paid each month. The money left over can be used for anything.

But should this leftover money be spent? What happens if a family has an expense it did not expect? A family needs to decide how to handle this leftover money. They may choose to save some so they are ready for an unexpected expense.

Knowing that there is only so much money to spend helps people make decisions on what to buy. Sometimes a buyer's decision may be not to spend any money at all.

You can choose to spend your money at a restaurant.

Ariel Skelley/Blend Images/Getty Images

Stop and Check

Talk With a partner, discuss the decision Jamie has to make. If you were Jamie, what decision would you make? Why?

Building Your Own Capital

You've learned that people get paid an income for the work they do. They use their income to buy the things they need and want and to save for the future. However, we don't always get paid for the jobs we do.

Your job right now is to go to school. You don't get paid an income for the work you do in school, but you're earning in other ways. The subjects you study in school help you "earn" or gain knowledge. This kind of earning is known as developing your **human capital**. Human capital is made up of the skills, experiences, and knowledge that will help you when you have a job and earn your own income. As you learn, you develop the tools you'll need to do different kinds of jobs.

A workshop can help you build human capital.

Hero Images/Fancy/Glow Images

There are different ways to develop your own human capital. One way is by going to school to learn new things and find out what interests you. Another way to develop your human capital is by being involved in activities in school and in your community. This will give you many different experiences. You'll learn new things from your different experiences. All the things you learn help you build your human capital. As a result, you become more valuable in your community and in your job.

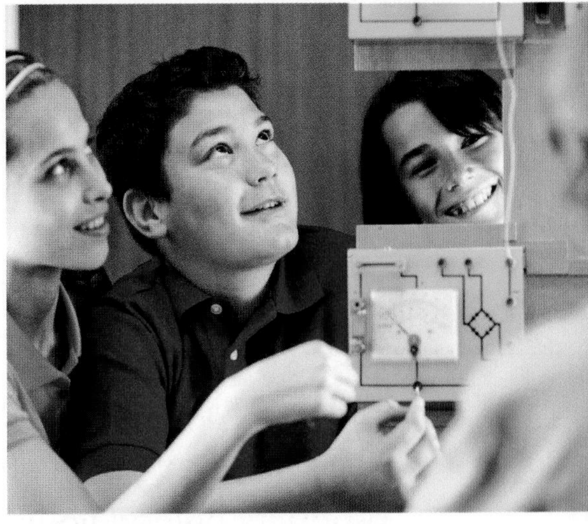

A school project also builds human capital.

Did You Know?

The word *capital* has many different meanings. In this lesson, *capital* means things that have value, such as human capital, money in the bank, and property that someone owns.

Capital also means the city in a state or country where the government is located. Sacramento is the capital of California.

In writing, a *capital* is an uppercase letter. Always begin a sentence with a capital letter.

What other meanings can you find for the word *capital*?

Stop and Check

Talk Discuss with a partner what *human capital* means. What could you do to build your own human capital?

What Do You Think? How can people spend money wisely?

Randy Faris/SuperStock

Connections in Action

Back to the EQ

Think about the chapter EQ, **"How do people in a community meet their needs?"**

- **Talk** with a partner about how innovations in technology have affected your community. How have new ideas or products helped your community meet its needs? What innovation do you and your partner think has had the most impact? Why do you think so?
- **Share** your opinion with another set of partners.

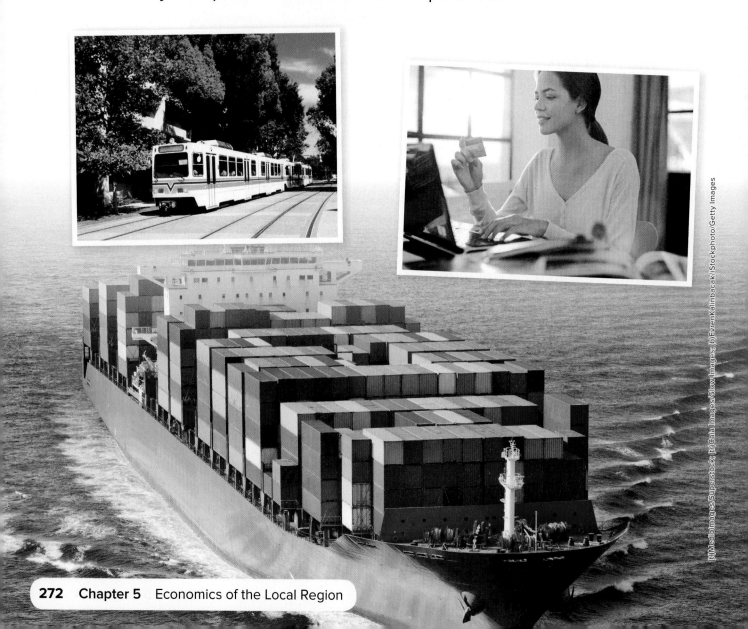

(tl)Medioimages/Superstock; (tr)Caia Images/Glow Images; (b)EvrenKalinbacak/iStockphoto/Getty Images

More to Explore

How can you make an IMPACT?

Give Advice

Imagine that your parents are thinking about buying a new car. Create a list of questions they should ask themselves before they make their choice. Then rank each question in order of importance.

Create a Sketch

Think about the definitions of *capital resources*, *human resources*, and *natural resources*. Select a business in your community. Sketch an example of each type of resource that this business uses. Label each sketch with the type of resource it shows.

Write a "Want Ad"

What do you want to do when you grow up? Imagine that you are an employer. You are hiring people in your career choice. Write a "want ad" describing the education and skills you expect the best person for the job to have.

Reference Section

The Reference Section has many parts, each with a different type of information. Use this section to explore people, places, and events as you investigate and take action.

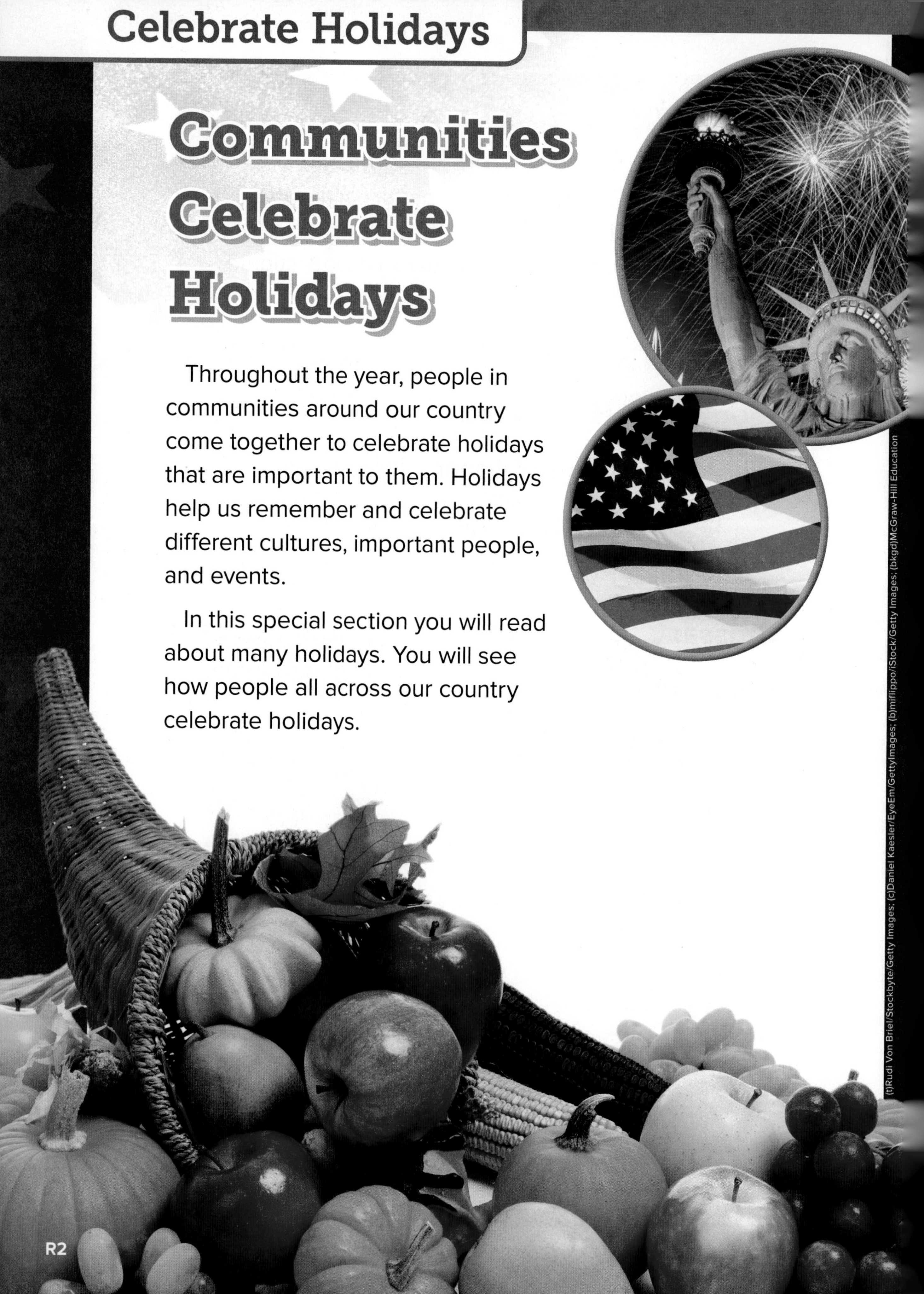

Communities Celebrate Holidays

Throughout the year, people in communities around our country come together to celebrate holidays that are important to them. Holidays help us remember and celebrate different cultures, important people, and events.

In this special section you will read about many holidays. You will see how people all across our country celebrate holidays.

(t)Rudi Von Briel/Stockbyte/Getty Images; (c)Daniel Kaesler/EyeEm/GettyImages; (b)mifflippo/iStock/Getty Images; (bkgd)McGraw-Hill Education

Martin Luther King, Jr., Day

World Journal Tribune, Library of Congress, LC-USZ62-111165

Dr. Martin Luther King, Jr., was born in Atlanta, Georgia, on January 15, 1929. He worked to make sure all people were treated fairly. In 1963 he made an important speech in Washington, D.C. He said, "I have a dream that my four children will one day live in a nation where they will not be judged by the color of their skin but by the content of their character..."

We celebrate Martin Luther King, Jr., and the dreams he fought for on the third Monday in January.

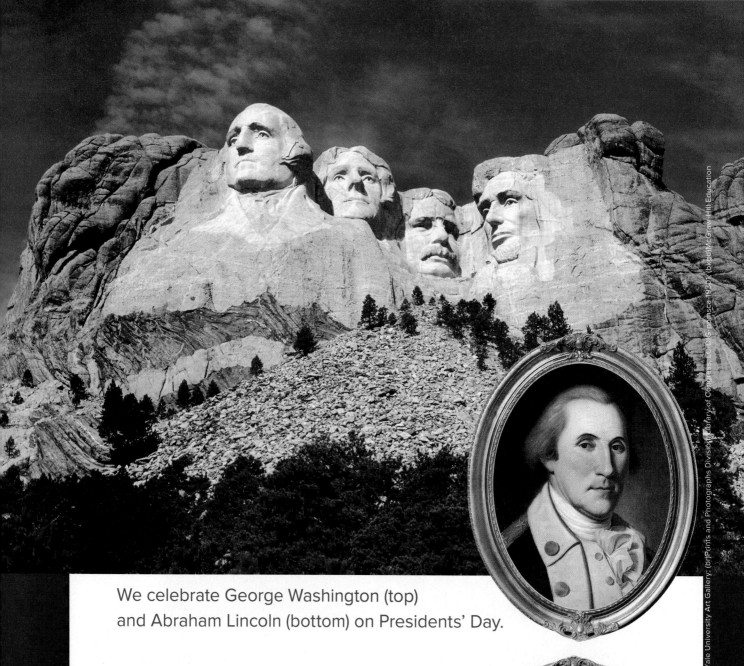

We celebrate George Washington (top) and Abraham Lincoln (bottom) on Presidents' Day.

Presidents' Day

Presidents' Day is celebrated on the third Monday in February. On this day we honor the work of all people who have served as President of the United States. Schools, banks, government offices and many businesses are closed to show respect for the people who have led our country.

(t)Purestock/Getty Images; (c b)kittimages/iStockphoto/Getty Images; (cr)Yale University Art Gallery; (br)Prints and Photographs Division, Library of Congress, LC-DIG-ppmsca-19301; (bkgd)McGraw-Hill Education

Cesar Chavez Day

Cesar Chavez Day is celebrated on March 31. Cesar Chavez made life better for farm workers. He worked hard and organized a union to make sure they were treated fairly. On this day we celebrate his life by doing service work for our communities. We clean up parks or plan community gardens.

Memorial Day

Memorial Day is celebrated on the last Monday in May. On this day we show respect for the soldiers who died in our country's wars. The holiday used to be called Decoration Day, because people would decorate the graves of soldiers who had lost their lives in war.

Many people celebrate this holiday by going to parades or visiting war memorials.

On Memorial Day, flags are placed on the graves of people who died fighting for our country.

(c)Malven/iStock/Getty Images; (bkgd)McGraw-Hill Education

Independence Day

Rudi Von Briel/Stockbyte/Getty Images

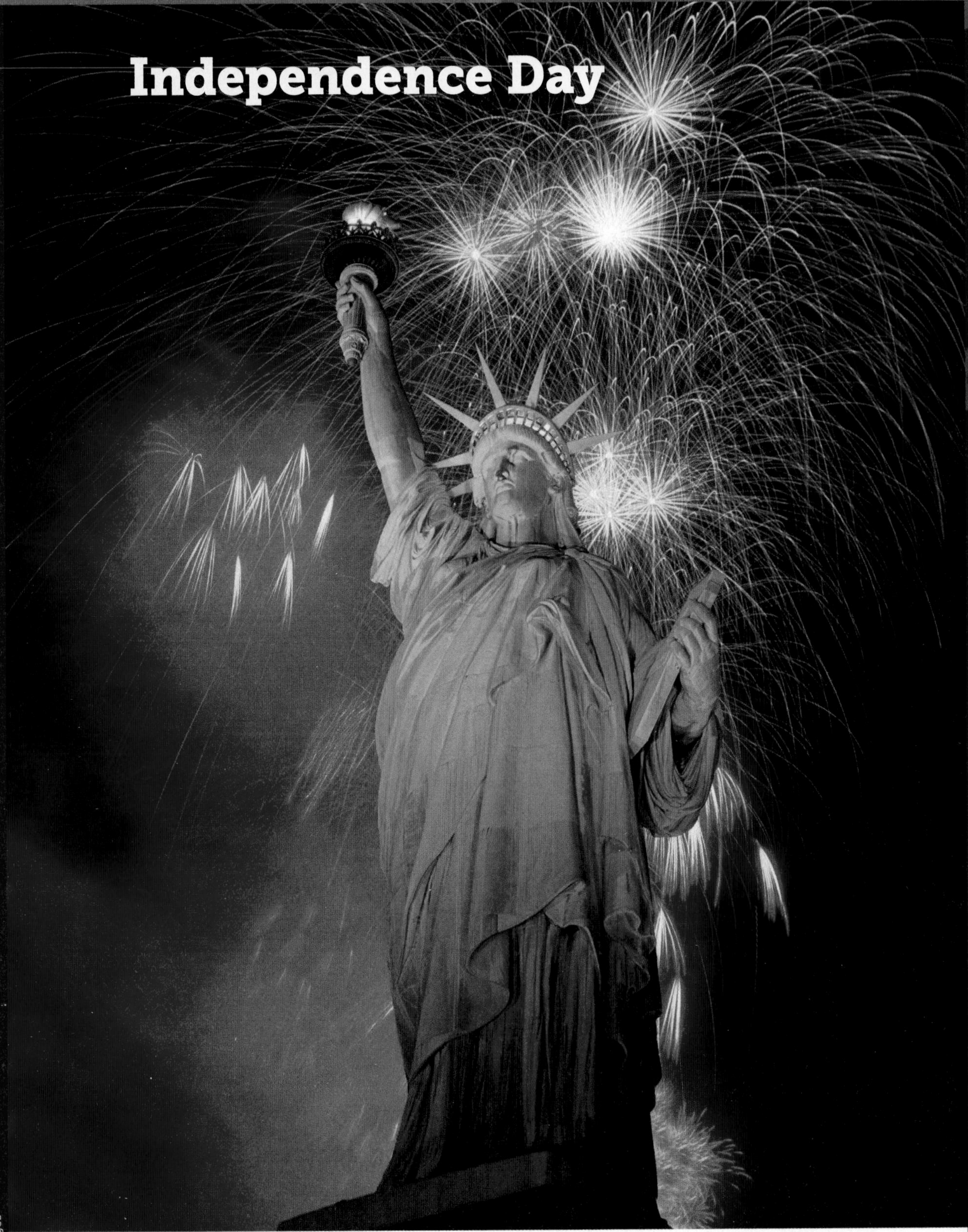

Independence Day, or the Fourth of July, honors our country's birthday. We remember that on July 4, 1776, we declared our independence from Great Britain. We celebrate with parades and fireworks to show that we are proud to be Americans.

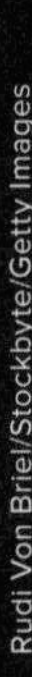

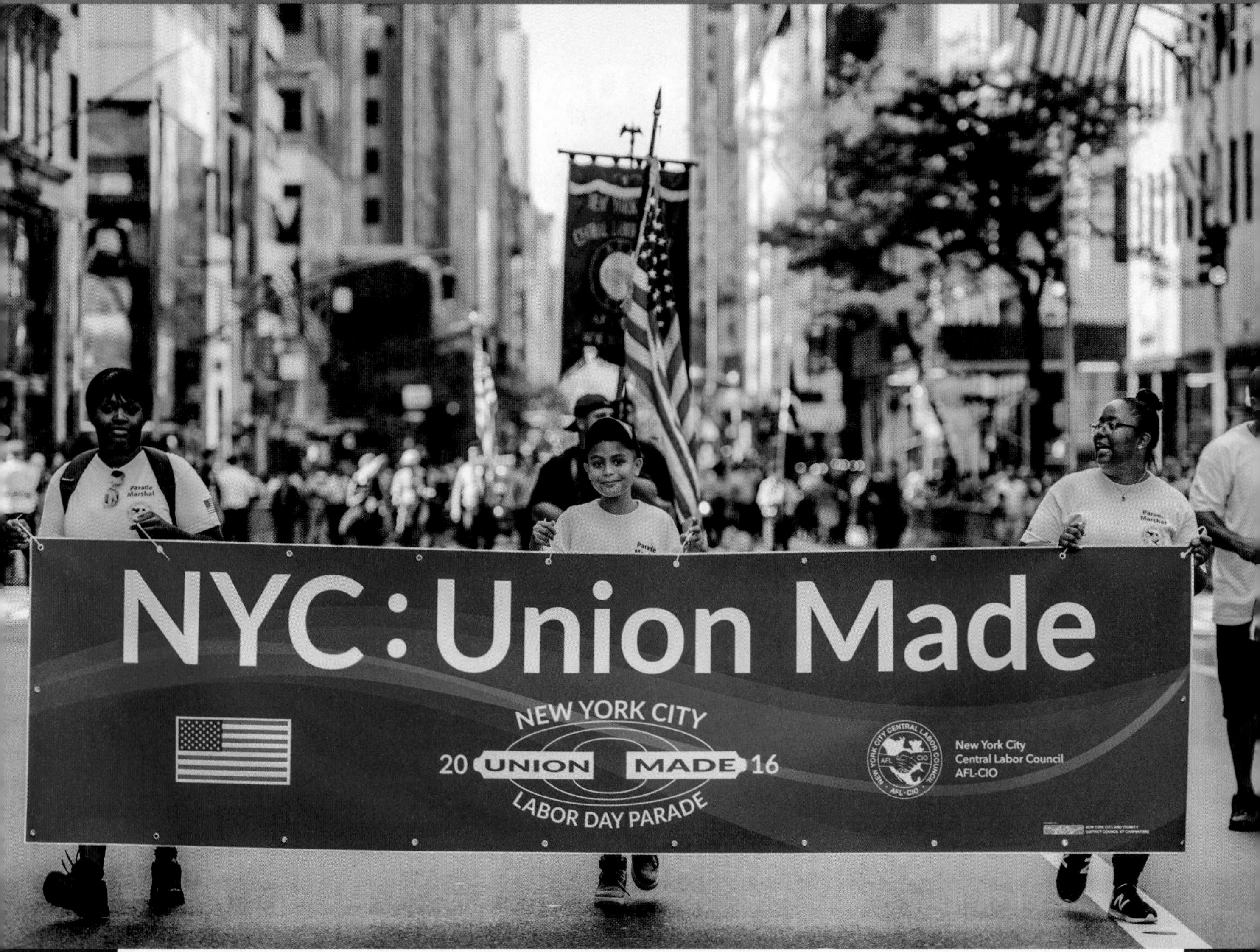

Parades are held on Labor Day to celebrate American workers.

Labor Day

Labor Day is celebrated on the first Monday in September. It was created to celebrate the contributions and achievements of American workers. Today, most people celebrate Labor Day by spending time with their friends and families and with picnics, parades, and festivals.

Erik McGregor/Pacific Press/LightRocket/Getty Images

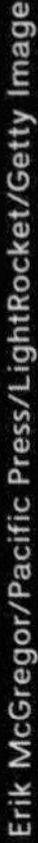

Thanksgiving

Thanksgiving is celebrated on the fourth Thursday in November. On this day we remember the feast shared by the Pilgrims and the Native Americans. We share a meal with family and friends and enjoy parades and celebrations. It is a time for us to be thankful for the many good things in our lives.

JGI/Blend Images LLC

The Themes of Geography

Geography is the study of Earth and the way people, plants, and animals live on it. Geographers divide geography into five themes. These themes are location, place, region, movement, and human interaction. They help us to think about the world around us.

Location

Location means a place on Earth's surface. A location can be defined in more than one way. One way is by street name and number.

Place

Every place has physical and human features that describe it. Physical features can include mountains and lakes. Human features include things like where people live, how they work, and what languages they speak.

(t)tupungato/iStock/Getty Images; (b)kropic1/Shutterstock.com

Region

A region is bigger than a place or a location. Regions cover large areas of land that share physical or human characteristics.

Movement

Geographers study why people have moved from place to place. They look at how movement changes the culture and physical landscape of an area.

Human Interaction

Geographers study how people and places change each other. People change the environment to meet their needs. For example, people build bridges to make travel easier.

(t)heyengel/iStock/Getty Images; (c)batuhanozdel/iStock/Getty Images; (b)Thinkstock/Comstock Images/Getty Images

Dictionary of Geographic Terms

1 **CANAL** A channel built to carry water for irrigation or transportation

2 **CANYON** A deep, narrow valley with steep sides

3 **COAST** The land along an ocean

4 **DAM** A wall built across a river, creating a lake that stores water

5 **DELTA** Land made of soil left behind as a river drains into a larger body of water

6 **DESERT** A dry environment with few plants and animals

7 **GLACIER** A huge sheet of ice that moves slowly across the land

8 **GULF** Part of an ocean that extends into the land; larger than a bay

9 **HARBOR** A sheltered place along a coast where boats dock safely

10 **HILL** A rounded, raised landform; not as high as a mountain

11 **ISLAND** A body of land completely surrounded by water

12 **LAKE** A body of water completely surrounded by land

13 **MOUNTAIN** A high landform with steep sides; higher than a hill

14 **MOUNTAIN PASS** A narrow gap through a mountain range

15 **MOUNTAIN RANGE** A row or chain of mountains

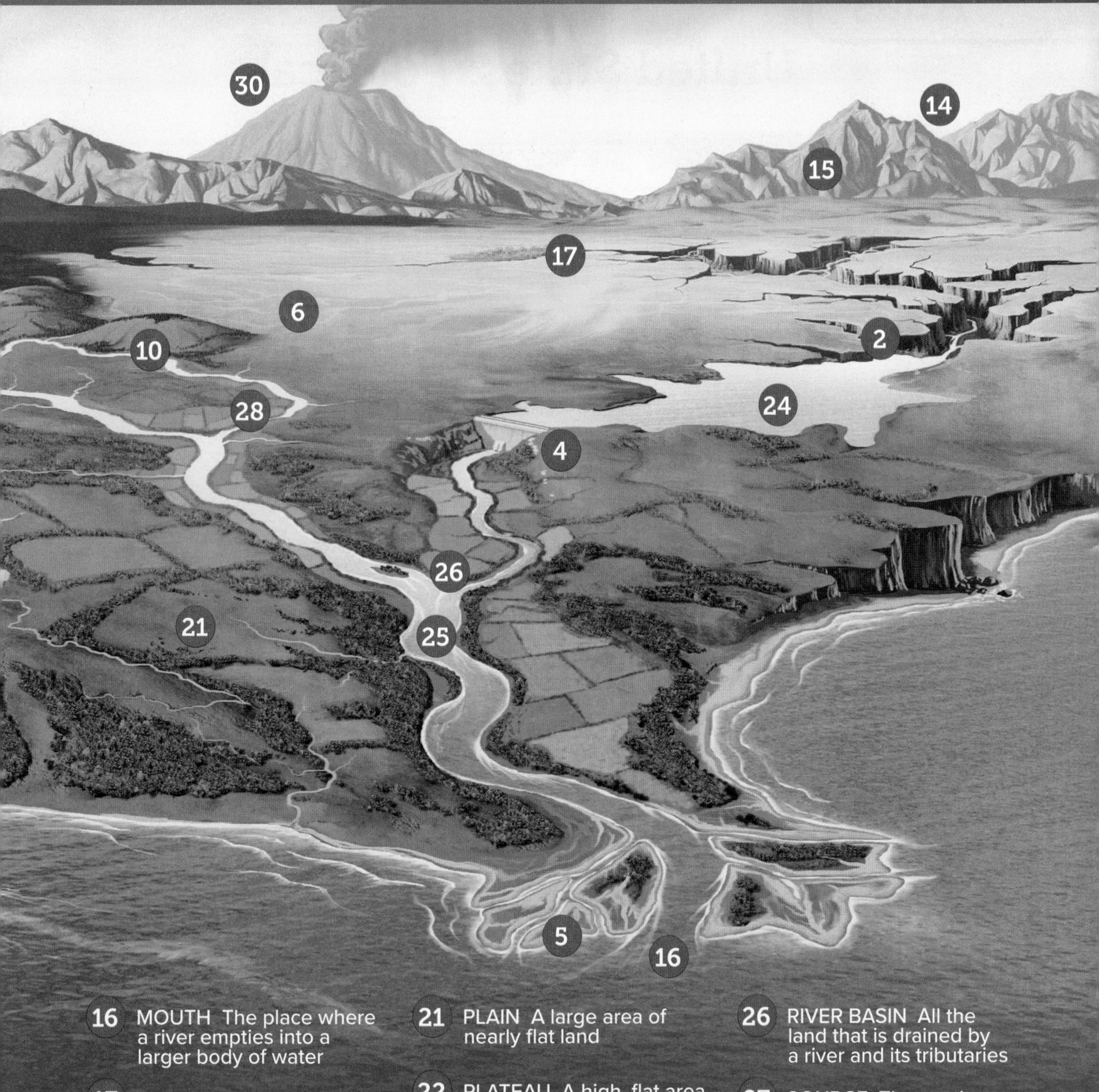

16 MOUTH The place where a river empties into a larger body of water

17 OASIS A fertile area in a desert that is watered by a spring

18 OCEAN A large body of salt water; oceans cover much of Earth's surface

19 PEAK The top of a mountain

20 PENINSULA A body of land nearly surrounded by water

21 PLAIN A large area of nearly flat land

22 PLATEAU A high, flat area that rises steeply above the surrounding land

23 PORT A city where ships load and unload goods

24 RESERVOIR A natural or artificial lake used to store water

25 RIVER A stream of water that flows across the land and empties into another body of water

26 RIVER BASIN All the land that is drained by a river and its tributaries

27 SOURCE The starting point of a river

28 TRIBUTARY A smaller river that flows into a larger river

29 VALLEY An area of low land between hills or mountains

30 VOLCANO An opening in Earth's surface through which hot rock and ash are forced out

United States: Political

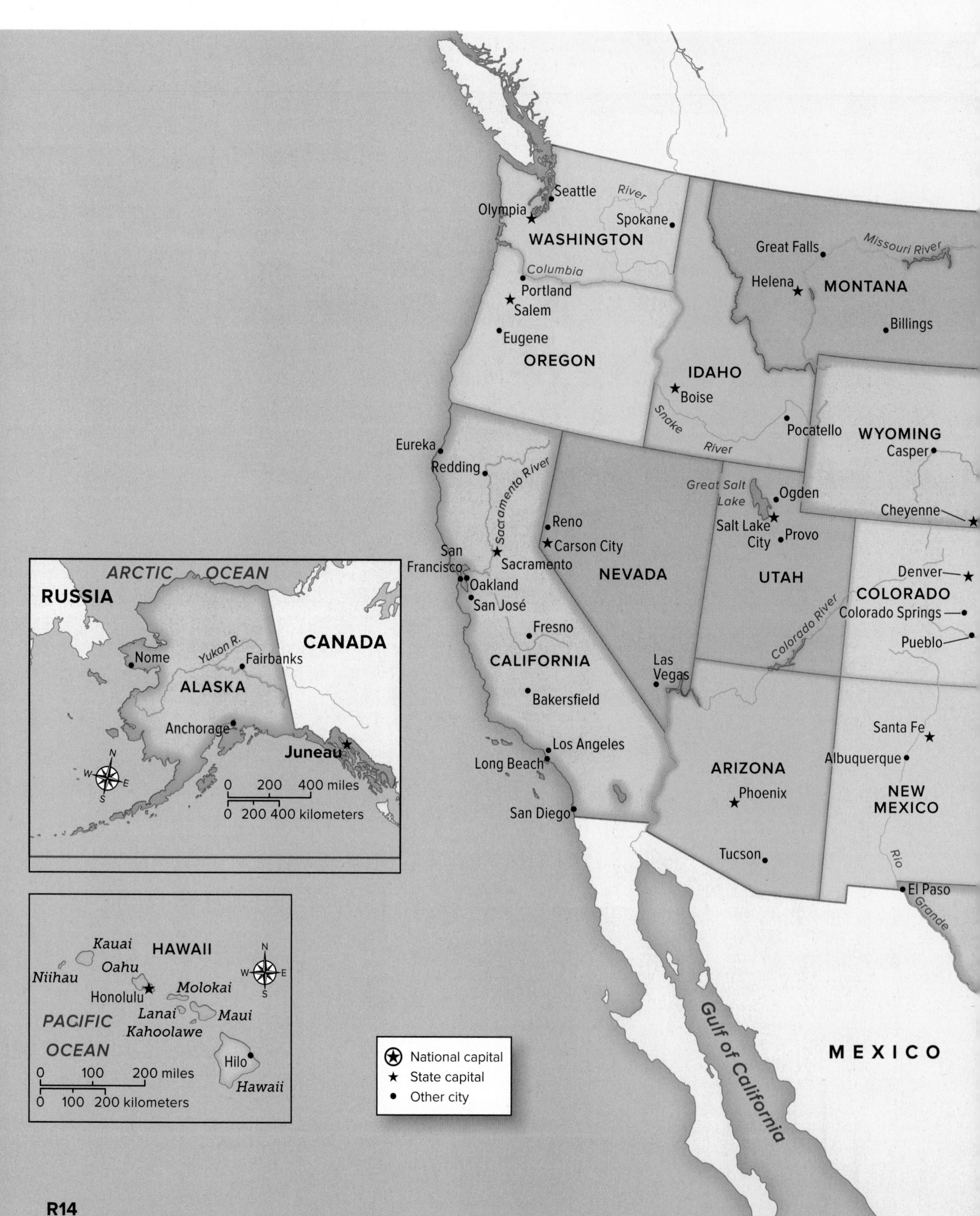

Seattle
River
Olympia
Spokane
WASHINGTON
Great Falls
Missouri River
Columbia
Portland
Helena
MONTANA
Salem
Billings
Eugene
OREGON
IDAHO
Boise
Snake
River
Pocatello
WYOMING
Casper
Eureka
Redding
Sacramento River
Great Salt Lake
Ogden
Cheyenne
Reno
Salt Lake City
Provo
Carson City
San Francisco
Sacramento
NEVADA
UTAH
Denver
Oakland
COLORADO
San José
Colorado Springs
Fresno
Colorado River
Pueblo
CALIFORNIA
Las Vegas
Bakersfield
Santa Fe
Los Angeles
Albuquerque
Long Beach
ARIZONA
Phoenix
NEW MEXICO
San Diego
Tucson
Rio Grande
El Paso
Gulf of California
MEXICO
ARCTIC OCEAN
RUSSIA
CANADA
Yukon R.
Nome
Fairbanks
ALASKA
Anchorage
Juneau
N
W
E
S
0 200 400 miles
0 200 400 kilometers
Kauai
HAWAII
Oahu
Niihau
Honolulu
Molokai
Lanai
Maui
PACIFIC OCEAN
Kahoolawe
Hilo
Hawaii
0 100 200 miles
0 100 200 kilometers
National capital
State capital
Other city

CANADA
NORTH DAKOTA
Grand Forks
Fargo
Bismarck
MINNESOTA
Duluth
Minneapolis
St. Paul
SOUTH DAKOTA
Pierre
Sioux Falls
WISCONSIN
Green Bay
Milwaukee
Madison
Lake Superior
MICHIGAN
Lake Michigan
Lake Huron
Grand Rapids
Lansing
Detroit
Lake Erie
Lake Ontario
NEW YORK
Buffalo
Albany
VERMONT
Montpelier
NEW HAMPSHIRE
Concord
MAINE
Augusta
Portland
Boston
MASSACHUSETTS
Providence
RHODE ISLAND
Hartford
CONNECTICUT
Newark
New York
Trenton
NEW JERSEY
PENNSYLVANIA
Harrisburg
Philadelphia
Pittsburgh
Baltimore
Dover
DELAWARE
Washington, D.C.
Annapolis
MARYLAND
IOWA
Cedar Rapids
Des Moines
Davenport
NEBRASKA
Omaha
Lincoln
Platte River
Missouri River
ILLINOIS
Chicago
Gary
Springfield
INDIANA
Indianapolis
Evansville
OHIO
Toledo
Cleveland
Columbus
Cincinnati
WEST VIRGINIA
Charleston
VIRGINIA
Richmond
Norfolk
KENTUCKY
Frankfort
Louisville
Ohio River
KANSAS
Topeka
Kansas City
Kansas City
Wichita
MISSOURI
St. Louis
Jefferson City
Mississippi River
Arkansas River
OKLAHOMA
Oklahoma City
Tulsa
ARKANSAS
Fort Smith
Little Rock
TENNESSEE
Nashville
Knoxville
Memphis
Tennessee River
NORTH CAROLINA
Raleigh
Charlotte
SOUTH CAROLINA
Columbia
Charleston
GEORGIA
Atlanta
Columbus
Savannah
ALABAMA
Birmingham
Montgomery
MISSISSIPPI
Jackson
Biloxi
Mobile
Red River
TEXAS
Dallas
Fort Worth
Austin
Houston
San Antonio
Laredo
Corpus Christi
Brazos River
Colorado River
LOUISIANA
Shreveport
Baton Rouge
New Orleans
FLORIDA
Tallahassee
Jacksonville
Orlando
Tampa
Miami
ATLANTIC OCEAN
THE BAHAMAS
Gulf of Mexico
N
S
E
W
0
200
400 miles
0
200
400 kilometers

United States: Physical

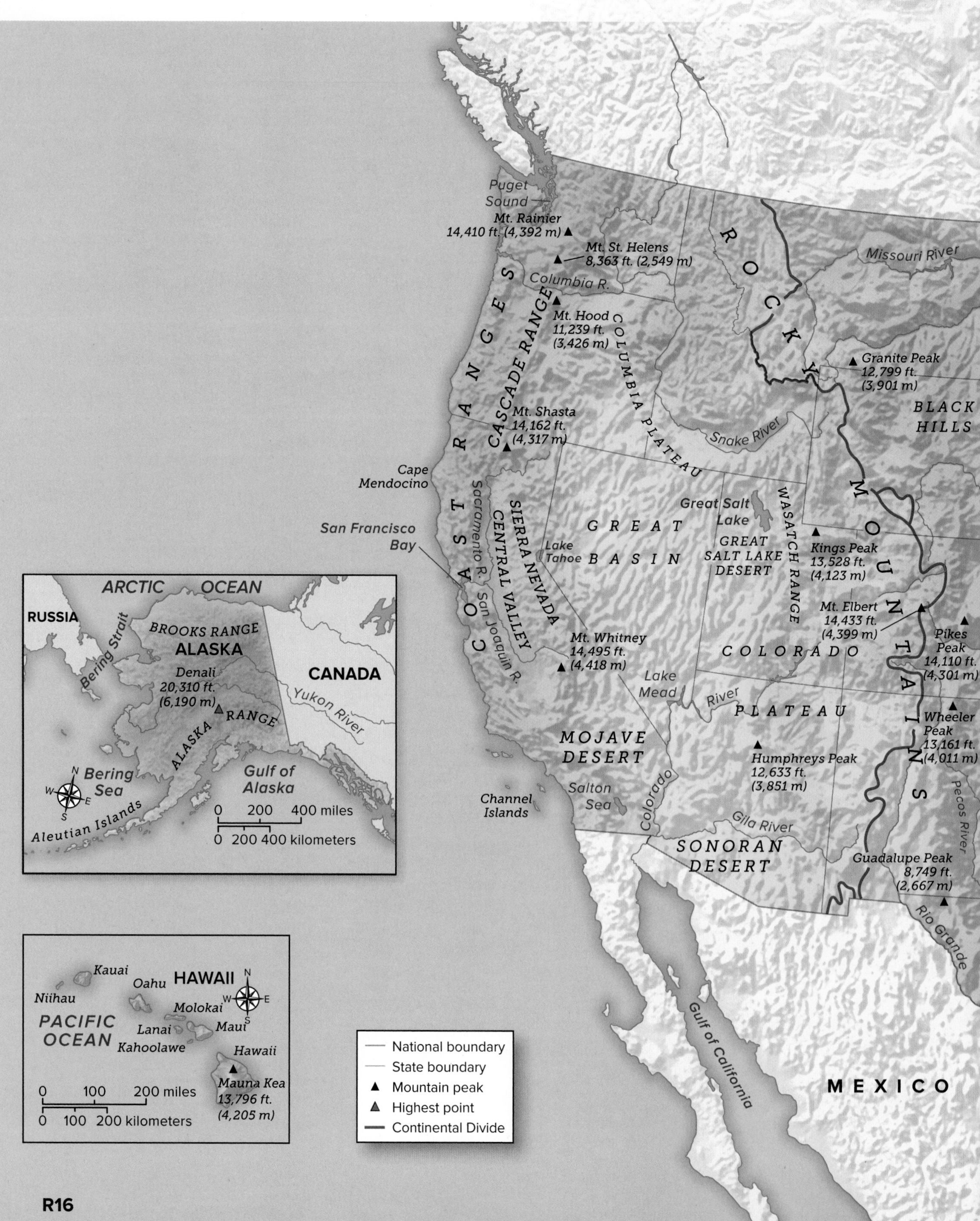
Puget Sound
Mt. Rainier 14,410 ft. (4,392 m)
Mt. St. Helens 8,363 ft. (2,549 m)
Columbia R.
Mt. Hood 11,239 ft. (3,426 m)
CASCADE RANGE
COAST RANGES
COLUMBIA PLATEAU
ROCKY MOUNTAINS
Missouri River
Granite Peak 12,799 ft. (3,901 m)
BLACK HILLS
Mt. Shasta 14,162 ft. (4,317 m)
Snake River
Cape Mendocino
Sacramento R.
SIERRA NEVADA
CENTRAL VALLEY
San Francisco Bay
Lake Tahoe
GREAT BASIN
Great Salt Lake
GREAT SALT LAKE DESERT
WASATCH RANGE
Kings Peak 13,528 ft. (4,123 m)
Mt. Elbert 14,433 ft. (4,399 m)
Pikes Peak 14,110 ft. (4,301 m)
San Joaquin R.
Mt. Whitney 14,495 ft. (4,418 m)
COLORADO PLATEAU
Lake Mead
River
Wheeler Peak 13,161 ft. (4,011 m)
MOJAVE DESERT
Humphreys Peak 12,633 ft. (3,851 m)
Channel Islands
Salton Sea
Colorado
Pecos River
Gila River
SONORAN DESERT
Guadalupe Peak 8,749 ft. (2,667 m)
Rio Grande
Gulf of California
MEXICO
ARCTIC OCEAN
RUSSIA
Bering Strait
BROOKS RANGE
ALASKA
CANADA
Denali 20,310 ft. (6,190 m)
ALASKA RANGE
Yukon River
Bering Sea
Gulf of Alaska
Aleutian Islands
0 200 400 miles
0 200 400 kilometers
Kauai
Oahu
HAWAII
Niihau
Molokai
PACIFIC OCEAN
Lanai
Maui
Kahoolawe
Hawaii
Mauna Kea 13,796 ft. (4,205 m)
0 100 200 miles
0 100 200 kilometers
National boundary
State boundary
Mountain peak
Highest point
Continental Divide

CANADA
0
200
400 miles
0
200
400 kilometers
GREAT LAKES
Lake Superior
MESABI RANGE
Lake Michigan
Lake Huron
Lake Ontario
Lake Erie
St. Lawrence River
WHITE MTS.
Mt. Washington 6,288 ft. (1,917 m)
GREEN MTS.
ADIRONDACK MTS.
Cape Cod
Hudson R.
Susquehanna R.
Long Island
ALLEGHENY PLATEAU
ALLEGHENY MTS.
Delaware Bay
Potomac River
Chesapeake Bay
Cape Hatteras
APPALACHIAN MOUNTAINS
PIEDMONT
ATLANTIC COASTAL PLAIN
Mt. Mitchell 6,684 ft. (2,037 m)
Savannah River
ATLANTIC OCEAN
GREAT PLAINS
Mississippi River
Missouri River
Platte River
CENTRAL PLAINS
Wabash River
Ohio River
Arkansas River
INTERIOR PLAINS
OZARK PLATEAU
OUACHITA MOUNTAINS
Red River
Tennessee River
Mississippi River
Alabama River
Chattahoochee River
Brazos River
Colorado River
EDWARDS PLATEAU
GULF COASTAL PLAIN
Mobile Bay
Galveston Bay
Mississippi River Delta
Lake Okeechobee
Gulf of Mexico
THE BAHAMAS
Florida Keys
Straits of Florida
N
S
E
W

World: Political

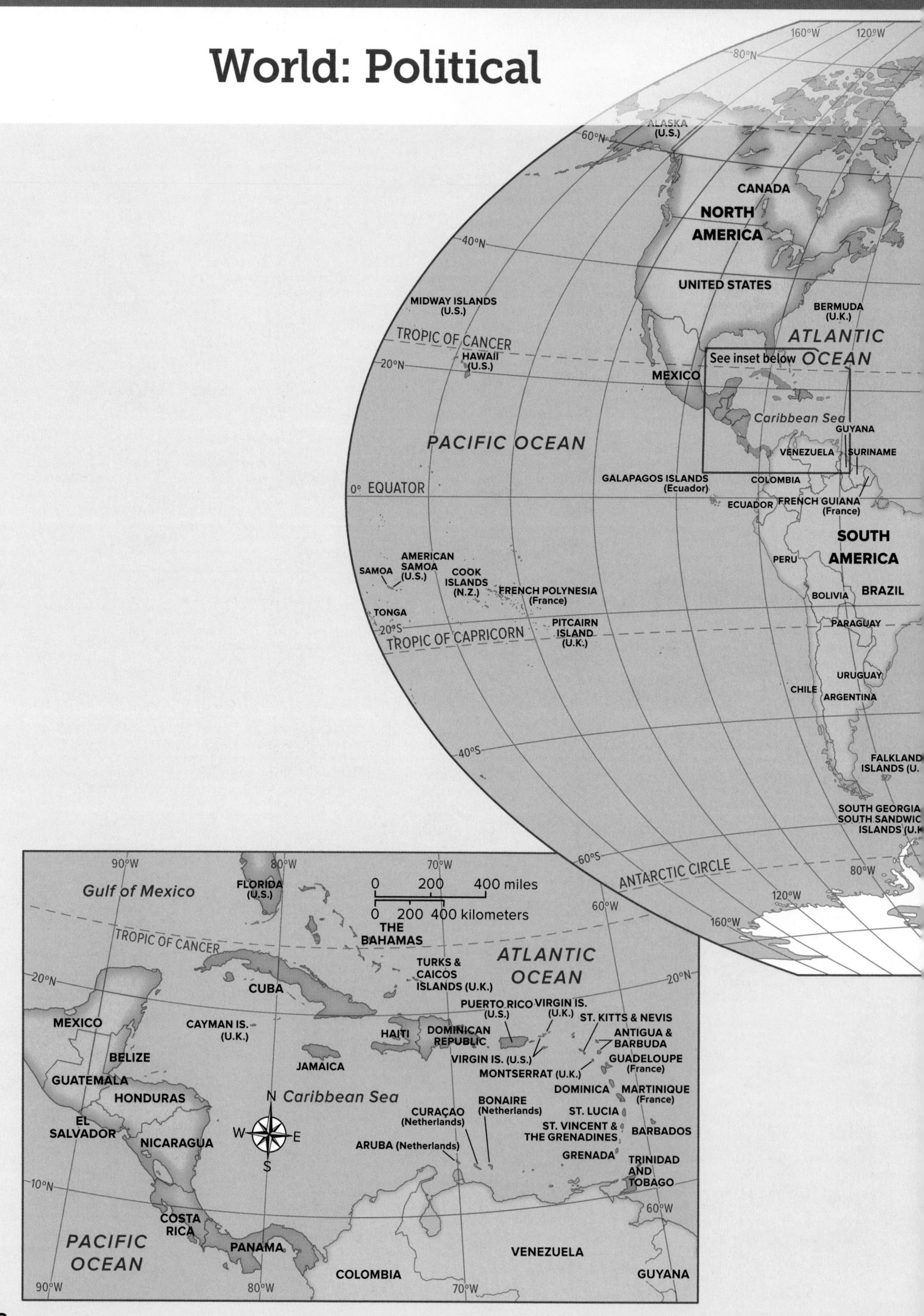
ALASKA (U.S.)
CANADA
NORTH AMERICA
UNITED STATES
MIDWAY ISLANDS (U.S.)
BERMUDA (U.K.)
ATLANTIC OCEAN
TROPIC OF CANCER
HAWAII (U.S.)
See inset below
MEXICO
Caribbean Sea
GUYANA
PACIFIC OCEAN
VENEZUELA
SURINAME
GALAPAGOS ISLANDS (Ecuador)
COLOMBIA
0° EQUATOR
ECUADOR
FRENCH GUIANA (France)
SOUTH AMERICA
AMERICAN SAMOA (U.S.)
SAMOA
COOK ISLANDS (N.Z.)
PERU
BRAZIL
FRENCH POLYNESIA (France)
BOLIVIA
TONGA
PITCAIRN ISLAND (U.K.)
TROPIC OF CAPRICORN
PARAGUAY
URUGUAY
CHILE
ARGENTINA
FALKLAND ISLANDS (U.
SOUTH GEORGIA SOUTH SANDWIC ISLANDS (U.K
ANTARCTIC CIRCLE
Gulf of Mexico
FLORIDA (U.S.)
0 200 400 miles
0 200 400 kilometers
THE BAHAMAS
TROPIC OF CANCER
TURKS & CAICOS ISLANDS (U.K.)
ATLANTIC OCEAN
CUBA
PUERTO RICO (U.S.)
VIRGIN IS. (U.K.)
ST. KITTS & NEVIS
MEXICO
CAYMAN IS. (U.K.)
HAITI
DOMINICAN REPUBLIC
ANTIGUA & BARBUDA
BELIZE
VIRGIN IS. (U.S.)
GUADELOUPE (France)
JAMAICA
MONTSERRAT (U.K.)
GUATEMALA
DOMINICA
MARTINIQUE (France)
HONDURAS
Caribbean Sea
BONAIRE (Netherlands)
CURAÇAO (Netherlands)
ST. LUCIA
EL SALVADOR
ST. VINCENT & THE GRENADINES
BARBADOS
NICARAGUA
ARUBA (Netherlands)
GRENADA
TRINIDAD AND TOBAGO
COSTA RICA
PACIFIC OCEAN
PANAMA
VENEZUELA
COLOMBIA
GUYANA

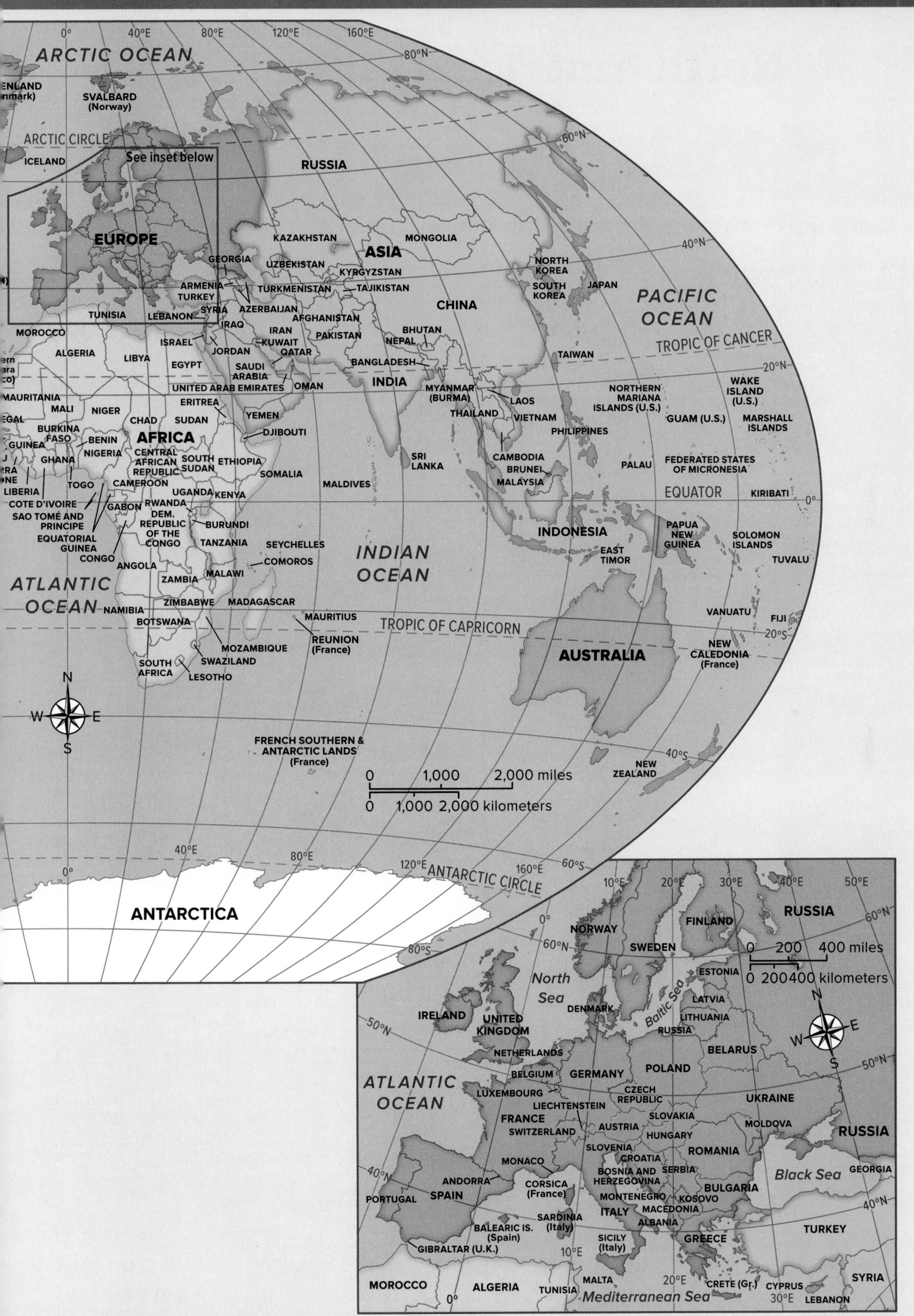
ARCTIC OCEAN
SVALBARD (Norway)
ARCTIC CIRCLE
ICELAND
See inset below
RUSSIA
EUROPE
KAZAKHSTAN
MONGOLIA
ASIA
GEORGIA
UZBEKISTAN
KYRGYZSTAN
NORTH KOREA
SOUTH KOREA
JAPAN
ARMENIA
TURKEY
TURKMENISTAN
TAJIKISTAN
AZERBAIJAN
CHINA
PACIFIC OCEAN
TUNISIA
LEBANON
SYRIA
IRAQ
AFGHANISTAN
IRAN
PAKISTAN
BHUTAN
NEPAL
MOROCCO
ISRAEL
KUWAIT
QATAR
TROPIC OF CANCER
ALGERIA
LIBYA
EGYPT
JORDAN
SAUDI ARABIA
BANGLADESH
TAIWAN
UNITED ARAB EMIRATES
OMAN
INDIA
MYANMAR (BURMA)
LAOS
NORTHERN MARIANA ISLANDS (U.S.)
WAKE ISLAND (U.S.)
MAURITANIA
MALI
NIGER
CHAD
SUDAN
ERITREA
YEMEN
THAILAND
VIETNAM
GUAM (U.S.)
MARSHALL ISLANDS
PHILIPPINES
BURKINA FASO
BENIN
AFRICA
DJIBOUTI
GUINEA
GHANA
NIGERIA
CENTRAL AFRICAN REPUBLIC
SOUTH SUDAN
ETHIOPIA
SRI LANKA
CAMBODIA
BRUNEI
MALAYSIA
PALAU
FEDERATED STATES OF MICRONESIA
TOGO
CAMEROON
SOMALIA
MALDIVES
LIBERIA
UGANDA
KENYA
EQUATOR
KIRIBATI
COTE D'IVOIRE
SAO TOMÉ AND PRINCIPE
GABON
RWANDA
DEM. REPUBLIC OF THE CONGO
BURUNDI
INDONESIA
PAPUA NEW GUINEA
SOLOMON ISLANDS
EQUATORIAL GUINEA
TANZANIA
SEYCHELLES
CONGO
COMOROS
INDIAN OCEAN
EAST TIMOR
TUVALU
ANGOLA
ATLANTIC OCEAN
ZAMBIA
MALAWI
ZIMBABWE
MADAGASCAR
NAMIBIA
BOTSWANA
MAURITIUS
VANUATU
FIJI
TROPIC OF CAPRICORN
REUNION (France)
MOZAMBIQUE
SWAZILAND
AUSTRALIA
NEW CALEDONIA (France)
SOUTH AFRICA
LESOTHO
FRENCH SOUTHERN & ANTARCTIC LANDS (France)
NEW ZEALAND
0 1,000 2,000 miles
0 1,000 2,000 kilometers
ANTARCTIC CIRCLE
ANTARCTICA
N
S
E
W
0°
40°E
80°E
120°E
160°E
80°N
60°N
40°N
20°N
0°
20°S
40°S
60°S
80°S
NORWAY
FINLAND
RUSSIA
SWEDEN
0 200 400 miles
0 200 400 kilometers
ESTONIA
North Sea
LATVIA
DENMARK
Baltic Sea
LITHUANIA
IRELAND
UNITED KINGDOM
RUSSIA
BELARUS
NETHERLANDS
BELGIUM
GERMANY
POLAND
ATLANTIC OCEAN
LUXEMBOURG
CZECH REPUBLIC
UKRAINE
LIECHTENSTEIN
FRANCE
SLOVAKIA
MOLDOVA
AUSTRIA
SWITZERLAND
HUNGARY
RUSSIA
SLOVENIA
ROMANIA
CROATIA
MONACO
BOSNIA AND HERZEGOVINA
SERBIA
Black Sea
GEORGIA
ANDORRA
CORSICA (France)
BULGARIA
PORTUGAL
SPAIN
MONTENEGRO
KOSOVO
ITALY
MACEDONIA
SARDINIA (Italy)
ALBANIA
TURKEY
BALEARIC IS. (Spain)
SICILY (Italy)
GREECE
GIBRALTAR (U.K.)
MOROCCO
ALGERIA
TUNISIA
MALTA
CRETE (Gr.)
CYPRUS
SYRIA
Mediterranean Sea
LEBANON
10°E
20°E
30°E
40°E
50°E
60°N
50°N
40°N

North America: Political

ARCTIC OCEAN
ASIA
Chukchi Sea
Bering Sea
Bering Strait
Alaska (U.S.)
Yukon River
Fairbanks
Anchorage
Gulf of Alaska
Juneau
Beaufort Sea
Banks Island
Victoria Island
Queen Elizabeth Islands
Parry Islands
Ellesmere Island
Greenland (Denmark)
Baffin Bay
Baffin Island
Nuuk
Davis Strait
Iqaluit
Labrador Sea
ICELAND
Mackenzie River
Great Bear Lake
Yellowknife
Great Slave Lake
Lake Athabasca
Hudson Bay
CANADA
Edmonton
Lake Winnipeg
Winnipeg
Island of Newfoundland
Quebec
Montreal
Ottawa
Lake Superior
Lake Huron
Lake Michigan
Lake Ontario
Lake Erie
Toronto
Detroit
Boston
New York
Philadelphia
Washington, D.C.
Vancouver
Seattle
Columbia R.
Portland
Snake River
Missouri River
Minneapolis
Chicago
Great Salt Lake
Salt Lake City
UNITED STATES
San Francisco
Denver
Colorado River
Arkansas River
St. Louis
Ohio River
Tennessee River
Mississippi R.
Los Angeles
Phoenix
Red River
Atlanta
Dallas
Houston
New Orleans
Ciudad Juarez
Rio Grande
ATLANTIC OCEAN
Bermuda (U.K.)
PACIFIC OCEAN
Miami
Gulf of Mexico
Monterrey
MEXICO
Guadalajara
Mexico City
THE BAHAMAS
Nassau
Havana
CUBA
Puerto Rico (U.S.)
ANTIGUA AND BARBUDA
ST. KITTS AND NEVIS
St. John's
DOMINICAN REPUBLIC
HAITI
Port-au-Prince
Santo Domingo
Roseau
DOMINICA
ST. LUCIA
JAMAICA
Kingston
ST. VINCENT & THE GRENADINES
GRENADA
TRINIDAD AND TOBAGO
Caribbean Sea
BELIZE
Belmopan
GUATEMALA
Guatemala City
HONDURAS
Tegucigalpa
San Salvador
EL SALVADOR
NICARAGUA
Managua
COSTA RICA
San José
PANAMA
Panamá City
SOUTH AMERICA
EQUATOR 0°
National capital
Other city
N
S
E
W
0 300 600 miles
0 300 600 kilometers

South America: Political

Caribbean Sea
CENTRAL AMERICA
Barranquilla
Maracaibo
Valencia
Caracas
Lake Maracaibo
Orinoco River
VENEZUELA
Magdalena River
Medellín
Gulf of Panama
Bogotá
Cali
COLOMBIA
Georgetown
GUYANA
Paramaribo
SURINAME
Cayenne
FRENCH GUIANA (France)
ATLANTIC OCEAN
N
W
E
S
Quito
ECUADOR
Guayaquil
Iquitos
Equator 0°
Negro River
Manaus
Amazon River
Belém
Tapajos River
Xingu River
Madeira River
Trujillo
PERU
BRAZIL
Recife
São Francisco River
Callao
Lima
Cuzco
Lake Titicaca
La Paz
Arequipa
BOLIVIA
Sucre
Salvador (Bahía)
Brasília
Paraguay River
Paraná River
Belo Horizonte
PARAGUAY
Antofagasta
Rio de Janeiro
São Paulo
Asunción
River
Tucumán
CHILE
Paraná
Uruguay River
Porto Alegre
Córdoba
Rosario
Valparaíso
Santiago
ARGENTINA
URUGUAY
Montevideo
Buenos Aires
Rio de la Plata
PACIFIC OCEAN
Concepción
Colorado River
ATLANTIC OCEAN
National capital
Other city
Falkland Islands (Islas Malvinas) (U.K.)
0 250 500 miles
0 250 500 kilometers
Strait of Magellan
Punta Arenas
South Georgia (U.K.)

California: Physical

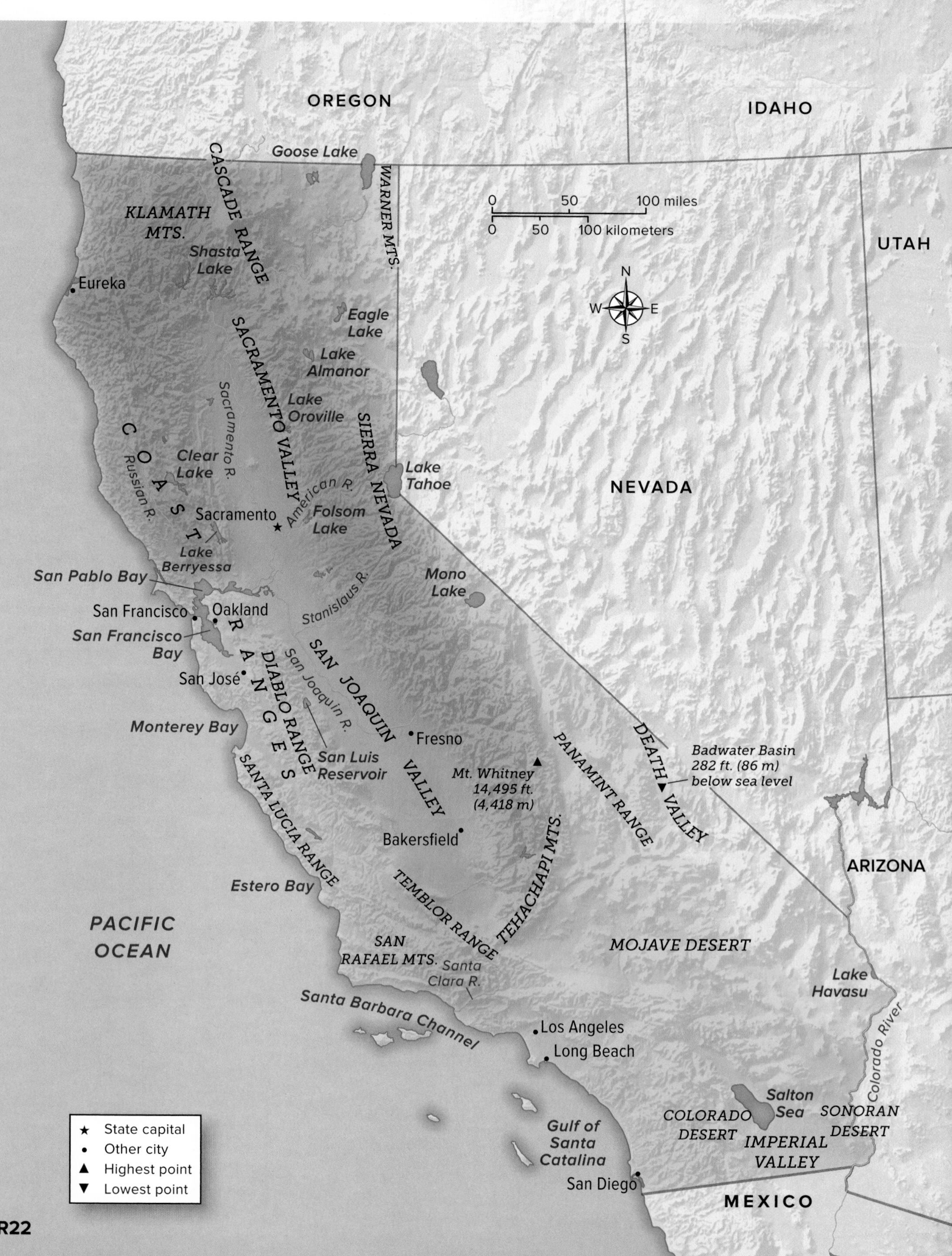

OREGON
IDAHO
UTAH
NEVADA
ARIZONA
MEXICO
PACIFIC OCEAN
Goose Lake
CASCADE RANGE
WARNER MTS.
KLAMATH MTS.
Shasta Lake
Eureka
Eagle Lake
Lake Almanor
Lake Oroville
SACRAMENTO VALLEY
Sacramento R.
SIERRA NEVADA
COAST RANGES
Russian R.
Clear Lake
Lake Tahoe
American R.
Sacramento
Folsom Lake
Lake Berryessa
San Pablo Bay
Mono Lake
San Francisco
Oakland
Stanislaus R.
San Francisco Bay
San José
DIABLO RANGE
San Joaquin R.
SAN JOAQUIN VALLEY
Monterey Bay
Fresno
San Luis Reservoir
Mt. Whitney 14,495 ft. (4,418 m)
PANAMINT RANGE
DEATH VALLEY
Badwater Basin 282 ft. (86 m) below sea level
SANTA LUCIA RANGE
Bakersfield
TEHACHAPI MTS.
TEMBLOR RANGE
Estero Bay
SAN RAFAEL MTS.
Santa Clara R.
MOJAVE DESERT
Lake Havasu
Colorado River
Santa Barbara Channel
Los Angeles
Long Beach
Salton Sea
COLORADO DESERT
SONORAN DESERT
IMPERIAL VALLEY
Gulf of Santa Catalina
San Diego
0 50 100 miles
0 50 100 kilometers
N
S
E
W
★ State capital
• Other city
▲ Highest point
▼ Lowest point

California Counties

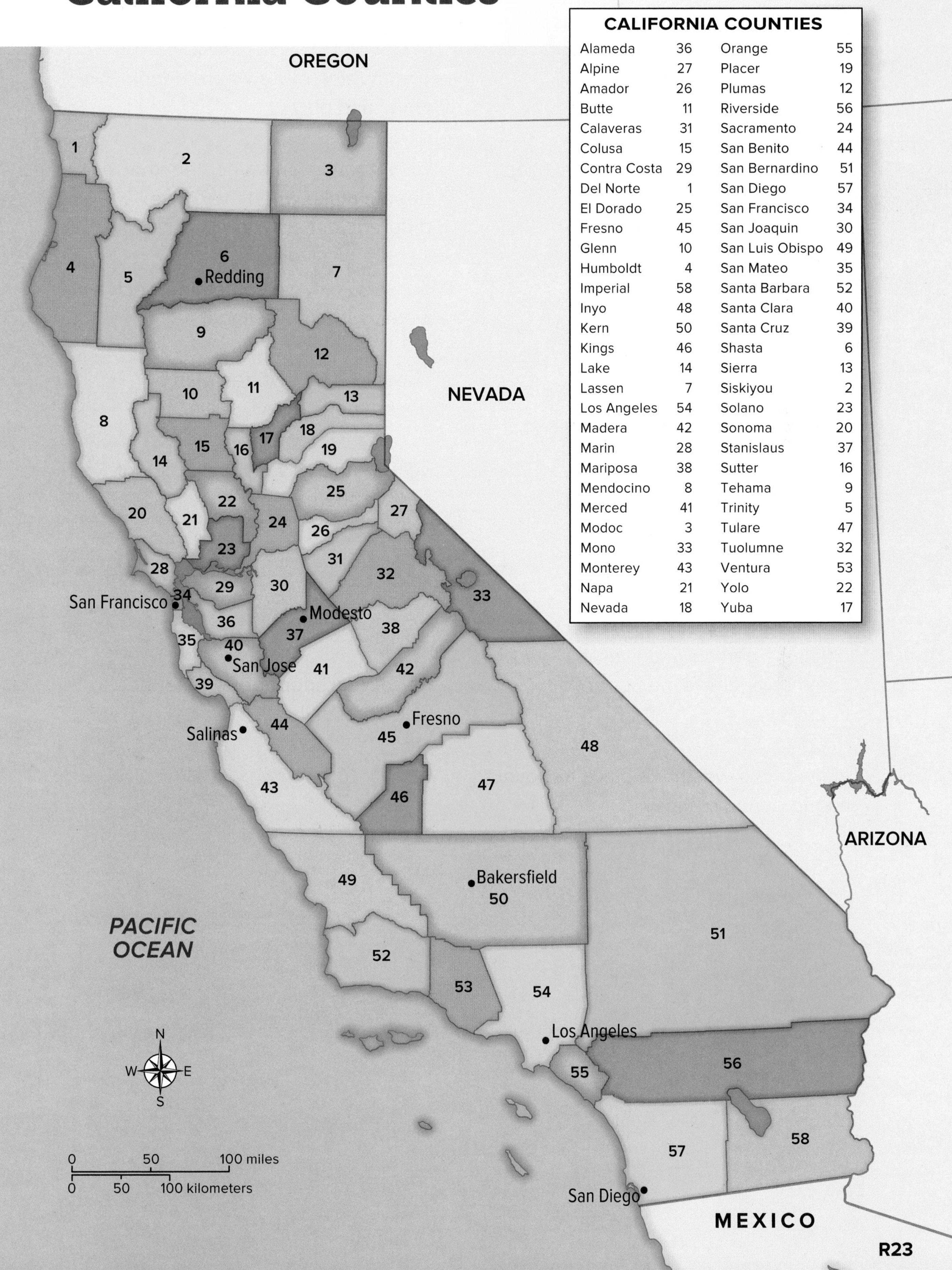

CALIFORNIA COUNTIES

County	No.	County	No.
Alameda	36	Orange	55
Alpine	27	Placer	19
Amador	26	Plumas	12
Butte	11	Riverside	56
Calaveras	31	Sacramento	24
Colusa	15	San Benito	44
Contra Costa	29	San Bernardino	51
Del Norte	1	San Diego	57
El Dorado	25	San Francisco	34
Fresno	45	San Joaquin	30
Glenn	10	San Luis Obispo	49
Humboldt	4	San Mateo	35
Imperial	58	Santa Barbara	52
Inyo	48	Santa Clara	40
Kern	50	Santa Cruz	39
Kings	46	Shasta	6
Lake	14	Sierra	13
Lassen	7	Siskiyou	2
Los Angeles	54	Solano	23
Madera	42	Sonoma	20
Marin	28	Stanislaus	37
Mariposa	38	Sutter	16
Mendocino	8	Tehama	9
Merced	41	Trinity	5
Modoc	3	Tulare	47
Mono	33	Tuolumne	32
Monterey	43	Ventura	53
Napa	21	Yolo	22
Nevada	18	Yuba	17

Glossary

amendment a change to a document

aqueduct a manmade channel used to transport water

benefit something that helps a person

capital resources goods such as tools and machines that businesses use to provide goods or services

century one hundred years

citizen a person who lives in a community or is a member of a country

climate the weather a place has over a long period of time

community place where people live, work, and play

compromise an agreement that people make when they have different ideas

conserve to use something, such as water, without wasting it

constitution a written plan of government

culture the way of life a group of people share

decade ten years

drought a shortage of water due to lack of rainfall

E

economy the production, buying, and selling of goods and services

elevation how high an area of land is above sea level

entrepreneur a person who starts and runs his or her own business

environment the surroundings or conditions in which someone lives

ethnic group a group of people who share the same culture

executive branch the part of government that makes sure that laws are carried out and followed

expedition a journey, especially by a group of people, for a specific purpose

explorer a person who travels to learn more about other places

export to send goods to another country for sale; an item transported to another country for sale there

F

federal national

harvest to gather in a crop; the crop that has been gathered in

human capital the skills and knowledge a person has to do a job

human resources people in a business who provide valuable skills

I

import to bring goods into a country from another country to sell; an item brought into a country for sale there

income money earned by working

industry a group of businesses that provides a specific product or service

innovation a new idea, piece of equipment, or method

J

judicial branch the part of government that decides what the laws mean

jury a group of citizens who are chosen to decide a legal case

L

legislative branch the part of government that makes the laws

M

manufacture to make products using machinery

migrate to move to a new area

mission a church or a settlement built around a church

N

natural resource something found in nature that people use

nomad a person who moves from place to place

P

pollution anything that makes the air, water, or soil dirty

population the number of people who live in one place

precipitation water that falls to the ground as rain, snow, sleet, or hail

profit money gained after operating expenses are subtracted

R

region an area of land with certain features that make it different from other areas

reservation land set aside for American Indians

right something that is due to everyone

S

settlers people who move to a new country or area in order to live there

tax money collected by a government

traditions beliefs or customs handed down from the past, such as from parents to children

vegetation plants found in a specific area

Index

This index lists many topics that appear in the book. It also tells you the page numbers where to find them. Page numbers after a *c* refer you to a chart, after an *m* refer you to a map, and after a *p* refer you to photographs or artwork.

C

S

Grade Three

Historical and Social Sciences Content Standards and Analysis Skills

History-Social Sciences Content Standards

Continuity and Change

Students in grade three learn more about our connections to the past and the ways in which particularly local, but also regional and national, government and traditions have developed and left their marks on current society, providing common memories. Emphasis is on the physical and cultural landscape of California, including the study of American Indians, the subsequent arrival of immigrants, and the impact they have had in forming the character of our contemporary society.

3.1 Students describe the physical and human geography and use maps, tables, graphs, photographs, and charts to organize information about people, places, and environments in a spatial context.

1. Identify geographical features in their local region (e.g., deserts, mountains, valleys, hills, coastal areas, oceans, lakes).
2. Trace the ways in which people have used the resources of the local region and modified the physical environment (e.g., a dam constructed upstream changed a river or coastline).

3.2 Students describe the American Indian nations in their local region long ago and in the recent past.

1. Describe national identities, religious beliefs, customs, and various folklore traditions.
2. Discuss the ways in which physical geography, including climate, influenced how the local Indian nations adapted to their natural environment (e.g., how they obtained food, clothing, tools).
3. Describe the economy and systems of government, particularly those with tribal constitutions, and their relationship to federal and state governments.
4. Discuss the interaction of new settlers with the already established Indians of the region.

3.3 Students draw from historical and community resources to organize the sequence of local historical events and describe how each period of settlement left its mark on the land.

1. Research the explorers who visited here, the newcomers who settled here, and the people who continue to come to the region, including their cultural and religious traditions and contributions.
2. Describe the economies established by settlers and their influence on the present-day economy, with emphasis on the importance of private property and entrepreneurship.
3. Trace why their community was established, how individuals and families contributed to its founding and development, and how the community has changed over time, drawing on maps, photographs, oral histories, letters, newspapers, and other primary sources.

3.4 Students understand the role of rules and laws in our daily lives and the basic structure of the U.S. government.

1. Determine the reasons for rules, laws, and the U.S. Constitution; the role of citizenship in the promotion of rules and laws; and the consequences for people who violate rules and laws.
2. Discuss the importance of public virtue and the role of citizens, including how to participate in a classroom, in the community, and in civic life.
3. Know the histories of important local and national landmarks, symbols, and essential documents that create a sense of community among citizens and exemplify cherished ideals (e.g., the U.S. flag, the bald eagle, the Statue of Liberty, the U.S. Constitution, the Declaration of Independence, the U.S. Capitol).
4. Understand the three branches of government, with an emphasis on local government.
5. Describe the ways in which California, the other states, and sovereign American Indian tribes contribute to the making of our nation and participate in the federal system of government.
6. Describe the lives of American heroes who took risks to secure our freedoms (e.g., Anne Hutchinson, Benjamin Franklin, Thomas Jefferson, Abraham Lincoln, Frederick Douglass, Harriet Tubman, Martin Luther King, Jr.).

3.5 Students demonstrate basic economic reasoning skills and an understanding of the economy of the local region.

1. Describe the ways in which local producers have used and are using natural resources, human resources, and capital resources to produce goods and services in the past and the present.
2. Understand that some goods are made locally, some elsewhere in the United States, and some abroad.
3. Understand that individual economic choices involve trade-offs and the evaluation of benefits and costs.
4. Discuss the relationship of students' "work" in school and their personal human capital.

Historical and Social Sciences Analysis Skills

In addition to the standards, students demonstrate the following intellectual, reasoning, reflection, and research skills:

Chronological and Spatial Thinking

1. Students place key events and people of the historical era they are studying in a chronological sequence and within a spatial context; they interpret time lines.
2. Students correctly apply terms related to time, including past, present, future, decade, century, and generation.
3. Students explain how the present is connected to the past, identifying both similarities and differences between the two, and how some things change over time and some things stay the same.
4. Students use map and globe skills to determine the absolute locations of places and interpret information available through a map's or globe's legend, scale, and symbolic representations.
5. Students judge the significance of the relative location of a place (e.g., proximity to a harbor, on trade routes) and analyze how relative advantages or disadvantages can change over time.

Research, Evidence, and Point of View

1. Students differentiate between primary and secondary sources.
2. Students pose relevant questions about events they encounter in historical documents, eyewitness accounts, oral histories, letters, diaries, artifacts, photographs, maps, artworks, and architecture.
3. Students distinguish fact from fiction by comparing documentary sources on historical figures and events with fictionalized characters and events.

Historical Interpretation

1. Students summarize the key events of the era they are studying and explain the historical contexts of those events.
2. Students identify the human and physical characteristics of the places they are studying and explain how those features form the unique character of those places.
3. Students identify and interpret the multiple causes and effects of historical events.
4. Students conduct cost-benefit analyses of historical and current events.

Continuity and Change

DNY59/E+/Getty Images

Chapter 1

Communities in California

ESSENTIAL QUESTION EQ **How does geography impact California communities?**

(t)David R. Frazier Photolibrary, Inc./Alamy Stock Photo, (b)powerofforever/Getty Images

Chapter 2

American Indians of the Local Region

How have California Indians influenced the local region?

(t)Spencer Grant/age fotostock, (c)rab-bit/iStock/Getty Images, (b)photoquest7/iStock/Getty Images

Chapter 3

How and Why Communities Change Over Time

How has life changed for people in my community over time?

(t)Pete Ryan/National Geographic/Getty Images, (c)i love images/Juice Images/Getty Images, (b)Sierralara/Shutterstock.com

Chapter 4

American Citizens, Symbols, and Government

How do our government and its citizens work together?

(t)TongRo Image Stock/Alamy Stock Photo, (b)©1976 George Ballis/Take Stock/The Image Works

Chapter 5

Economics of the Local Region

How do people in a community meet their needs?

(t)GomezDavid/E+/Getty Images, (b)asiseeit/iStock/Getty Images

Explore!

Welcome to the Weekly Explorer Magazine!

This magazine will give you a chance to explore the world.

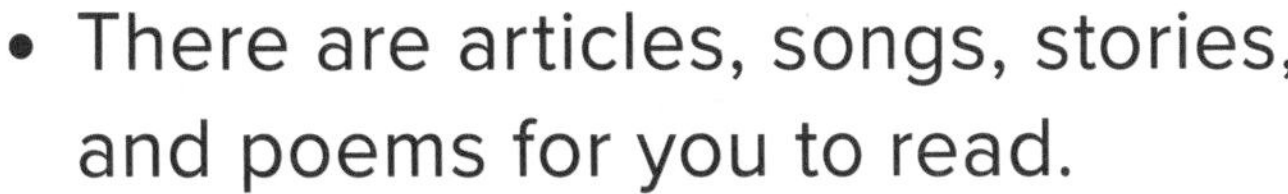

- There are articles, songs, stories, and poems for you to read.
- You will look closely at maps, diagrams, infographics, and other images.
- As you read, you will look for answers to an Essential Question (EQ).

drmakkoy/DigitalVision Vectors/Getty Images

The following steps will help in your exploration. You can take notes as you read.

1 Inspect

Read the text.

- What does it say?
- What are the details in the images?
- What are the main ideas?

2 Find Evidence

Reread the text and look at the images again.

- Look for more clues about the main ideas.
- What other details do you notice?
- How does the writer support the ideas?
- Be curious!

3 Make Connections

Think about what you've read.

- How does this connect to the EQ?
- How does it connect to other texts?
- How does it connect to you?
- What do you think?

Captain Yeo/Shutterstock.com

Let's go!

Chapter 1

Communities in California

How does geography impact California communities?

Table of Contents

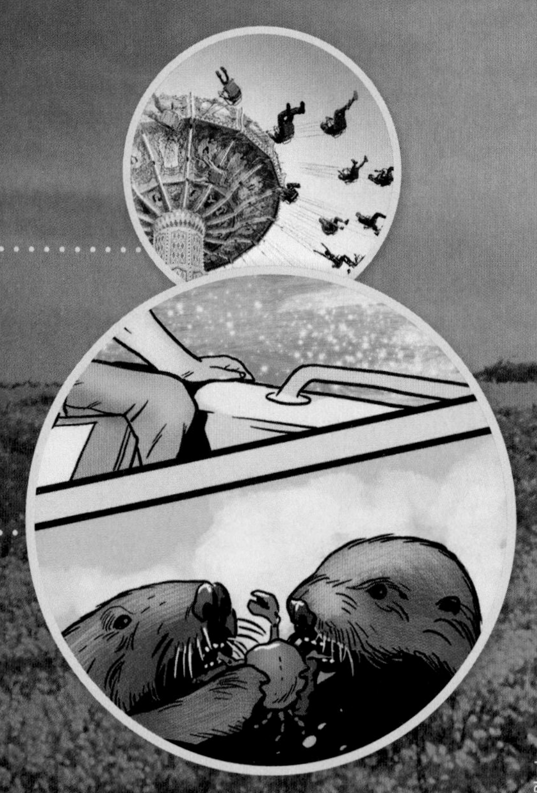

(bkgd spread)Marco Regalia Sell/Alamy Stock Photo, (t)Mimi Ditchie otography/Moment Open/Getty Images, (b)Andrei Stanescu/Shutterstock.com

Where Do Californians Live?

California is a big state. It is made up of many different types of land. Our communities are just as varied as our land!

Lake Tahoe is a large freshwater lake surrounded by mountains. People can do lots of outdoor activities here!

The Central Valley region is home to many people. Crops are grown here too, including grapes, peaches, and rice.

San Diego is the second largest city in California. Its warm and sunny climate makes beaches popular places to visit.

Some parts of California have a desert climate. Cacti and other desert plants thrive in these communities.

- What details do you see in the photos?
- What details are similar to where you live?

(tl)alacatr/E+/Getty Images, (tr)Michael Layefsky/Moment/Getty Images, (bl)David R. Frazier Photolibrary, Inc./Alamy Stock Photo, (br)North Light Images/age fotostock/SuperStock

OUR STATE, OUR FAIR

Then

CALIFORNIA STATE FAIR AND EXPOSITION

California State Fair entrance, 1964

Cattle contests have always been held at the California State Fair.

After gold was discovered in California in 1848, many people headed west. California's **population** boomed! California became a state in 1850. Californians wanted to prove that their state was about more than gold—it was also great for farming and industry. The State Agricultural Society decided to plan a fair to showcase their great state.

In 1854, the first California State Fair was held in San Francisco. As many as 15,000 people visited in a single day! Most exhibits were related to farming. People marveled at 2-inch-long peanuts, 72-pound beets, and a 10-pound carrot that was 3 feet long. Contests were held to judge livestock.

Over the years, exhibits became more elaborate. Around the turn of the last century, fair organizers even staged a full-sized train wreck! It remained a popular attraction until World War I.

(bkgd spread)Mimi Ditchie Photography/Moment Open/Getty Images, (l)Bettmann/Getty Images, (r)Jon Brenneis/The LIFE Images Collection/Getty Images

People raise and show animals at the fair.

Today's fair includes exhibits about agriculture and new technology. Farmers see DNA profiles of animals they're interested in. The fair is also about having fun. Students enter their best art work and win a prize. Rides and cultural celebrations add to the excitement. There's even a pie-eating contest! More than a million people visit California's state fair each year.

Today, visitors to the fair enjoy fun rides like this one.

(banners) I_Mak/Shutterstock.com, (t)Chieko Hara/The Porterville Recorder via AP/AP Images

CONNECT THROUGH LITERATURE

TO THE FAIR

by Kate Minor

Let's hitch up the buggy
And go to the fair.
We'll see all the people
And animals there.

Ma's packed up some jars
Of her strawberry jam.
Pa wants to see horses
And this year's new lambs.

We might see a strongman
Or maybe a race.
Last year my brother
Ate pie with his face!

So hurry up, family!
Let's get to the fair.
I can't wait to see
All the wonderful there!

WordBlast

What does the word **population** mean? What clue can you find in the text that helps you know the meaning?

A DAY IN THE LIFE OF A
MARINE BIOLOGIST
ROSA IS A MARINE BIOLOGIST. SHE STUDIES WILD ANIMALS THAT LIVE IN THE OCEAN. HER DAY STARTS EARLY!
GOOD MORNING, ED!
ARE YOU READY FOR YOUR FIRST DAY?
AQUARIUM
RESEARCH INSTITUTE
SHE IS STUDYING A GROUP OF SEA OTTERS. ED IS HER NEW HELPER.

ROSA USES A RADIO TO FIND THE OTTERS SHE HAS TAGGED.
THIS IS A MOTHER I'VE BEEN TRACKING. SHE HAS A PUP WITH HER!
TIME FOR BREAKFAST, KID!
OTTERS CAN DIVE DOWN AS FAR AS 300 FEET TO SEARCH FOR FOOD.
SHE'S BEEN DOWN THERE FOR ONE MINUTE. I BET SHE FINDS SOMETHING SOON.

SHE CAUGHT A BIG ONE! WHY DID YOU WANT TO KNOW HOW LONG THAT TOOK?

IT GIVES US AN IDEA OF HOW MUCH FOOD IS AVAILABLE.

SHE'S SHARING. THAT'S A GOOD SIGN, RIGHT?

OTTER PUPS RELY ON THEIR MOTHERS FOR FOOD.

YES. THAT IS A SIGN OF A HEALTHY ENVIRONMENT. WE'RE READY TO HEAD BACK.

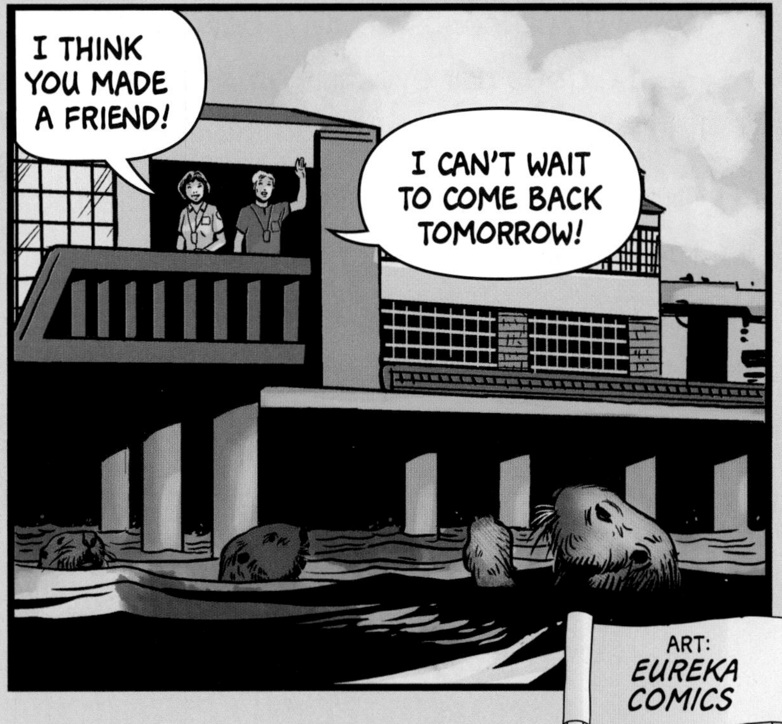

ART: EUREKA COMICS

TRASHING THE OCEAN

Imagine floating garbage stretching farther than your eye can see. It stretches from the west coast of North America all the way to Japan. Unfortunately, it's not imaginary. It's real, and it's called the Great Pacific Garbage Patch.

Trash that gets dumped or washed into the ocean floats. Currents of moving water carry the trash along. When multiple currents meet, an area of calm water can form. Once trash lands in the calm water, it stays there, trapped.

You might picture an island of trash. Really, the Patch looks like a lot of soupy water. Why? Because it's made mostly of plastic. Plastic does not ever **decompose**, or rot. It just breaks down into smaller pieces.

These tiny pieces cause huge problems. Turtles mistake plastic for jellies, their favorite food. Seabirds think the plastic is fish eggs. Eating plastic harms and often kills the animals.

So what can we do about the problem? We can limit our use of plastic. We can throw trash away in the right places. We can recycle. And maybe someday we can figure out a way to clean up the Garbage Patch.

WordBlast

What does the word **decompose** mean? How does the text help you figure out the word's meaning?

(bkgd spread)Ramunas Bruzas/Shutterstock.com, (inset)andrew payne/Alamy Stock Photo

How You Can Help

Groups work to remove trash from oceans and beaches all around the world. In 2015, nearly 800,000 people picked up more than 18 million pounds of trash!

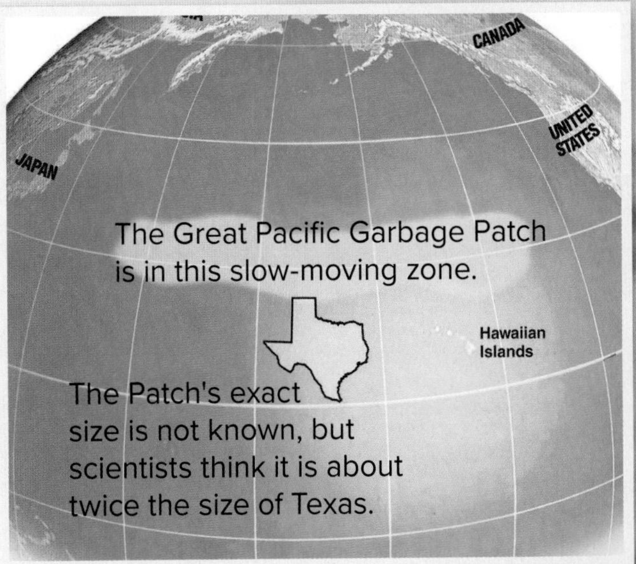

CANADA
UNITED STATES
JAPAN
The Great Pacific Garbage Patch is in this slow-moving zone.
Hawaiian Islands
The Patch's exact size is not known, but scientists think it is about twice the size of Texas.

You can plan your own beach cleanup. Here are a few tips.

- ☑ Wear heavy work gloves. You will need to protect your hands from anything sharp.
- ☑ Bring a refillable water bottle filled with fresh water. You can't drink the ocean!
- ☑ Bring bags and containers to hold what you pick up. Set up a place where you can dispose of the trash.

(t)Maschietto/Newscom, (b)Al Seib/Los Angeles Times/Getty Images

John Muir was born in 1838. He was both a woodsman and naturalist. He so loved the outdoors that he devoted his life to preserving it. A sequoia grove, glacier, mountain peak, and lake are all named for Muir.

At age 30, Muir climbed the Sierra Nevada Mountains. He spent the next five years learning about them. He would set off with his blanket roll and a rubber bag containing a little tea, flour, and maybe some oatmeal.

Muir would be gone for days or even weeks. He considered a fifty-mile hike in the rugged mountains a good "two day saunter."

Once he lashed himself to the top of a hundred-foot-high tree during a storm. He wanted to experience how a tree withstands the winds. During another storm, he was trapped overnight. His feet were frostbitten!

But that did not stop Muir from exploring. He learned more about the Sierra Nevada than anyone had ever known. He was the first to realize how glaciers had carved out the valleys.

(bkgd spread)©Pgiam/Getty Images, (inset)MCCAIG/iStock/Getty Images

John Muir and President Theodore Roosevelt visited Yosemite together.

When he was about fifty years old, Muir started writing articles about the importance of nature. These articles helped convince a group of powerful people to lobby Congress. They supported a bill to **preserve** the Yosemite Valley. Congress passed the Yosemite bill in 1890, creating a national park.

President Theodore Roosevelt was a fan of nature and of Muir's work. He helped pass more laws to protect forests. Roosevelt said that the sequoia trees in California needed protection "simply because it would be a shame to our civilization to let them disappear. They are monuments to themselves."

WordBlast

What does it mean to **preserve** something? Tell a partner something you can help to preserve.

PRIMARY SOURCE

In Their Words...

Now it is plain that the forests are not inexhaustible, and that quick measures must be taken if ruin is to be avoided.

—John Muir

This sign next to Yosemite Creek marks the site of a cabin built by John Muir.

TEXT: Muir, John. My First Summer in the Sierra. Boston, MA: Houghton Mifflin Company, 1911; PHOTO: (t)Library of Congress, Prints and Photographs Division [LC-USZ62-8672], (b)Russ Bishop/Alamy Stock Photo

WINTER IN DEATH VALLEY

Late on a winter night in 1849, Juliet Brier walked alone with her three sons. They were in one of the hottest and driest places on Earth. It was the desert of Death Valley. She carried her youngest boys, Kirk and Johnny. Eight-year-old Columbus struggled along in the dark. The trail ahead was faint. James, her husband, trudged far ahead with a few scraggly oxen.

The Briers were part of a large wagon-train company called the Sand Walkers. They started their journey from Salt Lake City, Utah, to the California gold mines in early fall, 1849. In two weeks, people disagreed about which trail to take. The Sand Walkers split up into smaller groups.

This illustration shows the Brier family.

TEXT and ILLUSTRATION: "Christmas in Death Valley." Highlights, December 2005.; PHOTO: (bkgd spread)HIT1912/iStockphoto/Getty Images, (inset)bayram/Getty Images

This modern photo shows what the trip across Death Valley might have been like.

The Briers followed behind a small band of about thirty young men called the Jayhawkers. The group followed a map that promised a shorter way to California. But there wasn't a shortcut. Instead, they blundered into Death Valley, wandering lost and near death for days. They were likely the first non-native people to enter Death Valley.

Juliet walked slowly with her children. When the Jayhawkers grew weak, they fell back. Juliet acted as a mother to them all. She tended the sick and inspired them to go on. The wagons had to be abandonded. Even though most of the cattle were killed for food, there was not enough. Thirteen men starved. But the Briers lived and carried on.

The group walked through Death Valley and the Mojave Desert to safety in Los Angeles. For many years, the Jayhawkers and the Briers held reunions to share memories of their journey together.

PRIMARY SOURCE

In Their Words...

I would get down on my knees and look in the starlight for the ox tracks and then we would stumble on.

— Juliette Brier

TEXT: Brier, Julia. "Our Christmas Amid the Terrors of Death Valley." The San Francisco Call, December 25, 1898, vol 85, no 25.
PHOTO: (bkgd)bayram/E+/Getty Images, (inset)David Bailey/Nashville/Digital Vision/Getty Images

THE HOOVER DAM

SHARING THE WATER

What do a glass of water in Phoenix, a sprinkler in Denver, a toilet in Los Angeles, and a fountain in Las Vegas have in common? It's likely that much of the water in each comes from the same place: the Colorado River.

In the early 1900s many states wanted to claim the river's resources. In 1922, a compact was created. This agreement divided the river's water equally among seven states.

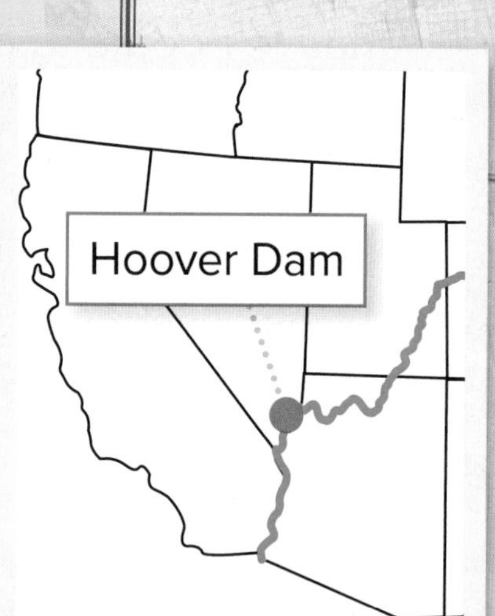

A REALLY BIG DAM

In 1931, work began on the Hoover Dam. It was to be the largest dam in the nation. It was built for a few reasons. It would hold back the Colorado River and prevent flooding. It would help regulate water. Perhaps most importantly, it would provide power through hydroelectric energy.

So how big is the Hoover Dam? It is 726 feet tall. That's 171 feet taller than the Washington Monument. Its base is as thick as two football fields laid end to end. The amount of concrete needed to build the dam could make a 4-foot-wide sidewalk all the way around the Earth at the Equator!

(bkgd spread)powerofforever/Getty Images, (inset)©Nova Development

AND A HUGE LAKE

When the Hoover Dam was finished and blocked the Colorado River, it created Lake Mead. Lake Mead is a huge **reservoir**. It can hold more water than any reservoir in the United States, enough to cover the entire state of New York in one foot of water. However, Lake Mead hasn't been filled all the way in many years. Drought and the demand for water have kept it at lower levels.

WordBlast

Lake Mead is a **reservoir**. What is a reservoir? Check a dictionary or the Glossary to be sure.

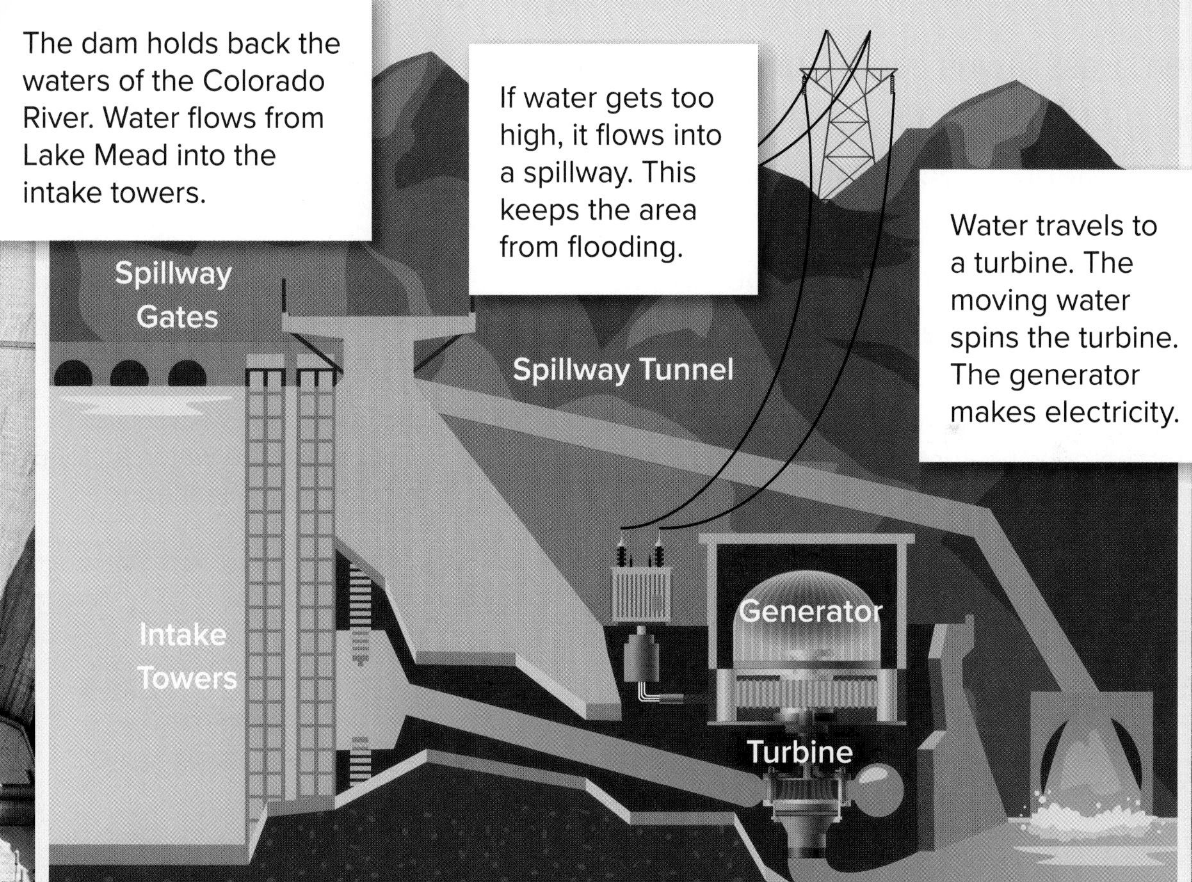

The dam holds back the waters of the Colorado River. Water flows from Lake Mead into the intake towers.
If water gets too high, it flows into a spillway. This keeps the area from flooding.
Water travels to a turbine. The moving water spins the turbine. The generator makes electricity.
Spillway Gates
Spillway Tunnel
Intake Towers
Generator
Turbine

EXPLORE the InfoGraphic

- How does the Hoover Dam provide power?
- What is the purpose of a spillway?
- Where does the water go after leaving the intake tower?

Your Yard Can Save Water!

Green grass lawns can be pretty, but they need a lot of water to stay alive. Using other kinds of plants in your yard can conserve water. That's good news for places where drought is a problem. Check out these drought-friendly plants.

This desert home is surrounded by plants but not the ones you usually see in yards.

Agave plants store water. They can survive for long periods without rain.

Cacti (the plural of "cactus") can store water AND filter it. They make the water systems around them cleaner.

Sagebrush is native to California. It uses little water and can help prevent erosion.

(bkgd)Bruce C. Murray/Shutterstock.com, (t)Andrei Stanescu/Shutterstock.com, (c)Robb Hannawacker/U.S. National Park Service, (b)Mark Herreid/Shutterstock.com

Take Action!

More to Explore

Here are some ideas for you to think about! You can research and discuss the questions below.

What is special about where you live?

What is Death Valley like today?

What are some other things you can do to save water?

WordBlast

- List two things that **decompose**. List one thing that does not.
- What caused the **population** of California to grow in the 1800s?
- Is it important to **preserve** natural areas? Explain.
- How does a dam create a **reservoir**?

Reflect

How does geography impact California communities?

Chapter 2

AMERICAN INDIANS OF THE LOCAL REGION

How have California Indians influenced the local region?

Table of Contents

(bkgd spread)Eyal Nahmias/Alamy Stock Photo, (t)photoquest7/iStockphoto/Getty Images, (c)rab-bit/iStock/Getty Images

CONNECTED TO OUR PAST

The California Indians are known as the first people of California. Their ancestors settled the area long before the Europeans came. There are many different groups of California Indians.

A Hupa Indian woman from long ago

Acjachemen Indian girls from today

- What do you notice in the older picture?
- What do you notice in the modern picture?

(l)Bettmann/Getty Images, (r)Spencer Grant/age fotostock

Citizenship

Sacred Sites

Each group of California Indians has special beliefs. They practice those beliefs at sacred sites. Two of those places are Mount Shasta and Medicine Lake. California Indians perform **traditional** dances and ceremonies at these sites. They gather healing herbs for good health.

MOUNT SHASTA

The Wintu have lived near Mount Shasta for hundreds of years. They believe that their ancestors came from a freshwater spring on the mountain. The spring runs into a beautiful area called Panther Meadows. Every August the Wintu hold sacred ceremonies in the meadows.

Today, many people from around the world visit Mount Shasta. They are drawn to its beauty and awed by its size. However, tourists don't always respect this special place. They place objects in the spring and use too much of its water. They damage plants in the meadows. The Wintu people are working to prevent this to keep their sacred place safe.

Mt. Shasta

WordBlast

What do you think **traditional** means? How does the text help you figure it out?

(bkgd spread)photoquest7/iStockphoto/Getty Images

Medicine Lake

MEDICINE LAKE

Medicine Lake is not far from Mount Shasta. It is a volcano that has filled with water over time. It is also a sacred place to many California Indians, particularly the Shasta, Modoc, and Pit River groups. These groups believe the lake is a place of great healing. In the lands that overlook the lake, many groups hold traditional ceremonies and gather herbs.

Some companies want to use the lands around Medicine Lake. California Indians are using the law to prevent this. They are working hard to keep their sacred site from harm.

A BIGGER VOICE

AB 52 was a bill that became a law in California in 2015. This law gave California Indians more power to make important decisions about their sacred sites. It also said that the state's public projects could not harm any place or object that was sacred to the Indians.

PRIMARY SOURCE

In Their Words...

Tribes are not formally recognized as ... experts on their cultural and historical resources. This bill will provide certainty to protect these important resources.

—Assemblyman Mike Gatto, author of Assembly Bill 52

TEXT:Gatto, Mike. "Assembly Committee on Appropriations." California: April 19, 2013.; PHOTO:(inset)Richard J. Rauenzahn/Alamy Stock Photo

The Mighty Redwood

Special Trees

Trees are important natural resources. They provide nuts, fruits, and berries for food. They also supply wood for building. The California coast redwood trees are among the oldest and tallest trees on Earth. They can reach higher than a 30-floor skyscraper. They can also live for more than 2,000 years.

The California Indians of long ago used fallen redwood trees very carefully. Nothing was wasted. They used redwood planks to build their houses. They also used hollowed-out logs from redwood trees to build canoes. They traded redwood materials with other tribes.

A California Indian house was understood to be a living being. The redwood used for the walls of a house was thought to be sacred.

(bkgd spread)GaryKavanagh/iStock/Getty Images

Redwood trees in California

Saving the Redwoods

As California grew in the 1800s, people needed lumber to build houses. They looked at the giant redwoods and saw just what they needed. The great trees were cut down and milled into boards. Soon, only a few stands of redwoods were left. People realized they had to protect the giant, ancient trees. They formed a group to protect the trees by buying land and making parks where the trees could not be cut down.

California Big Trees: A Paiute Legend

The Paiute Indians called the redwood trees *woh-woh-nau*. Say those sounds out loud. Do you sound like a bird? The Paiute word **mimics** an owl's hoot. The Paiute believed the redwood trees were watched over by owls. Cutting down a redwood tree or hurting an owl was thought to bring bad luck.

WordBlast

If you **mimic** something, what are you doing?

(t)Diane Diederich/Photodisc/Getty Images, (b)cyfrogclone/DigitalVision Vectors/Getty Images

POWWOW POWER

The term *powwow* comes from the American Indian word *pauwau*. Long ago, a powwow was a healing ceremony. It was led by a medicine man. American Indians held the ceremonies to celebrate and give thanks for a successful hunt.

Today, powwows are joyful social gatherings. Special clothes called **regalia** are worn at powwows. The clothes can be decorated with beads, feathers, ribbon, and yarn.

Powwows include drumming, singing, and dancing. They also can include handmade crafts and traditional foods like buffalo meat or acorn soup. You can find powwows all across the United States.

WordBlast

What is **regalia**? What kinds of decorations are used to make regalia?

(bkgdspread)Aurum/Alamy Stock Photo

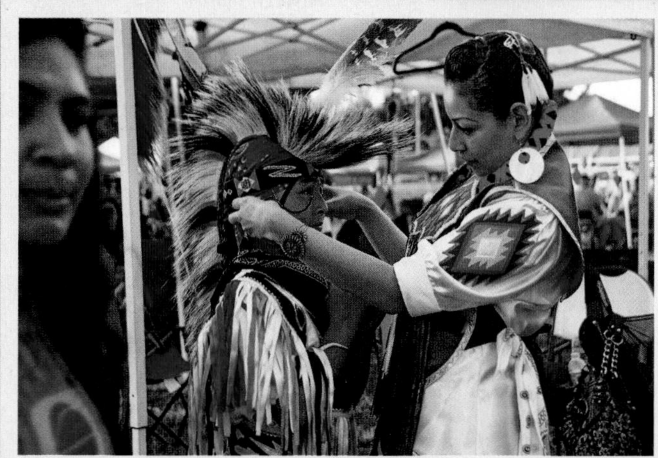

Families celebrate together at powwows.

THE POWERFUL DRUM

The drum is an important part of the powwow. It is treated with respect. American Indians say the drum brings the heartbeat of the Earth Mother to the powwow for all to hear and feel. Drums set the rhythm for the dances that happen in a circle. Everyone sits around the drum and hits the drum at the same time. The sound is very loud and powerful. It creates a beat that encourages singing and dancing.

Many dances are performed at powwows.

ck Photo,
nis/Los Angeles Times/Getty Images,
etty Images

CELEBRATING ACORNS

Did you know that people can eat acorns? It's true! For thousands of years, acorns were an important food source for many California Indians. The Miwok are one group that relied on acorns. Each fall, the Miwok gathered acorns. They ground the nuts into powder. Then they used the acorn powder to make bread, biscuits, and soup.

Today, acorns are not a big part of any group's diet. However, California Indians and others still celebrate and honor the acorn at the Miwok Acorn Festival near Sacramento.

This two-day festival is held every year on a weekend in September. Different groups gather to make and eat foods made from acorns. They also perform traditional dances, play games, and tell stories.

Miwok women ground acorns. Then they sifted the powder in baskets.

(bkgd spread)rab-bit/iStock/Getty Images, (l)George Ostertag/age fotostock/SuperStock, (r)Buyenlarge/Archive Photos/Getty Images

HOW TO ROAST ACORNS FOR EATING

With the help of an adult, follow these steps to roast acorns.

1. Gather ripe acorns or buy them online. The acorns of white oak trees are best to use.
2. Use a nutcracker to crack the acorns. Remove the shells. Put them in a pot of boiling water. Boil them for about 15 minutes. Change the water and boil them again until the water is no longer brown. This removes the bitter taste.
3. Preheat the oven to 350°F. Rinse and spread the acorns on clean towels to dry. Then, spread them on a baking sheet and place the baking sheet in the oven.
4. Roast the acorns for one hour. After the acorns cool, enjoy them on salads, in stews, or as a tasty topping for oatmeal.

EXPLORE the InfoGraphic

- How do you get rid of the bitter taste of acorns?
- How long should you roast the acorns?
- What are the best kind of acorns to use?

(inset)DAVID MCNEW/AFP/Getty Images

READY TO DANCE

AMERICAN INDIANS CALL THE OUTFITS THEY WEAR WHEN DANCING AT POWWOWS *REGALIA*. THEY NEVER CALL THEM COSTUMES.
HEY DENA, WHAT DO YOU THINK OF MY REGALIA?
YOU LOOK GREAT! YOU'RE READY FOR THE GRASS DANCE.

LONG AGO, IT IS SAID, YOUNG BOYS WERE SENT OUT TO FLATTEN THE GRASS BEFORE A CELEBRATION. THIS MOTION TURNED INTO A DANCE.
I HELPED MY MOM SEW THE FRINGE ON.
YOU SHOULD GET DRESSED, TOO. WE'LL BE DANCING SOON.

METAL CONES ARE SEWN ON THE DRESSES FOR THE JINGLE DRESS DANCE.
I CAN'T! LOOK! MOM DIDN'T NOTICE SOME CONES ARE MISSING.
EVERYONE'S REGALIA WILL BE PERFECT EXCEPT MINE.

WHERE IS YOUR MOM?
SHE LEFT EARLY TO PRACTICE HER BUCKSKIN DANCE.

THE BUCKSKIN DANCE IS ONE OF THE OLDEST DANCES. IT IS A BEAUTIFUL DANCE THAT INVOLVES A LOT OF PRACTICE AND SKILL.

YOU DON'T HAVE MUCH TIME. WE BETTER GET THOSE CONES SEWN ON.
I DON'T KNOW HOW TO SEW!

I DO! LET'S GET TO WORK!

PEOPLE WHO MAKE THE REGALIA ARE OFTEN VERY CLOSE RELATIVES OF THE DANCER.
WHO MADE THIS DRESS, DENA?
MY GRANDMOTHER.

IT LOOKS PERFECT! THANKS, PETE!

I HEAR THE DRUM!
WE BETTER RUN!
ART: EUREKA COMICS

IN OUR DAY

AMERICAN INDIAN RODEOS

What do you think of when you picture cowboys and cowgirls? You probably see people in cowboy hats riding horses and swinging ropes. And you would be right!

The tradition of cowboys and cowgirls goes back to the early days of cattle ranching. Spanish settlers brought horses and cattle to Southern California. California Indians living in the area learned how to use horses to herd cattle. It soon became a way of life for the American Indian cowboys and cowgirls.

Today, the tradition continues in the form of **rodeo**. Many weekends, American Indian cowgirls compete in barrel races. American Indian cowboys participate in bronco and bull riding. These competitions require a lot of skill and practice. They are a time-honored tradition for many American Indians.

WordBlast

What do you think a **rodeo** is? What words in the last paragraph help you figure out its meaning?

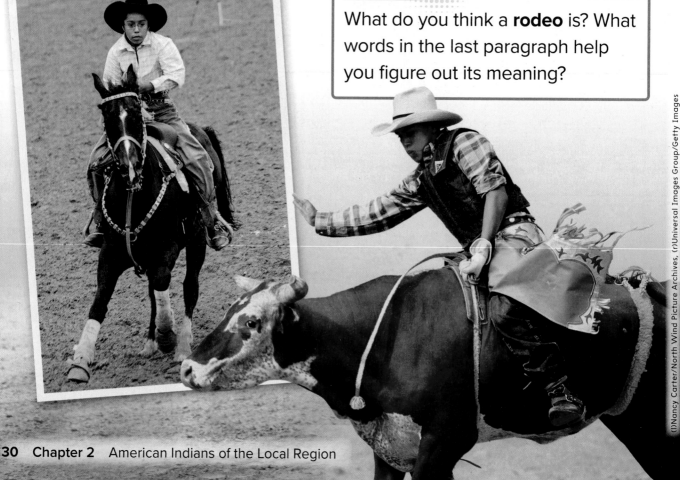

(l)Nancy Carter/North Wind Picture Archives, (r)Universal Images Group/Getty Images

Take Action!

More to Explore

What else do you want to know? The questions below have more ideas that you can research and discuss.

What other California Indian traditions would you like to learn about?

Where can you see redwood trees?

What are some ways to help keep sacred sites safe?

WordBlast

- How does the Paiute word for redwood **mimic** a sound in nature?
- What kinds of **regalia** are worn at powwows?
- What might you see at a **rodeo** today?
- What makes ceremonies at Medicine Lake **traditional**?

Reflect

How have California Indians influenced the local region?

Chapter 3

How and Why Communities Change Over Time

How has life changed for people in my community over time?

Table of Contents

(bkgd spread)bayram/E+/Getty Images, (t)Digiphoto/iStock/Getty Images, (b)i love images/Juice Images/Getty Images

A Neighborhood Changes

The first Chinese immigrants came to San Francisco in 1848. They built a community in the center of the city. Chinatown became a busy neighborhood.

Today, Chinatown is still busy. Shops, restaurants, and activities draw visitors from around the world.

What is different about the two photographs? What is the same?

(t)Library of Congress Prints & Photographs Division [LC-USZ62-98492], (b)Kris Wiktor/Alamy Stock Photo

GOLD!

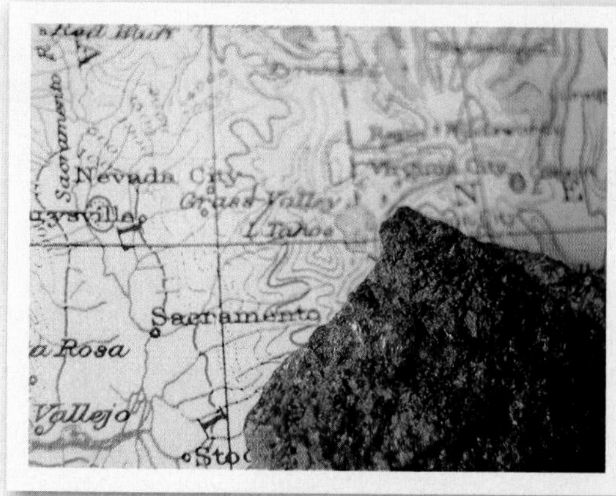

In 1848, gold was discovered in the hills of California. One year later, the Gold Rush was on! California became a **destination** for people looking for riches. They came by wagons from the eastern United States, Canada, and Mexico. Others came from places such as China and Chile by boat. Miners settled in central California and in cities like San Francisco.

WordBlast

What do you think a **destination** is? Check your answer in the Glossary.

People came from all over the world to find gold in California.

(bkgd spread)Pete Ryan/National Geographic/Getty Images, (t)Digiphoto/iStock/Getty Images, (c)TonyBaggett/iStock/Getty Images, (b)Library of Congress Prints and Photographs Division [LC-DIG-ds-04487]

A CHANGING WAY OF LIFE

The Maidu Indians lived in the Sierra Nevada where gold was discovered. Their home was quickly overrun by miners with gold fever. Many of the Maidu and other California Indians had to go to work in the mines as their lands disappeared. Miners and settlers took their land and changed their way of life forever.

Women played an important role in the Gold Rush.

WOMEN OF THE GOLD RUSH

Most gold prospectors were men, but women were also part of the Gold Rush. Some came west with their families or husbands. Some brave fortune seekers came to California on their own. Women discovered that they could make a living. Prospectors paid women to cook for them. Women also ran hotels.

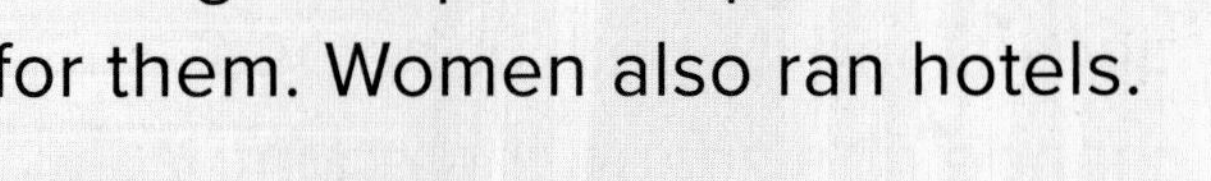

NEAR AND FAR

Miners came from near and far. African Americans hoped to start a new life. In many cases, they also hoped to earn their freedom. Other men came from China. They worked hard to earn money and build a new life. They were not always paid fairly. Gold seekers from Chile and Mexico faced similar challenges.

Chinese gold rush miners

(t)North Wind Picture Archives/Alamy Stock Photo, (b)Hulton Archive/Archive Photos/Getty Images

PAVING THE WAY WEST

ROUTE US 66

U.S. Highway 66, also called Route 66, was a famous highway. It was built in the 1920s, when the idea of highways—and cars—was still new. The road ran from Chicago to Los Angeles.

In the 1930s, thousands of people followed Route 66 as they moved west to escape the Dust Bowl. The road was not even completely paved. But it was still seen as the way to a better life.

In the 1940s during World War II, the government used the highway to move troops and equipment. After the war, gas stations, hotels, and restaurants opened all along the road. More people used the highway to move to California. California cities grew.

By the early 1980s, new modern highways had been built in place of Route 66. Today, there are still historic signs and museums along the old route. Route 66 helped **transform** the towns and cities along its path. It helped change and shape the country from the Midwest to California.

WordBlast

What do you think the word **transform** means? How do you know?

(bkgd spread)Franck Fotos/Alamy Stock Photo, (inset)lolon/DigitalVision Vectors/Getty Images

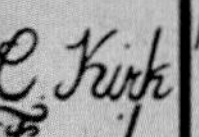

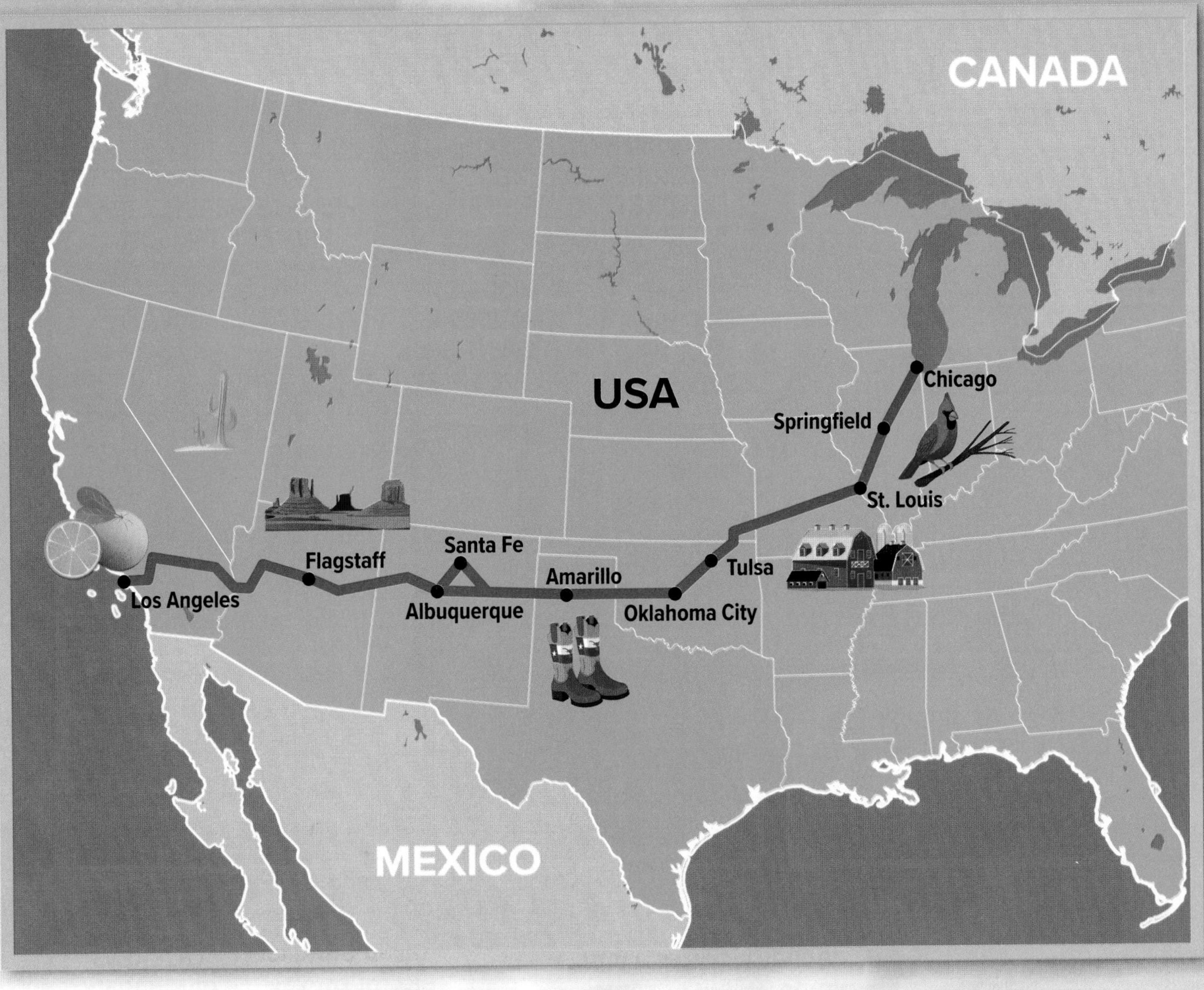

CANADA

USA

MEXICO

Chicago

Springfield

St. Louis

Tulsa

Oklahoma City

Amarillo

Santa Fe

Albuquerque

Flagstaff

Los Angeles

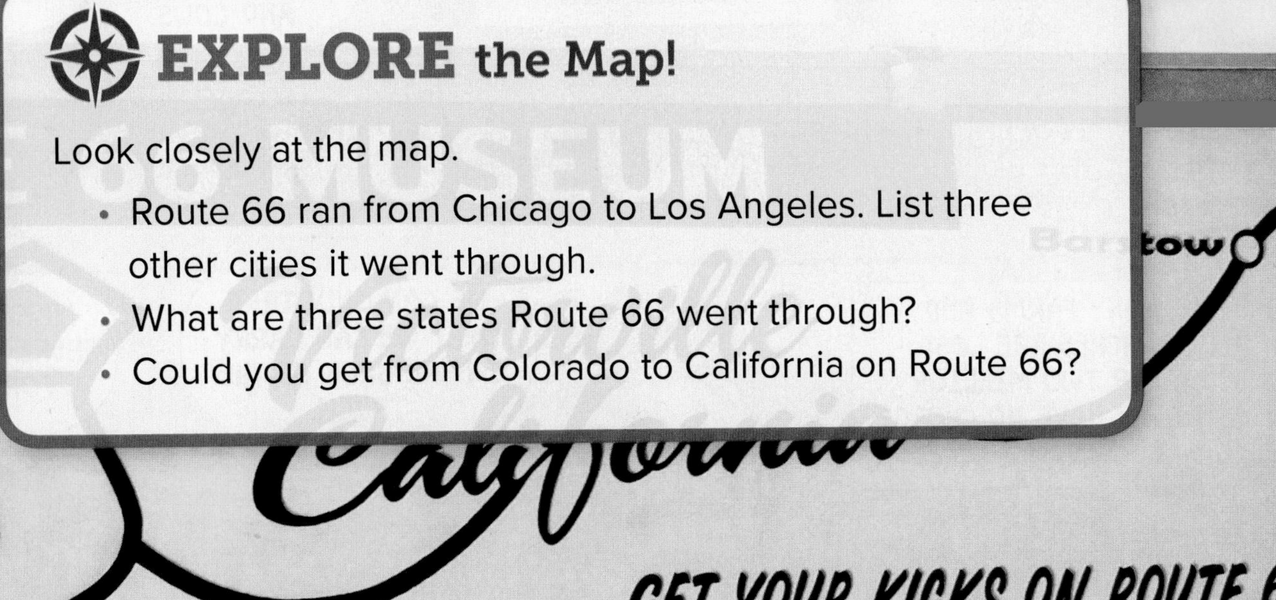

EXPLORE the Map!

Look closely at the map.

- Route 66 ran from Chicago to Los Angeles. List three other cities it went through.
- What are three states Route 66 went through?
- Could you get from Colorado to California on Route 66?

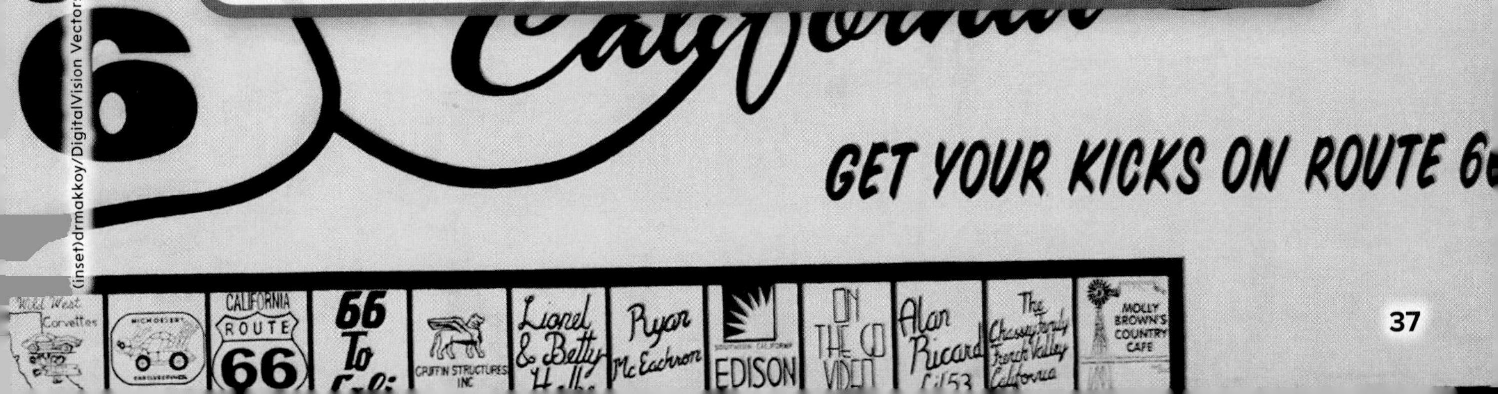

(inset)drmakkoy/DigitalVision Vectors/Getty Images

The Dust Bowl Migration

THE GREAT DEPRESSION HITS FARMERS HARD AS CROP PRICES DROP.

CORN ONLY SELLS FOR 8 CENTS A BUSHEL.

AT THAT PRICE, IT'S CHEAPER TO BURN CORN IN MY STOVE INSTEAD OF COAL.

SOME FARMERS MAKE CLOTHES FOR THEIR CHILDREN OUT OF EMPTY FLOUR AND SUGAR SACKS.

I'M GLAD MOMMA MADE ME THIS NEW DRESS.

I JUST WISH SHE USED A DIFFERENT SACK FOR MY SHIRT.

THE CROPS THEY GROW HAVE PUSHED OUT PRAIRIE GRASSES THAT PROTECT THE SOIL.
NOW WHEN THE WIND BLOWS, THE DIRT ITSELF IS CARRIED AWAY.

THEN A TIME OF DROUGHT COMES. WITH NO RAIN, DUST STORMS FILL THE SKY.

THESE STORMS ARE BLINDING THE HORSES AND COWS.

AND THE CHICKENS CAN BARELY BREATHE.

MANY FARMS AND RANCHES ARE LOST. OVER TWO MILLION PEOPLE HAVE NO CHOICE BUT TO MOVE ON.

WE CAN ONLY TAKE WHAT WE CAN CARRY IN THE BACK OF THE TRUCK.

MAKE SURE THERE'S ROOM FOR ME.

MANY TRAVEL WEST. SOME WALK AND SOME DRIVE.
WHERE ARE WE GOING?
WELL, I'VE HEARD GOOD THINGS ABOUT CALIFORNIA.

AT NIGHT, THEY CAMP IN TENTS OR SLEEP UNDER THE STARS.

THE GROUND IS AWFULLY LUMPY.

JUST MAKE SURE NONE OF THE LUMPS ARE SNAKES.

IF A CAR BREAKS DOWN, IT'S HARD TO GET PARTS TO FIX IT.

I HOPE THE BRAKES WILL WORK IN THE MOUNTAINS.

I HOPE THE PATCH ON THIS TIRE WILL LAST.

BUT WHAT AWAITS THEM IN CALIFORNIA IS NOT WHAT EVERYONE EXPECTS.

THIS JOB ONLY PAYS 20 CENTS AN HOUR!

THAT'S BETTER THAN STARVING.

SOME PEOPLE ARE STILL HOMELESS.
BUT WE CAN'T GO BACK. THERE'S NOTHING TO GO BACK TO.

YEARS PASS BEFORE MANY OF THE MIGRANTS TRULY SETTLE DOWN.

LIFE WAS HARD UNTIL WE FINALLY GOT OUR OWN HOUSE.

AT LAST CALIFORNIA FEELS LIKE HOME.

TEXT: *STEPHEN KRENSKY*
ART: *EUREKA COMICS*

Citizenship

It's Dry Out There!

A drought is a long period when there is not enough rain. In California, drought can be a serious problem. With little rain, fire danger increases. One spark in a dry area can start a fire. Once a fire starts, it can spread quickly. Wildfires can be big and scary, especially near homes. To **prevent** the spread of fires, new homes are built with materials that don't burn easily. Taking out dead plants and trees can also be a big help.

WordBlast

When you **prevent** something, what do you do? Look for clues in the paragraph.

Droughts can lead to wildfires.

(bkgd spread)Sierralara/Shutterstock.com; (inset)Chuck Place/Alamy Stock Photo

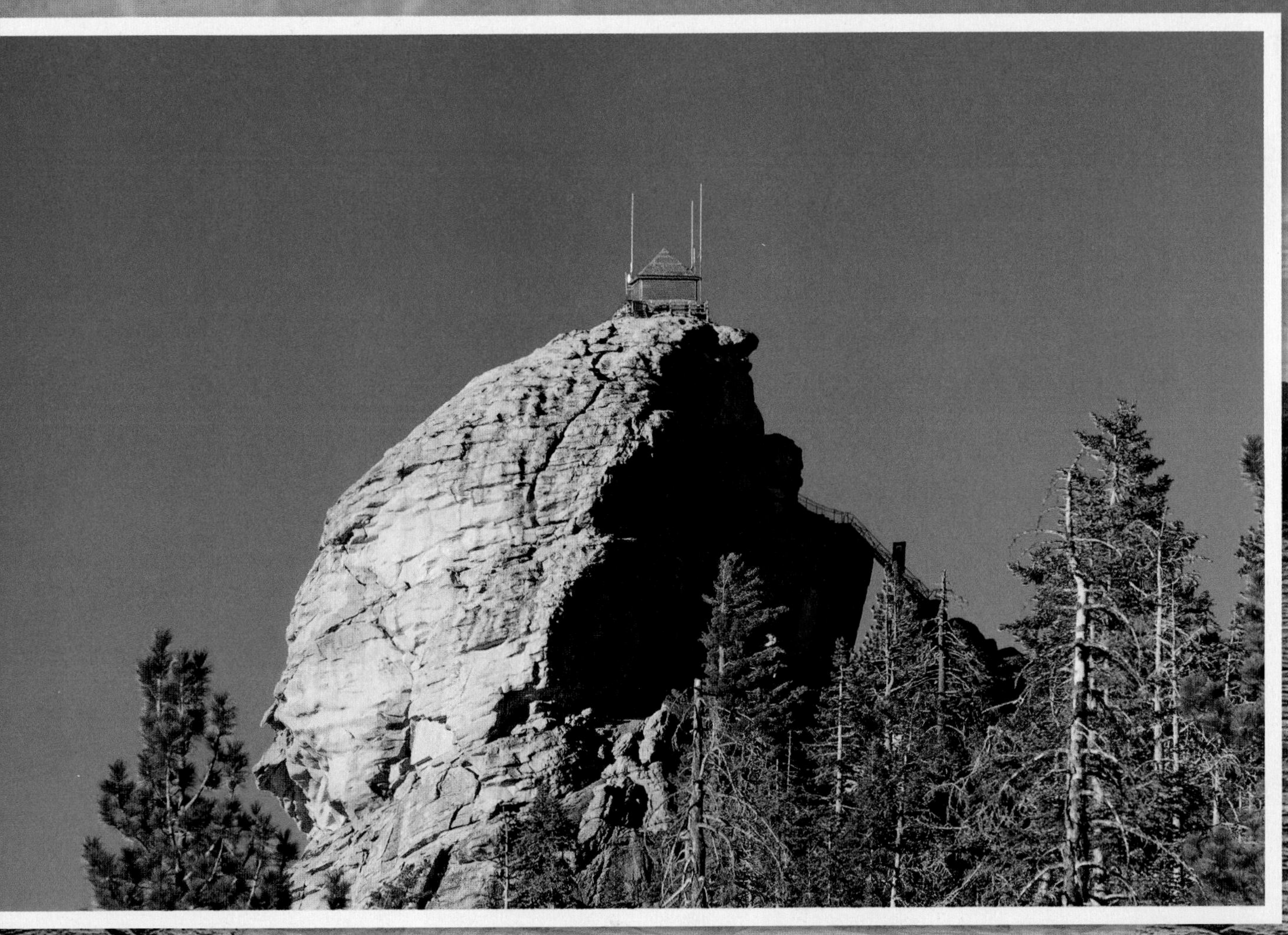

Fire Watchers Keep California Safe

To help prevent wildfires, the National Parks hire fire lookouts. The lookouts sit in watchtowers high above the trees looking below for any signs of fire. They must stay awake and alert so they don't miss a fire starting. When they see a fire, they call firefighters. Firefighters come and extinguish the blaze before it gets out of control. These fire watchers help protect the parks and all of us from wildfires.

(inset)George Ostertag/Alamy Stock Photo

THEN & NOW

HOORAY FOR HOLLYWOOD

Hollywood is a neighborhood in Los Angeles, California. It is known as the home of the movie business in the U.S. The movie-making business helped turn Los Angeles into a big city.

People called studio heads were in charge at the movie studios. They made actors into big stars. Shirley Temple was one of the biggest stars in the 1930s. She made her first Hollywood movie when she was only six years old! The little girl cheered up moviegoers during the Great Depression.

(bkgd, t)Bettmann/Getty Images, (b)Time Life Pictures/The LIFE Picture Collection/Getty Images

Grauman's Chinese Theatre in Hollywood attracts many visitors every year.

Today, moviemaking is still a big **industry** in Los Angeles. Those early studio heads would be surprised to see a movie today. Special effects make amazing worlds come to life. We still have real actors, but we also have computer-drawn ones!

WordBlast

What do you think **industry** means? Look at the other paragraphs for clues.

Mark Bassett/Alamy Stock Photo

Strawberry Season | Tiempo de fresa

by Guadalupe Lopez

Warm sunny days
Cool foggy nights

Summer on the Central Coast
Strawberry season is here!

Sweet ruby hearts
in fields of green

Pick now while ripe
For tomorrow they are gone

Cálidos días de sol
Noches de niebla

Verano en la Costa Central
Es tiempo de la fresa

Dulce fruta corazón
sobre manta verde

Hay que pizcarlas hoy
Pues mañana ya no hay

(bkgd)joshuaraineyphotography/iStock/Getty Images, (inset)i love images/Juice Images/Getty Images

Take Action!

More to Explore

What else do you want to know about? Here are some questions that you can research and discuss.

How has your neighborhood changed? How can you find out?

Which places along old Route 66 would you like to visit?

Other than gold, what brought people to California?

WordBlast

- Why was California a **destination** for so many immigrants in the 1840s?
- How did the movie **industry** change Los Angeles?
- Why is it important to **prevent** wildfires?
- How did Route 66 help **transform** California?

Reflect

How has life changed for people in my community over time?

Chapter 4

American Citizens, Symbols, and Government

How do our government and its citizens work together?

Table of Contents

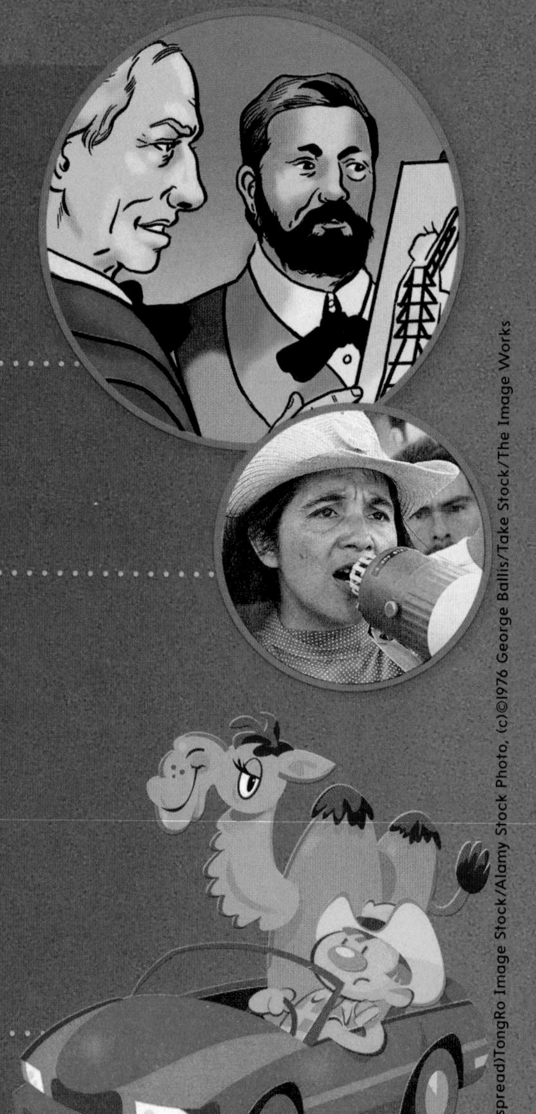

(bkgd spread)TongRo Image Stock/Alamy Stock Photo, (c)©1976 George Ballis/Take Stock/The Image Works

CELEBRATE OUR SYMBOLS

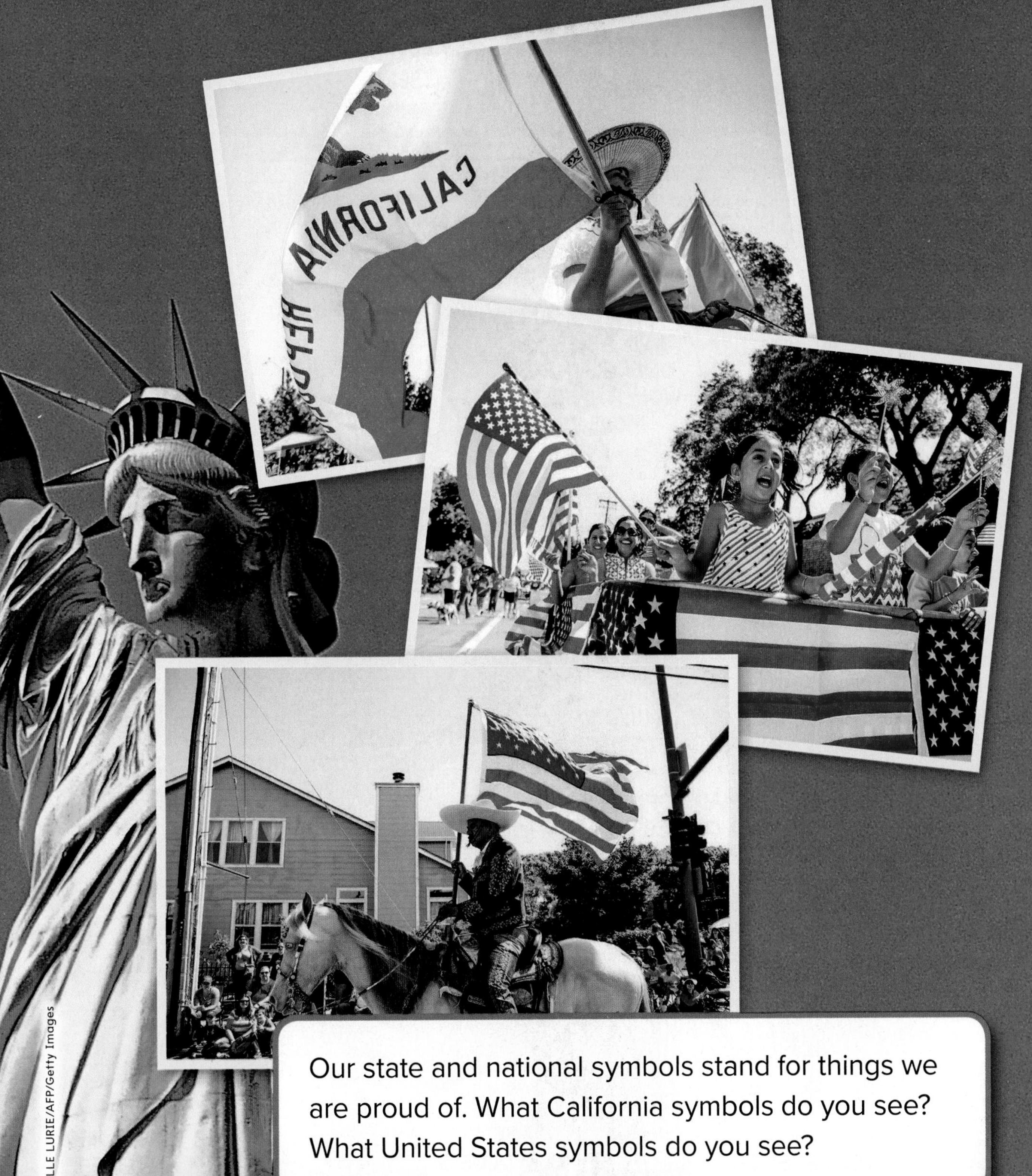

GABRIELLE LURIE/AFP/Getty Images

Our state and national symbols stand for things we are proud of. What California symbols do you see? What United States symbols do you see?

The Story Of The Statue Of Liberty

IN 1865, EDOUARD DE LABOULAYE HAS AN IDEA. HE HIRES FRÉDÉRIC-AUGUSTE BARTHOLDI TO SCULPT A MONUMENTAL STATUE.

IT WILL REPRESENT THE FRIENDSHIP BETWEEN FRANCE AND THE UNITED STATES.

AND THE IDEAL OF FREEDOM ITSELF.

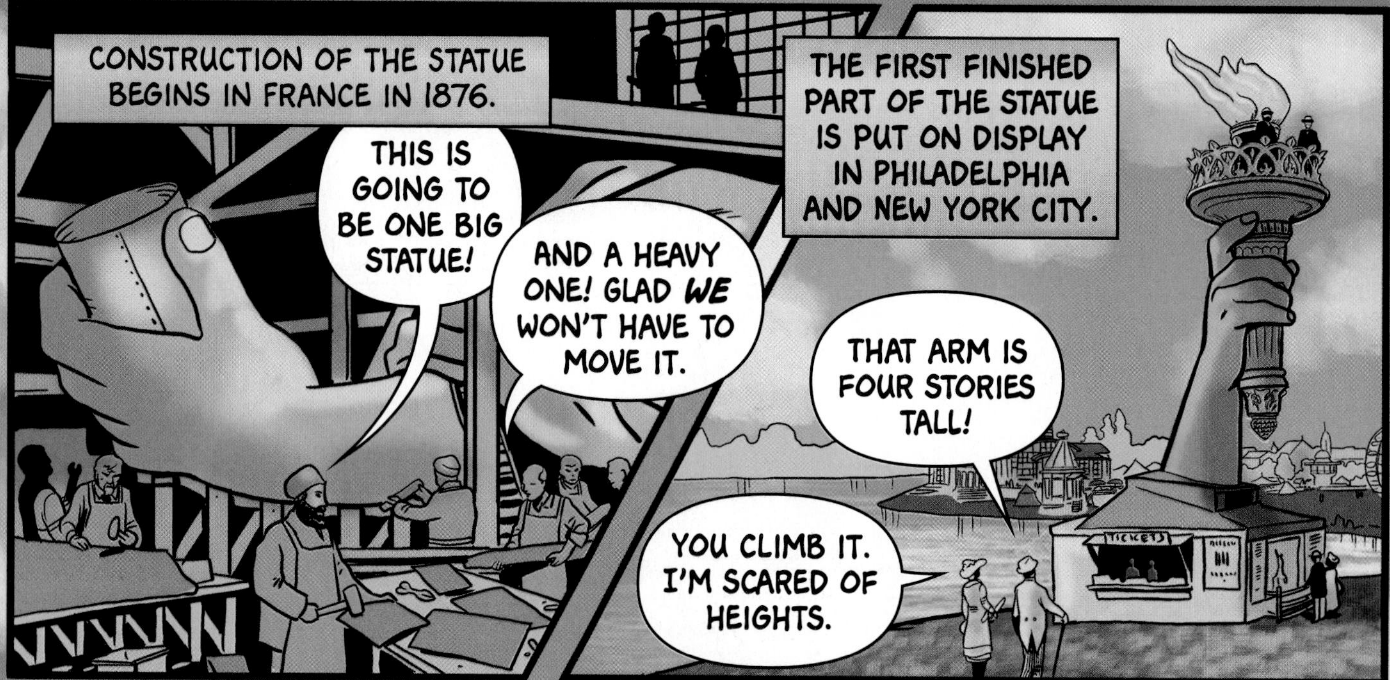

CONSTRUCTION OF THE STATUE BEGINS IN FRANCE IN 1876.
THIS IS GOING TO BE ONE BIG STATUE!
AND A HEAVY ONE! GLAD *WE* WON'T HAVE TO MOVE IT.
THE FIRST FINISHED PART OF THE STATUE IS PUT ON DISPLAY IN PHILADELPHIA AND NEW YORK CITY.
THAT ARM IS FOUR STORIES TALL!
YOU CLIMB IT. I'M SCARED OF HEIGHTS.
TICKETS

IN 1881, BARTHOLDI CALLS ON GUSTAVE EIFFEL, THE MAN WHO WILL LATER BUILD THE EIFFEL TOWER, TO FINISH THE STATUE.

IT WILL BE MADE OF COPPER, AND COPPER NEEDS SUPPORT.
I WILL MAKE A FLEXIBLE SYSTEM, LIKE A SKELETON.

THE YEAR IS 1885. THE STATUE OF LIBERTY ARRIVES IN NEW YORK HARBOR. MANY PEOPLE COME FOR THIS HISTORIC LANDING.

SO SHE'S HEADED OUT TO BEDLOE'S ISLAND.
YOU'LL BE ABLE TO SEE HER FROM ANYWHERE IN THE HARBOR!

DESIGNED BY AMERICAN RICHARD MORRIS HUNT, THE PEDESTAL TO HOLD THE STATUE IS FINISHED IN 1886.
ART: EUREKA COMICS
FIRST, BUILDERS ATTACH THE STATUE'S SKELETON. IT IS MADE OF IRON.
THEN, THE COPPER PLATES ARE ATTACHED TO THE FRAME. IT TAKES FOUR MONTHS TO PUT ALL THE PIECES TOGETHER.
AS YEARS PASS, THE COPPER WILL TURN GREEN FROM EXPOSURE TO AIR.
THE STATUE IS DEDICATED ON OCTOBER 28, 1886. A POEM BY EMMA LAZARUS IS ADDED TO THE BASE IN 1903. TODAY, MORE THAN FOUR MILLION PEOPLE VISIT THE STATUE EACH YEAR.

AN UNFAIR LAW

This illustration shows what Chinese workers in California looked like in the 1800s.

The United States is a country filled with people from other places. During the 1800s, many immigrants came to California from China. They worked in the gold fields, in factories, and on the railroads. However, some Americans wanted to stop people moving to the United States from China. They were afraid Chinese workers would take too many jobs.

In 1882, a law called the Chinese Exclusion Act was passed. When you **exclude** something, you do not let it in. The law stopped almost all Chinese immigration for ten years. It also made it hard for Chinese people already in the United States to leave and come back. Then, after ten years had gone by, the law was passed again. This time, it did not have an end date.

The law was not fair, but it stayed in place for many years. Finally, in 1943, President Franklin D. Roosevelt called the law a "historic mistake." He helped to make the law less strict. However, it was not fully **repealed** until 1965.

WordBlast

What word means the opposite of **exclude**?

WordBlast

The word *repeal* comes from an old French word that means "to call back." What do you think happens when a law is **repealed**?

DEA/A. DAGLI ORTI/De Agostini/Getty Images

LIFE ON ANGEL ISLAND

Angel Island is near the coast of San Francisco. It became an immigration center in 1910. Most Chinese immigrants had to pass through the island to enter the United States. It was often the hardest part of the journey. Men were separated from women and children. Everyone had to be tested for illness. People sometimes waited weeks or months before they could come into the United States.

The photographs show Chinese immigrants arriving at Angel Island.

(t)Fotosearch/Archive Photos/Getty Images, (b)FPG/Archive Photos/Getty Images

Citizenship

SPEAKING WITH SEVEN TONGUES

Dolores Huerta grew up in Stockton, California in the 1930s. She and her brothers lived with their mother and grandfather. Dolores learned to speak her mind early in life. In fact, her grandfather called her "Seven Tongues" because she talked so much—and so well.

When Dolores was a child, the United States was struggling through the Great Depression. Many of her neighbors were farm workers. They moved from place to place to pick the ripe crops. They were hired for short periods of time. They worked very long hours and were paid very little money. Dolores saw how hard their lives were.

migrant farm workers in the 1930s

After World War II, Dolores' mother ran a small hotel. She often let the farm workers stay there for free. Dolores learned about fairness and kindness from her mother. Dolores did not see her father very often, but she learned from him, too. He worked as a miner and as a farm worker. He showed Dolores that she could work to change things she didn't like.

(bkgd spread)ziss/iStock/Getty Images, (inset)Buyenlarge/Archive Photos/Getty Images

Growing up around farm workers led Dolores to want to help others. She wanted to be a voice for change. As an adult, Dolores became an **activist**. She used her voice and her skills to fight for the rights of farm workers. She and her friend Cesar Chavez started the Farm Workers Association to do just that.

It took several years, but their efforts made a big difference. The farm workers were able to ask for better wages and working hours. Dolores didn't stop there. She kept fighting for others, and she is still working and speaking.

Dolores Huerta uses her "seven tongues" to speak for those in need. She continues to work hard to help others today.

WordBlast

What does an **activist** do?

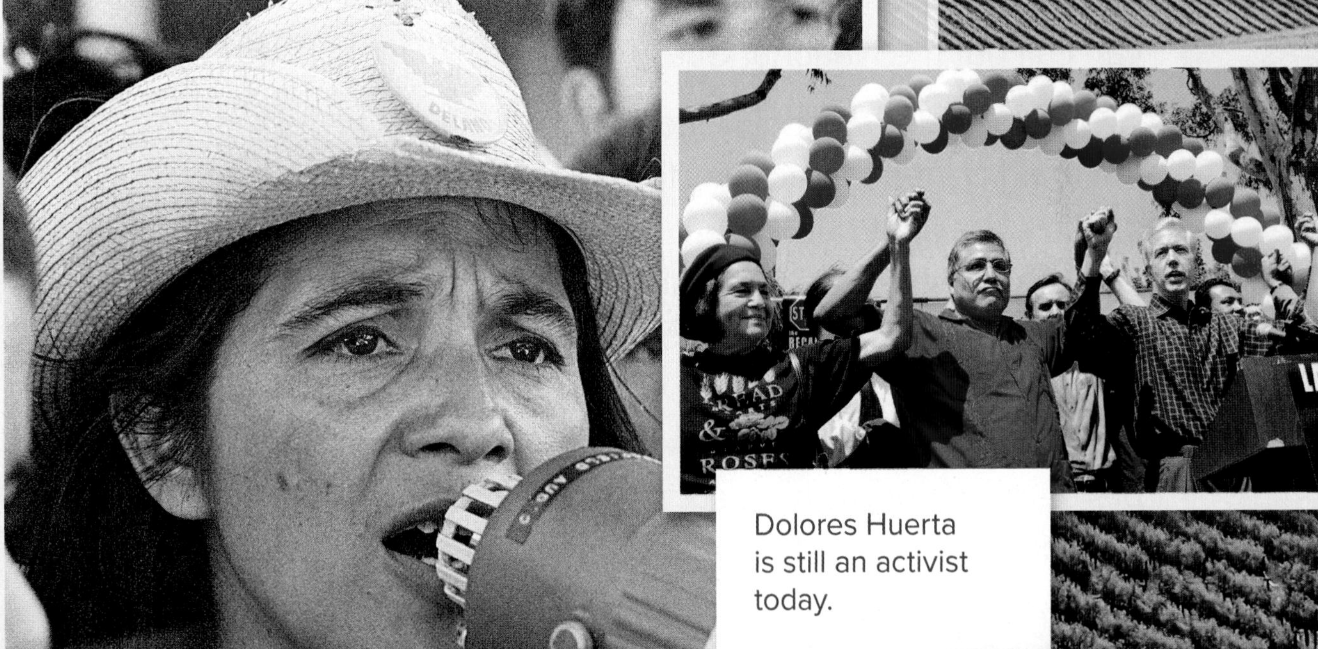

Dolores Huerta is still an activist today.

Dolores Huerta has spoken out for many years.

(l)©1976 George Ballis/Take Stock/The Image Works, (r)REUTERS/Alamy Stock Photo

DISASTER!

THE NATIONAL GUARD

Whom are you going to call if there's an earthquake, a hurricane, or a forest fire? Whatever the disaster, the National Guard is there to help!

The National Guard is a reserve military force for the United States. Their purpose is to be ready to protect and help Americans in an emergency. If there is a natural disaster, the governor of a state can call out the National Guard units.

A Guard soldier must be ready for anything. When tornadoes strike, Guard soldiers are sent out to clear fallen trees and other **debris**. When an area floods, the Guard might use boats to search for people who are trapped. They bring victims to shelters. They provide cots and blankets for people in need. And they don't just rescue people! One group, the Louisiana National Guard, has rescued more than 1,400 pets.

WordBlast

What do you think **debris** is? Check the Glossary to be sure.

A National Guard soldier views a forest fire from above.

(bkgd spread)Spencer Platt/Getty Images News/Getty Images, (inset)MixPix/Alamy Stock Photo

EXPLORE the Map

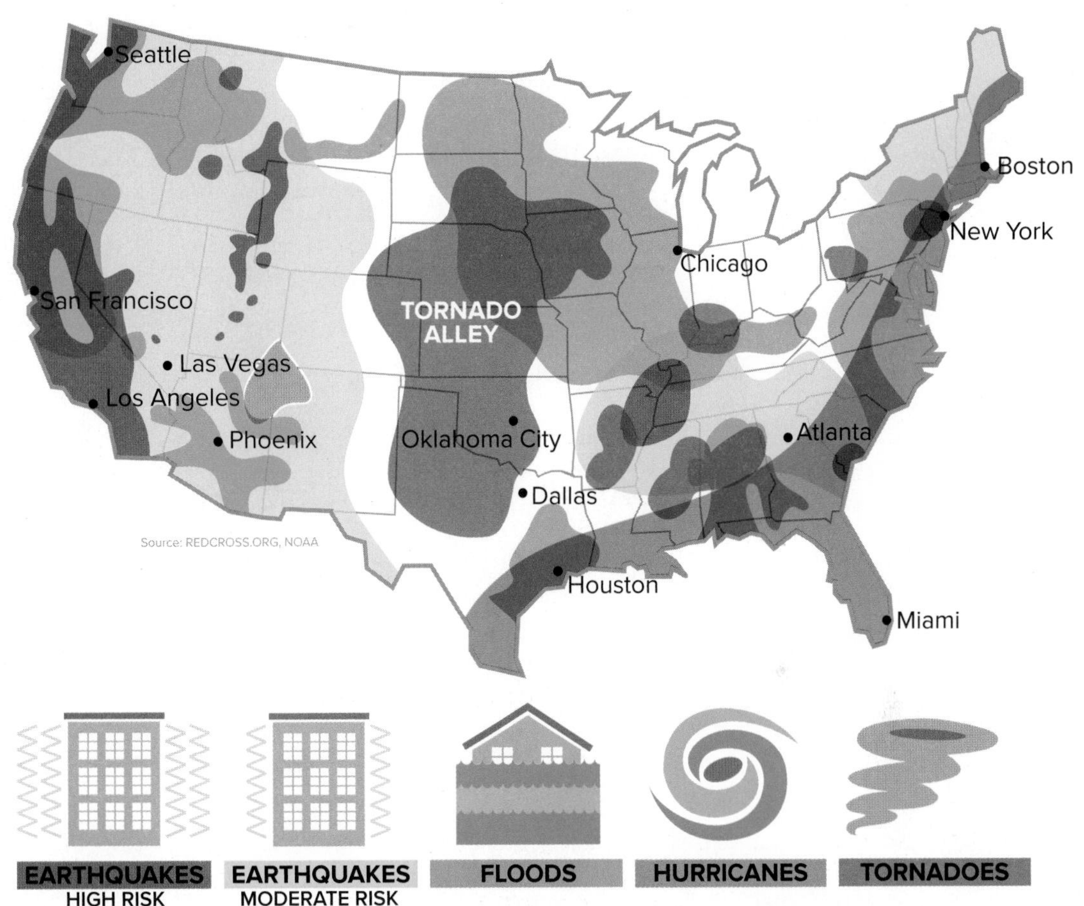

Use the map to answer the questions.

- On which coast are earthquakes more likely to happen?
- What does the orange color on the map show?
- What kind of disaster would the National Guard likely help with in Oklahoma?
- If you lived in Miami, what might you need to prepare for?

Welcome, New Friends

First Daughters

Every four years, the United States elects a president. Sometimes we vote to keep the same person for four more years. Sometimes we vote for a new person. But every time a new president takes office, the same thing happens. One family moves out of the White House and another family moves in.

Jenna Bush Hager and Barbara Bush are twins. They were teenagers when their father, George W. Bush, was elected president in 2000. The twins lived in the White House for eight years.

A new president named Barack Obama won the office in 2008. It was time for the Bush family to leave the White House. President Bush wrote a letter welcoming the new president. The Bush

(bkgd spread)Tetra images RF/Getty Images, (inset)TIM SLOAN/AFP/Getty Images, (b)Marc Bryan-Brown/WireImage/Getty Images twins also wrote a letter. Their letter went to President Obama's daughters, Sasha and Malia.

In the letter, the Bush daughters gave Sasha and Malia some good advice. They told the 7- and 10-year-old girls to have fun. They said it was okay to slide down the banisters. They told them to play on the White House lawn and have pets. They also said it was important for the girls to keep their good and loyal friends.

The Bush daughters didn't have to write a letter. But they wanted to help. They wanted to make the White House feel like a home for two little girls. And when the Obamas left the White House in 2017, the Bushes wrote them a new letter. It said welcome back to the "real" world!

CONNECT THROUGH LITERATURE

Inviting the Bears

A Retelling of a Tlingit Folktale

There was once an old man who was alone in the world. One day, the man saw two huge grizzly bears fishing in a stream. The bears snorted and growled when they saw the man.

But the man hid his fear. "Hello, great Grizzlies. I have no friends or family to share my table. Please come and feast with me this evening."

The bears looked at him quietly and nodded. The man rushed home to prepare for his guests. That evening he served the bears a great feast. After the meal, the largest bear turned to him. "I too have lost family and friends. The bears will always be your friends."

To this day, the Tlingit make friends by feasting together.

(t)Bill Clark/CQ-Roll Call Group/Getty Image, (c)Chip Somodevilla/Getty Images News/Getty Images, (b)Juniors Bildarchiv GmbH/Alamy Stock Photo

THAT BECAME A LAW?

Most laws make sense when you think about them. Buckle your seat belt. Do not litter. However, there are some laws that don't make a whole lot of sense today. Or maybe they never quite did!

ARIZONA: Even if your barn is full, it's against the law to let your donkey sleep in the bathtub.

MINNESOTA: It is illegal to eat hamburgers on Sunday in St. Cloud, Minnesota. Better get your burgers on another day!

NEVADA: It is illegal to drive a camel on the highway. Find another way to cross the desert!

WASHINGTON: You may not chase or bother Bigfoot, Sasquatch, or any other undiscovered animal. (Hopefully, they won't chase you either!)

Take Action!

More to Explore

Here are some ideas for you to think about!

What are some laws that you think are fair? What are some laws you think are unfair?

Who are some other people working to make changes today?

What other groups help people during and after disasters?

WordBlast

- What is something an **activist** might do?
- Why is **debris** a problem after a natural disaster?
- If you **exclude** someone from a game, how does that person feel? Why?
- How do you think the **repeal** of the Chinese Exclusion Act might have changed lives?

Reflect

How do our government and its citizens work together?

Chapter 5

ECONOMICS of the LOCAL REGION

How do people in a community meet their needs?

Table of Contents

(bkgd spread)Kit_Leong/iStock/Getty Images, (t)Ron_Thomas/E+/Getty Images, (b)Tina Stallard/The Image Bank/Getty Images

CALIFORNIA CROPS

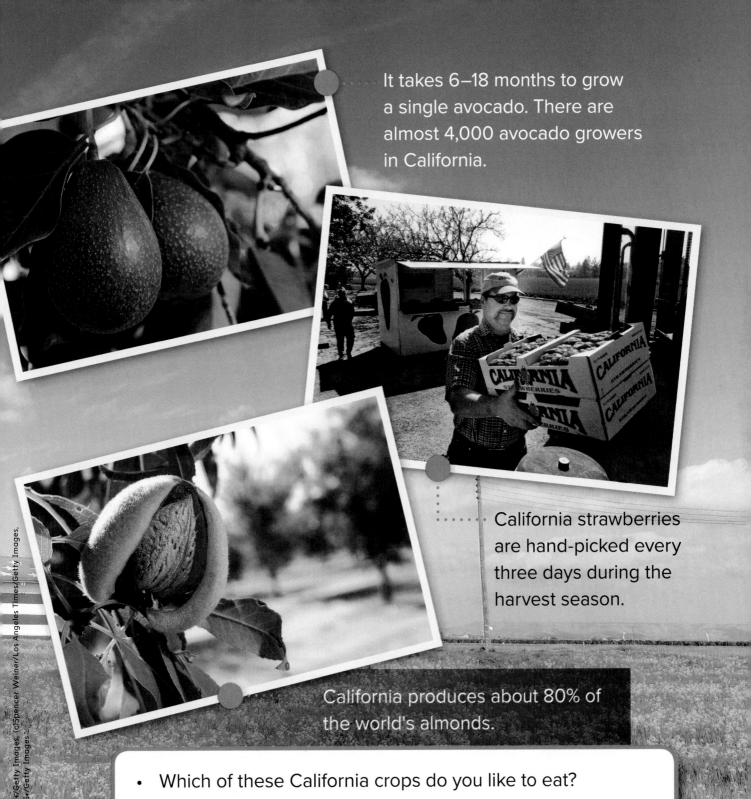

It takes 6–18 months to grow a single avocado. There are almost 4,000 avocado growers in California.

California strawberries are hand-picked every three days during the harvest season.

California produces about 80% of the world's almonds.

- Which of these California crops do you like to eat?
- Why do you think California is able to grow so many crops?

(t)GomezDavid/E+/Getty Images, (c)Spencer Weiner/Los Angeles Times/Getty Images, (b)GomezDavid/E+/Getty Images

POWERING THE FUTURE

Much of the energy we use comes from fossil fuels. These are things like coal, oil, and natural gas. Once the fuels are used up, they will be gone forever. The good news is that there are other **sources** of energy that will NEVER run out.

Solar power uses the energy of the sun. Special panels collect energy from the sun's rays. That energy is turned into electricity for homes and businesses.

Wind power is—can you guess? Yes! It is energy made using the wind. Giant wind turbines have blades that turn in the wind. The blades spin a generator. The generator makes electricity.

A sunny, windy day can be pretty POWERFUL!

WordBlast

What do you think the word **source** means? Check the Glossary to be sure.

There are more than 13,000 wind turbines in California.

California produces more solar power than any other state.

(bkgd spread)Tetra Images - Gary Weathers/Brand X/Getty Images, (inset)Ron_Thomas/E+/Getty Images

Make a Solar Pizza Box Oven

You can harness the power of the sun. Ask an adult to help you.

Materials: large cardboard pizza box, scissors, aluminum foil, tape, glue, plastic wrap, black construction paper, ruler

Directions:

1. On the top of the pizza box lid, draw a square. It should be about one inch in from each side of the box. Use scissors to cut along THREE sides to make a big flap. Fold the flap up. It should stand up when the box lid is closed.
2. Cover the inside of the flap with foil, shiny side up. Use tape to hold it in place.
3. Put foil on the inside bottom of the box and glue it in place.
4. Glue black construction paper over the top of the foil in the box.
5. Stretch plastic wrap across the hole in the lid. Glue or tape it in place.
6. Place the solar oven on a flat surface in bright sunlight.
7. Place food you want to heat on a plate. (Tortillas with cheese work well!) Put the plate in the oven.
8. Prop the flap open with a ruler. Turn the box so that the flap reflects sunlight right onto the food.
9. Wait for your treat to heat. It should take about 30–45 minutes. Turn the box as needed so the flap faces the sun. Enjoy!

Have you eaten a juicy, ripe peach? Tasted wildflower honey? Do you like fresh bread? The place you need to go is a farmers' market! There is so much to see and even more to taste. And it all comes from right around where you live!

California has more than 700 farmers' markets. That's more than any other state. The markets are fun, and they have the freshest foods. Farmers' markets are also good for farmers. They can sell their **produce** close to home.

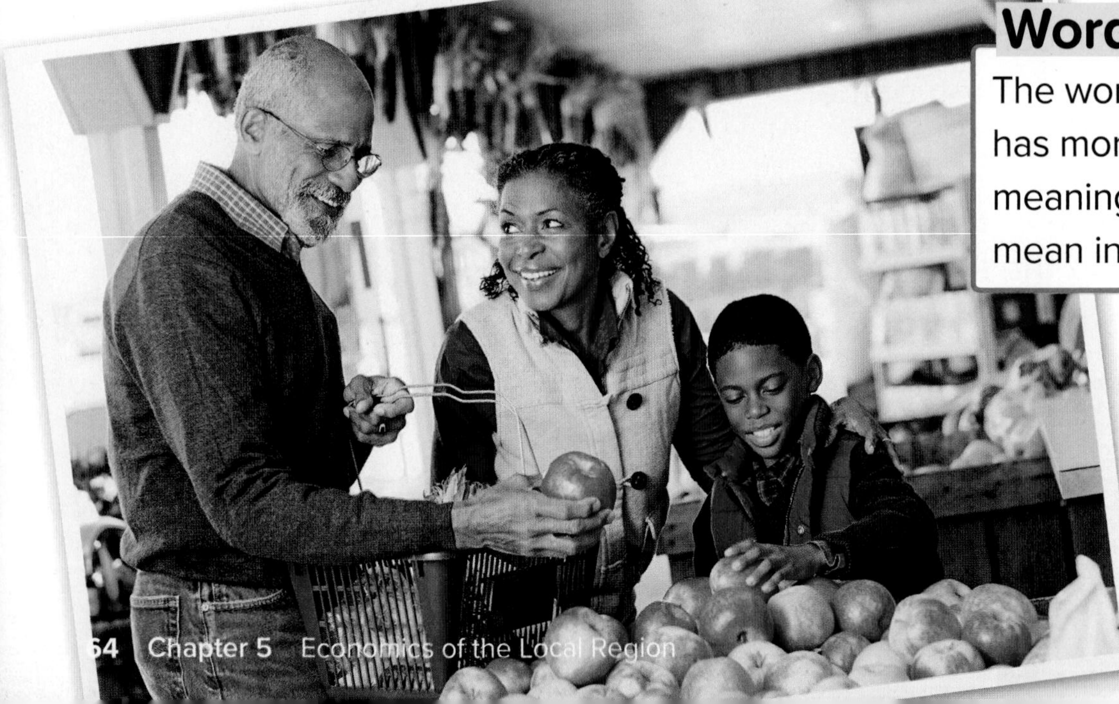

WordBlast

The word **produce** has more than one meaning. What does it mean in the article?

(t)Picsfive/Shutterstock.com, (b)Isadora Getty Buyou/Image Source

SUPPORT YOUR FARMER!

Farmers' markets aren't the only way to support farmers in your area. You can also ask your family to join a CSA. CSA stands for Community Supported Agriculture. In a CSA, people buy straight from a farmer. They pay the farmer, and the farmer delivers boxes of fresh produce to them.

Check out a farmers' market near you. Sign up for a CSA. You might find some new favorite foods!

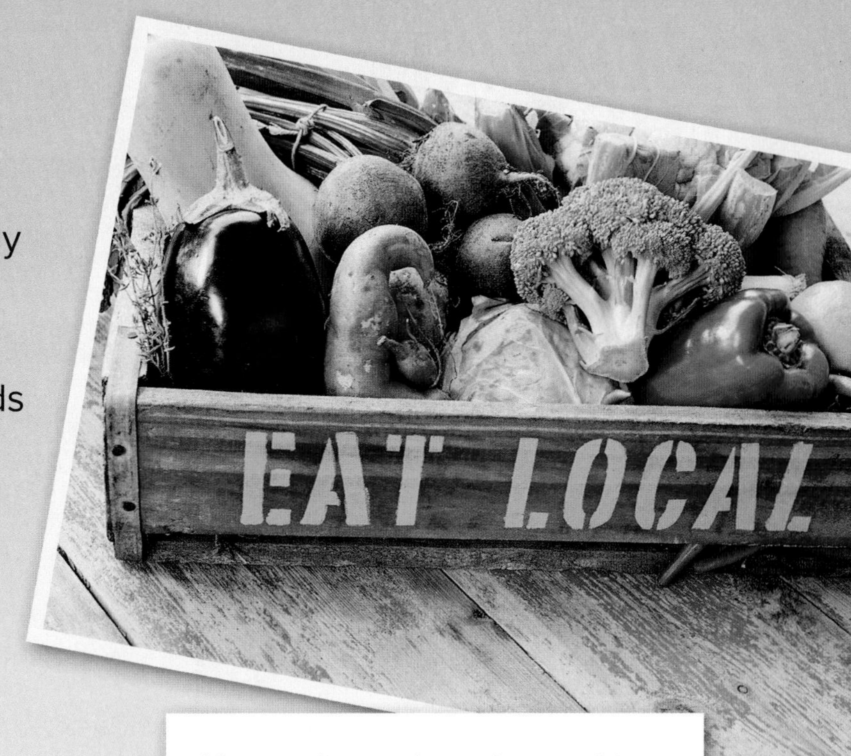

You can have a box of vegetables delivered to your home.

(t)David Malan/Photographer's Choice/Getty Images, (b)Tetra Images/Getty Images

A DAY AT THE DOCKS

IN BIG PORTS, SHIPS MOVE TONS OF GOODS IN AND OUT EVERY DAY.
LOU, THIS SHIP JUST CAME IN.
HEY, WHO'S THIS?
THIS IS MY DAUGHTER BRIANNA.
SHE HAS COME TO SEE WHAT WE DO AT WORK.

SOME CARGO SHIPS CAN BE UP TO FOUR FOOTBALL FIELDS LONG AND CAN CARRY 15,000 CONTAINERS.

HI, BRIANNA. I'M SAM, ONE OF THE CRANE OPERATORS.
THAT SOUNDS LIKE A COOL JOB!

CRANES LOAD AND UNLOAD CONTAINERS FROM SHIPS. OPERATORS "DRIVE" THE CRANES.
THAT'S THE CRANE I USE TO PICK UP AND MOVE THE CONTAINERS.
WOW! IT'S HUGE!

BY MOVING ONE LEVER, I CAN PICK UP AND MOVE 40 TONS OF CARGO.
YOU HAVE TO BE CAREFUL NOT TO DROP THAT.

A BUSY PORT HAS LOTS OF WORKERS. THEY MOVE AND STORE GOODS.
LET'S GET OUT OF THE WAY, BRIANNA.
WE'LL TALK TO SAM WHEN HE'S IN THE CRANE.

YOU MADE IT! HOW HIGH UP ARE YOU, SAM?
ABOUT 140 FEET. I'LL SEND A PICTURE TO SHOW YOU THE INSIDE.

WHAT ARE ALL THOSE LIGHTS?
THEY HELP ME KNOW WHEN IT'S SAFE TO PICK UP AND THEN DROP OFF A CONTAINER.

AFTER CONTAINERS COME OFF THE SHIP, THEY ARE PLACED IN A CONTAINER YARD.

TRUCKS AND TRAINS MOVE GOODS FROM THE PORTS TO PLACES ALL OVER THE UNITED STATES.

SAM'S JOB LOOKS EASY, BUT IT'S NOT.
I THINK IT LOOKS LIKE FUN!
ART: EUREKA COMICS

YOU GOT TO MOVE IT!

SHIPS IN, SHIPS OUT

Do you know where your bananas come from? You might think they come from California. After all, California grows so many fruits! But most bananas are **imported** from other countries. The last banana you ate probably came through one of California's shipping ports. Every day, tons of goods are imported and **exported**, or sent to other countries, through ports. In 2015, over 15 million 20-foot containers moved through ports in California.

TRAINS AND TRUCKS

Goods don't move just by ship in the United States. Huge amounts of products are transported across the country on trains and trucks. In fact, more than 49 million tons of goods are moved on trucks and trains each day. That's a lot of stuff!

WordBlast

What does the word **export** mean? If *import* is the opposite of *export*, what does **import** mean?

Bananas are unloaded from ships and into trucks.

Truck drivers move goods across the country.

(bkgd)Jetta Productions/Iconica/Getty Images, (inset)ELMER MARTINEZ/AFP/Getty Images

TRANSPORTATION

Ships carry containers filled with goods to a port. Some cargo ships can carry as many as 15,000 containers.

Trains and trucks transport the goods across the country. Some goods travel in the shipping containers.

A train can carry up to 200 containers. Trucks can move goods in or out of a shipping container.

Workers unload the goods. Trucks of all different sizes deliver them to stores close to where you live.

EXPLORE the InfoGraphic

- How many containers can a big cargo ship carry?
- How many containers can a train carry?
- Explain how a TV might move from China to a store near you.

Nucleartist/Shutterstock.com

Citizenship

CALIFORNIA KIDS HELP

REINS IN MOTION

Kids really can make a difference! Just ask the volunteers at Reins in Motion. It's a horseback-riding program in Livermore, California. People with disabilities learn to ride horses with the help of a teacher.

Students at a local middle school came to the rescue when the riding program needed a ramp for wheelchairs. They sold cups of hot chocolate, and in a week, they raised $300, enough to build the ramp. Now it's easier for riders to get on the horses. And it's all thanks to kids willing to help their community.

Reins in Motion and other groups like the one in the picture help people with disabilities learn to ride horses.

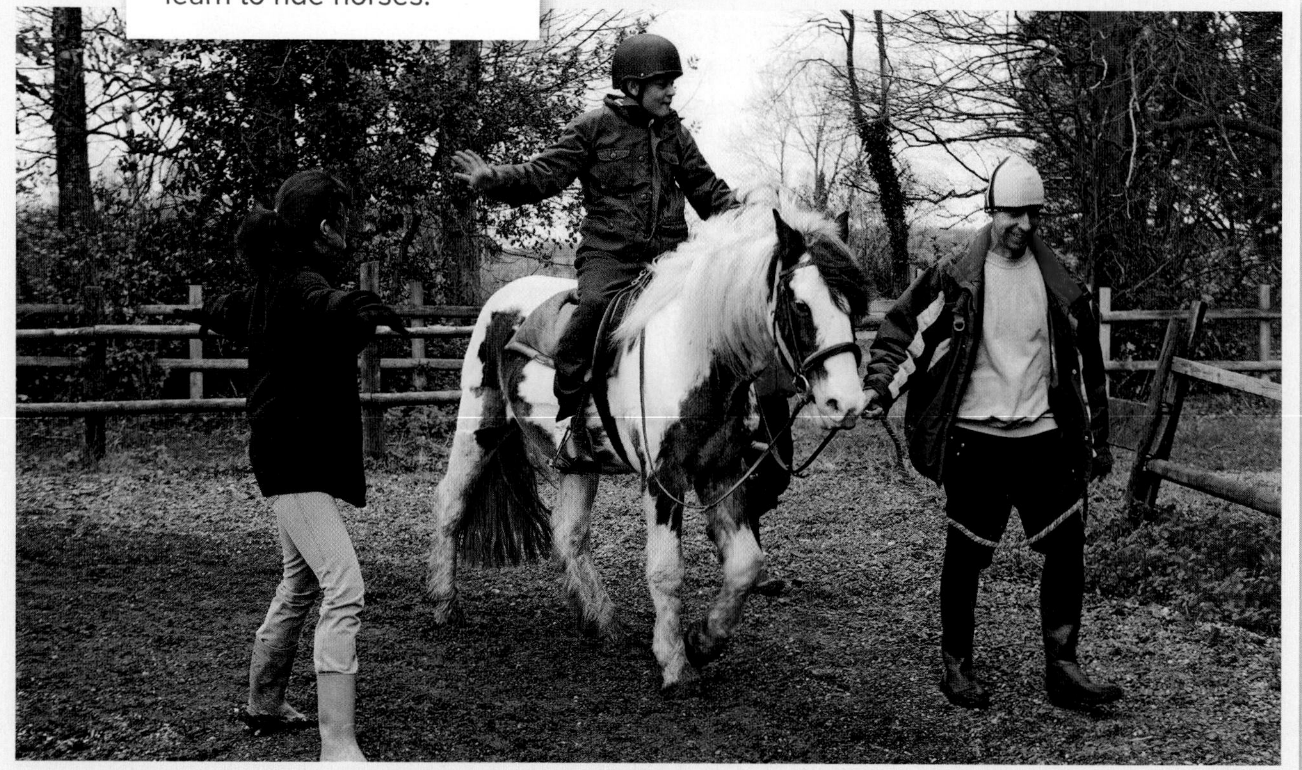

Tina Stallard/The Image Bank/Getty Images

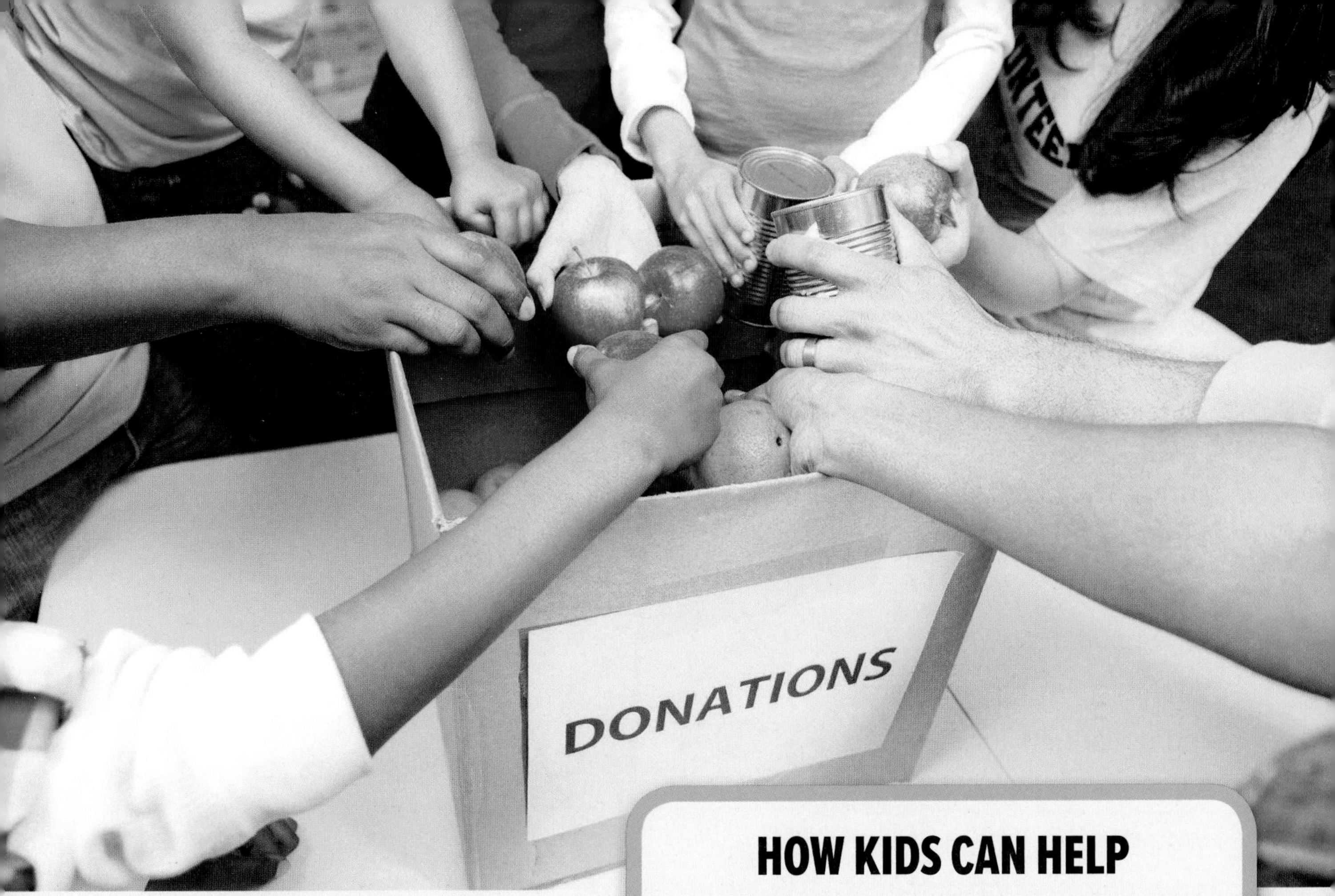

IZZY'S CORNER

In California, hundreds of thousands of people don't have enough food to eat. Izzy's Corner is part of a food bank in Orange County. Here, kids help other kids. Volunteers come one day a week to pack food. Then they distribute it to families in the area. At Izzy's Corner, small acts of kindness make a big difference.

HOW KIDS CAN HELP

Do you want to help your community, too? There are plenty of ways. These are just a few ideas. You might have some of your own!

- **Visit** a senior center. You can sing songs or read books together.
- **Volunteer** at an animal shelter. Maybe you can walk dogs.
- **Raise money** for a charity you care about. Organize a bake sale or a penny drive.
- **Sort cans** at a food bank, or plan a food drive to bring in donations.
- **Clean up** a park or a beach. Keep your community clean and safe.

POETRY CORNER

IF IT DID GROW ON TREES

by **Betsy Hebert**

Money, they say,
Doesn't grow on trees.

But what if it did?
What if the tree in my yard
Had dollar bills for leaves?

I would water that money tree
Every day, every night!
It would grow and grow.

I'd pick money any time.
New shoes, new games,
New every single thing I want.

Hmm.

And then what?

OlegErin/iStock/Getty Images

Take Action!

More to Explore

What else would you like to know about? The questions below have more ideas for you to research and discuss.

What crops are grown in California?

Where do they go?

How can you volunteer in your community?

How much solar power does the United States use?

WordBlast

- Why does a country **export** goods?
- Why does a country **import** goods?
- What are your favorite kinds of **produce** to eat?
- Name two **sources** of energy we use today.

Reflect

How do people in a community meet their needs?

What Do I Say?

Here are some ways you can talk with a partner or a small group.

Remember to . . .

Ask questions that add to the conversation.

- Why do you think the author said this?
- Why do you think that? Tell me more.
- I'm confused by . . . .

Why do you think that?

Christopher Futcher/E+/Getty Images

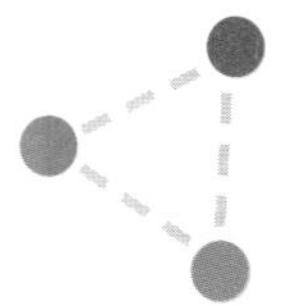

Connect ideas to other texts or situations.

- This reminds me of what we learned in . . . .
- This is a lot like . . . .
- This makes me think about . . . .

Help your partner explain more.

- Do you mean that . . . ?
- Can you explain that?
- Can you give me more examples?

Talk about what your partner said earlier.

- What you said made me think about . . . .
- I'd like to add to what you just said.
- I want to go back to what you said before.

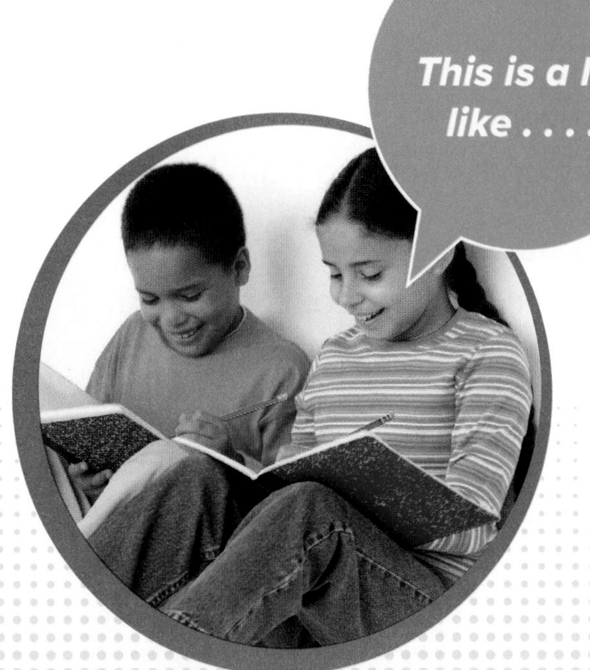

Ken Karp/McGraw-Hill Education

Challenge an idea.

- Where in the text did you find that evidence?
- Show me where the author says that.
- How do you know that?

Clear up misunderstandings.

- Okay, so what you're saying is . . . .
- What do you mean by . . . ?
- I'm not sure I know what you mean. Can you explain?

Disagree politely.

- I hear what you're saying. I also think that . . . .
- I'm not so sure. Maybe . . . .
- I see it differently.

Support your ideas with examples.

- In the text it says that . . . .
- For example . . . .
- The reason I think this is because . . . .

WordBlast

A

activist
a person who uses action to make change

D

debris
the remains of something that has been damaged or broken down

decompose
to break down, rot, or decay

destination
a place reached at the end of a journey

E

exclude
to keep someone or something out

export
to send goods to another country

I

import
to bring goods in from another country

industry
a business that provides a certain kind of good or service

M

mimic
to copy or imitate

P

population
the number of people, animals, or plants living in a place

preserve
to keep safe or protect

prevent
to stop something from happening

produce
fruits and vegetables grown by a farmer

R

regalia
special clothing, usually worn for important occasions

repeal
to end or do away with something

reservoir
a place to store liquids, such as a lake to store water

rodeo
a show or display of cowboy skills

S

source
the place or thing from which something comes

T

traditional
relating to customs that have been in place for a long time

transform
to change completely